LEADERSHIP AND POLITICS

STUDIES IN
GOVERNMENT AND PUBLIC POLICY

LEADERSHIP AND POLITICS

New Perspectives in Political Science

Edited by
BRYAN D. JONES

UNIVERSITY PRESS OF KANSAS

Published by the University Press of Kansas (Lawrence, Kansas 66045), which was organized by the Kansas Board of Regents and is operated and funded by Emporia State University, Fort Hays State University, Kansas State University, Pittsburg State University, the University of Kansas, and Wichita State University

Library of Congress Cataloging-in-Publication Data

Leadership and politics: new perspectives in political science /
edited by Bryan D. Jones.
p. cm. — (Studies in government and public policy)
Includes bibliographical references and index.
ISBN 0-7006-0407-3 (alk. paper) — ISBN 0-7006-0408-1
(pbk.)
1. Political leadership. I. Jones, Bryan D. II. Series.
JC330.3.L43 1989
303.3′4—dc20 89-33621
CIP

British Library Cataloguing in Publication Data is available.

Printed in the United States of America
10 9 8 7 6 5 4 3 2 1

The paper used in this publication meets the minimum requirements of the American National Standard for Permanence of Paper for Printed Library Materials Z39.48-1984.

Contents

Preface

Leadership in politics is one of the least tractable topics that political scientists deal with. To most people, leadership implies creativity, and creativity is not very amenable to the standard tools of analysis prevalent in political and other social sciences. These methods are more useful in studying the regularities in human behavior than they are in analyzing the creative changes in definitions of social understandings that, for example, Robert Tucker associates with leadership.

This does not mean that leadership is resistant to systematic inquiry. Indeed, I would not have undertaken this project had I so believed. It seemed to me that the study of political leadership could benefit greatly from more systematic examination than it had heretofore. I believed that there was much wisdom and theoretical insight concerning political leadership in the various subfields of political science but that academic boundaries had operated to limit the flow of information and insight on the subject. Hence I asked scholars from diverse parts of the discipline to contribute chapters to a volume that would focus on what we could learn about the general phenomenon of political leadership from their varied perspectives.

In principle, progress in the understanding of politics advances to the extent that we focus on integrative analyses. It is difficult for me, as an urbanist, to keep the literature on Congress or international relations in focus as I think about urban politics or the federal system. On the other hand, if someone with these specialties is willing to write about concepts that are useful or interesting to me, then I am able to bring research in diverse fields more quickly into my own realm of understanding.

Leadership is an integrative concept in another sense: the subject has been pursued from a variety of methodological perspectives. This is evident from the chapters in this volume. By putting these various methodological and substantive approaches together in one volume, I hope to give readers an appreciation for the variety of perspectives that may be used to study a single phenomenon.

There is a final sense in which leadership is integrative. Political scientists study institutions, they study the interaction between the political system and the economic system or social stratification, but they also study the behaviors of individual political actors. How are the behaviors of political actors related to social systems? How do social systems influence the behaviors of political actors? The study of political leadership offers one approach to this, the agency-structure problem.

Late in the development of this project, I became aware that the study of leadership was intertwined with another division in the discipline, a division that was more metatheoretical than methodological in the traditional sense of the latter word. Political scientists seemed to be approaching leadership, as well as a variety of other political phenomena, from one of two perspectives. In the first scholarly tradition, leadership is treated as part and parcel of a social world within which a social analogy of Newtonian causation holds. Political actors behave predictably according to incentive structures or institutional, cultural, and social constraints. They are pushed about by vectors in group theory or by vote maximization in public choice. The second scholarly tradition depicts a political world that is more similar to biology than to Newtonian physics. Understandable causation is certainly present, but outcomes are much affected by probabilistic unions of events and situational occurrences.

A more extended coverage of the "two worlds" of political analysis is contained in the introduction to this volume. I also asked Erwin Hargrove, who, as one of the reviewers of the first draft of this manuscript, was intrigued by the distinction, to write an essay putting some flesh on the bare bones of the basic distinction. He is to be commended for the promptness of his resulting essay.

The Political Leadership Project of the Department of Political Science at Texas A & M University, funded by the College of Liberal Arts Departmental Development Program, provided financial and secretarial support for this project. I am grateful for that support.

Bryan Jones

Introduction

1

Causation, Constraint, and Political Leadership

Bryan D. Jones

Like the Roman god Janus, the study of political leadership looks two ways: one toward the accomplishments of individual leaders, the other toward the economic, political, institutional, and cultural constraints on the exercise of leadership. On the one hand, some of the most insightful analyses of political leadership have been biographical or case studies, such as Robert A. Caro's works on Robert Moses and on Lyndon B. Johnson, or Edward C. Banfield's study of Chicago's Mayor Richard Daley.[1] Certainly these studies far surpass the study of the "man on horseback," but they nevertheless suffer from the tendency to attribute more influence to the subject of the study than may be warranted.[2]

On the other hand, systematic political science has emphasized the search for explainable regularities in political life and has generally thrown its lot in with the constraint school of thought. The biographical approach has pictured a political world that bends to the will of the dedicated leader, whatever that will may be.[3] The more systematic approach tends to depict leaders as products of social, economic, or political forces or as responding rationally to institutionally structured incentives.

These seemingly irreconcilable approaches suggest the desirability of more global theories; and in fact, there have been two recent attempts to take a comprehensive look at the phenomenon of leadership in politics.[4] These direct attacks have yielded considerable insight, yet they fall far short of providing comprehensive theories of leadership.[5] Indeed, as I suggest in this introduction, general theory would have to integrate somehow what I term the "two worlds" of political analysis. One of these "worlds" is characterized by economic rationality and Newtonian causation; the other, by probabilistic unions of events in ambiguously defined situations. The latter carries more of the spirit of the "great leader" approach but suggests more constraint; it suffers a diffuseness and lack of theoretical and mathematical rigor. The former offers rigor but virtually eliminates the possibility of creative leadership.

A major problem in making progress in the study of political leadership has been the increasing specialization in subareas of political science. The issue of *creativity* versus *constraints* in leadership arises in every area of the study of politics. Moreover, the study of leadership has the potential of overcoming some of this specialization. In this volume, an attempt is made to focus the contributions of subareas of political science on the general phenomenon of political leadership. We hope to illuminate the darkness with numerous flashlights, rather than one searchlight.

TWO ISSUES

Although there are many important facets of leadership, two issues are critical to the understanding of politics. These are, first, the issue of agency versus structure and, second, the issue of accountability to followers.

Agency and Structure. To what extent are the actions of leaders determined (or, put in a weaker form, constrained) by forces beyond the leader's control? To what extent is leadership dictated by structure, and to what extent is there room for independent action? The issue of structure versus agency is not quite a restatement of the old free-will debate, although elements of it are present.

In principle, *any* social force or institutional structure can limit the actions of leaders—for example, economic reality, patterns of cultural expectations, demands of followers, or constraints imposed by political institutions. In practice, political scientists have concentrated on the constraining factors that stem from political institutions, on the one hand, and on exogenous factors such as the economic structure, on the other.

In his essay in this volume, George C. Edwards III deals directly with the issue of personal agency with respect to the president's ability to get his legislative program through Congress. He concludes that the legislative skills of the president "do not appear to be a predominant factor in determining presidential support in Congress on most roll-call votes, despite commonly held assumptions to the contrary."

The limits on presidential leadership are, in major part, a consequence of the institutional character of American national government. John Robertson's essay concerning political influences on macroeconomic policies in cabinet democracies illustrates this point. Yet he also shows that the coalitional "style" that emerges within a parliamentary framework—a style that varies with time and place—also affects policy success. The implications are twofold. First, executive-legislative relations do exist in cabinet governments—at the level of coalition building and maintenance. Second, the style of a coalition influences the success of its policy, indicating a role for leadership skills in coalition building.

Many of the essays in this book suggest a role for political institutions in shaping the incentive and opportunity structures facing political executives. Leadership opportunities are highly contextual: what can be done and with what results are contingent on time and place. Yet political institutions are, to some extent, conscious creations. They have been reformed and modified before, and they will doubtless be reformed and modified again. Hence the argument that political institutions constrain and channel leadership is not a surrender to structure in the structure-versus-agency debate.

Accountability. The second issue concerns the interaction between leaders and followers. In one respect, the question of the influence of followers on the behavior of leaders can be subsumed under the issue of agency versus structure: Can leaders act independently of their constituents? On the other hand, there may be so much freedom of action on the part of the leader that little accountability to followers exists, so that we are led to the question of whether followers have any meaningful role in governance decisions at all.

If followers lack the ability to hold leaders accountable and if societal elites have the means and the motive to co-opt the leaders of mass-based organizations, Michels's iron law of oligarchy will result. Robert Harmel, in his rigorous empirical examination of that law, shows that oligarchy is not inevitable in party leadership, but it can occur—it is one path to the governance of society. Again, political context seems to matter.

THE "TWIN TENSIONS" OF CAPITALIST DEMOCRACY

Much writing in political science has been directed at the influence of the economic structure (or economic elites) on the policy actions of democratically elected politicians. One can find a panoply of positions taken on the issue, from Michels's contention that democratic politics are impossible, because of powerful incentives offered by the successful, to Joseph A. Schumpeter's claim (which has been defended by such authors as Allan H. Meltzer and Scott H. Richard) that democracy's redistributive tendencies would eventually destroy capitalism.[6]

One position that is being put forward with increasing acceptance among political scientists is (1) that elections matter and that they give constituents considerable potential power in a democracy, but (2) that powerful economic forces can and do strongly affect democratic politics, both through electoral means, such as campaign contributions, and through the need of politicians to induce rather than command business (as society's instrument of wealth production) to contribute to social goals. That is, democratically elected politicians must pay attention to followers because of the threat of elections, but they must also be sensitive to the fact that business elites cannot be compelled to be productive and that economic well-being is one of the things they will be held accountable for. Hence, business demands get special attention in the councils of government.

It would, however, be a gross oversimplification to assume that citizens, by demanding immediate consumption of the social product, are continuously opposed to business interests, which speak for investment. First, business elites often demand self-serving policies that consume rather than invest. Second, citizens themselves have a stake in the economic betterment of society and therefore are not continually re-forming themselves into consumption-oriented coalitions, as economists such as Mancur Olson would have us believe.[7]

The concept of dual imperatives in capitalist democratic society has been refined by work in the field of urban politics. From the old elitist-pluralist power debate, a new synthesis received its first analytic statement by Clarence N. Stone. Stone wrote in 1980 that public officials operate "under dual pressures—one set based in electoral accountability and the other based in the hierarchical distribution of economic, organizational, and cultural resources."[8] Stephen L. Elkin has refined this approach, arguing that the division of labor between state and economy has meant that governments must continually deal with the mandates of popular control and economic well-being. The manner in which the division develops will yield specific regimes, depending basically on the strength of political elites relative to economic elites.[9]

In his essay in this volume, Stone further develops his notion of preemptive power—the power associated with occupying the community leadership role *and* "being able to take the initiative and frame proposed actions as *community* responses." Because "formal public authority is weak," it is necessary for public leaders to construct governing coalitions, which normally involve business elites—the interaction between state and economy that defines political regimes for both Elkin and Stone. This political settlement yields a standing arrangement that is captured by the term "preemptive power."

These "twin tensions" that are present in capitalist democracies must play themselves out continuously at the level of the individual politician at all levels of government. That is, these dual social pressures are reflected in the decision-making choices of elected politicians everywhere.

As a starting point, we might cross-classify the extent of influence on leaders of economic circumstance (structure versus agency) and of followers (democratic accountability). This yields the classification in Table 1.1. This classification suggests four types of politicians, depending on their relationships to the two issues discussed above. Here, I limit structure and agency to the issue of economic limits on political leadership alone, although I recognize the cost of simplification.

TABLE 1.1

	Accountable	*Unaccountable*
Structure	Delegate	Lackey
Agent	Trustee	Entrepreneur

We might apply the label of *delegate* to the politician who has little independence from economic elites and who is accountable to his constituents. Presumably, this could occur only if the leader's constituents were in agreement with the views of economic elites. Just how this might occur is important, because agreement might be forged by common interest or by manipulation. An accountable representative who nevertheless is substantially free of control of economic elites might be called a *trustee.* The usage of these terms is not too far afield from that used by the authors of *The Legislative System.*[10] The politician who has little ability to chart an independent course and who is unaccountable to his followers is presumably controlled by economic elites—a classic capitalist *lackey.* Finally, the unaccountable leader who possesses independence from dominant elites might be termed an *entrepreneur,* to suggest his or her freedom to chart new political directions.

Table 1.1 suggests that the interaction of democracy and capitalism produces a limited set of types of politicians. Different kinds of political leaders will emerge in different proportions—depending on economies, cultural expectations, and institutional structure. Moreover, it is probable that each type of leader will bear a different relationship to social change. One might expect the delegate to reflect economic change through his followers; the trustee to be sensitive to elements of change that are not necessarily demanded by economic elites or by his or her followers, but that are generally in the interest of the followers; the lackey to be responsive only to demands of non-constituency-based economic elites; the entrepreneur to be free of either type of constraint and therefore less predictable.

THE TWO WORLDS OF POLITICAL ANALYSIS

The way in which we think about leadership is strongly influenced by our conceptions of social reality. At the risk of oversimplification, I suggest that modern political science has been dominated by two polar conceptions of the political world, conceptions that have resulted in two very different approaches to political leadership. In one world, Newtonian understanding of causation holds: politics consists of actions and reactions, forcings and adjustments, and well-understood, if complex, laws governing the resulting interactions. In the second world, probability and uncertainty are dominant, and public policy is the result of a fortuitous linking of events. Results are not incomprehensible, but they may be unpredictable. Adjustment among variables occurs, but it occurs in a world of limited search, of creative (or fortuitous) combinations of elements, in an imprecise and ever-changing manner. The analogy is biology, rather than Newtonian physics.

A NEWTONIAN WORLD

The issue of structure versus agency seems problematic in the Newtonian political world, because human actors so clearly have goals and intentions. If so, then how can they be bounced about like so many billiard balls? Are their goals irrelevant in the sweep of history? Perhaps, but economists have supplied another answer, an answer that many political scientists have seized upon. Social actors are utility maximizers. An actor is assumed to maximize some variable which presumably reflects his or her utility. In maximizing this variable, the actor forges the Newtonian causal link: as the variable changes, so must the actions of the utility-maximizing social actor. For example, the head of the corporation receives utility through the profits that his firm generates; hence he or she will maximize profits. In maximizing profits, he becomes the perfect adjustment mechanism: as technology or the competition changes, he adjusts so as to maximize profits. Thus it is that the corporate leader retains his human desires and intentions and yet becomes a pawn in the interplay of social forces.

Since the path-breaking work of Anthony Downs, the prevailing approach to the theoretical study of leader-follower interactions in mass democracies has been rooted in the notion of economic rationality.[11] Voters are preference revealers; politicians are vote maximizers. The assumption of vote maximization means that the role for political leadership is highly circumscribed, with the policy positions of leaders being completely dependent on the distribution of voter preferences.

Politicians, it is assumed, wish to win elections. In order to win, they must maximize votes. In order to achieve this, they promise policy packages that are "closest to" the most voters—the median voter, as can be proved. If the distribution of voters changes, the leader's policies change; otherwise, they do not. Political leadership is simply a direct reflection of mass preferences, and the source for political change is change in mass preferences. Accountability via elections is the strong force in politics; the second tension of capitalist democracy seems not to exist at all.

The political world envisioned by this analysis is one of high information and systematic predictable interactions among well-behaved variables. It is a world of certainty and clarity. Its actors are driven by single motives that can be achieved in straightforward ways, although the resulting social interactions can be enormously complex.

The influence of Newtonian causation is not limited to the public-choice approach, although it is easiest to see there. Interest maximization is not really so different from utility maximization; an interest just may be a little more difficult to find. In the group-theory approach, independent actions of politicians disappear in the confluence of vectors of influence generated by group interests. Public policy is forged at the balance point. In the pure form of group theory, leaders are mere lackeys of interests, but society achieves freedom from tyranny because of the plurality of interests and the openness of political institutions. Similarly, Eastonian systems analyses, in which public policies are forced out of the "black box" of the policy-making apparatus by a combination of demands and supports, are Newtonian in approach. The difference is that accountability to electoral majorities is played down, and influence by economic (and other, noneconomic) interests is stressed.

How far can we get by employing the utility maximization framework? The essay by Morris P. Fiorina and Kenneth A. Shepsle in this volume indicates that the approach can yield considerable insights into the nature of political leadership in certain situations—basically where "followers . . . lay down, *ex ante,* a contingent reward structure for their leader." The approach leads to an examination of the role of political institutions in providing that contingent reward structure—a very valuable exercise. However, these analyses are *follower driven,* in that the strategies of leaders are dictated by the preferences of followers and by the structure of political institutions. My essay stresses the problems of formal analyses related to the assumptions made concerning just what preferences voters have. Given that voters want to maximize utility, what exactly will they support? Are democratic voters consumption oriented, or will they support investment in the future economic health of society? In this analysis, leaders continue to be vote maximizers.

A Second World

Yet there are political scientists who envision a second political world, a more ambiguous and complicated (but not necessarily more complex) world. The differences between these two worlds are very easy to note in the aggregate but are not so easy to specify precisely. James Q. Wilson has suggested that the difference has to do with the assumption of fixed preferences: "Whereas economics is based on the assumption that preferences are given, politics must take into account the efforts made to change preferences."[12] However, this distinction does not seem to capture the difference between the two worlds. Economic preferences change, as do political ones. The key difference is that preferences in politics are less directly connected to goals than are those in economics, so that actors can more easily persuade others that a policy relates to their ends in politics. Put differently, in economics, preferences change only exogenously (e.g., through new technologies), whereas in politics, preferences can also change endogenously (e.g., through persuasion). Leaders may be able to convince others that their preferences correspond to the leader's policy proposal.

Jameson W. Doig and Erwin C. Hargrove applied this perspective to leadership in public agencies when they isolated major characteristics of leaders, including the identification of new missions for their organization and the development and nourishing of external and internal constituencies.[13] Leaders are not so much following the dictates of incentives as they are searching for new ways to convince relevant political actors that their goals can be achieved by doing what the leaders want them to do.

The public-choice theorist William H. Riker has argued that political leaders have ample room for manipulation even though they are faced with followers who have fixed, ordered preferences. The leaders can do so by controlling the voting agenda (the order in which alternatives are presented for decision), by strategic voting, and by the introduction of new policy dimensions. Riker calls this manipulation heresthetics. The third vehicle, the introduction of new dimensions along which preferences are ordered, is clearly important: Riker writes that "most of the great shifts in political life result from introducing a new dimension." Yet it also goes far toward undermining the well-structured world of the public-choice theorists. Riker is suggesting a political world that is considerably less determinant than the well-behaved world of the public-choice theorists, one in which new dimensions of conflict emerge and in which, presumably, others are destroyed; and the entire process is subject to manipulation by leaders.[14]

Political leaders can do more than pursue the three strategies suggested by Riker, however. Creative leaders can manipulate the connection between goals and policies that are perceived by other actors. Because the goals may be unclear (or, more likely, imperfectly ordered), political leaders may employ rhetoric to convince their followers that there is a connection between a policy proposal and the goals of the followers. The attribution of causation is subject to manipulation by leaders. At least in political rhetoric, *cause is not fixed.* In complex and ambiguous situations, political leaders may struggle over the attribution of the causal connection between means and ends.

If the goals of the actors are not directly related to preference, we ought to analyze just how social goals are attached to policies. If we do so, we enter a world of considerable indeterminancy. Michael D. Cohen and James G. March have described a set of organizations, termed organized anarchies, characterized by *problematic goals, unclear technologies,* and *fluid participation.* Their "garbage can" model of organizational choice conceives of a choice outcome as a function of the interplay of four streams within an organization: *problems, solutions, participants,* and *choice opportunities.*[15]

John Kingdon has used this work in his search for the genesis of policy proposals. His metaphors are purely biological: "The generation of policy proposals . . . resembles a process of biological natural selection. Many ideas are possible in principle, and float around in a 'policy primeval soup.' "[16]

The opportunities for leadership are considerably different in these two worlds. In the Downsian firmament, there is a role for creativity and innovation, but it is highly circumscribed by the institutional structure. Politicians may offer policy proposals ("platforms") to voters, but the acceptance or rejection of these ideas is controlled by elections. To paraphrase an old saw, the "parties propose, the voters dispose." But rational parties quickly converge on the median voter with their proposals, and creative change seemingly ceases—until the position of the median voter changes.

The "biological" world of Cohen and March, Kingdon, and others offers a world of considerably more room for political leadership. Leaders may be coalition builders, putting together "heterogeneous coalitions out of persons with changeable and incommensurable preferences in order to make binding decisions for everyone."[17] They may be policy entrepreneurs, defining a policy problem, recommending a policy proposal, mobilizing supporters, and shepherding the proposal through a complex policy process characterized by uncertainty and ambiguity. Or they may simply be spokespersons for a single social interest—("It's not that easy to be a pawn of labor," one Michigan state representative remarked several years ago).

In his essay in this book, Frank R. Baumgartner argues that what I term here the two worlds of political analysis have analogues in reality. Political actors are presented with situations that differ in the extent to which there is uniformity in the understanding of connections between means and ends. The firmer the social consensus on the connection, the more difficult major changes in policy will be.

A number of consequences flow from the relaxing of the analytical assumption of fixed social causation. The first is that actors are no less rational in the second world of politics. Indeed, a leader's preferences may be fixed with respect to, say, reelection, but—and this is the key point—they face other actors whose preferences are *not* fixed—for example, voters—with respect to things that are politically relevant. Second, because everyone's preferences are not fixed (or, perhaps it would be better to say that they are not affixed to political objects), the *definition of the situation* becomes extremely important in politics (and, therefore, in the study of political leadership). Robert C. Tucker, in his insightful essay on political leadership, has defined a situation as "a set of circumstances that someone endows with meaning because of the way in which they relate to that person's purposes and concerns."[18]

With the importance of definition of the situation comes the importance of culture. In his contribution to this volume, Aaron Wildavsky uses a cultural theory of leadership to trace varying leadership styles among political regimes. His classification of regimes is based on the number of cultural prescriptions extant in society and on the strength of social groups. Regimes vary in the nature of leadership they support. Wildavsky's essay makes clear that the "twin tensions" thesis detailed above is but one of a large number of possible cultural arrangements that affects leadership style.

Manus I. Midlarsky's essay, in which he compares Bismarck and Washington as national leaders, suggests the power of the cultural approach to leadership. The two men differed greatly in character traits and in strategies as leaders, but both "deeply reflected the particular norms of their time and place and acted upon those norms successfully without introducing any significant changes."

The essay by Kenneth J. Meier on leadership in public bureaucracies perhaps best suggests the complex mix of narrow rationality (utility maximization) and broader rationality, including preference formation, used by most political scientists to understand political leadership. On the one hand, compliance with leader directives can be achieved through inducements—the application of rewards and sanctions—that could be understood through narrow rationality framework.

On the other hand, certain facets of leadership in public organizations defy the standard utility-maximization approach—the appeal to solidarity or the attraction of more individuals who are receptive to purposive incentives than to private-sector organizations. That is, the people who seek membership are more likely to identify with organizational (rather than personal) goals in public organizations. This does not deter a utility-maximization approach; the organizational goal just would appear in the utility functions of these individuals. But the analysis could never be complete, nor would it "satisfice." Political analysts want to know the distribution of such motivations and to inquire under what conditions the organizational goal accomplishment motivates compliance. This is what Wilson means by the unwillingness of political scientists to take preferences as "given" in their analyses.

CONCLUSION

At this juncture in the study of political leadership, only the public-choice approach offers the possibility of a comprehensive theory of political leadership. Yet that approach is incomplete and must remain so, because preference formation and problem definition are so thoroughly important in politics: they are two aspects of political reality that are taken as givens in the utility-maximization approach. Nevertheless, in stable, structured situations, the power of the public-choice approach is impressive. Unfortunately, it is the unstable, changing event, in which situations are ill defined, that, according to Tucker, is the place in which leadership is most likely to emerge.

A reading of this collection of essays strongly suggests that any movement toward a more comprehensive theory of political leadership will have to deal somehow with three major aspects of leadership that have emerged from subdisciplinary attacks on the leadership problem. Each of these approaches has roots in particular parts of the discipline, but each seems barely recognized in other areas. A truly comprehensive theory would have to integrate these approaches by indicating the conditions under which each would hold.

First, a comprehensive theory of leadership must contain a role for maximizing behavior within a set institutional structure. Where institutional incentives are very strong, successful leaders are those who maximize. Second, such a theory must recognize and specify the conditions under which policy entrepreneurs can redefine the existing incentive structures, producing new missions for their agencies or new policies and ideas that will create new constituencies and demands (which other actors may respond to in a rational, maximizing fashion). These conditions are most likely to occur where ambiguity concerning the connection between policies and goals is high. Finally, no theory of leadership can afford to ignore the connection between the political and the economic worlds. Political scientists who study politicians within institutions have tended to ignore the role of economics; hence, the classic "vote-maximizing politician" is a unidimensional construct in a bidimensional (some would argue multidimensional) world.

Integrating these three considerations is an overwhelming intellectual task. As editor of this volume, I would be more than satisfied if these essays stimulated thinking about the limits of the dominant approaches within subareas of political science.

NOTES

1. Robert A. Caro, *The Power Broker* (New York: Vintage, 1975) and *The Path to Power* (New York: Knopf, 1982); and Edward C. Banfield, *Political Influence* (New York: Free Press, 1961).
2. This term is used by James MacGregor Burns, *Leadership* (New York: Harper & Row, 1978).
3. But see Jameson W. Doig and Erwin C. Hargrove, eds., *Leadership and Innovation* (Baltimore, Md.: Johns Hopkins University Press, 1987), for an attempt to systematize the biographical approach.
4. Burns, *Leadership;* Jean Blondel, *Political Leadership* (London: Sage, 1987).
5. Blondel (*Political Leadership,* chap. 6) readily admits that the study of leadership, even with progress in understanding, remains burdened with both conceptual and measurement problems.
6. Allan H. Meltzer and Scott H. Richard, "Why Government Grows (and Grows) in a Democracy," *Public Interest* 52 (Summer 1978).
7. Mancur Olson, *The Rise and Decline of Nations* (New Haven, Conn.: Yale University Press, 1982).
8. Clarence Stone, "Systematic Power in Community Decision-Making," *American Political Science Review* 74 (Dec. 1980): 984.

9. Stephen Elkin, *The City in the American Republic* (Chicago: University of Chicago Press, 1987).

10. John Wahlke et al., *The Legislative System* (New York: John Wiley, 1962).

11. Anthony Downs, *An Economic Theory of Democracy* (New York: Harper & Row, 1957).

12. James Q. Wilson, "The Politics of Regulation," *The Politics of Regulation*, ed. James Q. Wilson (New York: Basic, 1980), p. 363.

13. Doig and Hargrove, *Leadership*, p. 8.

14. William H. Riker, *The Art of Political Manipulation* (New Haven, Conn.: Yale University Press, 1986).

15. Michael D. Cohen and James G. March, *Leadership and Ambiguity*, 2d ed. (Boston, Mass.: Harvard Business School Press, 1986).

16. John W. Kingdon, *Agendas, Alternatives, and Public Policies* (Boston, Mass.: Little, Brown, 1984).

17. Wilson, "Politics of Regulation," p. 363.

18. Robert C. Tucker, *Politics as Leadership* (Columbia: University of Missouri Press, 1981), p. 16.

PART 1

Leadership and Public Choice: Prospects and Problems

2

Formal Theories of Leadership: Agents, Agenda Setters, and Entrepreneurs

Morris P. Fiorina and Kenneth A. Shepsle

Leadership is widely studied in sociology, psychology, and organization theory, as well as in political science. But from the perspective of social scientists not expert in the subject, there seems to be little cumulative advance in our understanding: the empirical regularities are neither robust nor compelling; the theoretical formulations are neither precise nor reliable. Perhaps leadership is epiphenomenal and derivative. Perhaps it is so dependent on contextual circumstances as not to permit holistic treatment.[1] In any event, in political science the literature on leadership is subfield specific. There are literatures on congressional leaders, executive leaders (presidents, governors, and mayors), party leaders, bureaucratic leaders, interest-group leaders, and leaders in various policy areas. From this fragmentation, few formal deductive treatments of the subject have emerged.

While there are few explicit formal treatments of leadership, there are several nascent conceptions of the phenomenon in the modeling literature. In many modeling settings, an individual looks like a leader either because she occupies a structural position in an institution or a temporal location in a sequential process or because she stands in a relationship to others. It is these more abstract aspects of leadership that we will explore in this essay. Specifically, in the first part we develop the theory of principals and agents; in the second, we report on the theory of agenda setters; in the third, we examine political entrepreneurs. In these three theoretical conceptualizations, formal modeling offers insights about some aspects of leadership. The three theoretical enterprises are neither mutually exclusive nor collectively exhaustive of the subject of leadership. In the fourth part, we discuss some of the overlaps as well as some of the lacunae.

LEADERS AS AGENTS

Henry Clay was elected from Lexington, Kentucky, as a freshman legislator to the Twelfth Congress. When that Congress convened in Washington on November 4, 1811, the freshman Clay was elected Speaker of the House. His acceptance speech was brief:

> Gentlemen. In coming to the station which you have done me the honor to assign me—an honor for which you will be pleased to accept my thanks—I obey rather your commands than my own inclination. I am sensible of the imperfections which I bring along with me, and a consciousness of these would deter me from attempting a discharge of the duties of the chair, did I not rely confidently upon your generous support.
>
> Should the rare and delicate occasion present itself when your speaker should be called upon to check or control the wanderings or intemperance in debate, your justice will, I hope, ascribe to his interposition the motives only of public good and a regard to the dignity of the house. And in all instances, be assured, gentlemen, that I shall, with infinite pleasure, afford every facility in my power to the despatch of public business, in the most agreeable manner.[2]

In stating that he would "obey rather your commands than my own inclination" and "afford every facility in my power to the despatch of public business in the most agreeable manner," Clay was adopting the classic role of leader as follower, or leader as agent. As Charles Jones has put it in a more contemporary context, "Rightly or wrongly, House leaders must attend to their majorities."[3] Implicit in this view of leadership is the belief that leaders are rational in whatever it is they pursue, that they choose and behave with these objectives in mind, and that an especially common motivation of leaders in these circumstances is some form of ambition that depends upon subsequent follower behavior. Put differently, leadership compensation is performance based and involves retrospective evaluation by followers. Exploring these notions is the province of agency theory. In a principal/agent (PA) model, followers (or principals) lay down, ex ante, a contingent reward structure for their leader (or agent). That reward structure ties the agent's ambition (to remain leader in the next period) to her performance (in the current period).

THE SIMPLE AGENCY FRAMEWORK

The economic theory of agency is concerned with delegation, decentralization, and the division of labor.[4] Since at least the time of Adam Smith, the division and the specialization of labor have been appreciated for the possibility they offer of enhanced productivity. The delegation of tasks to "specialists" is so natural in the modern world that individuals rarely serve as their own doctor, lawyer, financial advisor, or building contractor.

However, traditional economics, especially its neoclassical version, fails to distinguish between the *possibility* of enhanced productivity and its *implementation*. If one retains a doctor, a lawyer, a financial advisor, or a contractor to further some objective (such as good health or prudent investments) or to accomplish some task (to draw up a will or remodel a kitchen), how can the principal (P) be assured that the agent he retains will act in P's best interests? P may be convinced, in principle, that retaining an agent, A, is a sensible and economical thing to do. But P may worry that, in practice, she will look out for herself first, not for the principal.

There are several reasons for P's fears. First and most obvious, a self-interested principal would be less than prudent to assume that altruism rather than self-interest animated the behavior of agents. Thus, P will need to consider conflicts of interest between himself and his agent. The doctor or the lawyer might prefer to be out on the links on Wednesday afternoons rather than to remain available in the office for an emergency call from P.

Second, these conflicts may be subtle because of asymmetries in information. Presumably, some of these asymmetries led P to retain an agent in the first place: A is alleged to be an expert possessing specialized knowledge unavailable to P. But other of A's characteristics about which P is ignorant may have harmful consequences. For example, how does P know, when his financial counselor recommends a particular property to purchase, whether her recommendation reflects true economic worth or, alternatively, the fact that her brother-in-law wants to unload the parcel?

Another complication involves observability. Often the final outcome and P's ultimate welfare depend not only on the actions taken by A but also on events or actions outside of A's control (or even foreknowledge). Agent actions and exogenous events are often so inextricably intertwined that even fairly knowledgeable prinicpals are unable, after the fact, to determine the relative burdens of responsibility. With the link between A's actions and P's well-being weakened or mediated, so, too, might A's incentives to perform on behalf of P be weakened or mediated.

In short, conflicts of interest and informational asymmetries are problematical and can attenuate the advantages that might otherwise derive from a division of labor. These conflicts and asymmetries also set in motion the search for solutions that often entail the evolution of institutional practices. For example, if conflicts of interest between P and A are the only problem, then a "forcing contract" and institutions of exogenous enforcement may be sufficient to overcome them. A principal and his lawyer can sign an enforceable contract, called a "retainer," according to which the lawyer is on call, even if it means she will have to give up the occasional Wednesday afternoon of golf, in exchange for a fixed fee on top of her hourly rate.

In general, the theory of agency deals with solutions to various problems of this sort, especially those that arise when contracting is too costly or otherwise unavailable. This latter circumstance arises *a fortiori* when, as is typical in the political world, there are no institutions to enforce agreements exogenously. The parties typically seek out some mechanism involving incentives or monitoring that permits gains from exchange while discouraging cheating, reneging, or dissembling.

In the economic theory of agency, this problem is seen as belonging to the principal. The agent is simply a utility maximizer; she responds mechanically in utility-maximizing fashion to whatever incentives she faces. It is up to P to structure the situation, taking A's subsequent mechanical response into account. Thus, the theory assumes that P "moves first," choosing a reward structure, a fee schedule, an incentive scheme, or a monitoring institution. The agent "moves second," maximizing her utility contingent on the payoff structure that has been put in place by P.[5] Thus, it is taken as a given that A will behave opportunistically in her own interest, and the challenge to P is to structure the situation so that, as though there were an invisible hand, she will nevertheless be guided to act in his interest as well. A principal/agent relationship is in equilibrium when the agent is "best responding" to the principal's reward structure and when the principal has optimally anticipated the agent's response.

Theory of Agency and Leadership

The foregoing description should suggest why the theory of agency is a theory of leadership. In this view, *leadership is an institutional arrangement created by a P, or a collection of Ps (more on this below), in order to obtain some objective more efficiently, more effectively, or with higher probability than he, or they, could without the coordination and enhanced productivity provided by the leadership institution.* A leader, in effect, is retained as an agent for the singular or the collective P. Whether the speaker of a legislative chamber, the chairperson of a political party, or the chief executive officer of a firm or a city, she need not share the objectives of the principal(s) on whose behalf she is acting. If rewards are properly aligned, however, she will act to some extent as though she does.

Before examining some substantive studies and exemplary applications of the agency view of political leadership, we must call attention to a major analytical problem. The principal is assumed to have well-defined preferences. In most economic applications, for example, the principal is assumed to be a wealth maximizer, and outcomes are characterized in terms of changes in his wealth after he makes payment to his agent. In most political settings of interest, however, the political leader is the *common* agent for a *collection* of principals.[6] Multiple principals pose an additional layer of complexity. There may be conflicts of interest among the multiple principals so that the "principals' problem" is as much a game among themselves as it is one of controlling their leader-agent. The agent, on the other hand, may be faced with the problem of performing in behalf of *some* of the principals and compromising the interests of other of the principals.

To be more concrete, suppose a small number of farmers in a town want to drain a swamp in order to eliminate a serious health problem. They have a common objective—the elimination of insect breeding grounds; so they retain an agent (or choose one of their number) to help them coordinate their efforts. The agent is ambitious; she believes there are many similar problems facing the town; and therefore she wants to respond to this current problem in a satisfactory manner so that she might be retained for additional tasks. But in order to produce the public good, she must "tax" the members of the group—say, in terms of hours of work donated for clearing and draining. Each P is, in effect, being asked to trade off private goods (being required to donate time that might otherwise have been devoted to private productive activities) in exchange for the public good. Thus, the pursuit of a common objective is seen to entail the distribution of a burden. Whatever decision the agent makes is likely to evoke objections from some of the principals, for this is a classic conflict-of-interest circumstance in which each P wants to minimize his share of the burden.

In circumstances such as these, it is tempting to regard the problem as the agent's: she has to figure out how to distribute the burden. But it is important to see that it is also the problem of the Ps—they have to devise an institutional framework in which the agent has incentive (in terms of her ambition) to solve the problem in some fashion; otherwise, either no agent will "apply" for the job, or an agent, once in the job, will behave opportunistically, on the assumption that no "solution" will be judged as satisfactory. In most of the applications that we report, the "multiple principals problem" plays a central role.

Leader as Representative

The idea of a leader as agent, servant, delegate, steward, or ambassador has for many years been a familiar one in political theories of representation.[7] This rich philosophical tradition is what Fiorina sought to formalize in his model of representative behavior.[8] Essentially preagency theoretic in its origins, it nevertheless bears a relationship to at least one side of the principal/agent problem in that Fiorina has sought to articulate a theory of optimal agent behavior.[9]

The agent, a legislator, is faced with a choice in a roll-call voting situation which, at some subsequent time, will serve as a basis for retrospective judgment by her principals, the constituency. Fiorina took the agent's action as known and public (a yea vote, a nay vote, or abstain) and the reward/punishment that would be attached to her action as known in advance. In particular, it was assumed that the constituency was partitioned into groups of proponents of the bill and opponents of the bill—G_1 and G_2, respectively. Voting with G_i would yield an increment to A's probability of reelection equal to x_i, whereas voting against G_i would yield a decrement to her probability by an amount z_i. The credibility of these promised rewards and punishments was given by the parameter c_i, in effect the probability that G_i would actually deliver on its announced response. Thus, the expected value of voting with G_1—that is, voting yea on the bill—is $c_1x_1 - c_2z_2$, whereas the expected value of voting with G_2—that is, voting nay on the bill—is $c_2x_2 - c_1z_1$. The agent's optimal response will depend on these relative magnitudes. A bit of algebra produces the conclusions that she will support the bill if and only if c_1/c_2 exceeds $(x_2 + z_2)/(x_1 + z_1)$.

One of the driving features of Fiorina's model is a substantive assumption about the relative magnitudes of punishment and reward. Calling it the *ungrateful electorate hypothesis,* he assumes that a group's capacity and intention to punish exceeds its capacity and intention to reward. "That is, given that a group cares about an issue, we assume that the representative believes that a vote in accord with the interest of the group gains [her] relatively less credit than a vote against their interest loses."[10] This assumption generates a host of implications about an agent's optimal response to the electoral incentives that she faces.

Although this theory was developed before models of principals and agents appeared on the scene, it clearly resembles them. It is a model of group leader selection in which the leader is ambitious to remain leader and therefore behaves as an agent for (some of) her "followers," the constituency. Moreover, it anticipates the peculiar problems of leadership when the followers are not all of one mind—the "multiple principals problem," alluded to above. But it deals only with one part of the problem, that of optimal response on the part of the agent. It takes the principals' incentive scheme for their agent as fixed and exogenously given. Groups reward (x_i), punish (z_i), display ingratitude (the ungrateful-electorate hypothesis), and exhibit credibility (c_i) in a fixed fashion, which is usually known in advance. Put differently, the strategic issues that derive from the conflicts of interest among the principals are suppressed.

Generalizations of Leader as Representative

During the past decade a rather large literature on principals and agents has appeared, and several recent efforts have attempted to examine leadership within this framework. Kenneth Shepsle and Brian Humes, who were interested in institutional and partisan leadership inside legislatures, sought to integrate Fiorina's model explicitly with principal/agent theory.[11] In a manner that parallels his treatment of a representative of a heterogeneous constituency, they modeled the survival of a leader in a context in which the leader's party was rent by faction. Thus, like Fiorina's representative, the legislative leader makes choices and also receives rewards and punishments amidst conflicts among her principals. However, Shepsle and Humes were dissatisfied with the ungrateful-electorate hypothesis, in particular, and with the exogenous status of the incentive scheme that the agent is facing, in general:

> Still we are troubled by the ungrateful electorate hypothesis . . . for our problem (and perhaps Fiorina's as well) groups may be in a position to vary x_i, z_i and c_i. This is the other side of the agency framework—the principal's problem. In a sense, G_1 and G_2 are involved in a game against one another, a game to control the agent.

Shepsle and Humes look at a specific aspect of this game by permitting G_1 and G_2 to determine in advance (subject to certain logical constraints) whether they will be grateful or ungrateful—that is, whether they will set x_i larger or smaller than z_i. The effect is a two-by-two matrix, the rows and columns of which are the strategy choices of the two groups (grateful and ungrateful incentive schemes, respectively). The cell entries are the payoffs to the groups on the assumption of optimal response on the part of the agent. In this manner, Shepsle and Humes simultaneously incorporate both strategic behavior by principals and optimal responses by agents, contingent on the moves made by the principals. It is interesting to note that the *principals* are the strategic players; the agent is a "mere" best-response automaton.

In this very stylized setting, Shepsle and Humes find that G_1 and G_2 are indifferent as to whether they are grateful or ungrateful, since group strategic behavior has no effect on agent *choice,* only on agent *payoff.* This result is, in part, an artifact of the highly stylized setting of their model. By the authors' own admission the contribution of the paper lies, not in the particulars of the results, but rather in the first explicit formulation of the full principal/agent model as a framework for studying leadership.

In a related paper, John Ferejohn returns to Fiorina's original context—namely, constituents as principals seeking to control their leader-representative—and produces a model that is rich in results.[12] He exploits a repeat-play mechanism according to which both principals and agents take a multiperiod view, performing in one period with an eye on their respective aggregate payoffs over an infinite time horizon. His results are substantial not only because he employs the powerful method of dynamic programming, on the one hand, but also because he makes the strong assumption that the principals are homogeneous—theirs is a pure problem of agent control involving no conflicts of interest among themselves. In a concluding section he relaxes the homogeneity assumption.

In a sense, Ferejohn's approach is the mirror image of Fiorina's, because Ferejohn poses the problem of controlling the agent as the principals' problem. He acknowledges that in many static models "little attention is paid to the possibility that, once in office, the politician's preferences may diverge from those of [her] constituents." He goes on to note that "an 'enforcement' mechanism may exist to discipline politicians for failing to keep promises, but without a specification of the mechanism it is not obvious that it would be in the interests of the electorate to carry out threatened punishments."[13] Thus, his focus is on behavioral strategies both used by politicians and by their constituents which can actually be credible to carry out. A politician's promises, ex ante, are ignored by voters unless they believe that she, in her own self-interest, must carry them out. Similarly, voters' promises about subsequent rewards (punishments) are ignored by the politician unless she believes that a self-enforcing rationale renders those promises credible.

In Ferejohn's formulation there is an important additional feature that was not incorporated in previous modeling efforts. He supposes that voters are not able to observe the behavior of their agent; they only see the final outcomes, which they value. Thus, they cannot base their retrospective reward or punishment on the actual behavior of the agent. Moreover, they cannot infer such behavior by backward induction from the outcome that they observe, because "nature" intervenes. Specifically, the final outcome is the product of both agent effort, a, and a random variable, x (nature's intervention) which combine in a nonseparable way: a principal's utility function is given by $u(a,x) = ax$. He benefits both from high levels of agent effort and propitious conditions generated by nature, but he cannot untangle their joint effect. The agent, on the other hand, dislikes devoting effort—her utility function is decreasing in a—and she will do only as much as she "has" to. The elector-principal decision rule is in the form of setting a performance level, K: he will vote to reelect the agent if and only if $u(a,x) = ax$ exceeds K—that is, if and only if a is greater than K/x. If the selected level, K, is too high and/or if nature's intervention is too inauspicious (x is very small), then the agent will make the best of a bad situation: she will devote no effort at all to the principal's cause ($a = 0$); she will enjoy the perks of office for one period, knowing that she will be thrown out of office in the next. Information asymmetry is crucial here. At the time that the principal must establish the performance level, he has only probabilistic knowledge about the variable x. By the time that the agent must choose her level of effort, on the other hand, she knows both x and K and chooses optimally to further her own interest.

In the body of his paper, Ferejohn characterizes equilibrium strategies for both the principal and the agent; but we will ignore the details here. When, however, he seeks to relax the assumption of homogeneous principals, the results are less promising. Specifically, he shows that in the absence of any coordination among the principals to resolve their respective conflicts of interest, the agent will be uncontrollable because she will have "both the opportunity and the motivation to play off the voters against one another."[14]

Ferejohn's model is one of the richest in the literature in attempting to formulate and characterize both sides of the leadership equation. He focuses on optimal leader-agent behavior, which is contingent on (1) a stipulated reward scheme; (2) an optimal follower-principal reward scheme that anticipates optimal agent response; (3) the prospects of disincentives because of informational and observational asymmetries; and with less success, (4) the ever-present "multiple principals problem." One feature of the problem, which he does not explore, is *incomplete* (to be distinguished from *imperfect*) information.[15] Basically, Ferejohn assumes that all agents are alike; they are prepared to respond in an identical manner to whatever reward scheme they face. Thus, follower-principals have no preferences among different prospective agents; their problem is to control whoever their agent happens to be. Suppose, however, that all agents are not alike but that their respective differences are not readily apparent to followers. That is, suppose that the followers' information about the agent's *type* is incomplete, where the latter could refer to ideology or to ambition for another office, for example. This is the setting for a principal/agent model of legislative leadership, by Randall Calvert, and for a subsequent application to problems of leadership in hegemonic international regimes.[16]

Leadership and Incomplete Information

The setting for Calvert's model is a legislature in which there is a party of (heterogeneous) principals, one of whom is elected as leader. The principals share a common objective (say, a party program or platform), but they are not completely committed to it. From time to time, some of the principals may find it in their interest to desert the party, perhaps on a matter of conscience or constituency. If, however, the conditions under which desertion is permitted are too broad, then the frequency of desertion will increase, quite possibly jeopardizing the entire common objective. It is assumed that principals will prefer the public good (the common objective), even if they are required to sacrifice by forgoing some opportunities to desert. But this preference alone is insufficient to deter them from deserting when an opportunity presents itself, if such behavior carries no cost. This is the familiar free-rider problem in the theory of collective action.[17] The leader's task, therefore, is to administer punishments for desertion, thereby raising its cost, presumably diminishing its frequency, and possibly even deterring it altogether. Calvert's legislative leader is an agent much like the agent of our earlier story about draining a swamp.

The interesting features of Calvert's model are that it is costly for the leader to administer punishment and that only she knows these costs for certain. The costs of punishment derive from the fact that the leader, as the agent for her followers, needs their support to remain leader. If punishments are too frequent or too onerous, she will jeopardize that subsequent support. She would, therefore, like to avoid administering punishment; she would prefer voluntary follower compliance instead. But, if she fails to punish often enough, thereby encouraging revolt, common group objectives will not be achieved, and follower dissatisfaction with her leadership will emerge. As Calvert puts it, "The worse a leader's balance of collective goods provided against coercion imposed, the more likely followers are to reject the leader."[18] Calvert assumed that both leader and followers appreciate this paradox of leadership.

The theoretical wedge exploited by Calvert's leader is the followers' incomplete information about her costs. They are suggested by the payoff table (table 2.1), reconstructed from Calvert's figure 1:

TABLE 2.1

BEHAVIOR	LEADER PAYOFF	FOLLOWER t PAYOFF
Follower t obeys	a	0
Follower t rebels; Leader acquiesces	0	b
Follower t rebels; Leader punishes	$-x_t$	$b-1$

Calvert assumes that a is greater than 1 and that b is some positive number less than 1; x_t is a random variable equal to 1 with probability w and to 0 with probability $1-w$. Thus, if the follower obeys—by, say, voting with the party on a bill—the leader earns "credit" toward reelection while the follower's payoff is whatever value he places on the common objective (normalized, without loss of generality, to 0). If the follower rebels, voting against the party, then he earns a positive payoff, b, and the leader earns less than she would have if the follower had obeyed (again normalized, without loss of generality, to 0). Finally, if the leader chooses to punish a transgression, the follower will earn a negative payoff, while the leader's payoff will be either costless or costly depending on a random variable. The catch is this: the leader knows the value of the random variable *before* she must decide whether or not to punish rebellious behavior; the follower, on the other hand, has only beliefs about which value x_t has assumed—that is, an estimate of the probability, w, of costly punishment for the leader. Moreover, followers are endowed with a capacity to learn; they update their estimate of the probability of costly punishment for the leader on the basis of having observed her behavior in previous circumstances.

Ultimately, Calvert is interested in the attempt by leaders to develop *reputations*. If a leader is able to convince followers that the punishments she administers are mostly costless to her, then they will be more likely to obey. To develop a reputation for costless punishment, she might exploit the followers' capacity to learn by administering punishments early, even if they are actually costly to her. She does this in order to have an effect on followers' beliefs. But sophisticated followers will appreciate her incentive to "misrepresent" her cost schedule, so any analysis must take this kind of sophistication into account.

Calvert does this in a two-period (Stackelberg) reputation game. In period one, the first follower must decide whether to obey or rebel, and if he chooses the latter, the leader must decide whether to punish or acquiesce. In period two, the second follower and the leader make the same determinations, but this time, the decisions are contingent on what has already occurred in period one. Calvert shows that this two-period game has an equilibrium consisting of a strategy for the leader in each period, a strategy for each of the followers (who could be the same person), and the followers' beliefs. Each strategy is a "best response" to the other strategies, and the followers' beliefs are derived on the basis of previous beliefs according to Bayes's rule for probabilities. Together these features define a *sequential equilibrium,* a concept developed by David Kreps and Robert Wilson.[19]

In this very stylized setting, Calvert demonstrates that circumstances arise in which a leader, faced with the paradox alluded to above, finds it in her interest to engage in reputation building. "Reputation is really a problem of using the uncertainty of followers to the leader's best advantage, to make the most of whatever real resources the leader actually has."[20] But as he concedes, the setting is very stylized: there are only two periods; the followers rebel individually rather than in bunches; the details of the common objective (the party's program) are suppressed; the precise features of the leader's cost structure are given in truncated form; and the threat to depose the leader, as well as the coordinated collective action that this requires, is not explicitly analyzed.

Calvert's is the first model to address in a serious way the role that incomplete information can play in institutional analyses of leadership. What also impresses us is how complex even spartan models of incomplete information become. As modelers ourselves, we encourage efforts to address demands from substantive scholars to make models "more realistic." Calvert has done this by relaxing the often-criticized assumption of perfect and complete information, and he has done so in a natural and interesting way. But this, in turn, required major simplifications, and even with them, the resulting argument and propositions are delicate and complicated.

LEADERS AS AGENDA SETTERS

In the preceding section the connection between leaders and agents is straightforward once terminological confusions have been resolved. Leaders, in ordinary language, are "active," whereas in the principal/agent framework agents are "responsive." However, once it is admitted that leader activism is motivated by ambition and that leader success is controlled to some extent by followers, then it should be obvious that despite the apparent activism of leaders, they are in fact responding to incentives controlled by followers.

In contrast, the literature on agenda setting originally was premised on the idea of manipulation. Agenda setting provides an opportunity for those who possess agenda power to affect outcomes disproportionately to their individual voting power. By manipulating what is being voted on and in what order, it has been argued that the agenda setter can bias final outcomes in the direction of her own preferences. Thus, the agenda setter was not conceived of as working *for* a collection of principals. Rather, she was working for herself, and at most, the voting power of others constituted a constraint on her ambition. The early literature on agenda setting made this analysis precise. In this literature, the agenda setter was the only strategic actor; other members of the voting body were passive (in a manner to be made specific below). Second-generation models relaxed this unnatural assumption, allowing all actors to behave in a strategic manner. But still, the extraordinary powers granted to a distinguished actor—the agenda setter—were taken as fixed, given, and exogenous. Some recent efforts have been made to endogenize these features.

MAJORITY RULE AND CHAOS

The background for agenda-setter models is the spatial framework. For didactic purposes, imagine a two-dimensional space—say, the sheet of paper at which you, the reader, are staring. Each point in this space is a potential outcome of a voting process. The various actors have preferences over the points in this space. Specifically, there is a distinguished point—call it x^i for the ith actor—that is i's most-preferred point. For convenience we assume that i's preference for an alternative declines with distance from x^i: the more distant an alternative from x^i, the less preferred it is. Again for convenience, assume that the number of actors is odd and that the social decision rule is a simple majority rule. Finally, for any point in the space—say, y—define the *win set of y* as:

$$W(y) = \{x\text{: } x \text{ is preferred to } y \text{ by at least a simple majority}\}$$

$W(y)$ is the set of points that can defeat y in a majority-rule contest. Of course, if $W(y)$ is empty, then y is a majority-rule winner (or a *Condorcet point*).

Early models of majority rule in the spatial setting rediscovered a fact that had been known as early as the eighteenth century, namely that majority rule behaved very badly.[21] For almost any distribution of actors' most-preferred points, no point is a majority-rule winner. The win set for every point is nonempty, so that any point can be defeated in principle. This, in turn, suggested that majority rule was indeterminate and unstable, with any possible outcome vulnerable to being replaced by some other.

Moreover, Richard McKelvey has proved that under rather general conditions, for any two arbitrarily chosen points y and z, there exists a finite sequence of other points $x_1,x_2, \ldots x_t$ that has the following properties: (1) x_1 beats y; (2) x_j beats x_{j-1} for $j=2, \ldots t$; and (3) z beats x_t.[22] Known informally as the Chaos Theorem, this result establishes, for any two arbitrary points, that a finite path of alternatives exists between them, with each point losing to its successor in a majority-rule contest. From any commencement point, a majority-rule process can be driven to any final outcome with an appropriately chosen agenda.

Institutionalizing Agenda Power

Whether a point is beaten in fact depends on how contests between points are determined—that is, on how the agenda of comparisons is formulated. If some point were arbitrarily selected as the status quo and if contests against it were then determined by random selection from the space of alternatives, then chaos would in fact describe the process. For the given status quo, eventually an alternative would be selected that is an element of the status quo's (nonempty) win set and that would replace it. This new status quo, in turn, would be replaced by some point from its win set. And so on, ad infinitum and ad nauseam.

Random agenda formation is but one element in a family of agenda-setting schemes. Imagine, in contrast, a distinguished actor, called the agenda setter, who is empowered to structure majority-rule contests. That is, suppose agenda setting is institutionalized in the person of a monopoly agenda setter. There is an existing status quo, x^0, and the agenda setter may select a sequence of alternatives to be compared against x^0 by majority rule. In effect, the agenda setter is the leader of a majority-rule assembly, guiding it to a final legislative determination.

The Chaos Theorem tells us what will happen. Letting $y=x^0$ and $z=x^{as}$ (where the superscript stands for "agenda setter"), the theorem says there is a sequence of alternatives, and hence a sequence of majority-rule contests, that will produce as its final outcome x^{as}, the most-preferred point of the agenda setter. The agenda setter, by artful arrangement of the agenda, can produce his most-preferred point as the final outcome, no matter where the process commences. The leader extracts all of the advantage from collective action. Even the preferences of majorities are no constraint on his maximizing behavior.

Taken as theories of leadership, the early agenda-setting models conceived of leaders as manipulators. McKelvey's (Machiavelli's?) theorem made precise the degree to which such manipulation is successful. Experimental work by Charles Plott and Michael Levine, as well as theoretically inspired empirical work by Thomas Romer and Howard Rosenthal, gave considerable substance to the findings of McKelvey.[23] In an experimental setting (an agenda setter seeking to influence the fleet selection of a flying club) and an empirical setting (by agenda setting school boards in Oregon school districts), evidence was provided to support the claim that leaders (qua agenda setters) bias final outcomes toward their own preferences.

AGENDA SETTING WITH SOPHISTICATED FOLLOWERS

In discussing his result, McKelvey notes that one of the critical assumptions underlying his theorem is that of sincere voting.[24] Throughout the sequence selected by the agenda setter, it is assumed that each voter will vote for the alternative that he most prefers. He will engage in no strategic or sophisticated behavior; rather, he will vote myopically or sincerely at each voting occasion. Myopic followership permits manipulative leadership. But what if followers could incorporate an appreciation of what the leader is up to into their individual voting decisions? This is the question asked by Shepsle and Weingast and elaborated upon by Banks and McKelvey.[25]

In the Shepsle-Weingast formulation, the leader announces the agenda sequence in advance, and the followers determine their respective voting strategies by exercising foresight in Farquharson's sense.[26] Their voting strategies will not necessarily cause them to vote sincerely at each opportunity to vote; at times they may vote strategically for a less-preferred alternative over one that is more preferred. In these circumstances, McKelvey's theorem no longer applies. Anticipating sophisticated behavior on the part of her followers, the agenda setter must take this kind of behavior into account. Will sophisticated followers constrain a manipulative leader?

Shepsle and Weingast's results contain both good news and bad. The good news is that sophisticated followership does constrain manipulative leadership; the bad news is that it does not constrain it very much. Shepsle and Weingast demonstrate that McKelvey's theorem must be modified as follows when followers are sophisticated: for any arbitrary point y and for any other point z contained in the set U, there is a sequence of alternatives, x_1, x_2, . . . x_t, so that: (1) x_1 beats y; (2) x_j beats x_{j-1}, $j=2$, . . . t; and (3) z beats x_t, when followers vote in a nonmyopic, strategic fashion.

The critical difference is that now the points that are reachable by agenda manipulation are not all the feasible points in the space (as in McKelvey's theorem); rather, they are only the points contained in the set U. The latter is called the *uncovered set*. However, in most settings, U is "large," so that a leader's opportunities to manipulate remain substantial. Indeed, it will often be the case that the leader's most-preferred point will be an element of U so that even sophisticated behavior by followers will not impose any constraint on a leader's opportunities.

Endogenizing Agenda Institutions

At this point it is appropriate to examine why followers would submit to a leadership institution such as the one described above. We assume that leadership/agenda-setting institutions are not ordained by the heavens but that they are the creations of majorities. If such institutions as we have portrayed above possess manipulative opportunities for leaders at the expense of followers, then, surely, followers would do something about this.

Because, in the real world, we often observe presiding officers or agenda committees that appear to be much like the agenda setter described above, we need to ask what that "something" might be. Two possibilities, in particular, are suggested in this literature: procedural constraints on agenda setting and competition to be the agenda setter. Shepsle and Weingast (1984) analyzed the former and demonstrated that both decentralization (in the form of multiple jurisdictions, each possessing its own agenda-setting mechanism and germaneness rules that protect the sanctity of jurisdictions) and order constraints (e.g., voting the status quo, x^0, *last* rather than first) produce restrictions on a leader's manipulative opportunities. Gary Miller has explored the effects that competition for the agenda-setter position may have on final outcomes. He found that although biases toward agenda-setter preferences remain, they are considerably more muted than in the world of McKelvey's theorem.[27]

Leader as Agenda Setter: An Assessment

The literature on agenda setting was not formulated initially as a theory of leadership. In briefly reviewing this literature, it is *our* claim that an aspect of leadership consists of controlling the agenda of group decision making. Because models of agenda setting were not originally couched as a leadership theory, they left implicit the institutional connection between leader and follower. Rather, such models seek to determine what it is worth to be a leader, and thus focus on the manipulative opportunities provided by control of the agenda. In a sense, this literature shares with Fiorina's work an emphasis on the optimizing behavior of a distinguished actor.[28] The subsequent work, which we briefly summarized in the preceding subsection and which focuses on control of the agenda setter (through institutional procedures and competition), begins to look like the "other part" of the principal/agent story that we told in the first section of this chapter. A full-blown theory of agenda setting should parallel the full-blown theory of principals and agents; it should emphasize not only the opportunities for the manipulation of outcomes provided by agenda control but also the institutional constraints (incentives and monitoring) that followers impose on their leaders in their agenda-setting activities.

POLITICAL ENTREPRENEURS

The literature that is based on the concept of *political entrepreneur* (PE) comprises a third class of formal models that deal with aspects of political leadership. PE models constitute a more heterogeneous group than do the first two categories of models that we examined. While agency models focus on a particular type of relationship, and agenda-setter models focus on a particular type of activity, PE models focus on a variety of relationships that involve a variety of activities.

While the metaphor of political entrepreneur probably has an earlier history in the literature of political science, its use as an important concept in formal models dates from Richard Wagner's review of Mancur Olson's *Logic of Collective Action.*[29] Wagner agrees with Olson that groups of people with common interests often will not organize and press their demands on government, because potential members will not find it rational as individuals to contribute toward the provision of a collective good that they would benefit from independently of their individual contribution. But, Wagner continues, one should not conclude that group interests will not be furthered by the political process, because political entrepreneurs may advance the interests of particular groups as a means to satisfy their own private interests. Most obviously, candidates for office often champion the causes of groups such as the elderly, consumers, and taxpayers as a means to winning elections. Organizing and lobbying government is one strategy groups may use to advance their interests; remaining unorganized and simply supporting friendly candidates and parties is another. Presumably, the political marketplace will operate so that the most efficient strategies will be chosen. Thus, some groups will organize formally, while others will not; but both types will be achieving the maximum net benefit that overall political conditions permit.[30]

A number of scholars, in their own theoretical work, have employed the concept of the political entrepreneur. Norman Frohlich, Joe Oppenheimer, and Oran Young have offered an explicit theory of political leadership based on the concept.[31] Terry Moe has relied on the concept of entrepreneurial leadership to construct a theory of group organization and maintenance.[32] Most recently, as we noted earlier in this essay, new game theoretical models of leadership have been proposed, which do not explicitly mention the concept of PE but which clearly address what we view as the central problem that motivates the PE literature.[33] Simply stated, that problem is this: the potential for group gain exists, but for one of a variety of reasons, individual actions may not capture that gain. The PE helps group members realize the gain, getting something for herself in the process.

While we see uncaptured gains as the central problem that drives the literature on entrepreneurs, note that such uncaptured gains may exist for several reasons. This variety of reasons is what gives rise to the heterogeneity of the PE literature. Different models focus on different reasons for the frustration of group goals and on the different activities that entrepreneurs may undertake in order to overcome such frustrations. Our reading of the literature (undoubtedly not exhaustive) reveals at least two general aspects of leadership addressed by PE models: (1) leadership as coordination and (2) leadership as organization. We discuss each of these in turn.

Leadership as Coordination

The simplest function of a PE is to coordinate the actions of a group of people. Consider the noncooperative game (no communication, no agreements) depicted in table 2.2. Two individuals each must choose one of five strategies. The game has two equilibrium pairs (*b*,*e*) and (*c*,*a*) that, unfortunately for the players, are not interchangeable. That is, (*b*,*a*) and (*c*,*e*) are not equilibrium pairs. As shown, the interests of the two parties are completely in harmony—each does best when the other also does so. The parties are completely indifferent to which equilibrium pair they choose, so long as they choose one or the other. In this situation, both parties would welcome the presence of a third party, who would suggest which strategy each should play. They might very well be willing to pay the third party something for this service.

TABLE 2.2
Two-Person, Noncooperative Coordination Game

		Player 2 Strategies				
		a	*b*	*c*	*d*	*e*
Player 1 Strategies	*a*	0,0	0,0	0,0	0,0	0,0
	b	0,0	0,0	0,0	0,0	5,5
	c	5,5	0,0	0,0	0,0	0,0
	d	0,0	0,0	0,0	0,0	0,0
	e	0,0	0,0	0,0	0,0	0,0

The preceding logic illustrates political entrepreneurship in its simplest form—as coordination of individual activities. If the individuals were able to communicate, they could quickly coordinate their choices and attain their prize. In a sense they would have formed a group and achieved the group benefit. But if the individuals are unable to communicate, as assumed above, then a profit opportunity exists for a PE. If the opportunity costs she faces are less than the expected utility of this profit opportunity, she will attempt to lead—in the sense of coordinate—the group.

The Wagnerian PE will exercise leadership primarily in this sense of leadership-as-coordination. Consider a large group whose members vote but are represented by no formal organization. Then a candidate can appeal for group support, promising to advance the group's interests in the political process. She asks them to bear no additional cost—they already vote anyway. She only asks that they vote for *her.* This form of PE is only a large-number generalization of the logic sketched above.

One interesting question that arises in considering leadership as coordination is the question of defining the group. Groups are not mutually exclusive, so the PE must work to make group members more conscious of some group memberships than of others, presumably by making them focus on some group benefits and costs rather than others. The PE literature has little to say about this question, although other branches of formal theory hold some promise for exploring the strategic use of issue appeals.[34]

Leadership as Organization

For Wagner, the PE is a substitute for group organization. But following Robert Salisbury, most subsequent contributions to the PE literature have emphasized political entrepreneurship as a means of achieving group organization.[35] Frohlich, Oppenheimer, and Young have devoted their attention to situations in which "provision of collective goods requires an organization"; they operate on the basic assumption that "such goods will be supplied when someone finds it profitable to set up an organization (or make use of some existing organization), collect resources, and supply the goods in question. Any individual who acts to supply a collective good without providing all of the resources himself we will call a *political leader* or *political entrepreneur.*"[36] In a similar vein, Moe has discussed "three necessary conditions for associational emergence and survival": "An entrepreneur must offer potential members a set of benefits, some of these potential members must be willing to buy, and the costs and benefits involved must be such that both the entrepreneur and the members continue to expect a net gain on the exchange."[37]

The literature on PEs as organizers and maintainers of interest groups is replete with provocative insights about the calculations of group members and leaders, leadership strategies, the relations of groups to other aspects of the political environment, and so forth. As an aid in understanding the real world of politics, the PE literature is undoubtedly of more immediate use than are the principal/agent and the agenda-setter literatures. But the broader range and richer content of PE models comes at a price. For one thing, PE models are not nearly so well worked out as are the models in the other two areas, so that the implications of the PE models are not presently grounded on as firm a logical footing as are those of agency and agenda-setter models. Even more importantly, there is a major theoretical omission in the PE literature that renders all its findings conditional.

The omission is the familiar one of strategic interaction. In a system of exchange relationships, members will wish to buy cheap, and leaders will wish to sell dear. Thus, numerous bargaining games (generally unstable) over the distribution of group benefits and costs ensue. Moreover, PEs who successfully organize groups must then contend with rival PEs who head competitive groups. Do they compete for each other's members, or do they adopt (generally unstable) "hands-off" agreements? Do they coordinate efforts to achieve common ends? If so, how are the benefits and costs to be shared? PEs must also contend with opposing or "enemy" PEs whose activities frustrate group goals. What strategies should be followed, and what bargains negotiated? And finally, PEs must deal with challengers for their own positions. Do they sanction? If so, how and when? Analyses of a lone member's decision to join or not to join one group in isolation and of a lone leader's decisions about forming and maintaining one group in isolation are starting points, but such analyses quickly encounter serious sorts of objections once strategic interaction is considered.

In fairness, contributors to the PE literature explicitly recognize the current limitations of their analyses, and they speculate about the nature of the consequences that fully strategic analyses would have for existing simple models.[38] But until strategic considerations are more formally included and until their implications are more rigorously analyzed, PE models of leadership as organization will be of most value as heuristic devices that provide loose frameworks for empirical analysis.

CONCLUSION

In this paper we have attempted to provide an overview of formal theoretic approaches to the study of political leadership. We have divided these approaches into three broad categories. The principal/agent approach analyzes in detail the relationship between the leader and the follower, paying special attention to the means by which followers (principals) can ensure that leaders (agents) will act in the follower's best interests. The agenda-setter approach analyzes in detail the agenda-setting power of the leader and how that power can affect the group's or the electorate's choice of final outcomes. Both of these literatures are typical of the formal theory approach in that they adopt a narrow focus but probe deeply within that focus, extending and broadening the focus one painstaking step at a time. Indeed, those who work in the PA and AS areas refer to their models, not as leadership models, but simply as principal/

agent and agenda-setter models. Although the relevance that these considerations have for leadership is obvious, it is equally obvious that such considerations constitute only a part of political leadership.

A third approach that we reviewed—models based on the concept of political entrepreneurship—is both less narrow and less deep than the first two. Leaders engage in a variety of actions in an effort to coordinate the behavior of followers, to organize followers, and to utilize those organizations. This literature takes the broadest view of leadership, but the price is the least progress, beyond speculation and insight, into the realm of rigorous argument and well-founded conclusions.

All three approaches have in common the assumption that leadership is relational. A leader performs certain activities, but she anticipates that followers will react to her actions, and she chooses her actions with those reactions in mind. Leadership is not something that inheres in the person of the leader, nor is it situationally determined, although context—(and especially institutional context, as we note below)—will constrain it. Rather, leadership is a term we apply to one part of a web of mutually dependent anticipations, expectations, and choices. Leadership is both proactive, as traditionally conceived, and reactive, as many scholars have argued. *One cannot have leaders without followers, but going further, one cannot understand leadership without understanding followership.*

Not only do formal theoretical approaches analyze leadership as a relational concept, but the trend is to do so in an ever-more-explicit and self-conscious fashion. The early pre-agency-theoretic models and agenda-setter models treat the leader asymmetrically, as a distinguished actor who is fully cognizant of followers but who is calculating their reactions according to some simple probability functions or decision rules that followers are presumed to follow.[39] Essentially, such leaders optimize, subject to the constraint of nonstrategic followers. In each literature, however, later models impose greater symmetry; this permits followers to go through the full range of strategic calculations allowed leaders. In some cases this is probably not an empirically sensible assumption—the case of leaders of mass movements, for example. But in other cases, it would seem to be necessary to put followers on an equal strategic basis with leaders—the case of the chair of a congressional committee, for example.

Despite efforts to model the behavior of followers in a leader/follower relationship, it is nevertheless true that existing formal models generally focus on the distinguished actor—the leader. The efforts to bring followers in on an equal footing will strike many readers as rudimentary. The principal/agent models are most explicit about examining both sides of the relationship, but this importation from economics has encountered a number of special problems when applied to instances of political leadership. As mentioned, most political principals are collective, so we immediately encounter the impossibility of defining the collective preference on which the agent's incentive scheme is to be based.[40] Ferejohn has achieved strong conclusions when he has assumed that all voters have identical preferences; these conclusions have weakened considerably when he has abandoned that strong assumption.[41] In some situations, the agent does not know the identity of her principals. For example, the aspiring legislative leader in a high-turnover legislature may not know whether she will be seeking the majority or the minority leadership after the next election. Her principal is in a continual state of flux. Perhaps most interestingly, many political agents must first set up their principal. The agent as entrepreneur must create her interest group, construct her constituency, or build her coalition before she can reap the rewards of leadership. But this most fundamental aspect of leadership has not received a satisfactory treatment in the PE literature precisely because of a failure to incorporate the strategic calculations of followers.

A second substantive question that has not been well considered by existing models is that of competition for leadership. If leaders earn political rents, as the PE literature assumes, then there will be competitors, envious of those rents, who will seek to displace the incumbent leaders. The existing literatures on party competition and coalition formation can be viewed as general treatments of competition for leadership, but within the confines of the leadership models examined in this paper, only the most tentative moves in this direction are apparent.[42]

We end this paper with one negative and one positive note. On the negative side, there is no guarantee that further work on the kinds of models we have discussed will inevitably result in broader, more comprehensive models. It may be that the attempt to model competitive leaders who interact with strategic followers over time will result in models too complex to deal with. Indeed, we are already seeing signs of this in the PA literature. As we remarked in the discussion of Calvert's paper, even the attempt to treat one pair of behavioral alternatives for one leader and one follower over more than two time periods is technically tricky, because strategic possibilities multiply rapidly.[43] This does not give cause for optimism in dealing with multiple principals and competitive leaders over time, which is the general situation of political leadership.

But on a more positive note, the empirical contribution of formal models often lies less in the direct empirical applicability of their theorems than in more indirect insights that are stimulated by those theorems. For example, the chaos of majority rule, which we have described above, does not appear to describe the operation of real-world majority-rule institutions.[44] This lack of fit between theorem and reality suggests to many of us that the complex institutional structure of the real world, overlaid on the simple majority-rule mechanism, is what produces determinate outcomes.[45] The current interest of formal modelers in institutional structure, under the rubric of the "new institutionalism," has been stimulated by these initial results. In the leadership context, an analogous situation may hold. As we have described above, preliminary attempts to analyze sophisticated followers in AS models indicate that sophisticated followers cannot exert much constraint on the ability of an agenda setter to dictate the final outcome. Similarly, preliminary efforts to analyze competition for leadership indicate that competition constrains leaders, but its effects are not well understood.[46] In short, the analysis of leadership in a largely institution-free environment does not identify major constaints on the capacity of leaders to exploit their followers. Perhaps that is the reason why real-world leaders typically function within a complex pattern of political institutions. Rational followers would not enter leader/follower relations if the leader's appropriation of most of the potential gain was the predictable result. Procedural constraints are the mechanism by which rational followers can achieve an acceptable distribution of the gains from the relationship. Research on that subject has barely begun.

NOTES

1. Aaron Wildavsky, "Political Leaders Are Part of Political Systems: A Cultural Theory of Leadership" (mimeographed, University of California at Berkeley, 1986).
2. Henry Clay, *The Papers of Henry Clay,* ed. James Hopkins, vol. 1 (Lexington: University of Kentucky Press, 1959).
3. Charles Jones, "Joseph G. Cannon and Howard W. Smith: An Essay on the Limits of Leadership in the House of Representatives," *Journal of Politics* 30 (1968): 617–46.
4. For nontechnical developments see Michael Jensen and William Meckling, "Theory of the Firm: Managerial Behavior, Agency Costs, and Ownership Structure," *Journal of Financial Economics* 3 (1976): 305–69; and Terry Moe, "The New Economics of Organization," *American Journal of Political Science* 28 (1984): 739–77. For a more technical survey see Daniel Leventhal, "Survey of Agency Models of Organizations" (mimeographed, Carnegie-Mellon University, Pittsburgh, 1985).
5. There is a close resemblance, as well as a terminological confusion, between principal/agent models and Stackelberg games. The latter are games in which there is an explicit temporal structure. The player who moves first is called the Stackelberg "leader" (e.g., when IBM announces a price for its newest PC). The player who makes the second move, the Stackelberg "follower," reacts (say, one of the small IBM clone producers announces its price). The leader's initial choice, then, is predicated upon anticipation of the follower's reaction. In principal/agent models, P moves first, and then A reacts. So, P is a Stackelberg leader, and A is a Stackelberg follower. For an excellent discussion of Stackelberg games see James Friedman, *Oligopoly and the Theory of Games* (Amsterdam: North-Holland, 1977), chap. 4.
6. Douglas B. Bernheim and Michael Whinston, "Common Agency," *Econometrica* 54 (1986): 923–42.
7. Hannah Pitkin, *The Concept of Representation* (Berkeley: University of California Press, 1967).
8. Morris Fiorina, *Representatives, Roll Calls, and Constituencies* (Lexington, Mass.: Lexington Books, 1974).

9. We date agency theory with the seminal paper by Jensen and Meckling ("Theory of the Firm"), although a very brief early statement is found in Stephen Ross's "The Economic Theory of Agency: The Principal's Problem," *American Economic Review* 63 (1973): 134–39; see also Barry Mitnick, "Theory of Agency" (Ph.D. diss., University of Pennsylvania, 1974).

10. Fiorina, *Representatives,* p. 39.

11. Kenneth Shepsle and Brian Humes, "Legislative Leadership: Organizational Entrepreneurs as Agents," paper delivered at the Stanford Conference on Adaptive Institutions, Palo Alto, Calif., in 1984.

12. John Ferejohn, "Incumbent Performance in Office," *Public Choice* 50 (1986): 1–26.

13. Ibid., pp. 5–6.

14. Ibid., p. 21.

15. *Imperfect* information describes a condition in which an actor is uncertain about the consequences of his actions, either because of randomness or because of some unobserved (or undeducible) action taken by another actor. The principals in Ferejohn's model have imperfect information about the random variable x. *Incomplete* information describes uncertainty that is traceable to a lack of knowledge about the preferences of other actors, their strategies, or even who the other players might be. In the Ferejohn model, the prinicpals have complete information: they know who they are, what their common preferences are, and that the preference of their agent is to remain in office while putting forth as little effort as possible.

16. Randall Calvert, "Reputation and Legislative Leadership," *Public Choice* 55 (1987): 81–121; and James Alt, Randall Calvert, and Brian Humes, "Reputation and Hegemonic Stability: A Game-Theoretic Analysis," *American Political Science Review* 82 (1988): 445–66.

17. Mancur Olson, *The Logic of Collective Action: Public Goods and the Theory of Groups* (Cambridge, Mass.: Harvard University Press, 1965).

18. Calvert, "Reputation," p. 6.

19. David Kreps and Robert Wilson, "Sequential Equilibrium," *Econometrica* 50 (1982): 863–94.

20. Calvert, "Reputation," p. 27.

21. Charles Plott, "A Notion of Equilibrium and Its Possibility under Majority Rule," *American Economic Review* 57 (1967): 787–806.

22. Richard McKelvey, "Intransitivities in Multidimensional Voting Models and Some Implications for Agenda Control," *Journal of Economic Theory* 12 (1976): 472–82; and idem, "General Conditions for Global Intransitivities in Formal Voting Models," *Econometrica* 47 (1979): 1085–1111.

23. Charles Plott and Michael Levine, "A Model of Agenda Influence on Committee Decisions," *American Economic Review* 68 (1978): 146–60; and Thomas Romer and Howard Rosenthal, "Political Resource Allocation, Controlled Agendas, and the Status Quo," *Public Choice* 33 (1978): 27–45.

24. McKelvey, "Intransitivities."

25. Kenneth Shepsle and Barry Weingast, "Uncovered Sets and Sophisticated Voting Outcomes with Implications for Agenda Institutions," *American Journal of Political Science* 28 (1984): 49–74; Jeffrey Banks, "Sophisticated Voting Outcomes and Agenda Control," *Social Choice and Welfare* 1 (1985): 296–306; and Richard McKelvey, "Covering, Dominance, and Institution Free Properties of Social Choice," *American Journal of Political Science* 30 (1986): 283–315.

26. Robin Farquharson, *Theory of Voting* (New Haven, Conn.: Yale University Press, 1969).

27. Gary Miller, ''Experimental Results in Two-Party Agenda-Setting: What's It Worth to be a Party?'' paper presented at meetings of the Midwest Political Science Association, Chicago, 1980.

28. Fiorina, *Representatives.*

29. Richard Wagner, ''Pressure Groups and Political Entrepreneurs,'' *Papers on Non-Market Decision Making* 1 (1966): 161–70.

30. Arthur Denzau and Michael Munger, ''Legislators and Interest Groups: How Unorganized Interests Get Represented,'' *American Political Science Review* 80 (1986): 89–107.

31. Norman Frohlich, Joe Oppenheimer, and Oran Young, *Political Leadership and Collective Goods* (Princeton, N.J.: Princeton University Press, 1971).

32. Terry Moe, *The Organization of Interests* (Chicago: University of Chicago Press, 1980).

33. Calvert, ''Reputation.''

34. William Riker, *The Art of Political Manipulation* (New Haven, Conn.: Yale University Press, 1986).

35. Robert Salisbury, ''An Exchange Theory of Interest Groups,'' *Midwest Journal of Political Science* 13 (1968): 1–32.

36. Frohlich, Oppenheimer, and Young, *Political Leadership,* p. 6.

37. Moe, *Organization,* p. 38.

38. Frohlich, Oppenheimer, and Young, *Political Leadership,* chaps. 3 and 4; Moe, *Organization,* chaps. 3 and 4.

39. Fiorina, *Representatives;* and McKelvey, ''Intransitivities.''

40. Kenneth Arrow, *Social Choice and Individual Values* (New York: John Wiley, 1951).

41. Ferejohn, ''Incumbent.''

42. James Enelow and Melvin Hinich, *The Spatial Theory of Voting: An Introduction* (Cambridge: Cambridge University Press, 1984); Peter Ordeshook, *Game Theory and Political Theory* (Cambridge University Press, 1986); and Miller, ''Experimental Results.''

43. Calvert, ''Reputation.''

44. Gordon Tullock, ''Why So Much Stability?'' *Public Choice* 37 (1981): 189–202.

45. Kenneth Shepsle and Barry Weingast, ''Structure-Induced Equilibrium and Legislative Choice,'' *Public Choice* 37 (1981): 503–19.

46. Miller, ''Experimental Results''; Ferejohn, ''Incumbent.''

3

Leader/Follower Interactions in Mass Democracies: Follower-Driven Models

Bryan D. Jones

In their comprehensive review of formal approaches to the study of political leadership in this volume, Fiorina and Shepsle write: "Leadership is a term we apply to one part of a web of mutually dependent anticipations, expectations, and choices. . . . One cannot have leaders without followers, but, going further, one cannot understand leadership without understanding followership."

In this essay, I examine the role of the interaction between political leaders and followers in a democratic society. On the surface, this is a monumental task, given that the interaction is certainly affected by institutional context, cultural understandings, the personalities of the leaders, and the opportunity structure that the leaders face, to note but a few. I simplify the task by focusing on three formal approaches to the understanding of the interaction: the spatial approach, born of the focus on political parties as linkage mechanisms; the distributional-coalition approach, spawned by group theory; and an investment/consumption approach, which stems from political economy, broadly conceived.

Formal models of leader/follower interactions based on the assumption of rational utility maximization contain three basic elements: leaders, followers, and a set of institutional incentives for leaders that tie them to the wishes of followers. Regular elections are the primary institutional mechanisms that link leaders to followers. It is assumed that politicians want to win elections and that they attempt to maximize the number of votes in order to do so, because these models make the assumption that leaders in democracies are vote maximizers. Hence the wishes ("utility functions") of followers have substantive policy content (that is, followers want certain policies from the democratic policy process), but the wishes of leaders do not.[1] Hence, each model makes crucial assumptions about followers that can be evaluated.

In rational-choice approaches to politics, both leaders and followers are assumed to be maximizers. The controversial issue, however, centers less on the question of maximization and more on what maximization attaches itself to. I sometimes believe that maximization in politics fills a role somewhat similar to that of anxiety in psychoanalysis: the question is not existence; it is, rather, the object of attachment. At any rate, let us make the common assumptions that voters are utility maximizers and that governmental action affects that utility. Leaders are vote maximizers; that is, their welfare that is derived through the political process is entirely determined by how many votes they get in an upcoming election. The consequence of this assumption is that the behavior of leaders is determined once the function that relates the distribution of votes to the distribution of followers' utilities is known, because leaders are single-minded in what they want. In these models, then, leaders are completely controlled by mass preferences, in a manner similar to the control exercised by the consumer in the economic theory of the firm. This is clearly questionable, and it could be conceived as a definition of leadership taken right out of a volume purportedly on political leadership. But let us play out this assumption to see where it takes us.

SPATIAL MODELS OF LEADER/FOLLOWER INTERACTIONS

The classic formal statement of the relationship between leaders (political parties) and followers in democracies is that of Anthony Downs. Leaders are vote maximizers. Voters maximize utility, or their individual welfare. So far, so good. But here is the critical (and problematic) assumption: the spatial analogy. Voters adopt preference points in an issue-defined ideological space. Hence, leaders adopt positions in the ideological space that is "closest to" the largest number of voters in order to win elections. Downs reduces the issue of space to one dimension: "How much government intervention should there be?"[2] But he makes it clear that this is an analytical simplification. In such a situation the ideological positions of parties are dependent on the distribution of voters on the dimension. Indeed, one of the most interesting predictions of the model is that in a two-party system that has a normal or near-normal distribution of votes, the parties will adopt the position of the median voter.

This approach has spawned an academic generation of research aimed at expanding the model (for example, to multidimensional space) and relaxing various assumptions of the approach.[3] Although various researchers have relaxed various assumptions concerning voter distribution, the candidates' information about voter positions in space, and the relevance of the election procedures for candidate positions, spatial models obviously cannot relax what is the most unrealistic assumption of all: the spatial analogy itself. To understand just how demanding the spatial approach is for the average voter, let us quote from Otto Davis and Melvin Hinich:

> It is assumed that, at least conceptually, policies can be measured by certain indexes. . . . It is presumed that the population of registered voters is homogeneous in that the same indexes measure any given policy for all voters. Further, it is assumed that each voter has preferences concerning all issues of policy and that the ith voter's preferred position (or set of most desired policies) can be represented by the column vector $x_i = [x_{i1}, x_{i2}, \ldots x_{in}]$.[4]

The problems with these assumptions are well known; they were laid out by Donald Stokes as early as 1963.[5] Stokes attacked the spatial approach for what he contended were four unrealistic assumptions, or axioms: namely, unidimensionality, fixed structure, ordered dimensions, and common reference. Unidimensionality is the assumption of a single dimension of politics along which all political issues can be ordered. Fixed structure is the assumption that all dimensions are equally salient: "different dimensions should be given different weights at different times." The assumption of ordered dimensions implies that all issues are well-behaved quantitative issues ("position issues" in Stokes's terminology) and that no issues are valence issues (those linking "the parties with some condition that is positively or negatively valued by the electorate"). The axiom of common reference embodies the assumption that all relevant actors, especially voters and parties, share the same perceptual coordinate system.

In principle, all of these issues can be faced within the spatial framework, and, indeed, some have been. For example, the assumption of unidimensionality was relaxed years ago, and weights may be employed to adjust for dimensional salience. The assumptions of ordered dimensions and common reference are more difficult, but they could at least be subjected to empirical testing. Indeed, several researchers have examined the existence of ordered dimensions in the thought patterns of the electorate, with mixed implications for the Downsian approach. The extent of ideology as an orienting factor in the electorate, defined either as the extent of clustering among issues or as the use of the terms "liberal" and "conservative" to understand politics, seems to be low. Furthermore, measures of political attitudes are characterized by a considerable amount of instability, which, according to Donald Kinder, "reflects both fuzzy measures and fuzzy citizens." This instability is a result of the lack of coherent organizing principles within the mind of the typical voter and of "the fleeting attention commonly paid to politics, the preeminence of private desires over public ones."[6]

The picture of the ability of the mass public to respond to issue appeals by politicians, a demand of the Downsian approach, is not entirely bleak. First, there exists some evidence, obtained through the use of multidimensional scaling techniques, that candidate evaluation by the electorate proceeds along a limited number of dimensions.[7] Second, some members of the electorate do in fact exhibit high levels of conceptual sophistication when it comes to political matters, and these individuals tend to organize political issues on a liberal/conservative continuum.[8]

One might, therefore, develop a more complex model of communications in the electorate, in which the candidates and the ideologically sophisticated behave according to the classic assumptions of the Downsian approach and in which the rest of the electorate responds to some combination of set predispositions and cues from the politically sophisticated. This would mean dropping the assumption of an undifferentiated electorate, and it would complicate the analysis considerably. Indeed, John Aldrich has worked through the implications for party positions under the assumption of activist influence.[9] This direction would make analyses that rest on particular assumptions of the distribution of the electorate, including median-voter analysis, irrelevant, except, perhaps, as they apply to the distribution of activists. Because the distribution of activists is almost certainly bipolar, the implication of Downsian analyses of party convergence on the median voter would no longer hold.

The major problems with the spatial approach are its unrealistic assumptions about followers. Decades of careful public-opinion research have provided a picture of the electorate that is inconsistent with the stringent demands placed on voters by the Downsian approach. Most voters do not seem to evaluate politics by using a structured dimensional format. Without a more realistic model of the electorate, the spatial models are not likely to be helpful in the analysis of leader/follower behavior in mass democracies.

It can be argued that the validity of the spatial model does not hinge on the number of issue dimensions that are present in the electorate or on the salience patterns among dimensions or on whether or not some of the dimensions are characterized by only two values. None of Stokes's objections can call the generalized spatial modeling approach into question, because the issue is less the nature of the assumptions that go in and more the nature of the results that come out. Otto Davis has written: "Theory cannot be judged upon the basis of the reality of the assumptions. Theory should be judged on the basis of how well it performs in relation to its purpose."[10] Here, also, the spatial approach does not fare so well.

Work on the basic Downsian framework has suggested considerable dissatisfaction concerning the way the model fits with important aspects of political reality. This dissatisfaction has led to attempts at relaxing a number of Downs's assumptions, but each relaxation has made the analysis more cumbersome. A number of additions and modifications to the basic model have been made (e.g., the policy motivation of leaders; the distinction between political actives and passives), all with the consequence of making the approach more cumbersome, less elegant, and less parsimonious. Consider a spatial model that introduces, in the name of generalizability and realism, all of the following: the policy motivation of leaders, voter uncertainty, the issue of multidimensional space, the issue of salience, and differences between actives and passives. Could a model that is at once generalizable and realistic help us to understand politics any better than could the collection of facts and information it purports to organize?

Interestingly, the only way that parsimony can be restored is through the reintroduction of the very simplifying assumptions that have proved so empirically problematic. If candidates and voters could be placed on a limited number of ordered dimensions, with salience changing in regular ways, then the approach would be of enormous utility. Because this does not seem to be the case empirically, the spatial approach must be so burdened with relaxed assumptions that it is of little utility in studying the political systems. (These comments are meant to apply solely to mass/elite interactions. Where we can more plausibly assume that both followers and leaders are able to employ spatial strategies—e.g., Congress—spatial models are clearly appropriate.)

THE DISTRIBUTIONAL COALITION

It is possible that the democratic political world is basically a pork barrel. There is no particular reason that political scientists need to model politicians as operating in issue space; we can just as well conceive of them as acting in group space. Citizens are not so much alike because they occupy similar positions on policy issues; they are alike because their group memberships cause them to want similar things from the political process. The vote-maximizing politician must forge these diverse social groups into an electoral coalition that will be capable of carrying him or her into office. The politician does this, not by adopting a position in multidimensional issue space, but by appealing to as many groups as necessary by delivering (or promising) packages of policies tailored insofar as possible to the group. Policies are nothing more than vehicles for the delivering of group benefits.

The conception of politics as group based is at least as old as Arthur Bentley's *The Processes of Government,* and it reached its most elegant formulation in David Truman's *Governmental Process.*[11] Truman, however, left no room for the construction of electoral coalitions by politicians; governing energy comes primarily from group-based demands both in and between election periods.

The pluralistic formulation of Robert Dahl and others offers a more aggressive role for politicians.[12] They want to win elections; hence, they are responsive to the demands of groups. Indeed, they may create policy activities where little demand existed in order to construct coalitions that will serve them in future elections. Because of the uncertainties of an election somewhere in the future, politicians tend to be inclusive rather than exclusive in the construction of their coalitions.

The general idea that comes across from the pluralistic view of politics is that vote-maximizing politicians appeal to groups to construct election coalitions. Gary Cox and Matthew McCubbins have formalized this notion by continuing to assume that politicians are vote maximizers, but by changing the basic assumption about voters' utilities. Instead of being concerned about positions of candidates in issue space, voters want to maximize particularistic benefits that flow from the policy process.

Let $X_a = (x_{a1}, x_{a2}, \ldots x_{aG})$, the benefits that are promised by candidate A to the G groups in the electorate. Hence candidate A chooses X_a to maximize

$$EV_a\,(X_a, X_b) = \sum_{g=1}^{G} n_g\, P_{ag}\,(X_{ag}, X_{bg})$$

where $P_{ag}\,(X_{ag}, X_{bg})$ is the proportion of the gth group that will support A, given that A promises an amount X_{ag} to group *g;* X_{bg} is candidate B's promise to group *g;* G is the number of groups in the electorate; and n_g is number of members in the gth group. The distribution of benefits is subject to marginal returns; that is, as benefits that are delivered to a group increase, the incremental increase in support for the candidate will decline.

Under these conditions, candidates will adopt "strategies in which they invest little (if at all) in opposition groups, somewhat more in swing groups, and more still in their support groups." If politicians behave in this manner, "the core groups of a given candidate's or party's coalition will tend to get locked in and the fluidity of electoral coalitions which might be expected from a vote-maximizing standpoint will be mitigated."[13] That is, electoral coalitions will be relatively stable because of the actions of politicians in distributing benefits to their supporters and to their opponents—although this is somewhat dependent on how adverse to risk the politicians are.

Here we have an approach to the problem of leader/follower interactions in mass democracies that is much more consistent with prevailing views of democratic public opinion. Group-based understandings of the policy process have been found to characterize sizable segments of the electorate. Moreover, the use of group-based allegiances in the citizen's understanding of politics can be explained in terms of basic socialization processes.[14] In a broader sense, partisan identification can be seen as one type of psychological group membership, albeit one that has particular relevance for politics. This does not imply that group memberships are acquired but unchanging characteristics: clearly, there is considerable room for both individual and generational changes in group identifications. Indeed, changing group memberships (and changing the salience of group identifications in the case of multiple and overlapping identifications) can be an instrument of policy change if politicians are continuously constructing group-based coalitions in anticipation of the next election.

A POLICY TRADE-OFF BETWEEN INVESTMENT AND CONSUMPTION

The "distributional coalition" approach to the democratic-leadership issue postulates a very simple model of voters, especially when compared to the Downsian spatial approach. Voters want concrete policy benefits, regardless of the policy domain from which these benefits are plucked. There is also an implicit assumption that policy benefits are distributive goods, characterized by the ability to exclude some citizens (nonsupporters) from the benefits of policies.

What happens if we adopt the distributional coalition framework but add a second assumption about the wishes of voters? The voters are interested in the package of policy benefits that will be delivered, but they are also interested in the general state of the economy and its likely rate of progress. This, after all, determines far more than do specific policy benefits the probable future welfare of the individual voter. Moreover, both electoral research and common wisdom posit a relationship between the strength of the economy and the fate of the governing party. A considerable number of studies that rely on aggregate data have tended to find that general economic conditions are related both to presidential popularity and to voting for the House of Representatives. Several studies have also examined the relationships between individual personal circumstance, perceptions of national economic circumstance, and voting, but the results have been mixed.[15] Some of these studies have found relationships between individual circumstance and voting, but others have not. Donald Kinder and D. Roderick Kiewet have suggested that economic conditions affect the behavior of voters only when the voters see a national problem rather than an individual one.[16] In any case, the proposition that voters retrospectively evaluate incumbent politicians with reference to national economic circumstances has considerable empirical support in the literature.

One related issue is whether voters evaluate parties and candidates prospectively or retrospectively. That is, do voters compare policy packages that the parties promise, or do they compare the performance of the party in power against some explicit or implicit standard of performance? A third possibility is that the electorate compares the performance of the party in power to the prospective performance of the party out of power. This issue has generally been raised in conjunction with the issue of voter competence: if voters do not generally use structured, dimensional formats in evaluating policies, then they are not likely to perform the tedious and complex task of comparing the policy promises of parties that are competing for offices. On the other hand, voters seem to be perfectly capable of evaluating the performance of the party in power retrospectively and of commenting through the electoral process.[17]

Whether voters use a prospective or a retrospective process for arriving at evaluations of parties and candidates is not relevant, strictly speaking, to the issue of what they support. The voters may decide, retrospectively, that the incumbent party has not provided enough distributional benefits to an electoral coalition. Or the voters may decide, again retrospectively, that the party in power has failed to manage the economy successfully. The same results may be achieved via a prospective method. The point here is that the process (retrospective versus prospective voting) and the product (distributional versus collective benefits) ought not be confused.

Now it would seem that the politician has two choices: to invest in the future strength of the economy or to consume available resources to provide policy benefits to coalition members. For the moment, let us assume that there are no barriers to knowledge about which policies lead to economic growth and which ones detract from it (or are neutral). Nor do politicians have any problem in determining the optimal policy package for distributing benefits to supporters. The first option involves the provision of a collective good: the blessings of a growing economy cannot be denied to any segment of the population, although of course some segments may benefit more than others. The second involves dividing up the policy benefits of government to groups of claimants. Hence the politician must choose between providing distributional policy benefits or nondistributional collective goods.

WILL VOTERS SUPPORT FUTURE COLLECTIVE BENEFITS?

William Nordhaus has provided an analysis of one instance of this political choice: the trade-off between unemployment and inflation. Nordhaus has concluded on a pessimistic note: "The politically determined policy choice will have lower unemployment and higher inflation than is optimal," and "a perfect democracy with retrospective evaluation of parties will make decisions biased against future generations."[18]

However, the preferences of voters for the trade-off are crucial. It may not be the case that the voters prefer immediate consumption (which results in inflation) over the collective benefits that will accrue from more unemployment. Indeed, Douglas Hibbs has presented empirical evidence that the mass public is not likely to support expansionary policies, even though the unemployment rate is stable at a high level, if the inflation rate is moderate or higher.[19] In other words, the bias toward present consumption may not be as pronounced as Nordhaus and others have suggested.

The notion that voters may be oriented toward the provision of collective, rather than distributive, benefits is not new. Years ago, Edward C. Banfield and James Q. Wilson developed the concept of the public-regarding ethos among urban voters. Citizens who adhered to that ethos were supposed to be more likely to forgo individual, distributive benefits in the pursuit of community good. The authors found that middle-class Anglo-Saxon voters were more likely to exhibit public-regarding voting behavior than were working-class ethnic voters—a finding that subjected the entire concept to considerable criticism.[20]

The time has come for these ideas to be reexamined. In an attempt to begin to examine the support of voters for collective versus distributive benefits, I asked Texas voters a series of questions concerning support for public spending. This was part of the winter 1986 Texas Poll.[21] The results, from one state at one point in time, can be considered suggestive only. Nevertheless, the distrust of government that was evident in the Texas political culture and the state financial crisis brought on by the collapse of oil prices during that period made the issues posed by the poll salient. Each of these questions was prefaced by the phrase "To encourage economic development, state government should provide additional support for. . . ." I also asked whether citizens would support increased taxes to support economic development efforts.

Categorizing the issues by level of education offers the opportunity to juxtapose collective interests against (presumed) class-based interests. The results are presented in figure 1. First, every item except support for airports gained the approval of the majority in every category. Second, there was little evidence of class-based support for issues, with the exceptions of support for health and welfare, worker retraining, and taxes. Voters who had higher educational attainment were more willing to pay higher taxes but were less willing to support health-and-welfare and worker-retraining programs. The voters who had less education were also slightly less willing to support general government action to promote economic development, but support in that area was already at very high levels.

One can tentatively conclude that there is some support among Texas voters for policies designed to produce collective, rather than distributional, benefits and that this support is not class linked. If anything, lower-class individuals are more likely to support programs that are not in line with their distributional interests—particularly new-product research, tax breaks, and other incentives for industries. On the other hand, individuals who have higher educational levels are more willing to shoulder tax burdens on behalf of governmental efforts to secure economic growth. One can legitimately question whether "economic development" is such an emotionally charged term that indications of support are not to be trusted. Nevertheless, the data do suggest the limitations of models based on distributional benefits alone.

FIGURE 3.1 PUBLIC SUPPORT FOR EXPENDITURES TO PROMOTE ECONOMIC DEVELOPMENT

CAN GOVERNMENTS INVEST?

Support for economic growth by the mass public or by political leaders is irrelevant unless the government is capable of choosing between the policy options of investing in the future well-being of society, on the one hand, or distributing benefits to members of a prospective electoral coalition, on the other hand. The connective "or" is intended to be the inclusive variant; that is, it is not the case that the choice between investment and consumption needs to be a trade-off. Policies that result in improved economic performance can also have distributional benefits. Hence a politician can find him or herself in the fortuitous circumstance of having a coalition of supporters who desire investment policies.

A major issue concerns just which policy activities will promote economic growth and which will not; in other words, which policies can be considered investments in the future and which policies represent present consumption. A considerable body of literature, which derives from classical economic analysis, argues that most governmental activity is nonproductive and that public policies in regard to taxation and expenditure policies represent a transfer of social resources from productive activities to nonproductive ones.[22] Modern economists recognize that the government has a role in modern capitalist society, and they have analyzed situations in which markets will fail to produce optimally (basically, situations in which collective goods are needed).[23] Yet, neither economists nor political scientists have developed models to explain just which kinds of governmental activities are productive and which ones are not, nor have they developed any models of process which would explain why governments should invest rather than consume.

A number of studies have been conducted of policies pursued by state and local governments to promote economic growth. On the matter of industrial location, older studies have emphasized the irrelevance of public-policy actions, while later studies have found a more fundamental role for state action. Surveys of corporate officials and studies of aggregate data prior to about 1980 have found that the location of facilities was sensitive to access to markets, labor, raw materials, and transportation and to labor costs, and that variation in state and local tax rates and other public-policy variables were not important. More recent studies show that state tax and expenditure variables, education, and infrastructure expenditures are important, in addition to the traditional economic variables.[24] For example, Mark Schneider has reported that higher infrastructure expenditures are associated with increases in property values in suburbs.[25]

In studies of state expenditures, I have found that total expenditures are positively related to net business creation and that this relationship survives controls. (David Birch has shown that the creation of business is the key to economic expansion.)[26] Moreover, certain categories of state expenditures are more directly related to economic growth than are others. In particular, expenditures for education and local services are positively associated with the net creation of business, as well as increases in employment, whereas expenditures for welfare are associated with economic decline.[27]

The literature suggests that some public expenditures do promote economic growth. Other categories of expenditures probably act as a depressant on growth, while still others have no effect one way or another. These latter two categories of expenditures are consumption expenditures because they consume social resources without replenishing them. This certainly does not mean they ought not be pursued; it only means that they have different effects than do investment expenditures.

There is a final constraint. A tax structure that is too burdensome (and let us leave for the moment the definition of "too burdensome") can result in economic stagnation. This is most evident among localities within a single metropolitan region, where there are unlimited options for well-off citizens to move. The notion that high tax rates are related to economic decline also has support at the state level.[28] There is, then, a declining marginal effect to increases in investment expenditures and thus limits to pursuing a joint strategy of expanding expenditures for both consumption and investment.

THE CONDITIONS OF POLICY CHOICE

At this juncture, I have argued two points: first, that governmental expenditures can promote economic growth through their contribution to the human and physical infrastructure—a "supply side" approach to governmental expenditures—and second, that voters will support investment policies and that they therefore are more future oriented than current conceptions would suggest. I now turn to an examination of the conditions of policy choice—the conditions that will encourage politicians to advocate consumption policies over investment policies, or vice versa.

The first factor that will condition policy choice is spatial scale. The smaller the size of the governing jurisdiction, the more pronounced will be the impetus toward investment policies. The urbanist Paul Peterson has developed the thesis that cities are far more dependent on external factors than are nation-states. Peterson has further argued that these external forces strongly encourage investment expenditures (he calls them developmental policies) and that they operate against consumption expenditures (to Peterson, redistributive and allocational).[29] The relatively small size of municipalities (and for residents, the ready availability of alternative municipalities within which to live) causes city officials to follow a strategy of maximizing the tax base, the attempt to attract well-off citizens and productive businesses.[30]

At the other end of the spatial scale is the nation-state, which is less susceptible to the migration of the tax base but which is certainly not free to ignore the problem. Central governments in most developed democracies provide a panoply of consumption policies—from income supplements to farm subsidies—to a greater extent than do subnational governments. This specialization of function, which Peter Saunders has termed the dual state, can be overemphasized.[31] At every level of government, public policies are a mixture of investment and consumption. Nevertheless, incentives to invest are stronger for subnational governments than for nation-states.[32]

A second condition that affects policy choice is the nature of the distributional coalition that is constructed by the politician. If certain investment policies provide not only the collective good of economic growth but also divisible benefits to coalition members, then the pursuit of investment policies will be virtually painless.

Third, the existing state of the economy affects the choice between investment and consumption, but not in a simple fashion. At first glance, it would seem that investment policies would be more prevalent during periods of recession, while consumption policies would be more in evidence during inflationary periods, when demands generally are high. On further reflection, however, one might reason that deep recessions would generate increased demands for consumption expenditures, while periods of steady, noninflationary growth would allow investment policies to dominate.

In a study of expenditure growth in Michigan (which I chose for its "one-crop" automotive economy) between 1958 and 1983, I found that growth in educational expenditures (a "mixed function") and welfare (a consumption expenditure) tracked different paths.[33] Educational expenditures rose during the noninflationary growth years of the mid 1960s, leveled off during the inflationary growth years of the 1970s, and fell during the recession (in Michigan) of 1979–83. Welfare expenditures grew later than those for education, primarily from 1967 to 1973, and were level before and after. The growth years for welfare were relatively weak ones for the automobile industry but were not nearly so bad as the early 1980s, when welfare expenditures did not grow.[34]

All of this suggests that economic circumstances do affect the investment/consumption choice, but in highly complex ways. Economics affects, but does not dictate, political choice; but most of us already knew that.

A final consideration concerns the issue of information. The link between particular public expenditures and economic growth is not self-evident. Any group can make the claim that its preferred policies will lead to economic prosperity. Furthermore, changes in the economy mean that any policy initiative in the public sector is temporally limited in its beneficial impact. During the first half of the nineteenth century, canal building was touted as an investment in prosperity. Few people today would advocate such a strategy, even though the construction of the Tennessee-Tombigbee Waterway suggests the power of the pork barrel when it is connected to claims of economic progress. The uncertainty that surrounds the connection between policies and growth gives ample room to the force that argument, persuasion, and rationalization have in the policy process.

CONCLUDING COMMENTS

I have put forth the thesis that models of leader/mass interactions in democracies which are currently in vogue in political science are highly sensitive to specifications concerning the nature of followers. These models, including Downsian spatial models, distributional coalition models, and a model that I propose here involving a choice between collective and individual benefits, all assume politicians to be vote maximizers. These models differ, however, in their views of followers.

Spatial models make very strong assumptions about the nature of followers, assumptions that have generally been discredited by empirical research in voting behavior. One school of the philosophy of science argues that the assumptions of models are irrelevant and that outcomes (i.e., predictions) are critical. Nevertheless, given the struggle of Downsian analysts to relax assumptions and add complexities, it would seem that the simple spatial model is inadequate. Unfortunately, this work has tended to make the approach too cumbersome to be of much utility. I hasten to add that these remarks refer to elite/mass interactions only; in the case of sophisticated followers (i.e., in Congress) the models are more defensible.

A second approach drops the strong assumption of spatial thought and substitutes the notion that followers are benefit maximizers. Programs and policies are like jars holding jellybeans: politicians draw from them to construct benefit packages for members of their coalitions. Cox and McCubbins have shown how this group-based assumption yields the prediction of considerable stability to electoral coalitions as politicians try to add to their solid-core supporters without alienating them. It would be interesting to compare Downsian predictions with this approach to gain some sense of relative predictive power; certainly this approach requires far less of the voters.

Finally, I have developed a rudimentary model, which stresses a policy choice between providing consumption benefits to a distributional coalition and providing investment in future economic health. This approach probably makes more realistic assumptions about voters than do the other two approaches that I have discussed here. It also captures certain features of the policy process that are not incorporated by the other models, because in those models, policy effects are quite irrelevant. However, the conditions of policy choice are so difficult to specify that prior predictions are highly problematic.

The major weakness of all three approaches concerns the lack of attention to leader behavior. Leader initiative disappears, and followers become the driving force in electoral democracies. By calling attention to the dependence that well-articulated models of leader/follower interactions in democracies have on assumptions about followers, I hope that progress can be made in understanding both ends of the interaction; it is in this spirit that I offer this essay.

NOTES

I appreciate the comments that Jonathon Nagler and Clarence Stone made on an earlier draft of this paper.

1. Both the maximization assumption and the assumption of no policy motivations on the part of parties have been relaxed. On the latter see Henry W. Chappell and William R. Keach, "Policy Motivation and Party Differences in a Dynamic Spatial Model of Party Competition," *American Political Science Association* 80 (Sept. 1986): 881–99. Strong assumptions about voters remain, however.
2. Anthony Downs, *An Economic Theory of Democracy* (New York: Harper & Row, 1957).
3. See, e.g., Otto Davis, Melvin Hinich, and Peter Ordeshook, "An Expository Development of a Mathematical Model of the Electoral Process," *American Political Science Review* 64 (June 1970): 426–48; Robert L. Calvert, "Robustness of the Multi-Dimensional Voting Model: Candidate Motivations, Uncertainty, and Convergence," ibid., 29 (1985): 69–95; Gary Cox, "Electoral Equilibrium under Alternative Voting Institutions," ibid., 31 (Feb. 1987): 82–108.
4. Otto Davis and Melvin Hinich, "Some Results Relating to a Mathematical Model of Policy Formation in a Democratic Society," in *Mathematical Applications in Political Science,* vol. 3 (Charlottesville: University of Virginia Press, 1967), p. 15.
5. Donald Stokes, "Spatial Models of Party Competition," *American Political Science Review* 57 (June 1963).
6. Donald Kinder, "Diversity and Complexity in American Public Opinion," in *Political Science: State of the Discipline,* ed. Ada W. Finifter (Washington, D.C.: American Political Science Association, 1983), p. 397; see also Herbert Asher, *Presidential Elections and American Politics,* 4th ed. (Chicago: Dorsey Press, 1988).
7. Herbert Weisberg and Jerrold Rusk, "Dimensions of Candidate Evaluation," *American Political Science Review* 64 (Dec. 1970): 1167–85; Jerrold Rusk and Herbert Weisberg, "Perceptions of Presidential Candidates: Implications for Electoral Change," *Midwest Journal of Political Science* 16 (Aug. 1972): 388–410.
8. William Jacoby, "Levels of Conceptualization and the Liberal-Conservative Continuum," *Journal of Politics* 48 (1986): 423–32.
9. John Aldrich, "A Downsian Spatial Model with Party Activism," *American Political Science Review* (Dec. 1983): 974–90.
10. Otto A. Davis, "Notes on a Strategy and Methodology for a Scientific Political Science," in *Mathematical Applications in Political Science,* vol. 4, ed. Joseph Berund (Charlottesville: University Press of Virginia, 1969), p. 29.
11. Arthur Bently, *The Processes of Government* (Cambridge, Mass.: Belknap Press, 1967); David Truman, *The Governmental Process,* 2d ed. (New York: Alfred A. Knopf, 1971).
12. Robert A. Dahl, *Who Governs?* (New Haven, Conn.: Yale University Press, 1961).
13. Gary Cox and Matthew McCubbins, "Electoral Politics as a Redistributive Game," *Journal of Politics* 48 (May 1986): 385.

14. Kinder, "Diversity," pp. 405–6.

15. Herbert Asher, "Voting Behavior Research in the 1980's: An Examination of Some Old and New Problem Areas," in *Political Science,* ed. Finifter, p. 367; see also Heinz Eulau and Michael Lewis-Beck, eds., *Economic Conditions and Electoral Outcomes* (New York: Agathon, 1985).

16. Donald Kinder and D. Roderick Kiewet, "Economic Discontent and Political Behavior: The Role of Personal Grievances and Collective Economic Judgments in Congressional Voting," *American Journal of Political Science* (1979): 495–527.

17. The classic analysis is in Morris Fiorina, *Retrospective Voting* (New Haven, Conn.: Yale University Press, 1981). For a recent formal analysis see W. Robert Reed, "Retrospective versus Prospective Voting" (College Station: Department of Economics, Texas A & M University, 1988).

18. William Nordhaus, "The Political Business Cycle," *Review of Economic Studies* 42 (Apr. 1975): 169–90.

19. Douglas Hibbs, "The Mass Public and Macroeconomic Performance," *American Journal of Political Science* 23 (Nov. 1979): 705–54.

20. Edward Banfield and James Q. Wilson, "Public Regardingness as a Value Premise in Voting Behavior," *American Political Science Review* 58 (Dec. 1964): 876–87; and James Q. Wilson and Edward Banfield, "Political Ethos Revisited," ibid., 65 (Dec. 1971): 1048–62.

21. The Texas Poll is a quarterly survey of citizen opinion in the state of Texas by the Public Policy Resources Laboratory of Texas A & M University.

22. See Roger Freeman, *The Wayward Welfare State* (Stanford, Calif.: Hoover Institute Press, 1981).

23. James Buchanan, *The Public Finances* (New York: Irwin, 1970).

24. See John Blair and Robert Premus, "Major Factors in Industrial Location," *Economic Development Quarterly* 1 (Feb. 1987): 72–85; see also Rodney Erickson, "Business Climate Studies," ibid. (Feb. 1987): 62–71.

25. Mark Schneider, *The Local Market for Public Goods* (Pittsburgh: University of Pittsburgh Press, 1989).

26. David Birch, *Job Creation in America* (New York: Free Press, 1987).

27. Bryan Jones, "Public Policies and Economic Growth in the American States," paper prepared for presentation at the American Political Science Association Meetings, Washington, D.C., Sept. 1988; and Bryan Jones and Arnold Vedlitz, "Higher Education Policies and Economic Growth in the American States," *Economic Development Quarterly* (Feb. 1988): 78–87.

28. Robert Newman, "Industry Migration and Growth in the South," *Review of Economics and Statistics* 65 (Feb. 1983): 76–86.

29. Paul Peterson, *City Limits* (Chicago: University of Chicago Press, 1981).

30. Schneider, *Local Market,* chap. 2.

31. Peter Saunders, "Reflections on the Dual Politics Thesis," in *Urban Political Theory and the Management of Fiscal Stress,* ed. Michael Goldsmith (Aldershott, U.K.: Gower, 1986).

32. Paul Peterson, Barry Rabe, and Kenneth Wong, *When Federalism Works* (Washington, D.C.: Brookings Institution, 1986).

33. See Jones, "Public Policies"; Peterson, *City Limits,* chap. 5.

34. Bryan Jones, "Government and Business: The Automobile Industry and the Public Sector in Michigan," *Political Geography Quarterly* 5 (Oct. 1986): 369–84.

4

Two Conceptions of Institutional Leadership

Erwin C. Hargrove

Political leaders create new possibilities in history. The dominant issues, the terms of the debate, and the stock solutions of one era may give way to new conceptions articulated by leaders acting as agents of change. In the long interludes that separate periods of innovation, the task of a leader is to manage the social and political equilibrium established during the time of change. The first kind of leader is transforming and the second kind is transactional; one changes the paradigm, whereas the other maintains it.[1]

Leaders do not act alone. They move in concert with political trends. To view the ideal types of transforming and transactional leaders, one must understand the politics in which they do their work and the political and institutional resources that are available to them.

The social-choice model of decision making is most often used to describe transactional leadership. The political leader acts within a set of stable boundaries. The individual players know their preferences and act in predictable ways to maximize them. The role of the leader is to create coalitions for decision out of the range of preferences. Leaders most commonly do this by structuring institutional rules, by offering incentives to cooperate, and by manipulating situational factors. But no logical reason prevents transforming leaders from working with a social-choice framework to expand and rearrange the preferences of others. One analogue might be that of the business entrepreneur who creates new preferences among consumers.

The central focus of this chapter is the leadership of public bureaucracies. The term "social choice" is too broad for that subject; therefore the phrase I will use, derived from social-choice theory, is that of the "rational actor." The actor can be either a leader or a follower. In both cases the actor makes choices in behalf of his or her goals. Leaders maintain their leadership by appealing to the goals of followers. The latter may seek to control leaders by structuring institutional rewards and punishments in such a way as to require leaders to serve the followers' ends. In both cases, action follows incentives. The literatures on entrepreneurial leaders in voluntary organizations and on the leaders of public bureaucracy both exhibit this approach. My interest is in the latter.

The neoinstitutional model of politics, in contrast to the social-choice perspective, looks at the principles in politics and institutional life that bind people together. Politics is assumed to be primarily about such principles, rather than about the needs and goals of individuals or groups. Institutions are held together, in part, by shared meanings, language, symbols, and purposes. Such institutional traditions may have a long life, and one can only understand them through historical inquiry.

Neoinstitutional models provide plenty of room for the transforming leader. A central question is how people create and transform regimes and institutions. Politics is understood in historical terms. But the model has a place for the transactional leader who nurtures and continues established principles.

We may thus construct two continua with roughly parallel themes, yet permit a crossover from one continuum to the other at different points:

FIGURE 4.1

Transactional Leadership————Transforming Leadership
Rational-Choice Politics————Neoinstitutional Politics

Transactional leaders work within the stable confines of a fixed set of goals and purposes in a rational-choice world. They appeal to the incentives of individual actors. But it is also possible for transactional leaders to foster unity by appeal to principles that are generally shared, even when many individual goals differ.

Transforming leaders articulate the principles of creation and renewal in a neoinstitutional world. But they may also change goals in the perspective of a rational-choice model by stimulating new preferences, by creating new coalitions of interests, and by identifying new missions.

It is often assumed that social-choice approaches capture only the material interests of actors. This is not so. Rational choice encompasses all utilities, including material and ideological ones. The application of the model to the study of politics faces the obvious fact that individuals may seek more from politics than material gain. This is less the case when the analysis is of economic interest groups. But the question of how to extend the model to capture nonmaterial factors is important. One may handle this problem admitting other values while holding fast to the main elements of the rational-choice model: preferences are individual, fixed, and ranked. This is an atomistic model of politics.

The neoinstitutional model is often assumed to include only cultural and ideological factors. But there is no logical reason why material interests may not be captured by the model. However, such interests will inevitably cohere with larger principles that may best be characterized as cultural and ideological. Thus, an actor within an institution may pursue a material or a career interest, but that actor's understanding of that interest and the degree of legitimacy accorded it will have been shaped by the cultural or ideological themes by which the institution is organized.

LEADERSHIP AND RATIONAL CHOICE

The economist James M. Buchanan sees markets and politics as having the same structure. Each consists of individuals who seek to fulfill their goals through buying goods or through voting. Neither an economy or a polity has an existence or a purpose apart from the sum total of individual preferences. There is no public interest in this social-contract tradition, which, for Buchanan, includes the pluralist concepts of political science. The democratic polity is grounded on an assembly of individuals. Buchanan admits that other models of politics, such as organic, ruling-class, or force theories of the state, may also help explain politics. But they do not belong in a public-choice model.[2] All that is required for a "logical theory" of public choice is that "interests differ and that individuals act in accordance with their separate interests."[3]

For Buchanan, individuals act to maximize their expected utilities in terms of objectively identifiable magnitudes. These may be either material wealth or altruistic goals. Buchanan's polity may be a world of saints as long as their conceptions of heaven on earth differ. Supraindividual goals are ruled out.[4]

Terry Moe builds on Buchanan's insights to challenge the thesis of Mancur Olson that leaders keep interest groups together by side payments to members to induce the membership to pursue collective goods.[5] Moe argues that members of an organization will pursue political goals for their own sake, apart from material inducements to the membership.[6] Moe's central thesis, which he supports with empirical cases, is that once the assumption of economic self-interest as the only motive is relaxed, there are many grounds for individuals to participate in interest groups that seek collective goods for their members: for example, altruism, ideology, camaraderie, friendship, love, security, beliefs, racial prejudice.[7] Moe admits that it is hard to encompass such a range of motives in analytic formulation or models and that it is even more difficult to compare intangible units of prestige or loyalty. Many institutional norms and values emerge from group origins and processes of socialization and are important for understanding organizational cohesion and the strengthening of group norms.[8]

When such purposive inducements are important to the political goals of individuals, they may offer a better explanation of membership and participation than would a strictly economic model.[9] However, Moe does not expect unanimity. Nonmaterial incentives sow the seeds of instability, and political heterogeneity creates divisions.[10]

Rational-choice models of organizational leadership are most often applied to voluntary interest groups. The central question is asked by Olson: How can people be induced to join when they can be free riders who will automatically receive the collective good if others join? A public bureaucracy, which people join in order to be able to work, is not quite the same thing. The collective good that the organization is seeking is the achievement of its mission. How is that goal related to the goals of individuals? The public-choice literature has not explored this question. Fiorina and Shepsle point out that the literature about entrepreneurial leadership of interest groups does not satisfactorily cover the strategic interactions of leaders and followers.[11] This is even more the case with rational-choice theory about public bureaucracy.

Fiorina and Shepsle characterize the literature on leaders as agenda setters as assuming that leaders manipulate followers. Majority rule in an institution whose members have divergent preferences is both indeterminate and unstable, and a leader can drive a majority-rule process to any final outcome by constructing an agenda. Such authority is institutionalized in bureaucratic organizations.[12] Public bureaucracies are not governed by majority vote, but leaders do not govern bureaucracies by fiat alone. Leaders provide diverse inducements, not so much to elicit membership as to produce high levels of performance in the accomplishment of missions. Performance presumably has a positive relationship to the amount of external political and financial support that is given to the organization.

Anthony Downs's analysis of leadership in public bureaucracies looks at leadership in this way. Complex organizations contain people who have different perceptions of the interests at stake. Differences cannot be settled by voting, and a hierarchy is required. Central authority has some latitude in its autonomy when acting in zones of indifference to members of the organization.[13] Still it is necessary for leaders to appeal to the interests of employees. Downs is not explicit about how this should be done. He sets out an ideal type of optimal leader, whom he calls an advocate, who will seek to balance coherence and diversity.[14] Presumably diversity is resolved by coalition building, but in discussing coherence, Downs appears to be implicitly reaching for some goals or values that are shared in common by members of the organization and thus perhaps moves beyond rational-choice vocabulary altogether.

Gary Miller pursues the theme in a rigorous analysis in which he concludes that bureaucratic leaders are not able to achieve an optimal contribution from all members of the organization by appealing to self-interested incentives alone. Miller sees the organization as the arena for a number of prisoner's-dilemma games, in which the combination of player strategies is suboptimal for organizational performance. This is true even when the incentives go beyond material self-interest to include policy and group loyalties. Leaders who operate solely in terms of their self-interest will always seek to reward followers less than their followers wish to be rewarded. And organization members will always seek to perform at less than optimum in terms of their own interests.[15] Miller establishes this conclusion by modeling games in accepted social-choice terms. Both leaders and followers must transcend individual self-interest if long-run optimal outcomes for all are to be achieved, but the players have no short-run incentive to do so. The combination of players' rational strategies is suboptimal. The manipulation of incentives does not permit an organization to operate at optimal levels.

Miller argues that an effective leader has to move beyond individual incentives to the development of cooperation and trust within organizations. He uses the evidence of experiments in game theory to conclude that leaders may be able to create a "culture of cooperation."[16] He gives an importance to leadership skill that is not found in principal/agent models. He also gives an indeterminacy to outcomes: success is not guaranteed. Political leadership consists of "inspiring trust and creating expectations" to make all wish to work for optimal outcomes.[17] The highly effective business corporations that Peters and Waterman describe exemplify the creation of such corporate cultures.[18]

Miller concludes that an "ethics of simple self-interest maximization is insufficient" because the impossibility of matching individual and group interests will present ethical dilemmas for the individual. Management that appeals solely to the self-interest of its employees is therefore "deficient." Management must have an ethical component in which the interests of the whole are expressed.[19] Miller, to a greater extent than either Moe or Downs, has taken us beyond the rational-actor–social-choice framework altogether and toward issues that are treated by neoinstitutionalists because he posits common values.

Kenneth J. Meier's chapter in this volume makes clear that as understood by most political scientists, leaders appeal both to self-interest and to common values. He defines leadership as a "series of strategic choices by members of the organization's dominant coalition."[20] The goal of leaders is to acquire power for the organization by creating internal cohesion, expertise, and external support from clients. Leaders seek both organizational survival and policy achievement. The inducements that leaders offer take the form of exchanges based on incentives that can be material, purposive, or coercive. Organizations will vary greatly in the relative strengths of such incentives. Thus, the Marine Corps relies heavily on esprit de corps, the early Peace Corps relied on purposive incentives, and so forth. Meier does not give an example of a public bureaucracy that is built primarily on material incentives.

Indeed, he believes that government is likely to attract individuals who have purposive incentives. Otherwise, they would work in the private sector, in which material incentives are strong.[21]

Bureaucratic leadership must go beyond internal issues. Most institutions seek support from the environment, and most leaders build political coalitions for that purpose. The inducements offered to external groups by leaders to support work of the organization cover the same spectrum as those that they offer to people inside.[22] Political scientists may characterize this in the language of rational actors in the sense that leaders create coalitions of interests. The possibility that commonly shared values will exist across a cluster of constituencies seems remote to social-choice theorists.

William H. Riker has used social-choice conceptions to analyze the creation of coalitions by political leaders. His work does not focus solely on organizational leadership, but it can easily be applied to that subject. Riker looks at individual political leaders to understand how they may structure situations so as to cause others to support them. He looks at single decisions, rather than at continuing tasks of organizational leadership. But the general strategic approach would seem appropriate for continuing leadership. Riker has coined the term "heresthetic" to describe the strategy of manipulation within a rational-choice framework. The heresthetic uses language to manipulate other people when he "describes social nature, imparting to his description the exact twist that leads others to respond to nature as he wishes."[23] This is not rhetoric in which language is persuasive according to the merits of the argument. In heresthetic arguments, one makes a strategic case that the interests of others are served by doing what is suggested.

Riker's case studies of heresthetic leadership show how leaders manipulate support by setting and controlling agendas, making calculations about the strategic voting of others, and manipulating values that are important to others. The people to whom the appeals are made share only the group's official purposes. Their private motives are more important. "The heresthetic neither creates preferences nor hypnotizes. What he can do is probe until he finds some new alternative, some new dimension, that strikes a spark in the preferences of others."[24] Such analysis relies on a bedrock realism, even as the model includes nonmaterial motives. Leaders dominate by the manipulation of incentives even at the full tide of idealism.

Riker suggests the possibility of transforming leadership. The great shifts in political life come from the introduction of a new dimension to political conflict, such as the use of the slavery issue to break up the existing political equilibrium in American national politics. Lincoln and the Republicans were able to create a new equilibrium through heresthetics. Republican opposition to the extension of slavery to the new states in the territories put northern Democrats on the defensive and enabled the Republicans to create a new national coalition which would dominate national politics.[25] Riker sees such changes as actions to create new coalitions of interests through the creative structuring of issues.

Pluralist models of politics in political science usually parallel social-choice assumptions that politics is largely a process of bargaining among interests. The political leader creates coalitions out of interests.[26] But his resources are limited; they must be conserved and used strategically.[27] This is the picture of optimal presidential leadership developed by Richard E. Neustadt. Knowledge of the incentives of others is the first step toward the construction of alliances.[28] Stone, in this volume, applies the insights from public-choice and pluralist theory to the question of how a set of political leaders in a city are able to create, maintain, and modify a "governing regime." He uses the concept of preemptive power in which community leaders are able to control the public agenda and policy decisions by creating a coalition of dominant interests which competing coalitions cannot overcome. The leaders shape policy by making bargains within the governing coalition.[29]

We thus see a progression in a rational-choice approach from models of simple organizations that consist solely of individual material utilities to more complex entities in which goals are still diverse but go beyond material wants. There is a similar progression of leadership, which moves from the entrepreneur who is seeking to create a group out of diverse interests by offering inducements, on the one hand, to an administrative leader of a public bureaucracy who is the trustee not only of the survival of the organization but also of its achievement of policy goals. In the first case the leader provides inducements to persuade others to join. In the second case he must extract optimal productivity from those who work inside the organization.

NEOINSTITUTIONALIST PERSPECTIVES ON LEADERSHIP

"Neoinstitutional" is a term of convenience for a perspective held by those who see governments as having a history and sphere of operation of their own, apart from the constituencies in the society that they represent. Governmental institutions carry ideals, values, and expert capacities across time. Constituencies influence what a government does. But a government may also shape the patterns of politics and representation among its constituents.

The two principal variations of this approach are James G. March and Johan P. Olsen's "new institutionalism" and the "state capacity" school of Theda Skocpol, Stephen D. Krasner, and others.[30] March and Olsen focus on single organizations, as do Skocpol et al.; but the latter also compare the capacities of entire national governments in relation to their societies.

March and Olsen propose the new institutionalism as an antidote to what they regard as the prevailing norms in political science for the study of institutions. Theories of politics since about 1950, in their view, have seen politics as an extension of social conflict, as the aggregate consequences of individual behavior, as the result of calculated self-interest by individuals, as efficient in achieving a balance of interests, and as being primarily about the allocation of resources.[31] March and Olsen see rational-actor theories as having derived from economic understanding of markets, but they believe that the model has spread to political science. This has led to a perception of decision makers, whether citizens or leaders, as rational in knowing their preferences and how to achieve them.[32]

In the institutionalist view, preferences and meanings may develop through politics, and individuals will respond to the choices presented to them instead of imposing their goals on the process. Politics is seen, in part, as an interpretation of life in which shared and conflicting conceptions of society are discovered and expressed.[33]

It is logically possible that the leaders and all the members of an organization might, as rational actors, choose the goals of the organization as their personal goals. Would this occur in a rational-actor or neoinstitutionalist framework? Rational-actor theorists seldom explore this possibility, because they assume a diversity of interests. Even so, an organization of leaders and members who have identical goals would still be an atomistic collection of egoistic individuals. Institutionalists look at history in which symbols, language, norms, and values develop and cohere in a configuration. Even the contradictions within that pattern constitute an integral part of the larger configuration. The pattern cannot be reduced to individuals, because the whole is greater than, or at least different from, the sum of its parts. Much of the whole is not subscribed to in the form of self-conscious, calculating choice. One is socialized into it in the process of learning roles. Different individuals appropriate for themselves parts of the whole, and they act out the drama of the whole which, in this sense, has an institutional life of its own.

According to March and Olsen, the idea of leadership that creates willing coalitions among actors with known demands is implicit in modern political science. An alternative conception, which they advance, sees the transformation of preferences by the leader as educator, who presents new ideas and wins acceptance for them. They link the transforming leader with the new institutionalism.[34]

The actions of people in institutions, according to March and Olsen, are greatly influenced by the norms that are part of group life and that develop historically. Past experience is institutionalized in symbols and rules. Individuals within institutions may define their roles in terms of duties and obligations as well as by personal self-interest. They may also place high value on participation in the work of the institution, independent of policy outcomes.[35]

Finally, for March and Olsen, searches for alternative policies in organizations are understood not solely as problems looking for solutions but also as solutions looking for problems. There is an indeterminacy about decision making that rational-actor conceptions miss. Institutional leaders may prevail because they are able to join solutions to problems in completely unanticipated ways and thus are able to infuse the institution with a new understanding of its missions.[36]

The "new institutionalist" challenge to rational-choice theory is empirical. Can one find behavior that does not fit the concepts of rational choice? Some aspects of organizations which the new institutionalism might explore are the ways in which institutions either learn or fail to learn from experience, how historically derived norms shape the influence of internal interests, and the importance of institutional symbols and myths in guiding action and sustaining leadership.[37]

Skocpol cites Hugh Heclo's study of the development of twentieth-century social policy in Sweden and Britain as an illustration of the neoinstitutionalist approach. In both cases, civil servants, working from longstanding bases of expertise, influenced the development of welfare policies.[38] The professional capacities and normative orientations of civil servants shaped policy in conjunction with the political representation of interests. In contrast, those who use the "bureaucratic politics" approach in political science describe the calculations and actions of individuals and group actors without a complementary description of the instititutional logic that might shape such bureaucratic politics.[39]

Once adopted, policies become embedded in institutional memory, and they shape commitments and expectations. Aspirations for the future follow upon past achievement, if successful, and the past thus shapes the future. However, institutions may also possess the capacity for change in regard to strategies of action, bureaucratic competencies, and aspirations.[40] Such change usually takes place without undermining the broad institutional norms that have evolved. Krasner sees a "punctuated equilibrium" in which institutions are modified by short bursts of rapid change, followed by long periods of stability.[41] One might also conceive of gradual, continuous adaptations to new circumstances across institutional history.

The neoinstitutionalists emphasize institutional symbols and sagas. "Once established, a saga serves a prophetic function by linking past, present and future in an inspirational story to give participants the sense that they are taking part in a special process that is distinctly different from the mundane or corrupt world outside."[42]

The saga may guide adaptation to new circumstances, or it may become so entrenched that people in an organization are blinded to external change. Leaders may even seek to impose past, but now inappropriate, solutions on new problems. Institutions are not always efficient in adapting to historical change. The neoinstitutionalist view emphasizes the importance of organizational culture, conceived as the system of publicly and collectively accepted meanings held by its members. Culture includes symbols of the organization, the language that is characteristically used to depict organizational purposes, beliefs about what the organization should do and how, and myths and visions that are idealized conceptions of the organization and its mission.[43] Organizational leaders create culture by the invention and use of language, symbols, and myths and by the articulation of common purposes for the organization. In Andrew M. Pettigrew's description, entrepreneurs "make words walk" in the sense that ideas that leaders express become part of the culture, to be invoked in the future.[44] Ideas are sources of organizational direction and cohesion; and they also provide a resource as new problems are faced.

Neoinstitutionalists believe that pluralist theories of politics in political science suffer from the same weaknesses as social-choice theory. In pluralist descriptions of governmental decision making, individual leaders pursue their own goals in addition to representing the interests of others. Such pictures of leaders, neoinstitutionalists say, lack a conception of "institutional imperatives and constraints, including general political beliefs."[45] Pluralists are said to ignore the fact that organizational leaders are both empowered and constrained by institutional norms, practices, and capacities. The work of leaders is not adequately described if they are depicted as only having to create coalitions of self-interested actors in an atomistic organization.

SUMMATION

It should be clear that I regard both the rational-choice and the neoinstitutional perspectives as valid ways in which to try to understand institutions. Each approach may throw light on things that the other misses. The test of usefulness is empirical, but the task of interpretation is not easy. My purpose in the rest of this chapter is to explore the value of the framework that I present here, with a particular focus upon leadership.

The two continua of types of leadership and organization permit an elaboration into four ideal types of leaders. Type 1 is the coalition builder who works within fixed patterns of interests and incentives. Type-2 leaders transform utilities by creating new organizational missions and patterns of interests within the organization without altering the basic normative principles that guide the institution. Type-3 leaders are nurturers and maintainers of a stable institutional culture and a sense of purpose. Type 4 consists of transforming leaders who either create the organization according to normative conceptions of character and mission or redirect it in fundamental ways in response to a changing environment. They alter and adapt the normative principles that guide the organization. The central myth that has animated the organization is not apt to be discarded. Rather, the leaders will reinterpret it to fit new circumstances and missions.

FIGURE 4.2
TYPES OF LEADERS

	RATIONAL ACTOR	NEOINSTITUTIONAL
Transactional	Type 1	Type 3
Transforming	Type 2	Type 4

The assignment of an individual leader to a category is based on the leader's goals and the resources they invoke as leaders. Thus, type-4 leaders will rely on institutional myths more than type-2 leaders.

The distinction between transactional and transforming leaders is clear enough. Bertrand de Jouvenel has written about Rex and Dux, the two basic elements of leadership. Rex presides over a stable entity, whereas Dux creates new possibilities.[46] James MacGregor Burns draws the same distinction in his use of the terms "transactional" and "transforming."[47] Burns and de Jouvenel write about the leadership of entire polities. Neither draws the distinction that I draw here between rational actor and neoinstitutional models. Burns's transforming leader has a moral function in challenging the citizens of a polity to realize their highest moral potential in the kinds of political action that transform a society. He uses the example of Mao Tse-tung as the prototype of the transforming leader. Burns considers a democratic hero such as Franklin D. Roosevelt to be transactional because he rearranged interests to shore up the American Republic but did not create a new system of politics.[48]

In this essay, I refine and adapt the terms to serve other purposes. My focus is on organizational leadership, and I make distinctions between the strategies, resources, and instruments used by different types of leaders. The reader may object that the four ideal types are so pure as to be unreal. Surely, leaders in the real world reflect aspects of these tendencies, just as complex organizations are clusters of interests, united by one or several organizational cultures. The typology is only a point of departure and comparison for describing real leaders and organizations. It is difficult to imagine a neoinstitutional transforming leader who did not rearrange the coalition of interests. By the same token, a leader who transforms the pattern of interests within the existing cultural paradigm may certainly invoke that paradigm as an authority for the attempted changes. Transactional leaders may very well use both material and cultural resources as they manage the internal politics of the organization. In Riker's terms, the most skillful leaders may be both herestheticians and rhetoricians.

The difficult question is whether the mixes of types in the real world run together so much that they nullify the value of the typology. This is an empirical question. Differences are likely to be matters of degree and emphasis rather than of kind. Models of leadership and organization are most useful in teasing out competing hypotheses to explain behavior. The final test is one of plausibility in terms of the evidence. The best way to validate this scheme is to apply it in one case.

THE TENNESSEE VALLEY AUTHORITY: DEMOCRACY AND BUREAUCRACY AT THE GRASS ROOTS

The TVA is a good vehicle for understanding both transforming and transactional leaders because its history has seen great creativity at the beginning, then long periods of stability, punctuated by bursts of adaptation and renewal. The authority has embodied a strong belief in the superiority of a multipurpose governmental corporation for regional development which works to carry out its missions at the grass roots in close contact with the people of the valley. And yet, within this ideology, TVA has served the material interests of groups in the valley and also the professional and organizational interests of its employees. One can thus apply both rational actor and neoinstitutional lenses to the history of TVA as one seeks to understand the succession of transforming and transactional leaders.

The TVA was fifty-five years old in 1988. It has never been an organization at rest; it has continually changed and adapted to new missions and new politics. It is possible to compare several different TVAs across time, using Philip Selznick's idea that leadership is especially important at "critical turning points" in an institution's history.[49] When it was founded in 1933, the leaders of the new regional authority had a very broad statutory mandate to build dams for the generation of hydroelectric power and for navigation and flood control. TVA was to contribute to the agricultural development of the valley, as well as to husband natural resources in general.

The broadest goal was regional development, but the instruments for this were specific authorized missions. There were ambiguities. Was the authority to build distribution lines and sell power directly to consumers? Or was it to sell power to the existing private utilities in the valley? Was TVA to give technical assistance to farmers through its own organization or through the land-grant system of agricultural colleges and county agents? What authority was there for TVA to plan for the geographic, commercial, and industrial development of the valley? How was the TVA to relate to federal natural-resource agencies in the valley, such as the Corps of Engineers and the Soil Conservation Service? What were its relationships to be with the state and local governments of the seven-state region? Answers to these questions and many others like them had to be worked out by practice, through trial and error. These questions became the central issues of bureaucratic politics within the authority and in its relations with constituencies and opponents.

The period from 1933 to roughly 1939 was a period of definition. It was a highly creative time in which the central issues of purpose and mission were resolved after much internal and external conflict. The leaders of the TVA had to invent answers to the hard questions. The central task of leadership during this period was to overcome the ambiguity of the TVA mission by inventing plausible courses of action and purpose and by winning support for those goals.[50] David E. Lilienthal was the central character in this drama, and he can fairly be described as a transforming leader of the neoinstitutional kind who was able to fashion a pattern of interests around a set of leading ideas about the TVA mission. Lilienthal was the third chairman of the three-member TVA board. He was preceded by the first chairman, Arthur E. Morgan, and his successor, Harcourt A. Morgan. The first Morgan was a utopian who thought of the TVA as a demonstration model for the nation. It would have been enough if it had had one dam and power grid and one demonstration farm. They would have been beacons for imitation, as would new techniques of forestry, land use, and planning. A. E. Morgan had a strong sense of the need for the TVA to be a highly professional, nonpolitical organization, and he put his stamp on it permanently in that regard. He also insisted that the organization be as decentralized as possible, with many decisions being made at the operating level, and this norm has prevailed. However, A. E. Morgan lacked any sense of the need for the young institution to protect itself in the hard political world. He sought cooperation with the private utilities at the very time that they were suing in the courts to prevent TVA from distributing power.[51] Lilienthal had a much keener sense of the need to establish a program for the distribution of electric power through nonprofit municipal and rural distributors in order to create the base of popular support in the valley that TVA required. Harcourt Morgan was an agriculturalist who believed that the modernization of southern agriculture, in the form of the use of effective fertilizers and crop diversification, could best be achieved by having the TVA delegate the task of technical assistance to the land-grant colleges and county agents. The TVA would manufacture the fertilizer and oversee the entire effort. The idea of cooperation at the "grass roots" was H. A. Morgan's, and the theme of working with local governments and private groups, rather than displacing them, became the central theme of TVA.[52] It matched the idea of decentralization of decision making within the organization.

Lilienthal, who was chairman from 1940 until 1945, but who had been the effective leader under Harcourt Morgan's chairmanship from 1937 on, led the political fight for TVA against the power companies and with the president and Congress. He dramatized the authority to the people of the valley through speeches and demonstrations to introduce people to the many uses of electrical power. When the Interior Department sought to pull TVA under its administrative umbrella after 1939, Lilienthal fought back, by defending the virtues of a decentralized, multipurpose authority over the vices of separate and centralized

Washington bureaucracies. He articulated the TVA "myth" of grass-roots democracy in his book *TVA: Democracy on the March,* and he organized and led the organization internally so that the ideals of collaboration among professional fields in multipurpose functions and cooperation at the grass roots with citizens were the central themes of organizational culture.[53]

Lilienthal gave the TVA the ideology that held the organization together with a sense of purpose and guided its operations. In this sense he invented a myth. He also invented heresthetic strategies of self-defense, using the myth as protective cover. From the fight against Harold L. Ickes in 1939 through the Dixon/Yates fight during the Eisenhower administration, TVA was to rally its troops in the valley, as well as the congressional delegation, every time there was a threat to organizational autonomy.

A long period of organizational and mission stability, punctuated by periods of political insecurity, followed. The TVA actually began to fulfill its missions only during the war and immediate postwar years as the system of hydroelectric dams and power distribution was completed along with the work of navigation and flood control. As agriculture changed in the valley, TVA gave up technical assistance in favor of the development and manufacture of new kinds of fertilizer. The TVA became a power company with limited, residual missions in natural resource development. Gordon Clapp, who was Lilienthal's successor, had been the latter's right-hand man as general manager. Clapp was a professional public administrator who had risen to the top through the Personnel Department of TVA. That department had responsibility for the recruitment and training of employees and therefore their socialization; it was also the official source of ideas about organizational design and redesign. Clapp was the custodian of the missions developed during the Lilienthal period and the organizational norms of the decentralized, multipurpose authority.[54] His colleagues have described him as a leader who orchestrated TVA norms of decision making by insisting that ideas rise up to the board and that discussion by the board be highly collegial, with the directors of the separate departments also participating. Clapp led by a sort of indirection in which leaders throughout the organization were expected to get together on practical plans for action. During this postwar period, until Clapp left in 1954, the basic TVA missions were fulfilled, and the internal norms of management and decision making that have characterized TVA ever since became fully institutionalized.

The TVA structure was that of a three-person board, with a chairman, which concentrated on policy decisions. The general manager was the agent of the board, rather than a chief executive officer. He was a conduit between the board and the several mission offices, as they were called. This meant that the board had very little central capability for planning or program/budget analysis. The offices did most of the analysis. The autonomy of the office directors for the development of policy ideas and the implementation of programs was very great, and the decentralization of operations was the norm throughout the offices. This organizational structure matched the first generation of TVA missions of building dams, distributing power, straightening and deepening rivers, and assisting farmers, local businessmen, and state and local governments in projects of economic development and natural resource conservation projects.

The organizational culture that matched this structure of tasks and reinforced it was the "can do" outlook of the engineer. Give us the tools, and we will do the job. Central analytic capability was weak.[55] The power of expertise was in the offices, engineers, agriculturalists, foresters, and so forth. There was a great deal of overlapping of missions among the offices during the creative years. Power, navigation, and flood control had to be balanced in the management of dams. Assistance to farmers, who were in transition from row crops of corn and cotton to stock and pasture, required decisions in regard to soil erosion. Technical assistance to local and state governments on mosquito abatement and forest preservation; the transition of TVA libraries, established for construction workers on dam site; and many other such detailed matters, fostered internal cooperation.[56] It was dogma within the organization that such cooperation was best fostered by the flat hierarchy of a three-member board, a weak general manager, and continuous discussion at the board level among the office heads and other top officials.

During the period 1939 to 1954, each of the offices developed a subculture of its own within the broad, flexible framework of the TVA "myth" of a multipurpose organization working at the grass roots. Selznick described the offices of agriculture and of power in 1949. He saw two patterns of authority, which he described as two kinds of co-optation.[57] The TVA agriculturalists had delegated and had pretty much surrendered their authority over technical-assistance programs to the land-grant colleges and the extension service. This may have been the necessary price for the political support of agricultural establishments in the valley. It meant that the larger, more productive farmers would be helped, to the exclusion of marginal, subsistence farmers, both black and white. In this form of co-optation, an external group had managed to co-opt the authority of the agency. The other form of co-optation was in the power program, in which the TVA bureaucracy co-opted local power distributors into its system of rate setting and distribution. Lilienthal described the governance of municipal distributorships and rural cooperatives as grass-roots democracy, because the boards of such organizations consisted of local citizens. However, TVA set the power rates and insisted that local politicians not serve on the boards.

Both of these external authority systems could be justified within the broad myth of "grass-roots democracy." By "myth" I mean the ideal of organizational mission and the method of operation; I do not mean fiction. In both cases the TVA was working in a cooperative manner with citizens of the valley. Each office adapted the myth to its own purposes. All offices emphasized the centrality of specific professional expertise in operations, and all of the offices resisted efforts to introduce competing ways of looking at its mission. Neither power nor agriculture, for example, was hospitable to having economists used in evaluating its work.[58] The myth of decentralization within the organization protected office autonomy just as it permitted each office to develop its own authority relations with external groups. A third, a more diffuse, group within the TVA consisted of the apostles of the multipurpose ethos. These included the water people (navigation and flood control), the foresters, land-use planners, and a handful of staff assistants to the board, some of whom were economists.[59] These people were the guardians of the original H. A. Morgan belief that the TVA should work cooperatively with governments and private groups in the valley for regional development without developing a large bureaucracy of its own. Even more important, they were the strongest advocates of the belief that TVA was a regional development organization, not just a power and fertilizer company.[60] In this diverse group one saw the greatest cross-disciplinary interaction and the strongest commitment to broad missions. The influence of these people on the TVA's organizational ethos may have been greater than their actual authority in the organization, which could not compare to that of the power and agriculture offices.

Selznick saw the organization make two uses of the TVA myth. The first was to promulgate the myth of grass-roots democracy throughout the valley as a political resource for protecting the TVA's autonomy against anyone who would challenge it. TVA leaders have done this on numerous occasions when the authority was challenged by external opponents.[61] The second use of the myth was for purposes of internal socialization. TVA's formal and informal training programs propounded the leading ideas of the myth. One can trace the deliberateness of the effort from Lilienthal's external preaching of the myth to his work within the organization to ensure agreement on central tenets about organizational purpose and methods.[62]

In his theoretical analysis of administrative leadership, Selznick has drawn on the uses of the TVA myth to illustrate his argument that the central task of leadership is to infuse an organization with values beyond the technical task at hand.[63] The articulation of a myth is a strong resource for both external defense and internal unity. If the myth is shared by citizens, the efforts of opponents to weaken organizational autonomy will be weakened. Myth also serves as a glue for internal unity. An organizational culture is created from the myth, and the nurturing of that culture is the central task of leadership. It is perhaps not accidental that Selznick studied the TVA during the wartime and postwar years during which the two leaders of TVA were Lilienthal, who articulated the central myth, and Clapp, who nurtured and institutionalized it.

Knowledge of the importance of myth in TVA history leads one to the neoinstitutional perspective. Institutions have a life of their own which cannot be derived solely from their representative function. This life consists of ideas about what they should do and how they should do it. Thus the first generation of TVA leaders constructed a system of politics and organization that gave the TVA considerable autonomy in relation to the federal government and its agencies, to state and local governments, and to numerous private groups in the valley. Only in agriculture did the organization yield autonomy. The strength of the myth enabled the TVA to override competing federal agencies, such as the Corps of Engineers and the Soil Conservation Service; to prevent the takeover attempt by the Department of Interior; and in later years, in the Dixon/Yates episode, to protect the TVA from efforts by the Eisenhower administration to cut back the TVA's territory of operation. TVA leaders after Clapp used the myth, in its several aspects, as a resource not only for autonomy but also for the extension of mission. Strategies of organizational leadership were both rhetorical and heresthetic.

Clapp was succeeded by General Herbert Vogel, an experienced Corps of Engineers officer, who embraced TVA missions, to the surprise of Eisenhower-administration officials, who had sent him to Knoxville to curb the beast.[64] Vogel's achievement was to enhance TVA autonomy by working out the compromise that permitted the TVA to market its own bonds to pay for expansions of the power program within a fixed territory. The compromise of 1959, which came in the aftermath of the abortive Dixon/Yates initiative, satisfied both TVA's supporters and its critics. From then on, the authority was to raise most of its funds, except for a relatively small appropriation for the nonpower programs that were essential to its multipurpose mission. As a result of the compromise, congressional scrutiny of TVA was much reduced. The extensive program of nuclear-plant development from the mid 1960s on received little attention from Congress or the Bureau of the Budget.

Vogel was succeeded by Aubrey Wagner, a relatively new board member, who had been general manager under both Clapp and Vogel. Wagner was a Clapp protégé and disciple. Wagner had come up through the TVA navigation program; he was a water man who believed in the multipurpose mission and grass-roots methods.[65] With Wagner we begin to see the operation of the maxim that a possible form of organizational failure is persistence in the effort to repeat successes of the past.[66] Wagner was a proponent of the power program and, in particular, of the development of nuclear power, because he thought it would be cheaper and cleaner and thus would fulfill TVA's historic mission of cheap power for the people of the valley. But he was also a water man who did not want the TVA to be just a power company. By this time the agricultural work was reduced to the manufacture of fertilizer, and Wagner, a middle westerner, had never believed that southern agriculture could compete with the breadbasket of the nation. He turned to water projects as the means of keeping the TVA true to its multipurpose mission. Clapp had developed the idea of tributary development in which the TVA would build small dams on the watersheds of the Tennessee River and would assist small communities in developing economic capacities to take advantage of the new situation. Wagner established the Tributary Area Development program, and he directed much of the talent of TVA water people, including economists and planners, into the project.

The building of the Tellico Dam on the Little Tennessee River, which was first conceived in the 1960s but was not completed until the 1980s, was the showcase for Wagner's dream. He hoped to dramatize the new mission of economic development and to link it to the multipurpose, regional-development heritage.[67] The dam could not be justified by existing criteria—power, navigation, flood control—because the cost-benefit ratios were too weak. Wagner and his advisors developed the idea of purchasing the land around the dam reservoir and of estimating the effects of its development, especially for industry, as an extension of cost-benefit analysis. The TVA regional planners opposed the plan, thinking that it was utopian to put "factories in the fields." They preferred to work with small cities to develop industries, but their ideas were ignored. The water people in TVA favored the TAD and Tellico idea, and the Power Office also swung behind it in hopes that it could secure additional public appropriations.[68]

The debacle of Tellico is a long story. TVA pressed ahead with plans in the 1970s, despite opposition from farmers, whose valuable land would be flooded; Cherokee Indians, whose burial sites would be covered over; and fish and wildlife advocates, who opposed the damming up of the last natural river in the valley. The final blow to TVA came with the discovery of the tiny snail darter, a fish, which had to be protected under the Endangered Species Act. The dam was completed only because Senator Howard Baker of Tennessee was able to get Congress to pass a statute that exempted the project from the act.[69] The important story for our purposes is that the TVA persisted, despite strong opposition from its constituent groups in the valley. The organization, under Wagner, was true to the prevailing internal understanding of the historic missions of TVA. This is an example of organizational failure as a result of the attempt to repeat past successes.

Wagner's second term in the 1970s was a time of troubles in which the Tellico fight was accompanied by widespread criticism of the TVA's purchase and use of strip-mined coal, a dispute between TVA and the Environmental Protection Agency about air pollution from coal-fired steam plants, and, finally, the anger of ratepayers in response to increases in TVA power rates after the OPEC oil shocks. An additional irritant was controversy over the high price of the nuclear development plan, which at one time projected that the TVA would have seventeen nuclear reactors at work. In each of these controversies, Wagner was true to his understanding of the purposes of the TVA Act. He believed that he had the authority to develop missions for the TVA as long as he did not violate the language of the act, and he was strongly committed to the goals of cheap electric power and economic development, through the harnessing of both power and water.[70]

When S. David Freeman assumed command in 1978, he proceeded to do almost everything the opposite of Wagner but very much in the spirit of the TVA myths.[71] He settled the suit between the TVA and the EPA by complying with EPA requirements that scrubbers be placed on power plant smokestacks. This action was challenged by a group of TVA distributors in court, and it was the beginning of Freeman's alienation from the TVA's strongest constituency. He emphasized the conservation of energy in homes and industry with TVA technical assistance to families and manufacturers. He attempted to revive the economic-development mission, apart from water projects. He placed his own people in charge of the offices, and he strengthened the central program/budget analysis staff so that it could challenge proposals from the line agencies and evaluate programs in the field. A joke often heard in the TVA was that Freeman could not decide whether he was A. E. Morgan or D. E. Lilienthal and that Freeman changed his mind on alternate days. He charged a group of outside experts with having helped to develop ideas for TVA nonpower programs that were consistent with the original TVA ideals.[72]

Freeman did turn the authority in new directions, but he failed politically. The opposition of the power distributors to his attention to nonpower programs and the anger of ratepayers over increasing costs were enough to bring the TVA back into the orbit of congressional attention and criticism. In 1981 Senator Howard Baker advised President Reagan to remove Freeman as chairman and to replace him with Charles Dean, the head of the Knoxville distributorship. Baker's goal was to reduce controversy by adding a new face who would come to terms with the TVA's strongest constituents.

At some time between 1981 and 1985 the leaders of the TVA appear to have lost control of the organization. In 1981 a united board decided to cancel the construction of five nuclear reactors at two sites because the costs of construction and operation could not be justified in terms of projections of needs for power in the long-time future. This action was the last policy decision of the David Freeman period,and indeed, Freeman, who was still a member of the board, led the initiative. The TVA construction program was cut back drastically, the existing office for construction was abolished, and many of its engineers were assigned to the nuclear power division. In 1985 it was necessary to shut down the two reactors at the Sequoyah nuclear plant, and not long after that, three nuclear reactors at the Browns Ferry facility were closed because of operational problems. Licensing of the new Watts Bar nuclear plant was also delayed for the same reasons. The TVA fell under the critical scrutiny of the Nuclear Regulatory Commission. In January 1986 the TVA board hired retired navy Admiral Steven White as director of the nuclear program, independent of the power division, and charged him with returning the reactors to use.

Evidence suggests that the bureaucratic culture of the nuclear-power program was a deterrent to the correction of the construction flaws of the plants. The TVA power program had long been characterized by promotion from within, a strong premium on loyalty, resistance to external analysis, and the belief that its own experts could solve all problems. The symptom of these traits was the running succession of suits against the TVA by quality assurance engineers, who had been penalized by their superiors for having reported to the TVA board construction flaws and the failure to remedy those flaws. The TVA lost every one of these suits in the federal courts. The organizational problems that led to such turmoil were well documented in a report by Labor Department investigators.[73]

It is plausible to hypothesize that after the failures by both Wagner and Freeman to revive the organization in terms of the TVA myth, the several divisions of the TVA simply fell back on their own bureaucratic cultures and routines. The collapse of the nuclear program may be one symptom of that larger reality.

The TVA may have entered a new period in 1988 with the appointment of Marvin Runyon, president of Nissan-USA, as board chairman. Runyon announced that the TVA must reassess its goals by asking whether the nonpower programs were any longer activities in which the TVA should be involved. He also affirmed the goal of TVA's being the most competitive producer of power in the United States.[74] He subsequently announced substantial layoffs, a three-year freeze of TVA power rates, and budget cuts in the form of reducing overhead costs in the nonpower programs. Runyon announced that an uncompetitive TVA could not survive.[75] The authority was reorganized to take the form of a corporate model in which vice-presidents for power, nuclear power, and resource development would report to the chairman of the board through the former general manager, who became the vice-president and chief operating officer. A number of vice-presidents within each division would report to each senior vice-president, and vice-presidents in charge of staff units would also report directly to Runyon.[76] The place of the other two board members in the reorganization was not clear. The chairman was now more like a chief executive officer, and the office heads were directly accountable to him, working through a strengthened general manager, now an executive vice-president. The loose, bottoms-up strategy of governance of the long-established TVA organization appeared to have come to an end. It was too soon to say whether Runyon would seek to or be able to redirect the TVA in the direction of new missions or whether he would create new myths of organizational purpose. The opportunity to do so seemed to be present.

ANALYSIS

It is now possible to classify the TVA chairmen in terms of the typology of leaders that I set forth at the beginning of this chapter. Transforming leaders would be those who sought to do one of two things: either (1) infuse the organization with purpose by the intention or adaptation of a normative paradigm of goals and methods or (2) re-create purpose by building new coalitions of interests in terms of expanded missions. Transactional leaders would work to stabilize the organization, either by cultural leadership or by balancing competing interests. Each leader is examined in two dimensions. Did he seek to create a new paradigm of values and interests? Did he try to maintain the existing paradigm? Did he rely primarily on normative and cultural resources held in common in the TVA or, by contrast, on the manipulation of interests? The schema is too simple in the sense that the cells are too confining. Lilienthal was clearly a rhetorical leader who created the normative framework within which the TVA was to work for more than fifty years. He relied upon H. A. Morgan and Gordon Clapp to help him create the normative culture that would sustain his visions. A. E. Morgan had such a vision as well, although it was different from that of Lilienthal. The reason that Lilienthal won out was that he was both an idealist and a realist. He knew how to clothe the appeal to interests in terms of higher ideals to which individuals and groups would also respond. So it cannot be argued that Lilienthal and his lieutenants were blind to the need to manipulate interests. The way in which the uses of electric power were dramatized for people in the valley, as well as the link of the TVA with New Deal politics, suggests the contrary. But it would also not be accurate to describe these leaders as primarily manipulators of interests by clever heresthetics. A reading of Lilienthal's TVA diaries makes very clear that he regarded persuasion by rhetoric as his primary political resource with audiences both outside and inside the organization.[77] The original grass-roots theory, which was borrowed and adapted from H. A. Morgan, was first articulated in a 1940 speech to the Southern Political Science Association. Neither H. A. Morgan nor Clapp used rhetoric in such an effective way. But they were the cultural leaders in TVA's history; their primary contribution was to nurture the organizational folkways that they thought would be best for the identity and effectiveness of the institution. These leaders thus helped to establish and worked within a neoinstitutional framework.

Wagner and Freeman tried in different ways to restore the vitality of the TVA myth by defining new missions and adapting old ones. They sought to be transforming leaders within an accepted myth. They invoked the TVA myth even as they sought to adapt it to new challenges. Their primary strategies of leadership were the creation of new missions, as a means of tilting the balance of interests in the organization toward revival, and the strengthening of the goals of TVA as a multipurpose regional development authority. Wagner sought to keep the TVA from being just a power company by reviving and expanding the economic-development mission. Had he succeeded, the ideology of the TVA water people would have been predominant in the organization. Freeman used a variety of instruments. He challenged the authority of the offices with a new program-analysis staff. He put his own people in charge of the offices. He

FIGURE 4.3
TYPES OF LEADERS OF TVA

	Rational Choice		Neoinstitutional
Transactional	Vogel Dean		H. A. Morgan Clapp
Transforming	Wagner Freeman	Lilienthal Runyon?	A. E. Morgan

came close to being a Lilienthal kind of rhetorical leader in his efforts to mobilize external constituencies for energy conservation and a clean environment in the hopes that such pressures would affect internal TVA values. He was perhaps a clumsy heresthetician because, in so doing, he antagonized the TVA's strongest constituency, the distributors of electric power. The degree of political skill on Freeman's part may have been less important than the fact that his opportunities for building coalitions of support for TVA in the valley and in Washington were far less than those that had been available to Lilienthal.

It is possible that both Wagner and Freeman were prisoners of the myth created by Lilienthal. Their efforts to revive the organization in terms of the days of glory may also illustrate the weakness of the myth in later days, after the central missions had been largely fulfilled. They had relatively little success as transforming leaders, but the typology does not require success. The goals and strategies of the leader are the basis of classification. Part of their lack of success may have been due to the fact that they were not skillful herestheticians. They were not able to create new coalitions of interests to sustain the new missions they envisaged. Of course, it may have been beyond the skill of any leader to have done so. The organization may have achieved its original missions, and perhaps the basis for new ones was very limited.

Vogel and Dean were transactional leaders who maintained a balance among competing interests. Vogel's achievement was to ease the transition toward a new method of financing TVA sources of power, and this was achieved by compromise in the wake of exhaustion caused by the Dixon/Yates fight. Dean came into an organization that lacked strong animating forces other than the bureaucratic interests of the several TVA subcultures in the offices. The collapse of efficiency in the nuclear-power program went beyond the capacity of even the most clever transactional leader to lead by making bargains; it opened the way for a savior. Admiral White was the first manifestation, but Marvin Runyon was to inherit the savior mantle. The historical stage may have been set in 1988 for the invention of new myths about the TVA in accordance with new or adapted missions during a time of crisis. The dream of a multipurpose institution that was something more than a power company might be dead once and for all. At least, Runyon questioned it. Should this be the case, new myths articulating technological goals could be invented to fill the vacuum. The reorganization of the authority under Runyon might also be a means for transforming organizational culture in terms of new ideals. On the other hand, there is the possibility that Runyon might drain the organization of myth altogether and direct it toward the utilitarian, material ends of being strictly an efficient power company. It is not clear that any but the most simple rationale or myth would then be necessary. It is too soon to say in which direction he will go. But the situation would seem to be ripe for a transforming leader.

CONCLUSION

The analytic framework that I have developed here presents only teasing hypotheses for the understanding of the TVA's leadership and history. More intensive research would surely require some qualification of the hypotheses that I have given above. The more important question is whether the framework will point us to the important factors in understanding the role of leadership in changing and maintaining organizations. Is it not possible that the two continua, which make simple sense when presented in abstract form, contribute less when we try to place particular leaders and organizational histories within them? This would be the case if one were to insist on airtight cells along the continua. But the creation of cells is just the beginning of analysis. However, the original analytic distinctions are useful for suggesting the strategies of leaders and the primary resources that they used. We can tell transforming from transactional leaders, not so much in terms of what they have achieved, but by what they have tried to achieve. We know the instruments they have used and the resources they have invoked. Such knowledge is crucial for explanations of their relative success and failure. The leader is placed within the historical context of what was possible as defined by available resources and constraints on creative action. However, leadership is understood as an act of imagination which is influenced by, but is not determined by, the political environment. Indeed, the central act of creative leadership is to provide plausible strategies of action in an ambiguous environment.[78]

This study of organizational leadership is consistent with theories of the organizational life cycle.[79] New organizations must join technology, political support, and organizational culture in coherent complementary patterns; and the first generation of decisions will bias subsequent decisions in the same directions. But in the midlife of an organization, environmental changes will require new combinations of technology, politics, and culture. Creative leadership is critical at such junctures.[80] Theory about the conditions for the effective adaptation of organizations to such new challenges is the primary goal of any inquiry of this kind. Of course, instrumentalist notions of organizational success are incomplete. Organizations that contain solutions in search of problems—which was often the case with the TVA—may use politics for their own ends. Leadership through myth may be a form of manipulation.[81] Normative analysis that explores this question should be an integral part of research on organizational adaptation.

The study of leaders should not be subsumed by the study of institutions, as political scientists are inclined to do. We learn about institutional roles but not about leadership. However, the study of leadership should not be pursued by comparisons of individuals across institutions and across history without making any analysis of context. It is my hope that the framework presented and applied here will represent the kind of middle ground in the study of leadership that will enhance our understanding.

NOTES

I wish to thank Paul Conkin, Dan Cullen, John DiIulio, and Kenneth Finegold for careful readings and criticism of this chapter.

1. James MacGregor Burns, *Leadership* (New York: Harper & Row, 1978), pp. 18–23.
2. James Buchanan, "An Individualistic Theory of Political Process," in *Varieties of Political Theory,* ed. David Easton (Englewood Cliffs, N.J.: Prentice-Hall, 1966), p. 25. Buchanan uses the term "public choice" in his writing, and therefore I use it in the text in reference to his ideas.
3. Ibid.
4. Ibid., p. 28.
5. Terry Moe, *The Organization of Interests* (Chicago: University of Chicago Press, 1980), passim; Mancur Olson, *The Logic of Collective Action: Public Goods and the Theory of Groups* (Cambridge, Mass.: Harvard University Press, 1971).
6. Moe, *Organization,* p. 3.
7. Ibid., p. 113.
8. Ibid., pp. 14–15.
9. Ibid., pp. 126–27.
10. Ibid., p. 143.
11. Morris P. Fiorina and Kenneth A. Shepsle, "Formal Theories of Leadership: Agents, Agenda Setters and Entrepreneurs," in supra, pp. 35–36.
12. Ibid., pp. 28–31.
13. Anthony Downs, *Inside Bureaucracy* (Boston, Mass.: Little, Brown, 1967), pp. 52–56, 62–63.
14. Ibid., pp. 88–111.
15. Gary J. Miller, "Administrative Dilemmas: The Role of Political Leadership," Political Economy Working Paper, Washington University, June 1987, pp. 1–20.
16. Ibid., pp. 32–34.
17. Ibid., pp. 39–42, 48.
18. Ibid., pp. 43–44.

19. Ibid., pp. 48–51.
20. Kenneth J. Meier, "Bureaucratic Leadership in Public Organizations," infra, p. 268.
21. Ibid., pp. 269–72.
22. Ibid., pp. 276–77.
23. William Riker, *The Art of Political Manipulation* (New Haven, Conn.: Yale University Press, 1986), pp. ix–x.
24. Ibid., p. 64.
25. Ibid., p. 151.
26. Clarence Stone, "Paradigms, Power, and Urban Leadership," infra, pp. 155–56.
27. Ibid., p. 138.
28. Richard E. Neustadt, *Presidential Power: The Politics of Leadership from FDR to Carter* (New York: John Wiley, 1980), passim.
29. Stone, "Paradigms," pp. 146–49.
30. James G. March and Johan P. Olsen, "The New Institutionalism: Organizational Factors in Political Life," *American Political Science Review* 78, no. 3 (September 1984); Theda Skocpol, "Bringing the State Back In: False Leads and Promising Starts in Current Theories and Research," a working paper for the conference on States and Social Structures, Mount Kisco, N.Y., Feb. 1982. This paper was subsequently revised for publication as chapter 1 of *Bringing the State Back In,* ed. Peter B. Evans, Dietrich Rueschemeyer, and Theda Skocpol (Cambridge, Mass.: Cambridge University Press, 1985). The page citations are from the paper, rather than from the chapter.
31. March and Olsen, "New Institutionalism," p. 735.
32. Ibid., p. 736.
33. Ibid., pp. 739–40.
34. Ibid., p. 739.
35. Ibid., pp. 741–42; Stephen D. Krasner, "Approaches to the State, Alternative Conceptions and Historical Dynamics," review article, *Comparative Politics* 16, no. 2 (Jan. 1984).
36. March and Olsen, "New Institutionalism," p. 740.
37. Ibid., pp. 743–44.
38. Skocpol, "Bringing the State Back In," pp. 20–21; Hugh Heclo, *Modern Social Politics in Britain and Sweden* (New Haven, Conn.: Yale University Press, 1974).
39. Krasner, "Approaches," p. 224.
40. March and Olsen, "New Institutionalism," pp. 744–46; Krasner, "Approaches," p. 235.
41. Krasner, "Approaches," pp. 42–43.
42. Lee G. Bolman and Terrence E. Deal, *Modern Approaches to Understanding and Managing Organizations* (San Francisco, Calif.: Jossey-Bass, 1984), p. 223.
43. Andrew M. Pettigrew, "On Studying Organizational Cultures," *Administrative Science Quarterly* 24, no. 4 (Dec. 1979): 574.
44. Ibid., p. 578.
45. Krasner, "Approaches," p. 227; Skocpol, "Bringing the State Back In," p. 9.
46. Bertrand De Jouvenel, *Sovereignty: An Inquiry in the Political Good* (Chicago: University of Chicago Press, 1957), pp. 298–300.
47. Burns, *Leadership,* pp. 18–22.
48. Ibid., p. 394.
49. Philip Selznick, *Leadership in Administration: A Sociological Interpretation* (New York: Harper & Row, 1957), pp. 40–41.
50. Robert C. Tucker, *Politics as Leadership* (Columbia: University of Missouri Press, 1981), chap. 1.

51. Erwin C. Hargrove, "The Task of Leadership: The Board Chairman," in *TVA: Fifty Years of Grassroots Bureaucracy,* ed. Erwin C. Hargrove and Paul K. Conkin (Urbana and Chicago: University of Illinois Press, 1984), pp. 90–95.

52. Ibid., pp. 95–98.

53. Ibid., pp. 98–101; Erwin C. Hargrove, "David Lilienthal and the Tennessee Valley Authority," in *Leadership and Innovation: A Biographical Perspective on Entrepreneurs in Government,* ed. Erwin C. Hargrove and Jameson Doig (Baltimore, Md.: Johns Hopkins University Press, 1987); David E. Lilienthal, *TVA: Democracy on the March* (New York: Harper & Brothers, 1944).

54. Hargrove, *TVA,* pp. 101–5.

55. Erwin C. Hargrove, "A Strategic Planning System for the Tennessee Valley Authority," in *The Nineteen Seventy-nine Summer Policy Study: The Role of TVA Programs in Regional Development* (Tennessee Valley Authority, 1981).

56. Lilienthal, *TVA,* chaps. 7 and 8.

57. Philip Selznick, *TVA and the Grass Roots: A Study in the Sociology of Formal Organization* (New York: Harper Torchbooks, 1966), pp. 217–19.

58. Norman Wengert, *Valley of Tomorrow: The TVA and Agriculture* (Knoxville: University of Tennessee Bureau of Public Administration, 1952), pp. 44–46, 53–54, 119–20, 124–26; Marc J. Roberts and Jeremy S. Blum, "The Tennessee Valley Authority," in *The Choices of Power: Utilities Face the Environmental Challenge,* ed. Marc Roberts (Cambridge, Mass.: Harvard University Press, 1981), pp. 78–81.

59. Author's interview with John Krutilla, Sept. 8, 1987, in Nashville, Tenn., and conversations with Richard Freeman and Vernon Rutan over a period of years, 1979–86. These three men were members of the TVA policy planning staff during the 1950s.

60. Rexford G. Tugwell and E. C. Banfield, "Grassroots Democracy: Myth or Reality?" *Public Administration Review* 10 (Winter 1950): 47–55.

61. Examples are the fights over building the Douglas Dam in the 1940s and the Dixon-Yates controversy in the 1950s.

62. Hargrove, "David Lilienthal," pp. 52–54, 56–57.

63. Selznick, *Leadership,* pp. 17, 151–52.

64. Hargrove, *TVA,* pp. 105–8.

65. Ibid., p. 108–12.

66. Robert H. Miles, chap. 13 in *The Organizational Life Cycle: Issues in the Creation, Transformation and Decline of Organizations,* ed. John R. Kimberly, Robert H. Miles, and Associates (San Francisco, Calif.: Jossey-Bass, 1980), pp. 443–44.

67. William Bruce Wheeler and Michael J. McDonald, *TVA and the Tellico Dam, 1936–1979* (Knoxville: University of Tennessee Press, 1986), chap. 1.

68. William Bruce Wheeler and Michael J. McDonald, "The New Mission and the Tellico Project, 1945–70," in *TVA,* ed. Hargrove and Conkin, p. 174.

69. Wheeler and McDonald, *TVA and the Tellico Dam,* p. 212.

70. Hargrove, "Task of Leadership," p. 110.

71. Ibid., pp. 113–17.

72. *Nineteen Seventy-nine Summer Policy Study.*

73. *Mansour Guity vs. Tennessee Valley Authority,* Investigation Report, United States Department of Labor, Apr. 28, 1986, Nashville, Tenn.

74. *Nashville Tennessean,* Jan. 26, 1988, pp. 1A–2A.

75. Ibid., Apr. 27, 1988, pp. 1A, 4A.

76. Ibid., May 19, 1988, pp. 1A, 4A.

77. David E. Lilienthal, *The Journals of David E. Lilienthal,* vol. 1; *The TVA Years, 1939–1945* (New York: Harper & Row, 1964), pp. 53–54, 79–80, 106–7.

78. Erwin C. Hargrove and Michael Nelson, *Presidents, Politics, and Policy*

(Baltimore, Md.: Johns Hopkins University Press, 1984), chap. 4; Jameson Doig and Erwin C. Hargrove, "Leadership and Political Innovation," chap. 1 in *Leadership and Innovation*.

79. Kimberly, Miles, and Associates, *Organizational Life Cycle.*

80. Selznick, *Leadership in Administration*.

81. Sheldon Wolin, *Politics and Vision: Continuity and Innovation in Western Political Thought* (Boston, Mass.: Little, Brown, 1960). See Wolin's criticism of Selznick's conception of institutional leadership based on myth.

I am grateful to Ira Strauber for advice on the importance of normative analysis to avoid sheer instrumentalism.

PART 2

CULTURE, ECONOMICS, AND SITUATION

5

A Cultural Theory of Leadership

Aaron Wildavsky

"The concept of leadership," Cecil Gibb has written in the *Encyclopedia of the Social Sciences,* "has largely lost its value for the social sciences, although it remains indispensable to general discourse."[1] If all of us (including social scientists) find this term indispensable, however, why has it been so unsatisfactory in social research? Some say leadership is so general a concept that researchers cannot tell what it refers to; others say the term is too specific to cover the vast range of possibilities. What makes leadership so vast a subject that it cannot be encompassed?

STUDIES OF LEADERSHIP IN THE SOCIAL SCIENCES

Despite the claim that leadership is a dead issue for scholarship, the topic continues to spawn extensive studies. If leadership is an endangered species, it is not extinction that threatens it. Rather, the tendency of the concept to engulf the very factors that are supposed to distinguish it is what makes it an amorphous, indefinable subject. An analytic history of the leadership debate will help us understand why it has come to a dead end.

Early on in leadership studies, leaders were assumed to be self-evident agents who had certain physical or psychological traits that explained their rise to power. Leaders were shown to be generally heavier and taller, though in two of nine studies, some leaders turned out to be shorter. In 1915, E. B. Gowin found that university presidents were taller than college presidents; railroad presidents, than station agents; and insurance executives, than policyholders.[2] But once this relatively safe physical haven was left behind, disappointment became the daily fare of the "traitists." It must have been disconcerting when they discovered that the correct number of essential traits varied from two to between nineteen and thirty.[3] Universal traits stubbornly refused to reveal themselves. Worse, people who were amply supplied with the hypothetical traits often did not assume leadership positions, however broadly defined. Did leaders exhibit a drive to dominate? At the most frequently reported correlation of .20, this would mean that only 4 percent of total variance could be attributed to dominance.[4]

Worse still, if leaders were distinguished by their traits, then the generic quality called leadership inhered in individuals. If that were so, there could be as many types of leaders as there were individuals or traits. The generalizations of social science would give way to the particularities of individuals. Because individuals confer meanings on objects, moreover, leadership would have to be what society thought it was, thus requiring a social agreement on the importance of traits that was never forthcoming. One way or another, by the back door if not the front, social relations would enter the bastion of leadership by individuals.

Dominance as a trait led inevitably to the question of leadership styles. Was there no difference between coercive leaders, who enforced their power with brutality, and those who dominated through persuasion? As a trait, "dominance" suggested dangerous ideological overtones. Alfred R. Lindesmith and Anselm L. Strauss—writing not long after the struggle against Nazism—attributed fascination with traits to "current popular conceptions of leaders as being in some way unusual beings possessed of extraordinary powers alien to the common run of mankind. As such, they are objects capable of being transformed into the 'magical helpers' sought by those whose need for security is resolved by finding some powerful authority upon whom they can become dependent."[5] Similarly, Daniel Bell found that almost all the literature, which was based on Aristotle and Machiavelli, conveyed the "image of the mindless masses and . . . the strong-willed leader."[6] Robert Tannenbaum added: "Classical models of bureaucracy share with these elite conceptions an authoritarian bias in their emphasis on the exclusive prerogative of leaders to command the unquestioning obligation of subordinates to obey."[7] The evident ideological overtones in the effort to democratize the concept of leadership, together with the experience of World War II, did make social scientists aware that the term could be made to serve different social purposes. Leadership by persuasion was different from leadership by coercion. Connections between the style of leadership and the form of social organization languished, however. Philip Selznick did issue a call to connect leadership to different kinds of organization, but that call remained unanswered.[8]

The trait approach seemed ill conceived from the start. One could not imagine leaders without considering followers; perhaps, then, there was something in the followers—some ineffable clue—that led leaders to them? Exit the "hero in history," and enter group dynamics—more prosaic but perhaps more profound. Again it turned out that there were almost as many dynamics as groups. Sometimes group members were led; sometimes they did the leading; often the observer, in the midst of exponentially increasing interactions, could not tell which.

Not so fast. The insights of the social-relations school were abandoned almost as soon as they were formulated. For if followers were essential to leaders—indeed, if the ability to attract followers were virtually a defining aspect of leadership—then it followed ineluctably that leadership was an organizational phenomenon. Once followers had been brought in, they would either become leaders themselves or they would be converted into the very ones who conferred that status on individuals. The designation usually given to patterned relationships between people, including relationships between followers and leaders, was organization. And if organizations differed, so would those leaders who developed followers. Before the organizational path that Max Weber opened up could be followed, however, a new consideration intervened.

Perhaps there had been an oversight? Leaders and followers were embedded in history. They interacted in regard to something, and that something was called "the situation." "Situationists" entertained a variety of opinions. Ralph M. Stodgill concluded that the "qualities, characteristics and skills required in a leader are determined to a large extent by the demands of the situation in which he is to function as a leader."[9] Since separate situations make different demands on leaders, A. Bavelas suggested that we must instead try to "define the leadership function that must be performed in these situations and regard as leadership those acts which perform them."[10] But situations are potentially infinite in their variety. Every situation then might be explained as a product of still other situations in an infinite regress.[11] Situations, then, were even more varied than followers, who, in turn, were more diverse than leaders.

What, indeed, is a situation? W. I. Thomas and F. Znanieck's famous "definition of the situation" is composed of kitchen-sink variables: beliefs, values, groups, the physical environment, tasks, perception of all the above, and, for good measure, the surrounding culture.[12] Not surprisingly, A. Paul Hare has concluded that "the major finding of this research is that there are more differences between situations than between the two leader styles" tested in his research.[13]

Sometimes "situation" appears to designate an event such as the shooting of a czar or a series of similar events, such as revolutionaries who raise money by robbing banks. Does situation include both singular events and organized patterns of power relations—hierarchy or anarchy as systems of rule? Apparently the answer is "all of the above." Yet a single episode may have different implications from a series; and a pattern of rule is different from a series of situations. Theorizing depends on seeing (or imposing) regularities on what may originally appear to be disparate happenings. Treating situations as discrete events would make theoretical interpretation impossible. There would be as many leaders as there were different situations: history would be reduced to narrative; interpretation, to repetition. Without having a theory of interpretation to impose meaning on disparate events, piling up an infinity of "situations" is bound to prove stultifying.

Do situations somehow give rise to leaders who, in those circumstances, are able to attract followers? Is it leaders who seize upon situations in which they can attract followers? Or is it followers who find leaders to help them get through difficult situations? Or is it some combination thereof? In the midst of all this causal-cum-conceptual confusion, what is the poor social scientist to do? How best to avoid criticism? Easy; just do it all.

LEADERSHIP IN A STEW

To understand the tendency for social-science studies to include everything, it is worth looking at the separate components of the leadership syndrome—from groups of followers, to situations, to traits—as they were piled up willy-nilly on top of one another. As ontology was once said to recapitulate phylogeny, with the individual passing through all stages of the species, so each approach to leadership ends up, willy-nilly, by incorporating the others. Each conceptual nationalism becomes its own research imperialism. Every native dish turns out to be a stew.

Begin with the group. If anything is evident, it is that individuals are not isolated. According to Cecil Gibb: "A group is characterized by the interaction of its members, in such a way that each unit is changed by its group membership and each would be likely to undergo a change as a result of changes in the group. In this case there is a dependence of each member upon the entire group, and the relation between any two members is a function of the relation between other members."[14] Thus the blurring begins; as social life becomes a seamless web, connectedness replaces separability.

On what basis, however, are groups organized? Simply saying that life is a social activity is a truism. Specifying forms of social organization and relating each to different types of leadership would reduce, instead of expand, the realm of relevant leadership behavior. But this is never done. Instead, Harold Proshansky and Bernard Seidenberg assert that group members "share a common set of norms, beliefs, and values."[15] Without quite realizing it, they define out of existence two of the great questions in the study of leadership: Are (Should) leaders (be) like followers? Should (Can) leaders transform the values and beliefs of followers? Imperceptibly, description becomes prescription; mutual dependence comes to imply equality. Group norms become a code word for consent.

Once leadership comes to depend on relevance within a group, group members lead as well as follow. Kenneth F. Janda has concluded: "Clearly, a member cannot be salient unless he can be differentiated from other group members on one or more criteria, and, of course, almost every group member can be differentiated from other group members on the basis of one or more of these criteria. From this realization, it is just a short step to conclude that every group member can be, and often is, a leader.''[16] How nice! ''The individual who engages in leadership events,'' as Gibb puts it, ''becomes a sometimes leader.''[17] By a stroke of the pen, everyone gets a turn at leadership. Subtly, the everyday understanding of leadership is reversed: leaders no longer tell followers where to go; rather, leaders help followers get to where they want to be. ''Leadership,'' D. Cartwright and A. Zander have asserted, ''is viewed as the performance of those acts which help the group achieve its preferred outcomes.''[18] Are all groups devoted to equality of influence, or are there other groups for whom power asymmetry is a guiding principle?

We are all one big happy family, especially when one realizes that leadership is part of the ''general process of role differentiation, by which a group develops 'specialists' in the performance of recurring functions.''[19] Leadership not only has been equalized by the group approach, it has also been decomposed. It has become part of the specialization and division of labor in society through which people adopt different roles varying with time, place, and circumstance. Unfortunately, if some people are specialized to ''leadership roles'' and others are specialized to followership ones, the division of labor will reintroduce the inequalities that the group approach is supposed to obliterate.

Despite serious methodological difficulties, which make inferences of cause and effect dubious, most studies seem to show that leaders have some sensitivity to group concerns.[20] Is it true, therefore, that members of a group (another euphemism for followers) approve of leaders who show them ''consideration'' and who side with the group in disputes with outsiders or higher-ups?[21] This reverse-twist approach to traits, however, is undermined by situational findings. D. C. Pelz discovered that most white-collar workers—aware of the need for someone to run interference for them outside the work group—preferred a supervisor who was well connected in the hierarchy, even if that meant the supervisor wasn't exactly one of the boys.[22] These findings were rationalized by positing a difference between task and emotional leadership; it seemed that sensitive leadership made the group happy, but not necessarily effective. And then there are circumstances. Colonel Nicholson in the movie *Bridge over the River Kwai* is superb in circumstances that call for sticking to the rules, but he is rigid when he should be flexible.

It isn't easy to depart from the obvious, because it keeps coming back at you. Expecting leaders to follow, to abide by (even if to change) group goals, requires some doing. Happily, E. P. Hollander is up to the task. In a creative construction called ''idiosyncrasy credit,'' he suggests that leaders first perform a series of services for their followers, thus building up credit, then trade in those credits for permission. (This, of course, assumes that the people who are involved will remember.) The contrary position, which may be attributed to experienced politicians, is known as "What have you done for me lately?" Asked which position prevails, a reasonable person no doubt would say that it depends on who the people are, who the politician is, and what situation they are all in together.

Again, I am indebted to Gibb's invaluable surveys of the literature on leadership for the ultimate synthesis, which he calls "interaction theory," possibly because it covers all conceivable relations. A comprehensive theory of leadership, in Gibb's words, must not only include the personality of leaders, followers, groups, and situations; it also "must recognize that it is not these variables per se that enter into the leadership relation, but rather the perception of the leader by himself and by others, the leader's perception of those others, and the shared perception by leader and others of the group and the situation."[23] No base is left untouched.

The difference between maintaining a system and changing it—shoring up the existing order versus altering it—has occasioned comment from the beginning of recorded political philosophy.[24] What is attempted can differ drastically; so, then, must the characteristics of leaders who will be capable of achieving either modest maintenance or grand changes.

Enter charismatic leadership. Desiring to distinguish between small, repetitive choices that reinforce existing institutions, on the one hand, and large, unusual ones that create new designs, on the other hand, Max Weber classified political systems by the kinds of authority that legitimate leadership. He saw traditional authority repeating itself, rational-legal authority making minor adjustments, and charismatic authority introducing new patterns of action, new values, and new institutions. Weber's charismatic leader is distinguished by a divine call to duty—or, at least, so the leader thinks—that is transmitted to and shared by followers because of a certain glow that radiates from the source. The confusions that this classification generates—for example, naming the cause after the effect, mixing inspiration within deification, confusing personal qualities with kinds of regimes—have led others to try to clarify the concept. Observing that charismatic traits are attributed to people who perform perfectly ordinary secular roles, Edward Shils has suggested that "charisma not only disrupts social order, it also maintains or conserves it."[25] Order is essential in every society. Why shouldn't the prophets of order as well as disorder—sometimes, I might add, in the same person—share the mantle of charisma?

What interests Shils is not the concentration of charisma but its dispersion in society. A society in which people are civil to one another, Shils says,

> entails not only the imputation of charisma to the mass of the population by itself; it also requires that the established and effective elite impute charisma to the mass as well, that the elite regard itself, despite all its differences as sharing some of the charisma that resides

> in it with the rest of its society. It requires, too, that the virtues implicit in this widespread and consensual dispersion of charisma should be practiced in and with respect to the central institutional system—government and law, above all.[26]

Somewhere in between asserting the right to rule and accepting that rule, charisma is becoming close to legitimacy. The more equally charisma-cum-legitimacy is distributed, to be sure, the more it characterizes entire populations. Charisma has become authority over oneself.

Charisma has been democratized, by becoming a mass as well as an elite trait, and deradicalized, by supporting stability as well as change. If charisma is a substitute for legitimate authority, what sort of political regime will try to organize itself without a binding source of rules? No answer is given, because charisma, removed from its essential mooring in a particular political regime, has become a quality for all seasons, essential to all regimes, and, therefore, capable of distinguishing among none.

In socializing and democratizing leadership, leaders have ceased being all-powerful; they merge imperceptibly with the crowd of jostling humanity from which they came. How, then, can we distinguish the presence from the absence of leadership?

LEADERSHIP AS "CAUSE"

With interdependency so rampant, there might be leadership, but how could researchers point to leaders? If leadership is everything in general, the question is, can it be anything in particular?

No one who knows the field will doubt that there is "widespread disagreement" about the meaning of leadership.[27] The difficulty is, not that students of the subject cannot think up definitions, but that, following the multifaceted feature of the concept, their definitions are so different.

Leaders have been defined as those who occupy high-level positions, who have been elected by a group, who are most influential in setting goals (or in helping to achieve them), who influence others whether or not goals get accomplished, who try hard or often to exert influence but do not succeed, or who do succeed more often than anyone else.[28] Leadership, some scholars say, is what leaders do. Unfortunately, expectations of the leadership role vary so widely that it is hard to know what parts of a leader's life count. Alternatively, "leader behavior may be defined as any behavior that makes a difference in the behavior of the group."[29] Thus, attention shifts from leader as cause to leader as effect. Is leadership, one wonders, the tower of power or the tower of Babel?

A glance at a thesaurus, our repository of related meanings—influence, power, prestige, esteem, charisma, magnetism, sway, reign, rule, mastery, dominance, upper hand, persuasion, supremacy, primacy, authority, effectiveness—will reveal that it is not of much help.[30]

"Although students of the subject are often troubled by the obvious differences in the phenomena selected for study by these various criteria," Kenneth F. Janda has reported wryly, "they reluctantly do what Festinger did and include studies under a heading of leadership 'only because those reporting such studies call it leadership.' "[31]

Recently a convergence of minds has been observed in defining leadership as the exertion of power or influence.[32] Leaders are those who make things happen that otherwise would not come about. The criterion can be strengthened by adding that power wielders get their way against opposition.[33] The definition can be made more precise by converting it into a statement of forgone alternatives—the economist's concept of opportunity costs—in order to exercise power.[34] The probability of exerting influence would vary with what had to be given up in order to achieve that sway. Power might vary also with the difficulty of the attempt or the importance of the issue.

Conceiving of leadership as a causal relationship is an advance. Even more so is the stipulation of the domain of causality: power is an interpersonal relationship in which some people exercise power over other people. Immediately the study of leadership falls victim to the same difficulties that are suffered by those who study power, influence, control, and other synonyms for "cause."[35] There are as many types of leaders as there are kinds of causes, and there is much difficulty in distinguishing one from the other or in assigning them relative weights in different situations. Clearly, some things must be held constant if we are to be able to observe variations in leadership.

The most imaginative attempt to link leadership to power, influence, and cause is made by Andrew S. McFarland, who has proposed this setup for research:

> Let us outline some important considerations for the study of leadership, defined as influence. First, we must establish the limits of a person's action in terms of general social forces, although this is obviously difficult. Second, we "think away" the existence of the particular leader, and consider what might have happened if the leader had not lived. Third, we compare the more probable "might-have-been's" with the actuality in order to assess the magnitude and significance of the influence (causality) the leader has exercised on human events. Finally, such judgmental-probabilistic reasoning need not be restricted to past events but can be applied to future possibilities.[36]

This thought experiment describes well what goes on in the mind of the analyst, but it would not be easy to get agreement on such creative leaps. How, for instance, can one limit the scope for individual action as against the constraints imposed by "general social forces"? How can one imagine away or account for the influence of "the particular leader"?

In a valiant effort to rehabilitate the utility of personality in political analyses, Fred I. Greenstein has tried to break up these big questions into more precise and answerable units, speaking of "action dispensability" (Would it matter if an action were different?) or "actor dispensability" (Would it matter if the individual actor were different?). Greenstein says:

> The objection to studies of personality and politics that emphasizes the limited capacity of single actors to shape events does not differ in its essentials from the nineteenth and early twentieth century debates over social determinism—that is, over the role of individual actors (Great Men or otherwise) in history. In statements of this objection emphasis is placed on the need for the time to be ripe in order for the historical actor to make his contribution. Questions are asked such as, "What impact could Napoleon have had on history if he had been born in the Middle Ages?" Possibly because of the parlor game aura of the issues that arise in connection with it, the problem of the impact of individuals on events has not had . . . much disciplined attention. . . . The impact of an individual's actions varies with (1) the degree to which the actions take place in an environment which admits of restructuring, (2) the location of the actor in that environment, and (3) the actor's peculiar strengths or weaknesses.[37]

What are these environments that admit of restructuring? Are they situations—that is, kinds of events—or are they social organizations—that is, patterns of social relationships? I shall argue that as long as the emphasis is on the individual and not on the regime in which action takes place, variety will always overcome commonality.

There we have it: the circle of social relations has bedeviled all efforts to study leadership. Every effort to separate leaders from those who are led is followed by corrective efforts to put leaders in their place. With increasing sophistication, scholars have succeeded only in making leadership indistinguishable from other phenomena.

If leadership is equivalent to cause, the greatness of the cause determines the importance of the leadership. Should we attribute great leadership, then, to anyone who has drastically changed the lives of other people, whether for good or ill? Do the moral ends or objectives of leadership not matter? Carl J. Friedrich has declared: "To differentiate the leadership of a Luther from the leadership of a Hitler is crucial for a political science that is to 'make sense'; if a political science is incapable of that, it is pseudo-science, because the knowledge it imparts is corrupting and not guiding.''[38] Alas, alas, leaders may both guide and corrupt, as with a Hitler, a Stalin, or a Pol Pot.

What about leaders who coerce obedience to their commands? ''Coercive strategies need not detain us here,'' James M. Burns has swiftly asserted (thus disposing, like many other authors, of an ancient issue by fiat), ''since we exclude coercion from the definition of leadership.''[39] Are dictators not leaders? What about those mixed cases in which leaders use force and yet appear to gain consent? One of the distinguishing aspects of leaders may be the degree to which they coerce followers.

The identification of leadership with legitimate moral purpose seeks to relate organizational objectives to the consent for carrying them out. Philip Selznick maintains in his *Leadership in Administration* that the purpose of leadership is to imbue administrators with a vision of the ultimate importance of their work by evoking objectives that establish a relationship between what they are asked to do and what is desirable. ''The problem,'' in Selznick's view, ''is always to choose key values and to create a social structure that embodies them.''[40] Whose values, however, are to be key? If values have been articulated and rejected, did the failure to adopt them lie in the leader or in the potential followers? ''Our dilemma, then, is not an absence of leaders,'' Benjamin Barber has observed, ''but a paucity of values that might sustain leaders, not a failure of leadership but a failure of followership, a failure of popular will from which leadership might draw strength.''[41]

If one multiplies the kinds of leaders by the types of followers by the samples of situations, more intellectual variety is produced than anyone can manage. Looked at in this light, leadership is an impossible subject for study; and it has not proved to be a useful way to look at ''politics'' or ''society.''

What can be done about all this interrelatedness? Cecil Gibb says that ''progress will best be made by using simpler and less multidimensional concepts.''[42] But Nevil Sanford wants all facets of leadership to be dealt with under a single set of categories, for ''to concentrate on any one of these facets of the problem represents over-simplification of an intricate phenomenon.''[43] To restate the question that has occupied us, why doesn't the social-science literature on leadership get anywhere?

Observing that ''some frustrated political scientists have tended to throw up their hands and settle for tracing circular patterns of influence between leaders and followers, without coming any closer to determining the nature of leadership,'' Lewis J. Edinger has deepened the difficulty:

> If it is difficult, if not impossible, to discover what causes people to follow a leader, it is equally difficult to ascertain the motives which determine the leader's behavior. . . . The individual may deliberately conceal his ''real and true motives,'' he many rationalize them and accept them himself as ''real and true,'' or he may not even know

> what they are because they are "unconscious motives." The complexity of motivations and the difficulty of discovering, identifying, and attributing motives makes it practically impossible to satisfy the requirements.[44]

If Edinger is right, then we need an approach to leadership that either does not require attribution of motives or that infers from them the more accessible dimensions of the regimes, a shorthand term for political cultures, within which leadership is exercised. Leadership, in a phrase, has to be made a part of politics.

LEADERSHIP WITHOUT POLITICS

The status of social-science research into leadership may be ascertained by asking what kinds of questions it cannot answer. John Miller has asked in his exhaustive review, "Why has no amount of data massaging been capable of establishing consistent relationships between leader behavior and organizational outcomes?"[45] A plausible answer is that neglect of regimes attenuates the relationships between leaders and the organizational imperatives they face. Miller has continued his quest by asking, "Why is it that well-planned and well-executed attempts to change leadership styles by various training procedures have such unpredictable—even dysfunctional—outcomes?" "Because separating leadership from regime keeps apart the requirements of organizational context from personal performance," I would reply; style by itself is bound to lack predictive value.[46] The type of organization and the kind of leadership must be part of the same phenomenon; otherwise, not only leaders but also followers would be interchangeable, like reversible clothes—just turn them inside out at will and *voilà,* you have a new type of leader-cum-followership.

Miller has come close to answering his own question with another that reveals an anomaly: "If the effectiveness of leadership behavior is situationally contingent and prescriptive models call for leader flexibility, why are observed leadership styles so stable?"[47] If leadership is a function of regime, as I claim, leadership should vary more with regime than with situation.[48] How leaders respond, this cultural hypothesis goes, depends more on the social relationships that they are trying to justify than on whatever is inherent in the situation with which they are faced, or, much more accurately, with their interpretation-via-reformulation of the situation as they wish to perceive it. Because facts cannot speak for themselves and because no one can pay attention to everything simultaneously, it is not so surprising that regimes confer significance on situations. People use the relationships among them, their interpersonal relationships, to interpret their environment. People internalize their preferred social relations so as to decide what to prefer.[49]

The blending of description with prescription that is found in the study of leadership cannot be eliminated without doing violence to the subject itself. The leadership literature asks, "Who shall lead?" as if it didn't matter where. "Perhaps," Gabriel Almond has written, "the confusion [between types of leadership] arises because . . . the focus is on the leader as the 'causer,' and not what is being caused."[50] This will not do. From a strictly descriptive standpoint, as Arthur Bentley argued in his life work, the actor and the activity must always be kept together because their meaning lies in the process of which they are a part.[51] Leader and follower are always in the act of choosing among regimes. And when they choose whom to associate with and how to associate with them, they also choose what kind of leaders they will follow. We should ask not only "What is the purpose of leadership?" but also—and together—"Which regime has been chosen?" Classifying leadership according to its consequences in different regimes is essential if we are to understand why we get the kind of leadership we do, what kind we want, and what we have to give up in order to get it.

In the micropolitics of everyday activity, leadership is getting people to do things they otherwise would not do. In this sense, as used in ordinary politics, leadership is equivalent to power, influence and control, in that all these terms are effectively synonyms for cause. But if we ask what causes cause, what way of life or what general theory makes sense out of politics, we get no answer. It is hard to play the game if you do not know the rules. Small politics has to be placed within grand politics, the macroregimes from which the micromaneuvers take their meaning.

MODELS OF REGIMES

Leadership is a function of regime, or political culture. These macropolitical regimes constrain the micropolitics of individual encounters. If we do not find what we expect—the type of leadership that ordinarily goes with the kind of regime—we know when to be surprised. This approach permits us to examine characteristics of leaders, their interaction with their followers, and their performance in various situations within a limited number of political contexts.

Referring to regimes would warn against placing too much stress on the details of political maneuvering that prove at once so fascinating and so exasperating—fascinating in their human detail, exasperating because the study of them outside their political context leads to so few insights. There is complexity but not clarity. It may be, of course, that great leaders alter regimes. Indeed, the ability to alter regimes is a measure by which we determine force of personality. By the same token, leaders can create regimes in which they do badly or which reject them entirely. Without understanding what type of leadership goes with what type of regime, however, one cannot judge the degree to which a regime has been changed by the impact of a dynamic person. By placing personality within a context of political regimes, it should be possible to do justice to both.

My two criteria for classifying regimes and leadership are the usual ones: parsimony and persuasiveness. Categories should be few in number and clear in concept; they should also convince the reader that they fit the phenomena in question. Knowing what kind of regime we are talking about should enable us to anticipate what sort of leaders it will generate and what kind of difficulties its leaders will face.

Like others who choose to break their bones on the rocky shoals of a general theory, I seek the smallest number of dimensions with the largest payoff in predictive and retrodictive power. Thus, the questions asked and the answer given in these dimensions are generalizations of generalizations. I do not ask "To what nominal group do certain people belong?" Rather, I ask about whether and to what extent they seek to be attached to groups at all. It would be hard to find questions more basic than "Who am I?" The question of identity may be answered by saying that the individual belongs to a strong group, a collective, that makes decisions binding on all members or by saying that the individual's ties to others are weak in that choices bind only the individual. Nor do I ask which specific norms an individual should obey; rather, I ask whether an individual internalizes many or few norms. The question of action—"What should I do?"—is answered at a very general level by responding that the individual is subject to many or few prescriptions of required behavior.

My purpose in this paper is to apply the theory to leadership, not to expound the theory itself. Nevertheless, it will obviously be easier for readers to follow if they have some idea of what this cultural theory is all about.[52]

Strong groups that have numerous prescriptions combine to form hierarchical collectivism. The dimensions of group strength and few prescriptions form an egalitarian culture, a life of voluntary consent, without coercion or inequality. Competitive individualism joins few prescriptions with weak boundaries, thereby encouraging endless new combinations. When group boundaries are weak and prescriptions are strong, so that decisions are made by people outside the group, the group's controlled culture is fatalistic. I call the combination of hierarchy and egalitarianism social democracy, after the European nations that add a strong egalitarian element to the sacrificial ethic of hierarchy. Wherever egalitarianism and individualism combine, so that equality of opportunity is believed to lead to equality of results, as in the Jacksonian era of American political history, I call the mixture "American individualism." Extreme individualism, in concert with the dominion of authoritarianism, brings forth state capitalism. Authoritarianism, together with hierarchy, breeds totalitarianism. And in the middle, preferring to get by without coercing others or being coerced by them, is a hermit political culture.

The important decisions that individuals make are simultaneously choices of culture. People discover their preferences by continuously constructing and reconstructing their culture through decision making. Just as—but on a more cosmic scale—identification with a party enables individuals to cut their information costs in choosing among political parties, the continuing reinforcement and rejection of existing authority relationships helps them learn what to prefer as external circumstances change. Put plainly, people decide for or against existing authority.

Let us suppose that, as often happens, something goes wrong. Who is to blame? Egalitarian regimes blame "the system," the established authority that introduced unnatural inequality into society. Hierarchies blame deviants, who harm the collective by failing to follow its rules. Market regimes fault the individual—for example, for failing to be productive—or the government—for restricting transactions (not allowing the best bargains to be made). Suppose that a new development occurs. Without knowing much about it, those who identify with each particular way of life can guess whether its effect will be to increase or decrease social distinctions—guesses that are made more definitive by observing what like-minded individuals say. It does not take much for members of a market or a sectarian regime to figure out whether they oppose or approve of a progressive income tax, or for a member of a hierarchical regime to surmise that strengthening the state through a central treasury is better than the fragmentation of finance. Nor would extrasensory perception be required to understand that hierarchy makes it easy and equality makes it hard on leaders.

For a study of leadership, it is important that each regime bring with it a characteristic style of leadership. Knowing the regime, I claim, should enable an analyst to predict the style of leadership, which will usually—that is, more often than not—be associated with it.

I leave the reader with the chart of nine models that combine the dimensions and give these well-known names to the categories of political culture they make up. In this paper, I shall work out the implications for leadership of the four basic cultures out of combinations of which all possible political regimes are made up.

THE SCOPE AND DURATION OF LEADERSHIP

Our interest is in leadership as a function (consequence, if you like) of regime. Among many of its aspects, we need to know whether leaders in each regime will be obeyed over a wide or narrow spectrum of affairs (the *scope* of leadership) and whether they will exercise leadership all of the time or, like the temporary dictatorships of Rome, only some of the time (the *duration* of leadership).

Under fatalistic regimes, leadership is *despotic*—continuous and total; under equities, leadership is ipso facto inegalitarian, and therefore *illegitimate,*

MODEL 5.1
NINE MODELS OF CULTURES

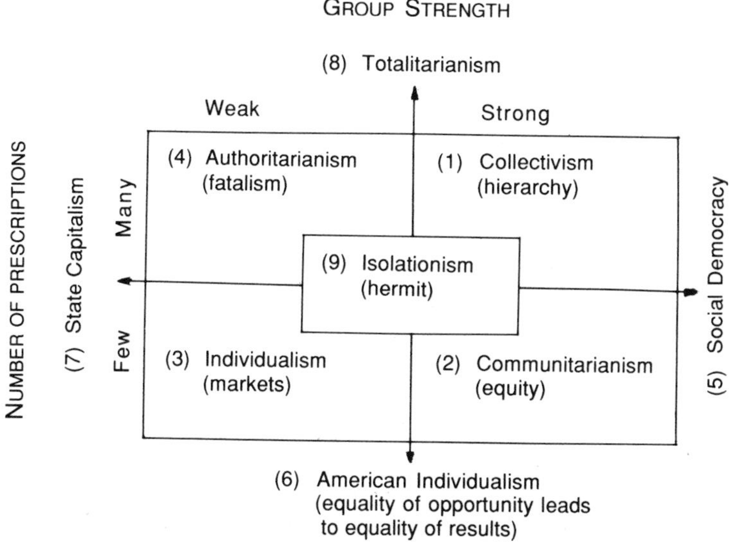

or it is *charismatic*—a legitimate bringer of new law that is unlimited in scope. Hierarchic regimes have *autocratic* leaders; within their spheres these leaders are supreme, but their scope is limited. Market regimes are led by *meteoric* leaders who flame bright and burn out quickly—the right person in the right place at the right time for the right purpose!

Reading model 5.2 as a series of predictions, we see that when followers are fatalistic, leadership is total: it is unlimited and continuous. Rulers may change, but fatalists still have rulers. As good a definition of despotism as any comes from Carlos R. Alba in regard to Francisco Franco of modern Spain: "His position as Head of State . . . consisted of a power that was exceptional, arbitrary, and without limits in its exercise, except those deriving from his own will."[53]

In equities based on voluntary association, equality of condition is the only legitimate political norm. Hence, leadership is discontinuous, but when present, it is unlimited. An all-or-nothing dichotomy occurs because charisma is the substitute for authority.

The nature of the cultural theory that I am expounding may become clearer if it is understood that power relations among participants constitute the political aspect—which I call regime—of its organizational culture. Charisma is a replacement for the law, a reestablishment of order based on the unusual

MODEL 5.2
STYLES OF LEADERSHIP BY POLITICAL REGIMES

1. *Fatalistic* Unlimited Continuous DESPOTIC	3. *Hierarchical* Limited Continuous POSITIONAL
4. *Markets* Limited Discontinuous METEORIC	2. *Communitarian* Unlimited Discontinous CHARISMATIC

personal qualities of the leader on whom the spirit of God shines or who exudes perfect egalitarian behavior. Hence, the charismatic leader can never arise in a hierarchical, a market, or an apathetic regime. The hierarchy already has its rule establishing social order—a place for everyone; everyone in his or her place. Hierarchical leaders, therefore, can be famous, popular, even wonderful or terrible; but they cannot (in cultural parlance) be charismatic because they come to uphold or to modify the old law, not to reject and replace it with a new one. Because individualists in market regimes do not want a new law anymore than they want an old or any other kind of law other than the minimum one required to respect property rights, a charismatic leader would be anathema, a purported leader without followers. Network builders are another matter. Individualists may follow an entrepreneur who appears to be doing well in order to share in the rewards. But individualists do not believe in the leader; they believe only in the results, in the bottom line. Not a new law, but better results under a market regime, capture their allegiance.

Fatalists are ruled from above. Old or new law makes no difference to them. They must be converted to sectarianism, voluntary rather than involuntary consent, before charisma would matter to them. First the liberation; only then, if ever, the conversion.

Egalitarianism is the home of the charismatic leader, the only home, according to cultural theory, that charisma can have. For it is only when social relationships are characterized by an effort to achieve near-perfect equality of condition—when everyone is allowed, even encouraged, to do everything—that social roles become deeply ambiguous. When all are equal, who is supposed to do what is unclear. In time of trouble, however, egalitarians may seek out a perfect exemplar to save them, a charismatic leader who will provide a substitute for authority.

Endless factional struggles beset regimes that have no internal authority and thus no mode of settling disputes except by starting one's own sect. Ordinary leadership is anathema because it represents a prima facie instance of inequality. Egalitarians do believe in minimal prescription, but they are also part of collectives that have strong boundaries to maintain. The voluntary and collective character of equities extends to the necessity of gaining agreement on each and every issue, rather than just the most important ones. Thus, there is no disposition to follow merely because an erstwhile leader tells you to do so.

Egalitarian regimes often engage in tearing down leaders as soon as they rear their ugly heads. When life sends up challenges, however, especially when they are subject to foreign invasion, equities get desperate. By that time, things are so bad that equities must invest leaders with both virtue and heroism, thus fitting them to exercise total power.

Virtue is the vice of equities. For as perfect equality makes leadership difficult, it also makes leadership necessary. How will children be socialized if not by the same strict education that is condemned in hierarchies? Many enemies have been made, but how will battles be fought without generals? Thus, leadership in equities, when it appears, is charismatic, if by that we mean leadership of supreme virtue and of short duration which encompasses all aspects of life.[54]

It is easy to understand why leadership is continually being exercised in hierarchies; but why is it limited in scope? As the classical scholars who studied traditional societies from Sir Henry Maine to Max Weber have maintained, obligations were reciprocal: the rules and statutes that enabled the top to give orders down the line also, by virtue of their binding character, limited what leaders could do to followers.[55] "I must obey here, but you have no right to give orders there." The numerous motion pictures on military life—I think of John Ford's *She Wore a Yellow Ribbon*—which show sergeants being deferential to officers on the battlefield but using customary practice to avoid encroachment on their family life—the colonel cannot give orders to the sergeant's children or invade his home—fit the picture. You can't have one—specialization or division of labor—without the other—acting according to the authority vested in one's rank and station.

In the market regime, leadership is both limited and discontinuous. It may not exist at all; self-regulation through bilateral bargaining may suffice. When leadership does exist, it will be limited in duration and confined to specific purposes. Why? No one is obliged to be a leader or to acknowledge those who claim to be leaders. There has to be a contract in which followers hire leaders before any mutual obligation exists. This contract has a narrow focus and a short time period, for if leaders should become permanent, they could dictate their terms, thus abrogating freedom of contract.

Enter the headless horseman. Leaders arise only for limited purposes and for short durations. The right to shift alliances so as to assure balance among the segments is the essence of the matter. Coalitions are reformulated until they are relatively even in strength; this leads to bargaining and stalemate. Although the family or clan may be quite hierarchical, it comprises the units of interaction, which are fiercely jealous of their autonomy, coming together with others just long enough to meet immediate needs and then dissolving.[56] Hence, leaders last only as long as there is a conglomerate entity to lead. Market regimes perform a delicate balancing act between having leaders when they are needed and getting rid of them when they are not.

Comparing these headless regimes (or segmentary systems, as Meyer Fortes and E. E. Evans-Pritchard named them after African experience) with equities, the difference in leadership is striking.[57] At first examination, these occasionally organized anarchies appear to be open to charismatic leadership. True enough, leadership is evanescent and personal. But market regimes do not subscribe to total leadership. They give up only as much autonomy as they need to for each engagement—that much and nothing more.

(ANTI)LEADERSHIP

The strength of leadership that is exercised within political regimes flows directly from the way they answer basic questions about political life. Hierarchies and fatalism favor strong leadership; sects and market regimes do not. This is too simple-minded, almost a matter of definition. We can do better by addressing a common political query to these categories of regimes: How does the demand for leadership compare to the support for it? The model contains two additional dimensions—balance (the gap between demand and support) and level (the direction of the gap so as to promote leadership or hinder it). The balance dimension suggests that what matters is not only the level of desired leadership but its relationship to the support provided.

The third model—"Political Balance in (Anti)Leadership Systems" (the "anti" in parentheses is a reminder that leadership may be absent as well as present)—specifies the gap between demand and support for leadership. The greater the gap between demand and support, the larger the leadership problem.

Although it is all too easy to speak about leadership as an unalloyed good—the more the better—people in a market regime may be quite content with the less the better; they may choose or accept leaders only when indispensable and thereby avoid having to pay the price that leaders often impose.

In hierarchical and market regimes, demand and support for leadership balance each other. This does not mean that such leadership is desirable, only that it exists in a balanced context. Because markets are organized to reduce the need for authority, having little authority is sufficient. The main difference is that hierarchies are balanced at a high level of reliance on authority, whereas markets are balanced at a low one. So long as these regimes operate properly, leadership is not problematical. To be sure, hierarchies may be tempted to use excessive force, thereby forcing people into fatalism; and markets may have so little leadership that they fall apart, because many of its adherents have become fatalists, subject to the desires of others. Change is ubiquitous. But as long as

MODEL 5.3
POLITICAL BALANCE IN (ANTI)LEADERSHIP SYSTEMS

SUPPORT	DEMAND: Low	DEMAND: High	
High	1) Fatalism support → demand unbalanced	3) Hierarchy support → demand balanced	LEADERSHIP SYSTEMS
Low	4) Individualism demand → support balanced	2) Communitarianism demand → support unbalanced	ANTI-LEADERSHIP SYSTEMS

markets and hierarchies last in recognizable form, whether or not they have sufficient leadership is not their problem. Their leadership may be either effective or ineffective, but the quantity of leadership is suited to their organizational condition.

Problematic leadership is a sign of unbalanced relationships: demand and support are out of whack. Fatalism is unsatisfactory because there is too little demand and too much support. Equities are in trouble because there is too much demand and too little support; they need leadership to stay together, but they manufacture, so to speak, antileadership antibodies.

HIERARCHIES VERSUS EQUITIES

Hierarchies support leadership; equities suspect it. The hierarchy gives its leaders an extra push; an equity holds them back. If that is all there is to it—starting with their right to give orders versus having to justify this right every time—leadership would be entirely static, stronger in one regime but weaker in another. There is more to the story: hierarchic regimes work actively to build leadership up, whereas regimes of equity work to tear it down. Like the roaches attempting to climb out of the tub, where the leader is pulled down by his fellow creatures as soon as he nears the top, equities actively undermine leadership. By what mechanisms do hierarchies strengthen leadership while equities weaken it?

Let us begin with an assumption about human nature that is usually accepted in hierarchies: human nature is flawed, but it is not so hopelessly evil that it cannot be mended by good institutions. If men are naturally evil, institutions that embody hierarchies are naturally good. Institutions complete the work of the creator. Human nature is perfected only in institutions.

Institutions imply permanence. The placement of rewards and punishments inside hierarchic regimes enables those regimes to undertake long-term ventures. Regime maintenance requires the ability to set directions and to keep to them over generations. Thus, individuals must be taught to sacrifice the short term for the long run, the personal for the group interest. Momentary passions, fleeting impulses, and ecstatic experiences must be eschewed in favor of sober self-sacrifice. Salvation is collective.

By the same token, as the good things are shared in hierarchies, so are the bad. Everyone is jointly responsible for whatever happens. Thus, leaders share in the credit but are generally absolved for the blame by the diffusion of responsibility. Blame shedding and blame sharing are characteristic of hierarchies; so are its standard operating procedures—secrecy, mutual protection, investigations aborted or never held.

To show the difference, equities blame both outsiders (because these adherents of foreign ways embrace inequality) and insiders (because they have secretly introduced impure practices), thus explaining why there may be breaches in equities' wall of virtue. They can pass blame to the outside, but they cannot share it on the inside. Hence, internal conflict is either driven underground or projected onto evil external forces.

In hierarchies, human beings who love institutions are called natural, and those who hate them are called unnatural—that is, perverts. Unnatural vice, to employ redundancy for emphasis, is opposed to established institutions. The establishment is good for you; if you are disloyal, it follows that you are bad. Q.E.D. Those who do not follow the rules, as Soviet behavior shows, are treated as if they were insane.

The protection of institutions is enhanced if individual opposition is nullified. The rationale is that evil spreads. The remedy is the same as for any disease that is considered catching—namely, isolation. The theory that immoral—that is, antiestablishment—behavior is contagious (viz. the discussion of the acquired immune deficiency syndrome) is a standard charge made by hierarchies. The weapon they use is boundary maintenance. They exert control by condemning behavior in which "lowerarchs" seek to usurp the position of hierarchs, or in which someone somewhere plays a role for which he has not been chosen.

For the same reason—for example, the vulnerability of the young, and their need for training in the values of the hierarchy—education assumes importance. The young are segregated from contaminating influences and are indoctrinated into prevailing practices. They must feel what is right; they must be able to recite the right before they can claim to know it. Institutional allegiance is rendered automatic, and the suppression of dissent, where it cannot be compromised, is justified.

Strong collective boundaries provide a dimension that equities share with hierarchies. Hence the two regimes share purification rites and an obsession with cleanliness. But the kind of corruption that each fears is different. Because all members of an egalitarian regime claim immediate and unmediated access to higher principles, their "filth" is the imposition by others of practices members do not accept. In equities, in short, leadership is close to corruption. In hierarchies, by contrast, evil is disobedience, acting against the practices imposed by hierarchical leaders.

LEADERSHIP IN A CULTURAL CONTEXT

In cultural analysis, context is crucial. For one thing, each culture takes on its coloration from its opposition: an equity that opposes a market regime will look different from an equity that opposes a hierarchical regime. For another thing, adherents of equities need not be entirely egalitarian; nor do members of markets need to be wholly individualistic. Members deserve their classification (according to carefully specified quantitative procedures) in comparison to others who differ from them in regard to the relevant measures of group incorporation and degree of prescription.[58] No culture exists in a vacuum. All societies or institutions above the most rudimentary level of organization are compounds of different cultures. How strong or weak each culture is relative to the other cultures that operate in the same arena exercises a crucial influence over its behavior. A nation such as Sweden, which has very strong hierarchies and moderate-strength markets and equities, is quite different from the United States, which has a strong market culture, a weak hierarchy, and moderate-strength equities. The regulation of industry is much more friendly in Sweden, where all major interests are part of the national family, to be dealt with by mutual persuasion; in America, on the other hand, major interests are just other special interests, to be coerced in the name of equality. Consider the Cambodian Khmer Rouge. It is (and was) an equity devoted to creating a perfectly egalitarian rural society. Had it been constrained by other cultures, the Khmer Rouge might have become just another fringe group fighting for its right to protest. Propelled into power and surrounded by a decayed royal hierarchy and institutionally weak market forces, it undertook fearful measures to realize its vision.

The kinds of demands that regimes make upon their leaders, and hence the personalities who can be successful in them, differ dramatically. The meteoric leader in a regime of individualism requires an almost instantaneous capacity to spring into action upon demand, together with the quite different ability to endure long periods of latency. Although meteoric leaders will be rewarded handsomely, they are expected to leave as soon as their task, such as winning a war, is over. Because these twin demands clash, meteoric leaders such as General George S. Patton of the United States or Moshe Dayan of Israel, who having readied themselves like coiled springs, excelled upon being called into action, did poorly during peacetime conditions or in the lulls between battles—moody, irascible, disappointed, out of focus, lashing out in socially disapproved ways.[59]

Would-be egalitarian leaders are in trouble before they start. Leadership implies followership—in other words, inequality. Mutual persuasion is what equities approve of. Meetings are lengthy, discussions interminable. Would-be leaders must dissemble, at once being persuasive about the right course to follow and self-effacing. For if they push themselves forward, attempting to lead rather than merely convening or facilitating discussion, they would soon be attacked for attempting to lord it over others. Civil rights and feminist organizations, when organized on an egalitarian basis, are fertile sources of examples.[60]

Exercising leadership in hierarchies is a lot easier. Prospective leaders are expected to lead; their authority inheres in their position. The regime that guides and constrains them gives consistent advice: leadership is necessary and therefore should be supported. The larger the hierarchy, however, the more numerous and diverse its parts, the more leaders are torn between their roles of mediating and guiding. On the one hand, hierarchical leaders must adjudicate statuses so that the parts that make up the whole are still willing to cooperate. Without agreement on jurisdiction—who has the right to do what?—internal conflict will prevent concerted action. At the same time, however, especially when danger threatens, leaders are expected to chart a definite course. Just as being merciful and being ruthless are difficult qualities to combine in the same person, so the leader who is both diplomatic and decisive is hard to find.

Made out of amalgams of opposites—be firm, be flexible, gain consent without coercion—leadership has proven to be both a protean and an elusive subject. Now, at least, following the guidelines of cultural theory, we know something about why leadership has so stubbornly resisted analysis. Political regimes are composed of two dimensions—the strength of group boundaries and the number and variety of prescriptions. When these dimensions work at cross-purposes—a collective regime that requires leadership but denies authority on grounds of equality—leadership becomes precarious. Even when supply and demand are more congruent (market regimes reduce the need for as well as the acceptability of leadership, while hierarchies increase the demand and the support for leadership), contradictions arise because it is difficult to satisfy the requirements of two such different dimensions equally well. Strong leadership, for instance, threatens the self-regulation of market regimes and the compromise among the elements or subunits that make up a hierarchical regime. The spanning of these conflicting requirements in the same personality provides a perennial source of strain. Leaders often do not meet our expectations because our demands are contradictory or, when they are consistent, because satisfaction requires the integration of opposing demands. I chose the title for my book about the leadership of the biblical Moses—*The Nursing Father*—because that phrase captures so well the union of opposites (nurture plus discipline) that leaders are expected to achieve.

What about personality? I recommend studying the operation of different personalities within regimes, by holding the cultural context constant. In *Dilemmas of Early American Presidents from Washington through Lincoln: A Cultural Analysis*, Richard Ellis and I have derived a series of dilemmas—in which leaders are pulled in opposite directions. Thomas Jefferson's and Andrew Jackson's dilemma, for instance, was how to act forcefully as president when their followers were opposed to central executive authority because it was perceived to be a device for increasing inequality. Jefferson solved his problem by incessant behind-the-scenes wheeling and dealing. Jackson solved the same problem in quite a different way, by building a mass party and by using the office that he held to reduce the size and scope of government. The evident differences in personality between the two men explain a great deal, but not until they are seen in cultural context.

Could personality be more important than culture? That would tell us a great deal about the fit (or lack thereof) between leaders and followers. Above all, individualists fear the leader who overstays his welcome, for such a leader would substitute his authority for their consent. More than anything, hierarchists fear the charismatic leader who would replace the ordered chain of being with his own personality: such a one might skip over organizational positions by intervening at any level. Fatalists have no leaders; passive people cannot develop active leaders.[61] Egalitarians usually have no leaders, because leadership, to them, represents a prima facie case of inequality. Only in desperation, fearful that their incessant attack on existing authority as being corrupt and illegitimate might lead to extermination, then and only then, when the leader shapes the culture in his own image, does personality become dominant. Only against a background of formlessness (equality as nondifferentiation) can a personality stand out against the structures within which the rest of us find ourselves.

An aphorism from the Old World had it (courtesy of Nelson Polsby) that when a poor man eats a chicken, one of them is sick. In a similar spirit, when you know more about what a third baseman is likely to do by knowing his personality than by understanding the rules and customs of baseball, one of you is crazy. Whether you will be seen to be out of your mind or whether your views will become normative, hence your designation as a charismatic leader, depends not only on your behavior but also on the cultural context that alone gives it meaning.

PUTTING MACROPOLITICS BACK INTO THE STUDY OF MICROLEADERSHIP

The most remarkable feature of the literature on leadership is the nearly total absence of large-scale politics. Political situations proliferate. But there is little discussion of types of regimes as productive of different kinds of leadership.

The social-science literature on leadership, in conclusion, either ignores regimes or jumbles them together in a woefully wide definition of situation. I have tried to unpack "situation" by deriving, from their cultural contexts, four political regimes and the kinds of leadership associated with them. By showing how leadership is shaped through a limited number of possible regimes, it may yet be possible to restore order in the house of leadership.

NOTES

This chapter is a more theoretical version of material published in my book *The Nursing Father: Moses as a Political Leader* (University: University of Alabama Press, 1985).

1. Cecil Gibb, "Leadership: Psychological Aspects," in *International Encyclopedia of the Social Sciences,* ed. David L. Sills (New York: Macmillan, 1968), vol. 9, pp. 91–101.
2. Cecil Gibb, "Leadership," in *Handbook of Social Psychology,* ed. Gardner Lindzey and Elliot Aronson, 2d ed., vol. 4 (Reading, Mass.: Addison-Wesley, 1969), p. 216.
3. Alvin W. Gouldner, "Introduction" to *Studies in Leadership,* ed. Alvin W. Gouldner (New York: Russell & Russell, 1965), p. 25.
4. Gibb, "Leadership: Psychological Aspects," pp. 98–99.
5. Quoted in Gouldner, "Introduction," p. 23.
6. Daniel Bell, quoted in *International Encyclopedia of the Social Sciences,* 9:102.
7. Robert Tannenbaum, Irving R. Weschler, and Fred Massarik, *Leadership and Organization: A Behavioral Science Approach* (New York: McGraw-Hill, 1961), p. 23.
8. Philip Selznick, *Leadership in Administration: A Sociological Interpretation* (New York: Harper & Bros., 1957).
9. Quoted in Tannenbaum et al., *Leadership and Organization,* p. 23.
10. Quoted by Gibb, in "Leadership," p. 228.
11. Gouldner, "Introduction," p. 46.
12. Quoted by Gibb in "Leadership: Psychological Aspects," p. 93.
13. A. Paul Hare, "Situational Differences in Leader Behavior," *Journal of Abnormal and Social Psychology* 55 (July 1957): 134.
14. Gibb, "Leadership," p. 207.

15. See Harold Proshansky and Bernard Seidenberg, *Basic Studies in Social Psychology* (New York: Holt, Rinehart & Winston, 1965), p. 377.

16. Kenneth F. Janda, "Towards the Explication of the Concept of Leadership in Terms of the Concept of Power," *Human Relations* 13 (Nov. 1960): 345–63.

17. Gibb, "Leadership: Psychological Aspects," p. 93.

18. Ibid., p. 94.

19. Ibid.

20. Gibb, "Leadership," p. 224.

21. Ibid., p. 239.

22. Ibid.

23. Gibb, "Leadership," p. 268. Gibb adds: "No doubt Sanford (1952) was right when he predicted that studies focusing on any one of these aspects alone will continue to yield 'positive but unexciting correlations.' What is needed is a conception in which the complex interactions of these factors can be incorporated." This I have tried to supply with "regimes."

24. See Carl J. Friedrich, "Political Leadership and the Problem of the Charismatic Power," *Journal of Politics* 24 (Feb. 1961): 3–24; and Arnold Tannenbaum, "Leadership: Sociological Aspects," *Encyclopedia of Social Sciences,* vol. 9, pp. 101–7.

25. Edward Shils, "Charisma, Order, and Status," *American Sociological Review* 30 (Apr. 1965): 199–213.

26. Ibid., p. 211.

27. Tannenbaum et al., *Leadership and Organization,* p. 22.

28. See the lengthy list in Janda.

29. Comprehensive studies include Robert T. Morris and Melvin Seeman, "The Problem of Leadership: An Inter-Disciplinary Approach," *American Journal of Sociology* 56 (Sept. 1950): 152–53.

30. *Roget's International Thesaurus.*

31. Janda, "Towards the Explication," p. 350.

32. Ibid., p. 353.

33. See Robert A. Dahl, *Who Governs?* (New Haven, Conn.: Yale University Press, 1961).

34. John Harsanyi, "Measurement of Social Power, Opportunity Costs, and the Theory of Two-Person Bargaining Games," *Behavioral Science* 7 (Jan. 1962): 67–80.

35. See Herbert Simon, *Models of Man* (New York: Wiley, 1957).

36. Andrew S. McFarland, *Power and Leadership in Pluralist Systems* (Stanford, Calif.: Stanford University Press, 1969), pp. 157–58, 161.

37. Fred I. Greenstein, "The Impact of Personality on Politics: An Attempt to Clear Away Underbrush," *American Political Science Review* 61 (1967): 629–41.

38. Friedrich, "Political Leadership," p. 19.

39. James MacGregor Burns, *Leadership* (New York: Harper & Row, 1978), p. 417.

40. Quoted ibid., p. 455.

41. Quoted ibid.

42. Gibb, "Leadership," p. 205.

43. Tannenbaum et al., *Leadership and Organization,* pp. 23–24.

44. Lewis J. Edinger, "Political Science and Political Biography: Reflections on the Study of Leadership (I)," *Journal of Politics* 26 (May 1964): 431–32.

45. John A. Miller, "Structuring, Destructuring Leadership in Open Systems," Management Research Center, University of Rochester, Technical Report no. 64, Office of Naval Research (Mar. 1973), p. 3.

46. Ibid.

47. Ibid.

48. Elihu Katz and his colleagues approach but do not quite reach this understanding. Inquiring into the conditions under which leaders survive from this to that situation, Katz et al. conclude that "leaders change not with every change of activity but only with changes to markedly different kinds of activity—that is, to activities which may no longer be compatible with the leader's talents" (Elihu Katz et al., "Leadership Stability and Social Change: An Experiment with Small Groups," *Sociometry* 20 [Mar. 1957]: 37). Such qualitative changes in kind would be changes in regime.

49. Aaron Wildavsky, "Choosing Preferences By Constructing Institutions: A Cultural Theory of Preference Formation," *American Political Science Review* 81: 1 (March 1987), pp. 3–21.

50. Gabriel Almond, "Approaches to Developmental Causation," in *Crises, Choice, and Change: Historical Studies of Political Development,* ed. Gabriel A. Almond, Scott C. Flanagan, and Robert J. Mundt (Boston, Mass.: Little, Brown, 1973), pp. 1–42.

51. See Lewis A. Dexter's splendid introduction to Arthur Bentley's *The Processes of Government* (New York: Transaction, 1982).

52. See Mary Douglas, *Natural Symbols: Explorations in Cosmology* (London: Barrie & Rockliff, 1970), and "Cultural Bias," in her *In the Active Voice* (London: Routledge & Kegan Paul, 1982); see also Mary Douglas and Aaron Wildavsky, *Risk and Culture* (Berkeley: University of California Press, 1982).

53. Carlos R. Alba, "The Organization of Authoritarian Leadership: Franco's Spain," in *Presidents and Ministers,* ed. Richard Rose and Ezra Suleiman (Washington, D.C.: American Enterprise Institute, 1980), p. 258.

54. Max Weber's idea of the routinization of charisma is tempting but troublesome. If leadership is regularized, it is not charismatic. Leaders may want to disperse their charisma, but when the carriers of the creed become a regular and predictable institution, they are, in my opinion, better called a hierarchy.

55. What is here called a hierarchic regime is a combination of Max Weber's traditional and rational legal authority. I think the concept of hierarchy serves well enough in discussions of leadership without loading it with distinctions that have proved elusive in practice. What exactly is passed along when leadership is traditional? I object to this usage because it is historical, whereas the types of leadership to which it is compared are social. See Reinhard Bendix, "Reflections on Charismatic Leadership," in *State and Society,* ed. Reinhard Bendix (Boston: Little, Brown, 1968), pp. 616–29; and Shils, "Charisma, Order and Status."

56. The classic description of a market regime as an "ordered anarchy" is from E. E. Evans-Pritchard, *The Nuer: A Description of the Modes of Livelihood and Political Institutions of a Nilotic People* (New York and Oxford: Oxford University Press, 1940). The political puzzle that Pritchard is trying to explain is that "the lack of government organs among the Nuer, the absence of legal institutions, of developed leadership, and generally, of organized political life is remarkable. . . . The ordered anarchy in which they live accords well with their character, for it is impossible to live among Nuer and conceive of rulers ruling over them" (p. 181).

57. Meyer Fortes and E. E. Evans-Pritchard, eds., *African Political Systems* (Oxford: Oxford University Press, 1940).

58. See Steve Rayner and Jonathan L. Gross, *Measuring Culture* (New York: Columbia University Press, 1985).

59. See Ian V. Hogg, *The Biography of General George S. Patton* (New York: Galley Books, 1982); Naftali Lau-Lavie, *Moshe Dayan: A Biography* (London: Vallentine, Mitchell, 1968).

60. See Jo Freeman, ed. *Social Movements of the Sixties and Seventies* (New York: Longman, 1983); Jo Freeman, *The Politics of Women's Liberation* (New York: Longman, 1975); and Emily Stolper, "The Student Non-Violent Coordinating Committee," *Journal of Black Studies* 8 (1977): 13–28; and in Freeman, *Social Movements,* pp. 320–34.

61. See my *The Nursing Father.*

6

Strategies of Political Leadership in Diverse Settings

Frank R. Baumgartner

In his introduction to this volume, Bryan Jones makes the distinction between biological analogies to political leadership and those drawn from the world of physics. In the world of Newtonian physics, actions cause predictable reactions, and forces lead to movement in a certain direction; but in the evolutionary world of biology, a number of unrelated streams come together and disengage in apparently random fashion. Of course, many phenomena in the physical world are extremely complex and involve seemingly random events, but we shall consider the two analogies as sufficiently different to distinguish between political leaders who operate in different environments. Some leaders operate in areas that can be easily understood, where their actions can be said to stem from single or few causes and where the consequences of those actions are also relatively straightforward. Other leaders work in areas where choices are ambiguous, where participation is fluid, where arguments depend more on symbols than on objective facts, and where certain time periods are more propitious for change than others. Simply put, it is more difficult to predict, explain, or even to understand what is going on in some circumstances than in others.

The importance of the biological analogy to political leadership is that ambiguous and shifting situations leave more room for individual leadership than do well defined and objectively understood ones. This chapter seeks to illustrate how individual leadership strategies must be adapted to divergent situations. Leadership exists only in relation to the people or organizations to be led; therefore, the understanding of leadership requires an understanding of the range of contexts within which leaders act. Both the biological and the physical analogies to the study of political leaders have important lessons. This chapter attempts to illustrate how both the "biological" elements of unrelated events and the "physical" elements of rational calculation must be studied in order to understand the contexts and the nature of leadership.

The aspect of leadership on which this chapter focuses is the ability of political and bureaucratic leaders to manipulate debates and to put them into those arenas of policy making that are most amenable to their own ideas. Different types of leadership are needed in different situations, so the successful bureaucratic leader may have few of the same skills as the successful political leader. In some cases, the most successful bureaucratic leaders may work by coordinating with political entrepreneurs, but in other cases, those leaders may be most successful by avoiding the political arena. Similarly, political leaders can sometimes show their leadership skills by keeping consideration of an issue limited to specialists, but on other occasions they may be most successful by "going public." There are many different strategies for the successful leadership of policy. The most successful use of strategies depends on the proper fit with the context in which they are being used.

LEADERSHIP IN AMBIGUOUS SITUATIONS

The portrayal of an issue determines who will decide it. One person's "simple technical measure designed to increase efficiency" is another's "politically motivated attack on the working class." Policy makers do not have complete freedom in asserting or denying the political importance of an issue; the national importance of some issues cannot be denied. Except for the most extreme cases, however, policy makers have great leeway in portraying issues according to their interests. This simple fact creates tremendous possibilities for those hoping to influence the outcome of national debates. Changing other people's minds is not easy, but the sophisticated political leader does not need to attempt this. Because different groups of actors are likely to become attracted to issues depending on how they are portrayed, political leaders can attract or avoid particular groups of participants by affecting the way in which people perceive the issue. Leadership is often a matter of rhetoric.

E. E. Schattschneider has written that the scope of a debate is the most important determinant of its outcome. There is no fixed roster of participants in the policy process; the definition of who will become involved in a given debate is often the most important determinant of its outcome. Therefore, heresthetically skilled policy makers often focus their efforts on affecting the scope of a debate.

> The most important strategy of politics is concerned with the scope of conflict. Imagine what might happen if there were a hundred times as many spectators on the fringes of the conflict who sympathized with Able rather than Bart. Able would have a strong motive for trying to spread the conflict while Bart would have an overwhelming interest in keeping it private. It follows that conflicts are frequently

> won or lost by the success that the contestants have in getting the audience involved in the fight or in excluding it, as the case may be.[1]

Generally speaking, the losers of a policy debate have an interest in expanding participation, while winners try to keep participation restricted: "It is the weak who want to socialize conflict, i.e., to involve more and more people in the conflict until the balance of forces is changed."[2] As Schattschneider wrote almost thirty years ago, "nothing attracts a crowd as quickly as a fight." Political conflicts do not expand in a random fashion; they grow because of specific appeals made by the losers in the original debate. These strategic policy makers direct their appeals toward those whose involvement, they hope, will tip the balance of forces to their side. The policy community expands in a particular fashion as the winners and the losers each attempt to influence who will be involved.

Political leadership is often the art of attracting the right group of participants to a policy debate. Sometimes, this involves appealing to large numbers of new participants, and sometimes it involves avoiding a broad consideration of the issue. A quiet consensus by all those concerned can forestall greater awareness of a question, and this is to be hoped for when the balance of opinions might change with that increase in participation. For example, policy making for the social-security program in the United States was first consensual but later became conflictual. As conflict increased, participation grew. During the early years, social-security policy was

> made by a relatively constricted and autonomous set of actors with a strong sense of proprietorship in the program. Decisions about social security were generally made in isolation from decisions about other government activities, both structurally and financially. Within the proprietary group, there was a high level of consensus about guiding principles. Initiatives and choices gradually followed paths well defined by programmatic doctrines and were treated as if they were technical matters.[3]

The small policy-making community that dominated social-security policy during its early years was the result of an absence of conflict, not the cause of it, according to Martha Derthick. When this consensus broke down, the policy community was transformed. Nonspecialists, who had previously shown no interest in the program, suddenly became interested in it. The program became the topic of increased interest to political generalists, as well as the subject of greater media attention. The presence or absence of conflict was the single most important variable in explaining the change in the nature of the policy-making system that surrounded social security, according to Derthick. Sponsors of the program were successful in their leadership strategy; they pushed through an ambitious social reform as long as they were able to avoid public controversies. By avoiding links with "welfare" and by making sure that their program was understood as a "self-insurance" pool, their portrayal was culturally acceptable, and it grew tremendously. When the circumstances changed, however, this strategy no longer worked. Strategies must be adapted continually to changing situations.

The issue of child abuse in the United States was transformed, just as social-security policy was, by a change in the degree of conflict among those involved. After years of being considered only in specialized policy groups, this issue suddenly began to appear on the national political agenda. An increase in conflict among those involved was one of the two most important criteria for explaining why this change occurred.[4] In fact, the second criterion noted by Barbara J. Nelson, "social versus scientific and technical construction of the problem," is the means by which political leaders altered the terms of the debate in order to attract the attention of a larger group of participants.

In the cases of both social security and child abuse, political and bureaucratic leaders, operating within environments of conflict or consensus, followed strategies that no longer worked when the nature of the environments changed. In the case of social security described by Derthick, the most successful political leaders built up their program by avoiding any broad discussion of it, while in the case of Nelson's study of child abuse, pushing this topic onto the agenda was essential for enacting important changes in public policy. This view of leadership as sometimes avoiding, but sometimes seeking, public attention is contrary to many previous studies of the topic. Building up the social-security program in the United States was no less a feat of political leadership because the successful strategy was to avoid, rather than to attract, attention. In fact, it is all the more cunning because of this counterintuitive aspect.

Schattschneider was the first to point out the importance of the scope of political conflict, and many political scientists since him have noted the empirical relationship between conflict and participation. Michael Hayes noted that the members of Congress react differently to issues depending on the degree of conflict surrounding the issues.[5] Public salience and conflict determine the incentives for congressmen to become involved in a given issue. Where public salience is low and conflict is nonexistent, specialists need not fear interference from nonexperts; when salience and conflict increase, a greater number of congressmen become involved. David E. Price has described the case of aviation policy, in which a specialized community made policy with little interference from outside actors until the issue became controversial.[6] This increased the public salience of the issue and created the incentives for many more members of Congress to become involved, thereby changing the nature of the policy community. Policy makers know that the degree of consensus or conflict that they exhibit before Congress will influence the way in which the members of Congress react to them.

Elected officials are especially attuned to questions of controversy, and they adopt a very simple decision rule when faced with a question of apparently no conflict: they go along with the advice of the "experts." For the policy experts hoping to retain control over an issue, presenting a "united front" before Congress is of considerable importance.[7] Political conflicts lead to greater participation, and they increase the chances that political generalists, rather than only technical specialists, will become involved. This is true not only in the limited case of the U.S. Congress; policy makers everywhere react differently to different types of issues. By portraying issues in different ways, therefore, astute leaders can affect the types of other participants who will be attracted or repelled.

In his contribution to this volume, Kenneth J. Meier discusses William T. Gormley's ideas about salience and complexity. Gormley demonstrates how different types of participants are attracted to different types of policy situations. Politicians, according to Gormley, are "attracted to salience, repelled by complexity." Contrasting portrayals of a given issue make this process still more complicated and still more open to manipulation by skilled leaders. In some situations (e.g., the "biological" world of ambiguous choices), even complex issues can be treated in a symbolic rather than a technical way. This gives political leaders more lee-way than even Gormley implies, since they can manipulate the debate. The best leaders are those who manipulate the arguments so that the issue is considered in the most advantageous arena. In the "physical" world of clear choices, the possibilities for redefining issues may be much more limited. Leaders in those situations may not be as successful.

Political events "are largely creations of the language used to describe them,"[8] and policy makers explain issues in different ways depending on the audience they are hoping to draw into the conflict. Those hoping to restrict the conflict to the smallest possible group explain an issue in technically complex terms: "Perhaps the most effective way to restrict or to localize the scope of an issue is to redefine it technically so that most people will not understand it."[9] Similarly, those hoping to expand participation focus on symbols that are more easily understood and more politically charged. In the fluoridation controversies during the 1950s and the 1960s, "this issue was redefined by antagonists to be, not a health issue . . . , but rather a matter involving the violation of individual rights and the intrusion of government into private realms."[10] The more ambiguously an issue can be defined, the more emotional and the less technical it can be made to appear, the greater the chances that the issue can be expanded to include the general public.[11] In the hands of a skilled political strategist, even an effort to fight tooth decay can become a "Communist plot."

Symbols play a preeminent role in the definition of political conflicts, according to Charles D. Elder and Roger W. Cobb. Policies must be explained with reference to symbols of some sort, and policy makers fight over the attachment of symbols to their policies because they know that different symbols will attract different participants. "What is at stake in any particular conflict is a matter not simply of the facts of the situation but of what facts are considered relevant and of the meanings people assign to them. Who has what at stake, then, is often itself an issue. Those whose definition attracts the greatest and most intense support are likely to prevail."[12] Contrasting symbols urged by proponents of different policy outcomes form the basis for political conflict, and these are the methods that leaders use to manipulate the debate to their benefit.

Schattschneider noted the importance of the scope of the conflict; several writers have demonstrated a relationship between conflict and participation; and Edelman and Cobb and Elder have focused on the terms of the debate as the mechanism by which conflicts can be expanded or contracted. The strategic behaviors of political leaders and their efforts to manipulate the terms of a debate are not unique to any country or to any policy area; but they are a constant and important part of the policy process across Western democracies. Politicians and other policy makers are adept at manipulating arguments to suit their needs. In one of the first major controversies of the Chirac government in France in 1986, a proposed sale of a state television channel was transformed by opponents into a much broader question. The *New York Times* describes the considerable rhetorical skill with which Socialist opponents of the proposal transformed the issue into a broadly symbolic one: "The proposal . . . has already generated the widest public protest of any Government measure so far, with many groups here contending that the state-owned stations are an inalienable part of the national cultural heritage."[13] Selling off the cultural heritage is not a popular position in France, and opponents of the sale could kill the measure if they succeed in portraying it in that way, whether or not they believe that the measure actually is related to France's cultural patrimony.

The strategy of expanding an issue is used with equal skill by politicians of both the Left and the Right in France. In the case of the sale of the public television station in 1986, the Socialists were the expanders, but similar tactics were used by the Conservatives when they were in the opposition from 1981 to 1986. Socialist antitrust proposals for the newspaper industry were portrayed as an attack on the "freedom of the press"; plans to nationalize businesses were seen as attacks on the "freedom to conduct business"; plans calling for increased accountability for governmental subsidies to private schools were portrayed as attacks on the "freedom of education." By continually stressing one of the most value-laden terms in the French national psyche (liberty: *"la liberté de la presse"; "la liberté d'entreprendre"; "la liberté de l'enseignement"*), opposition politicians scored a great tactical victory. While the government attempted to play down the symbolic implications of each of these issues, the opposition was able to generate such rhetorical hot air that these decisions became the subject of widespread public awareness and political debate, and the government was forced to justify itself in their terms.[14] The government's inability to dictate the terms of the debate resulted in a major political disaster for the Mitterrand administration, and accounts for much of the reason for its defeat in the 1986 elections. Conservatives were particularly adept in their relentless attacks on common, easily understood symbols. When the roles were reversed after the March 1986 elections, the Socialists proved equally capable of injecting some rhetorical hot air into many debates that the government would have preferred to treat at a lower political altitude.

The French may seem particularly adept at portraying seemingly routine issues in ideological ways. In fact, the issues that hit the national political agenda in most Western countries are only sometimes the "most important" ones. Politicians in the United States often portray mundane issues in ideological ways, invoking such themes as "anticommunism," "states' rights," or "equality." Several authors have recently noted the ability of American politicians and other political leaders to redefine issues to suit their needs. "Heresthetics" refers to the efforts of strategic policy makers to redefine a situation to their advantage. "The heresthetician uses language to manipulate other people," according to William H. Riker.[15] By reformulating a debate or by convincing others that two issues somehow are related, the heresthetic political leader can transform defeat into victory. Riker describes several examples of strategic policy makers who altered the terms of the debate to suit themselves, including such diverse politicians as Abraham Lincoln and Pliny the Younger. In one example, a United States senator was opposed to a Defense Department proposal to transport dangerous nerve gas through his state. As long as the issue was framed in terms of where the gas would go, he was certain to lose, because the majority of his colleagues were relieved that his state had been chosen rather than their own. He was careful to find another plausible way of portraying the issue, however, one that he knew would lead to a much more favorable result. Since the material was coming from an overseas base covered by treaty agreements with Japan, he was able to assert that the decision to remove the nerve gas represented a change in the status of the treaty relationship and that the Senate had not been informed of this. What the Defense Department had portrayed as a simple question of which state would be the depository for this nerve gas, Senator Warren Magnuson was able to transform into a debate about the "unconstitutional usurpation of the Senate's power to ratify treaties." Since the senators were not willing to vote against their own power in opposition to the executive branch, especially in the aftermath of the Vietnam War, when this debate took place, this strategically skilled senator transformed his losing position into the winning one.[16]

John W. Kingdon has described how policy entrepreneurs link problems and solutions by redefining one of them so that other policymakers will be convinced that the two are related. Skilled policy entrepreneurs link their pet solution to whatever problem happens to emerge on the national agenda. "A problem captures the attention of important people, and participants hook their proposals onto it, arguing that they represent solutions, even though advocacy of these proposals originally had nothing to do with the new problem."[17] The important point for the entrepreneurs is to redefine the issue so that it will attract the attention of a different group of participants. Proponents of federal aid to urban mass-transit programs, for instance, first portrayed their solution as an answer to the problem of "traffic congestion in the cities," according to Kingdon. When this problem was no longer of intense interest among the politicians, they redefined their solution to be the answer of the next popular problem on the agenda: "the environmental movement. . . . The environmental movement faded, and what was the next big push? You guessed it: energy."[18] By portraying the same solution in three different ways, proponents of this program were able to generate support for many years. Besides their success in generating support, they could be proud of their rhetorical and navigational skills. They succeeded in maneuvering their issue to that area of the political system where they could garner ever-increasing support.

American policy makers seeking funds for education in the 1960s showed their strategic skills when they established a link between the Soviet space program and the U.S. educational system. Nelson W. Polsby has described with apparent awe how supporters of education were able to maneuver their issue into the wake of Sputnik:

> The fact that Sputnik spurred our primary space effort is . . . an expected outcome, since anybody can see the connection between the Soviet space effort and the United States space effort. The task of leading official thinking to make a connection between the perceived "threat" of imminent Soviet space exploration and inadequate funding of schools and colleges is of a different order of complexity, and suggests that entrepreneurial talent of a very high order was at work.[19]

The redefinition of an issue can be used to generate opposition to a proposal, just as well as to generate support. James G. March and Johan P. Olsen have described how opponents of an administrative reorganization plan under the Roosevelt administration established a link between it and a variety of other issues, ultimately leading to the abandonment of the plan. Some of the connections that they established were evidence of great rhetorical skill. They argued that the reorganization plan was related to a diverse collection of unpopular issues, including the Supreme Court controversy, allegations of corruption within the Democratic party and in other administrative departments, and even an antilynching bill that happened to be under discussion at the same time. "The result of this garbage-can collection of issues was that a reorganization that was first received with indifference or moderately positive attitudes was transformed into a major confrontation and defeat for the President.''[20]

In a recent book Samuel Kernell has described the strategic decisions that American presidents have made to appeal to the public in order to put more pressure on Congress to get their bills passed into law.[21] The ability to shift the debate from the relatively quiet negotiations with Congress to the general political arena is one of the greatest strengths of the presidency, as Kernell points out. Political leaders are those in a position where they can choose the arena in which a debate will be discussed. Just as Kernell has shown the importance of ''going public,'' Cary R. Covington has noted how American presidents have often won by ''staying private.''[22] When their strategic calculations indicate that their interests will best be served by moving an issue either up or down on the political agenda, presidents, like other policy makers, attempt to move issues to different arenas. In a hot-air balloon, higher is not necessarily better, if the winds are blowing in the wrong direction at those altitudes. Strategic policy makers, like skilled navigators, seek out not a particular altitude, but the one that will carry them most quickly in the direction they want to go.

Policy makers manipulate the policy process by redefining issues to change the roster of participants. Depending on the balance of power in different policy communities, policy makers attempt to force the issue onto the general agenda, to restrict it to a small community of experts, or to shift it from one group of specialists to another. The sponsors of mass-transit policy described by Kingdon or the education-policy entrepreneurs cited by Polsby followed a sophisticated strategy of policy making, redefining their issues to change the balance of power among those involved. Like the balloonist who has no power to change the direction of the prevailing winds, strategic policy makers generally have little power to force others to agree with them. Rather than accepting the current roster of participants and the terms of the debate as presented to them, however, the policy makers follow the balloonist's example: they alter the terms of the debate, heating up or cooling down the political controversy in order to find the arenas where the prevailing winds are the most favorable.

Of course, for each loser in a battle there is a winner, and winners are not likely to stand idly by while their opponents redefine an issue to shift the balance of power away from them. Much of the political battle takes place in this way: one side attempts to redefine an issue to its benefit, while another side attempts to prevent the redefinition of the issue. For those attempting to manipulate the policy debate, nothing is inherently better about any particular definition of a given issue; each definition has a different implication for who will become involved and who will win. In an important sense, therefore, the most effective leaders are simply those who have the greatest skill at manipulating policy arguments, hitting the right cultural symbols to induce support from the needed groups while avoiding those contrasting portrayals of an issue that might lead to opposition.

It is clear that no single strategy of political leadership is likely to be universally successful. Even the most astute rhetorical strategy can sometimes fail in the complex interaction of unrelated events which makes up the biological world of politics. A particular leader or leadership strategy is only as good as its fit with the environment. The most skillful leaders are not necessarily the most successful ones, nor can their strategies of leadership necessarily be transported from one area to another. Each strategy must be specially defined to fit with the situation. The study of leadership must therefore include a study of the fit between the leader and the environment.

LEADERSHIP IN FRENCH AND AMERICAN POLITICS

The institutions of the U.S. government were purposely designed to thwart leadership, while the centralized institutional structures of the French Fifth Republic were designed with almost the opposite concerns. The drafters of the latter's 1958 constitution wanted to make sure that effective leadership would be facilitated, and indeed, French governmental leaders do have more success in seeing their policy proposals carried through than their American counterparts usually can count on. These institutional differences only go so far, however, in explaining success in leadership. French leaders can face enormous problems in getting their policies enacted, just as skilled manipulators of the political symbols dear to Americans are sometimes able to show their leadership skills. The institutions of government are only one aspect of the environment of leadership, however. Other important factors are the social and interest-group context and the symbolic associations that leaders are able to create for their issues. The same issue, considered in two different social and historical contexts, may become associated more easily with different cultural symbols.

Institutional differences between France and the United States abound, but there are also important differences among issue areas within each of the countries. The organizations associated with some issues are divided and conflictual, while other organizations exhibit great homogeneity and consensus. In order to note the importance of both the institutional and the social dimensions, I describe in this section two issue areas in each country: education and nuclear energy. The institutional structures that surround French education could not be more centralized, whereas American education is governed at the local level by thousands of school boards and could not present greater problems for leadership. Despite these institutional differences, however, a divisive interest-group structure surrounds French education, and close links to some of the most potent political symbols makes leadership difficult to observe in France. In the United States, the area of education represents the single greatest commitment to public spending, and it enjoys broad political support. In contrast to the area of education, in which social conflict makes leadership difficult in the French case, nuclear energy represents an area in which the disjointed policy process and the lack of shared goals in the United States make it virtually impossible for clear leaders to emerge, whereas in France a coherent set of state elites creates a leadership steam roller.

Leadership depends on the ability to control the nature of the debate surrounding an issue. The most successful leaders are those who can ensure that their issues will be debated in terms that will attract supporters and that will not arouse the interest of potential opponents. Centralized institutional structures often help leaders to have more control over the debate. These structures are not sufficient, however, to ensure effective leadership. Social groups may be organized in a way that will inhibit the generation of consensus or in a way that will encourage it. Related to the organization of social groups are the symbols to which leaders can appeal in framing the debate. Leaders can be most powerful where they operate in environments that combine institutional control with organizational consensus. This allows issues to be defined in the most advantageous ways for the leaders, as in the case of French nuclear-energy policy. In areas with no internal consensus, each attempt by one group to redefine an issue will lead to countermobilization by those opposed to the redefinition, and the result often is stalemate. This can occur in areas of tight institutional centralization, as in French education, or in any other area that exhibits a lack of consensus, such as American nuclear policy. Where leaders operate within areas of relative social consensus and where they may appeal to powerful symbols without fear that opponents will raise equally powerful symbolic arguments to counter them, leaders may be able to provide effective leadership even in the absence of tight institutional control, as the case of American education shows. The combination of institutional and social contexts within which leaders operate determines much of their ability to portray issues in the most advantageous ways. Leadership depends on formal institutions, on the social environment, and on the skills of the leaders.

EDUCATION

Education in the United States is one of a few areas of public spending that enjoy widespread public support. While controversy surrounds many other areas of social spending, the symbol of equal opportunity, which depends on a vast system of public education, allows public support to be generated more easily around this question than around many others. The link between education and important positive cultural symbols in the United States does not guarantee that proposals for expanding it will be endorsed unanimously.

Important conflicts surround certain areas of American education, to be sure. Still, many questions surrounding education can be portrayed in ways that will elicit generalized support from the broader public. Attacks on the value of public education are not common.

Education in France is associated with a number of other cultural symbols, some of them positive, others very divisive. Because of the historical importance of Catholic education in France, the expansion of the public education system became inextricably linked to the great ideological conflict between anticlericals and supporters of the church, between Left and Right, and between Republicans and Monarchists. Whereas the dominant symbols associated with American education—in particular, equality of opportunity—are essentially positive, many of those associated with education in France elicit hostility on one side of the political spectrum or another.

Besides the relevant cultural symbols and the institutional organization of the government, the relative cohesion of the interest-group environment is also of importance. In this area, differences between French and American education could not be more stark. The French minister of national education sits at the top of a hierarchy within which every teacher and every classroom in the country has its place. The United States secretary of education, on the other hand, oversees the activities of thousands of local school boards over which he and his small federal bureaucracy have little direct control. The politics and policy making surrounding education in France are rife with conflict, however, and this partially mitigates any advantages that may come from centralized control. The policy process is divided among a number of competing unions and associations of specialists, many of which are in competition with one another for members. Furthermore, most of these associations maintain links with different political parties. Therefore, the Ministry of Education operates in an environment in which each conflict within the specialized community of experts has the potential for being translated into a broader fight between Socialists and Communists, between Conservatives and Leftists, or between Clericals and Anti-Clericals.[23] Furthermore, the extreme centralization of the system encourages single, national battles over issues in France which in the United States are made by a variety of independent local decisions, none of which has the profound importance of a national policy. The decentralization of the American system helps avoid its politicization.

Even purely pedagogical issues can lead to political conflicts in France. The Left sees the educational system as the means by which elites are reproduced,[24] while the Right sees the leftist teachers' unions as the cause of mediocrity and entrenched interests. Because each of the major actors within the educational-policy community has a distinctive political ally, issues are easily transformed from the pedagogical to the political and the ideological. While conflicts within the American education-policy community rarely explode onto the national political agenda, education in France periodically surfaces on page one of *Le Monde.*

Unlike American groups, French organizations in the area of education are often in competition for members, as several unions may dispute the representation rights to a single category of teachers or employees. In a mail survey conducted in 1984 of all groups involved at the national level in educational policy in France, almost 90 percent of French educational groups reported the existence of competing organizations, while only about 25 percent of American educational groups that were contacted in a similar survey conducted in 1983 reported that they engaged in "continuous competition for members or resources with other associations in the field." This competition over members which the French groups experience often translates into substantive conflict, as each group seeks to differentiate itself from its rivals. Of the French educational groups, 72 percent reported other organizations "with which [they] often find [themselves] in disagreement," and the vast majority of these groups described the disagreements as "fundamental matters of principle" rather than only "questions of detail." In the United States, by contrast, only 29 percent said that "some organized groups oppose the policy aims of this organization."[25]

Often, controversies stem from the jurisdictional and membership battles in which the different unions in France are engaged. These fights, which often have little to do with policy content, nonetheless serve to complicate the policy process and to push the issues higher up the administrative and political hierarchy. Issues that might otherwise be dealt with by educational specialists alone may take on political and ideological overtones, thereby attracting the attention of political leaders. When medical students objected to the institution of a new examination system in 1983, they found natural allies in the political parties of the opposition in their efforts to shift the debate from the specialized community of medical-educational experts, where they had little influence, to the general political agenda, where they had more success. Parliamentary spokesmen for the opposition were happy to defend a vocal constituency against the Socialist government, and they used the forum of the parliamentary debate on the bill to focus national attention on an issue that previously had been the subject of only restricted interest among specialists. The issue was transformed from a purely pedagogical one into a political and ideological one because of the organization of interests surrounding it and because of the strategic appeals of the losers to their allies in the general political arena.[26]

Of course, particularly skillful leaders can score important policy successes even within the difficult environment of French education. One high administrator searched for ways to find significant amounts of money to refurbish several national museums that he found in disrepair when he came into office in 1981. With some research, he established that each of four major buildings had a strong link with previous governments of the Left. Two museums dated from the Convention of 1792, and two others from the Popular

Front government of 1936. By focusing on the ideological legacy of the French Left, he argued that the restoration of these "cultural jewels" would show that the new Socialist government had greater respect for the traditions of the Revolution and for France's cultural legacy than had the previous governments of the Right. Such rhetorical flourish proved successful in moving this dossier out of the normal bureaucratic channels of negotiation between the Education Ministry and the Ministry of Finance. Further, it could not be attacked on ideological grounds, as can many other policies surrounding education in France. This strategic bureaucrat was rewarded with hundreds of millions of francs in new budgetary authority despite the "rigorous" budgets of the time. This bureaucratic heresthetician commented in an interview in 1984, "If there had been a government of the Right in power, I would have had to think up different arguments!" A clever leader can make his skills shine even in the difficult environment of French education.

In the United States, the internal consensus among educational specialists has allowed them to avoid the politicization of pedagogical issues which occurs periodically in France, despite the more complicated institutional structures within which they operate. One of the most important consequences of the greater consensus surrounding education in the United States is this nation's greater financial commitment to the area. Education is one of the few areas of the welfare state in which American public expenditures per capita far exceed those of European states. While the United States lags far behind other countries in most areas of public expenditure for social programs, its commitment to education is extraordinary.[27] French education, unlike American, is not the subject of any societal consensus.

It should be apparent that the coincidence of diverse and conflictual cultural symbols associated with education in France and the divided and conflictual interest-group environment surrounding it is not the result of mere chance. Interest groups were built up around the important societal cleavages of clericals versus anticlericals; public-school supporters versus supporters of the private schools; Socialists versus Communists; and along jurisdictional grounds. Once such a diverse set of organizations was in place, this compounded the difficulties for political leaders attempting to avoid the mobilization of contrary interests, each armed with powerful symbolic associations in support of their mutually hostile goals. The relatively consensual set of organizations representing educational professionals in the United States both reflects and facilitates this nation's greater social consensus on the importance of public education.[28] The cultural symbols available to political leaders as they attempt to generate support for their proposals are therefore likely to be closely intertwined with the mobilization of organized interests in society. This combination can make leadership virtually impossible, as in the case of French education, or surprisingly realistic, as in the case of the United States.

NUCLEAR ENERGY

The institutional structures surrounding nuclear energy in France and in the United States differ in much the same ways as those surrounding education. In the French case, policy makers in charge of the nuclear industry operate within a centralized system of administrative control inside the executive branch of the national government, and they limit their relations with outside actors as much as possible. In the United States, a disjointed group of executive-branch regulatory agencies, state and local governmental authorities, legislative committees, and judicial bodies creates an environment within which it is difficult for leadership to emerge. French nuclear authorities are able to take advantage of these institutional strengths, whereas their counterparts in education could not. The nuclear authorities maintain a tight internal consensus and are able to appeal to powerful cultural symbols, while the education officials do not. Nuclear-energy proponents in the United States have not been able to generate strong support for their policies because of the disjointed nature of the institutional environment and because of the lack of consensus among those involved. This makes it impossible for the proponents to portray the issue in the most advantageous way. Policy makers on both sides of the issue follow strategies of expansion and contraction, just as would be expected, but the different organization of interests makes it possible for the French to be much more successful than the Americans in the case of nuclear energy, whereas the opposite is generally true in the case of education.

From the beginnings of the nuclear program in France, as elsewhere, the development of the new technology was hailed as a guarantee of national independence. This argument was first applied to its military applications, but after the 1973 oil embargo, it also became a strong argument in favor of domestic sources of energy in general. With few indigenous sources of energy, France embarked on the world's most ambitious program of nuclear development in 1974. The percentage of electricity generated by nuclear power in France increased steadily but slowly until the 1974 decision to embark on a vast construction program began to see its fruits in the late 1970s. In 1976, France ranked behind the United States in the percentage of electricity generated by nuclear power, at approximately 8 percent, as compared to 11 percent in the United States. By 1980, France had increased the relative share of nuclear power to 24 percent of its electricity, while the percentage of nuclear power in the United States remained at 11. By 1985, France was getting more than 65 percent of its electricity from nuclear energy, while the industry remained in virtual stagnation in the United States.

There is no surprise in the French government's desire to develop this new source of energy. Many other countries proposed massive investment in it as well. The striking feature of the French case is its enormous scale and its successful implementation. The groundwork for the successful implementation of this massive policy decision was laid in the twenty preceding years through skillful manipulation of the debate; then it was carried through because of the consensus among those involved and the weakness of any organized opponents. Proponents of nuclear energy in the United States use many of the same arguments in urging that it be expanded. The difference between these proponents and their French counterparts is their striking lack of success. The same leadership strategies, followed by different groups in different environments, have led to opposite results.

Partisans of the extension of nuclear energy programs in France have been able to avoid links to the political parties and effectively to insulate themselves from partisan conflicts, a remarkable achievement in comparison with their collegues in education. From the beginning of the nuclear program after World War II, those involved have been able to portray the technology as the guarantor of national independence and international prestige.[29] Electricity of France (EDF), the national electricity company, dominates the process, along with the Atomic Energy Commission (AEC) and only a few other large institutions. Compared to the United States, where a variety of manufacturers deal with a large number of public and private utilities, the French have centralized the process to the highest degree.

> EDF, which serves in the capacities of architect-engineer, owner and operator of its plants, currently buys all its reactors from one manufacturer, Framatome, and all its turbines from another manufacturer, Alsthom-Atlantique. . . . In this country [the U.S.], more than 100 plants have operating licenses; the plants are operated by 50 different utilities and were designed by 17 architect and engineering firms.[30]

Because of the tight-knit nature of the French nuclear industry, it is able to avoid the politicization of debates surrounding it much more easily than would otherwise be possible.

The nuclear-power industry in France operates within an environment of consensus, reinforced by tight control over the regulatory process. Graduates of the prestigious Ecole polytechnique and the Ecole des mines dominate a process in which proponents of the industry exclude those who are opposed and prevent them from voicing their concerns. While the courts have been an important venue for opposition success in the United States, the rules of standing make it virtually impossible for opponents of new nuclear power plants in France to make use of the civil courts, thus limiting the options open to opponents of the plants to shift the debate to another venue where they might have more success.[31] Furthermore, local governmental authorities have neither the power nor apparently the interest in opposing Parisian plans to site nuclear facilities. In the United States, requirements that state and local governments cooperate in the planning of new plants have allowed opponents to focus their efforts on state governors who may be very happy to be put in the position of "protecting the safety of the citizenry," especially if they happen to be running for president. Uncertainties associated with potential delays during the regulatory process present one of the greatest problems for those hoping to build nuclear plants in the United States, but unpredictable delays during the public-hearing process are rare in France. Only those individuals who live within five kilometers of a proposed plant are entitled to be heard, and their complaints must come in writing during a period of only eight weeks. Considering the rural areas in which nuclear plants are built, the five-kilometer rule limits the public hearing process to a minimum.[32] Finally, organizations that oppose nuclear energy in France are politically marginal, since all the major parties have adopted a pronuclear stance, albeit for different reasons and with varying levels of enthusiasm. The combination of limited institutional options and low organizational strength makes the antinuclear movement in France no match for the powerful nuclear industry there.

National independence is a typical argument used by pronuclear activists in all Western countries, just as "nature" or "the environment" is for antinuclear ones. Just as one portrayal may hit cultural chords more easily in some countries than in others, national independence has been an extremely powerful argument in France. One paradox that should make it clear how this portrayal is subject to elite manipulation is that such arguments were not heard when they would have gone the other way. During the 1960s, French elites decided to abandon the indigenous design for nuclear plants and to adopt American technology. Opponents to this decision could easily have focused on the national-independence idea, but De Gaulle himself, who was not known for his willingness to follow American leads in other areas, made the decision in order to cut costs and to allow the quickest possible expansion of the nuclear facilities. So, paradoxically, abandoning national research and development for adopting a foreign design was championed as the key to "national independence" when it suited the needs of the cohesive elite. While American constructors built plants of many different designs, the French abandoned their independent design efforts and built nothing but Westinghouse pressurized water reactors—all in the name of "national independence."

American nuclear-energy policy is controlled by no one, apparently, as the courts, regulatory agencies, executive departments, local governments, outside interest groups, many committees of both the House and the Senate, and a complicated myriad of public and private utilities and constructors attempt to make decisions. In France, nothing of the sort occurs, and the consensus among all the pronuclear decision makers allows forceful decisions not only to be made but also to be carried through.

The same strategies may not work in different cultural settings. For example, antinuclear activists in France have attempted to focus on such topics as "protecting nature," as have their counterparts in other countries. In Germany, where the forest and nature strike important cultural chords, these arguments are much more successful. Similarly in Great Britain, where the countryside has likewise been a part of the cultural myth, not only do these arguments hold great sway, but a ready-made system of organizations defending "nature" already exists. In Sweden, where objective pressures for adopting nuclear energy are at least as strong as in France, an ambitious plan was eventually abandoned after the issue became entwined in partisan battles.[33] In the United States, of course, "the environment" became a rallying cry for opponents to many types of economic development in the 1960s, and an extensive network of groups was built up around it. So, cultural values not only affect the ability of leaders to strike the right chords in attempting to mobilize people through favorable portrayals of given issues, but they also affect the existing mobilization of bias through the pressure-group system.

CONCLUSION

Individual leaders need to be skilled manipulators of rhetorical debates. Leaders focus on the most positive symbols associated with their policies, while avoiding those that might attract opponents. These strategies of policy making and consensus building are the means by which policy makers attempt to achieve their goals. Manipulating the portrayal of issues may be the most important way of doing this. However, the ability to alter the portrayal of an issue can be determined in part by the nature of the social and the institutional environment surrounding it. In the evolutionary world of complex decision making, considerable leeway is apparent for strategies of individual leadership. Policy makers' attempts to manipulate the portrayals of issues are clearly a part of this entrepreneurial enterprise. It is clear, however, that policy makers operate within environments that structure their behavior. Policies are made neither in Kingdon's "primeval soup" of completely random couplings of problems, solutions, actors, and choice opportunities nor in Weber's rational world of problems needing solutions. While the real world leaves much room for individual strategies of leadership, some situations clearly are more amenable to effective control than are others. In this chapter, I have attempted to show some of the circumstances that can lead to a combination of the physical and the biological analogies to political leadership.

Political leaders operate in situations of ambiguity or of rationality. The interaction of their leadership strategies, the cultural symbols that they are able to manipulate, and the institutional and social contexts within which they operate determine their success. The ambiguity that is apparent in many situations creates the opportunity for leadership to emerge. Effective leaders thrive on ambiguity, since it creates choices and opportunities for them to portray their issues in different ways, seeking out the arena in which they will be most successful. In areas where a single dominant portrayal of an issue is apparent, leaders can be most successful by maintaining internal consensus and by ensuring that they maintain control over the issue. This is apparent with the case of the most successful group of all that were considered here: French nuclear authorities. Armed with powerful control over the policy process, with a strong internal consensus, and with powerful cultural symbols, they have enacted a massive policy of building nuclear plants which could not have been possible in other circumstances or with less skillful leaders. In areas where leaders cannot control the portrayal of a debate, as in American nuclear energy or in French education, leadership is much more difficult, since each attempt to launch a new program or to adopt some change will lead to a counterattack by opponents willing and able to bring opposing cultural symbols into play. This may occur within a system of centralized institutions, as in French education, or in a disjointed institutional structure, as in United States nuclear policy. Even where the institutions may be well controlled, if social groups outside of government are divided, single dominant portrayals will emerge with difficulty. Even in such a disjointed institutional structure as American education, if a dominant cultural portrayal emerges and is reflected in the organization of interests, then strong leadership becomes more likely. Leadership is a function of individual skills and the manipulation of symbols, as the biological analogy notes, but it is severely constrained or enhanced by the institutional and social environment, as the physics analogy reminds us.

NOTES

1. E. E. Schattschneider, *The Semi-sovereign People* (New York: Holt, Rinehart & Winston, 1960), p. 4.

2. Ibid., p. 40.

3. Martha Derthick, *Policymaking for Social Security* (Washington, D.C.: Brookings Institution, 1979), pp. 7–8.

4. Barbara J. Nelson, *Making an Issue of Child Abuse: Political Agenda Setting for Social Problems* (Chicago: University of Chicago Press, 1984).

5. Michael Hayes, ''The Semi-sovereign Pressure Groups,'' *Journal of Politics* 40 (1978): 134–61.

6. David E. Price, ''Policy Making in Congressional Committees,'' *American Political Science Review* 72 (1978): 548–74.

7. John W. Kingdon, *Congressmen's Voting Decisions* (New York: Harper & Row, 1973), pp. 243–45.

8. Murray Edelman, *Politics as Symbolic Action* (Chicago: Markham, 1971), p. 65.

9. Roger W. Cobb and Charles D. Elder, *Participation in American Politics: The Dynamics of Agenda-Building*, 2d ed. (Baltimore, Md.: Johns Hopkins University Press, 1983), p. 45.

10. Ibid., pp. 44–45.

11. Ibid., pp. 112–24.

12. Charles D. Elder and Roger W. Cobb, *The Political Uses of Symbols* (New York: Longman, 1983), p. 129.

13. Richard Bernstein, "Bills Introduced in France on Immigrants and TV," *New York Times*, June 12, 1986.

14. See Pierre Mauroy, "M. Mauroy: La Défense des libertés est un des axes fondamentaux de notre politique," *Le Monde*, June 21, 1984.

15. William H. Riker, *The Art of Political Manipulation* (New Haven, Conn.: Yale University Press, 1986), p. x.

16. Ibid., p. 110.

17. John W. Kingdon, *Agendas, Alternatives, and Public Policies* (Boston, Mass.: Little, Brown, 1984), p. 191.

18. Kingdon, *Agendas*, p. 181.

19. Nelson W. Polsby, *Political Innovation in America: The Politics of Policy Initiation* (New Haven, Conn.: Yale University Press, 1984), p. 170.

20. James G. March and Johan P. Olsen, "What Administrative Reorganization Tells Us about Governing," *American Political Science Review* 77 (1983): 281–96.

21. Samuel Kernell, *Going Public: New Strategies of Presidential Leadership* (Washington, D.C.: Congressional Quarterly Press, 1986).

22. Cary R. Covington, " 'Staying Private': Gaining Congressional Support for Unpublicized Presidential Preferences on Roll Call Votes," *Journal of Politics* 49 (1987): 737–55.

23. See, for examples, John S. Ambler, "Equality and the Politics of Education," in *The French Socialist Experiment*, ed. John S. Ambler (Philadelphia: Institute for the Study of Human Issues, 1985), "Neocorporatism and the Politics of French Education," *West European Politics* 8 (1985): 23–42, and "Constraints on Policy Innovation in Education," *Comparative Politics* 20 (1987): 85–105; Antoine Prost, *Histoire de l'enseignement en France, 1800–1967* (Paris: Armand Colin, 1968); James M. Clark, *Teachers and Politics in France: A Pressure Group Study of the Fédération de l'Education Nationale* (Syracuse, N.Y.: Syracuse University Press, 1967).

24. See Pierre Bourdieu and Jean-Claude Passeron, *Les Héritiers* (Paris: Editions de Minuit, 1966).

25. See Frank R. Baumgartner and Jack L. Walker, "Educational Policy Making and the Interest Group Structure in France and the United States," *Comparative Politics* 21 (1989): 273–88.

26. See Frank R. Baumgartner, "Parliament's Capacity to Expand Political Controversy in France," *Legislative Studies Quarterly* 12 (1987): 33–54.

27. See Arnold J. Heidenheimer, "The Politics of Public Education, Health and Welfare in the USA and Western Europe: How Growth and Reform Potentials Have Differed," *British Journal of Political Science* 3 (1973): 315–40; Anthony King, "Ideas, Institutions, and the Policies of Governments: A Comparative Analysis," ibid., pp. 291–314, 409–24.

28. For a more detailed description see Baumgartner and Walker, "Educational Policy Making."

29. See Lawrence Scheinman, *Atomic Energy Policy in France under the Fourth Republic* (Princeton, N.J.: Princeton University Press, 1965); Peter De Leon, *Development and Diffusion of the Nuclear Power Reactor: A Comparative Analysis* (Cambridge, Mass.: Ballinger, 1979).

30. James M. Jasper, "French Lessons: Can They Help the U.S. Nuclear Industry?" *Resources* (quarterly journal of Resources for the Future), 1987, p. 15.

31. See Dorothy Nelkin and Michael Pollak, *The Atom Besieged: Extraparliamen-*

tary Dissent in France and Germany (Cambridge, Mass.: MIT Press, 1981); Herbert B. Kitschelt, "Political Opportunity Structures and Political Protest: Anti-Nuclear Movements in Four Democracies," *British Journal of Political Science* 16 (1986): 57–85; Michael T. Hatch, *Politics and Nuclear Power: Energy Policy in Western Europe* (Lexington: University of Kentucky Press, 1986); Philippe Garraud, "Politique electronucléaire et mobilisation: Le Tentative de constitution d'un enjeu." *Revue française de science politique* 29 (1979): 448–74.

32. See Nelkin and Pollak, *Atom Besieged.*

33. See Mans Lonnroth, "Le Rôle de l'énergie nucléaire dans les divers scénarios suédois," in *Energie nucléaire et société,* ed. Michel de Perrot (Paris: Pergamon Press, 1981).

7

Paradigms, Power, and Urban Leadership

Clarence N. Stone

Leadership in the urban community has long been a subject of study. Classic examinations of community power, in particular Robert Dahl's *Who Governs?* and Edward C. Banfield's *Political Influence,* are centrally concerned with leadership by elected executives. More recent studies, such as the *Ungovernable City* by Douglas Yates and *Governing the Ungovernable City* by Barbara Ferman, are similarly focused on mayoral leadership.[1] Even writers who are concerned mainly with the impact of an impersonal market on city policy and politics, notably Paul Peterson in his influential *City Limits,* contrast more-effective and less-effective forms of executive leadership.[2] While there is a common tendency to treat leadership in highly personal terms, the lasting studies, such as those mentioned above, never stop at that. They show a high level of awareness of the context in which leadership is exercised, and they embody some underlying conception of what the leadership task is.

In this chapter, I want to follow in that tradition and to extend it. Specifically, I want to focus attention on the question of leadership's task, conceptions of power that are intertwined with that question, and the contextual dimension of power and leadership. I do not propose to talk in detail about these issues here. Instead, I want to consider how we come to think about these questions. In the following pages, I will argue that our understanding of power and leadership in the local community is shaped by the paradigms we apply to the study of urban politics. From an initial paradigm of modernization, we have moved to an economistic paradigm, and we now stand on the threshold of a regime paradigm. Each of these paradigms shapes how we look at power and what we think the nature of the leadership task is.

By focusing on paradigms, I aim to show not only why it is important to see urban leadership in broader terms than the skills and abilities of individuals who occupy the office of mayor but also why it is important that we be fully aware of the conception of the leadership task that is embodied in our analyses.

None of this is intended to deny that at the community level mayors are our most visible leaders. And I do not mean to characterize the personal qualities of mayors as inconsequential. They are significant. But I think the proper beginning point is the nature of the leadership task. To understand that, we must begin by looking at different conceptions of the community and what its governance entails. As will be evident, my preference is for the regime paradigm. At the same time, I hope to show that there are connecting threads that tie the regime paradigm to its predecessors.

THE MODERNIZATION PARADIGM

As I indicated above, two of the most important books in urban political science are Robert Dahl's study of New Haven, *Who Governs?* and Edward Banfield's study of Chicago, *Political Influence.* Both did much to focus attention on mayoral leadership, and both rightly are considered pillars of pluralism. My labeling of them here as pillars also of the modernization paradigm may strike some readers as odd or even perverse. Why talk about a modernization paradigm when pluralism is already a widely used and much discussed term?

One reason for talking about a modernization paradigm is that it is indeed a new label—one that I hope will enable readers to see some classics in a new light. A second reason for using the term "modernization" is to emphasize that both Dahl and Banfield saw urban politics in a context of social change. Neither saw city politics as static. Dahl, in particular, made extensive use of a historical perspective. For Banfield, too, although the point is made more emphatically in the book he coauthored with James Q. Wilson, city politics is to be understood as an activity shaped by the transition from a traditional ethos of private regardingness to a modern ethos of public regardingness.[3] For example, in Banfield's eyes, Mayor Richard Daley was not merely a skillful broker of particular conflicts; he was also the master broker between Chicago's tradition-minded inner wards and its modern-minded outer wards.[4] Dahl made a related argument. He described New Haven's move away from politics based on ethnic conflict, arguing that assimilation had blurred the class character of the original cleavage between Yankee Protestant and Catholic immigrants. Dahl's counterpart to public regardingness is the set of policies that New Haven's Mayor Richard Lee engineered, policies that emphasized "shared benefits to citizens in general rather than specific categories."[5] As further evidence of the change away from the old ethnic-based politics of patronage, Dahl suggested that the significant new actors so visible under Mayor Lee were professionally qualified program specialists. Dahl concluded that the new power actors "in local politics may very well prove to be bureaucrats and experts—and politicians who know how to use them."[6] These new figures in New Haven politics received follow-up study in books by Raymond Wolfinger and Russell Murphy.[7]

Banfield gave less attention to bureaucrats and experts, but he nevertheless described the Chicago political landscape in "modernized" terms. He did not ignore the machine, of course, but he did not make it the center of his explanation of city policy. Instead he observed that civic controversies, from which policy in Chicago grew, arose "out of the maintenance and enhancement needs of large formal organizations."[8] He, like Dahl, saw these isuses as being resolved in a context of popular control and against a background of consensus on fundamentals.

For reasons that I will explore below, both Banfield and Dahl treated urban politics as a matter of many small, nonclass conflicts. If the two differed much, it is that Dahl placed more emphasis on the autonomy of political leaders and their capacity to activate latent support for an ambitious policy agenda. New Haven's entrepreneurial mayor, Richard Lee, stands in contrast to Chicago's political broker, Mayor Richard Daley. Whereas Dahl talked about the "potential of the cunning, resourceful, and masterful leader,"[9] Banfield offered a classic rendition of pluralist brokerage:

> According to the Chicago view, a policy ought to be framed by the interests affected, not by the political head or his [this was before Jane Byrne's mayoralty] agents. In this view, the affected interests should work out for themselves the "best" solution of the matter (usually a compromise). The political head should see that all principally affected interests are represented, that residual interests (i.e., "the general public") are not entirely disregarded, and that no interest suffers unduly in the outcome.[10]

Of course, it was easier to talk in such terms as the 1950s came to a close—the time in which Banfield and Dahl wrote their classics. At that time the mayors of New Haven and Chicago seemed to represent the spectrum of effective city leadership. The urban scene, after all, appeared basically tranquil, with issues confined largely to narrow-gauge conflicts between the parties immediately affected by particular policies. Yet, it would be highly unfair to Banfield and Dahl to suggest that they were merely reporting what was visible at the time. Their analyses were much too penetrating for that. To be sure, their conceptual "blinders" prevented them from foreseeing the turmoil ahead, but they were still able to probe an underlying character of political arrangements. For this reason, we need to consider further the label "modernization" as an adjective for the paradigm they employed.

Modernization

Modernization can be defined in various ways. Banfield, in particular in his work with James Q. Wilson, talked about urban conflict primarily in terms of a cleavage between a provincial and tradition-minded ethos linked to machine politics and a cosmopolitan and modern-minded ethos linked to good government reform.[11] This cleavage, rather than class or racial conflict, was the focus of Banfield and Wilson's understanding of city politics. Dahl differed mainly in placing more emphasis on consensus than on conflict. Yet, while both Banfield and Dahl were much influenced by the concern with political culture and political socialization so prevalent at the time they were writing, both also had a more profound understanding of what modernization is about.

For both, modernization meant social differentiation and a high level of role specialization. That understanding of modernization informed their understanding of conflict: for them, conflict occurred along lines of highly refined social differentiation, not along the broad break of class associated with early industrialization. Perhaps the key sentence in Dahl's *Who Governs?* is this: "political heterogeneity follows socioeconomic heterogeneity."[12] From the early differentiation between social notables and business elites to Mayor Lee's introduction of program experts and policy professionals into an increasingly middle-class community, Dahl's New Haven story is about how socioeconomic heterogeneity fosters political heterogeneity and forms the foundation for a pluralist distribution of power. In *Political Influence,* Banfield was much less historical; nevertheless, he reached the related conclusion that "Chicago is too big a place, and the interests in it too diverse, for agreement to occur very often."[13]

According to both Dahl and Banfield, social differentiation causes fragmentation, and *the* political task is to cope with that fragmentation. According to Banfield, Daley accomplished this by being the master broker. He brokered a necessary amount of cooperation in a community with "limitless opportunities for obstruction."[14] For Dahl, Mayor Lee was an extraordinary public leader because he created an executive-centered coalition capable of promoting a broad program of action. According to Dahl, this program generated substantial popular support, and it represented a major achievement because it was brought about in a situation in which "the centrifugal forces in the system were . . . persistent and powerful."[15] Lee's political skill was evident in his ability to prevent the elements in his coalition "from flying off in all directions," despite a natural tendency to do so.[16]

Power as a Cost-of-Compliance Problem

Both Banfield and Dahl base their view of power on this view of modernization as a fragmenter of social life. For both of them, power represents a cost-of-compliance problem. They draw on the Weberian formulation that power is the capacity of A to get B to do what B would not otherwise do. Seen in this way, power in a complex system is inevitably distributed in a pluralist pattern. As Dahl has argued, "control is almost always to some extent costly to the ruler."[17] To obtain B's compliance A has to expend resources. Banfield observed: "In a system in which the political head must continually 'pay' to overcome formal decentralization and to acquire the authority he needs, the stock of influence in his possession cannot all be 'spent' as he might wish."[18] Given that compliance never comes free of charge, one can argue that control, particularly in a formally democratic system, can be exercised only over a small domain and a limited range of activities, especially if more than a thin level of compliance is being sought.[19]

The linking of this line of argument to Weber's definition of power is notable. In a premodern world, control might be expanded by sacred myth, but Weber argues that the modern world has been "disenchanted." Furthermore, in such a world, a world of instrumental rationality, specialists acquire autonomy as their expertise removes them from effective control by their superiors.[20] When functional specialists are brought together bureaucratically, Dahl reminds us that formal organizations develop an impulse toward independence.[21] Compliance is costly because, in Chester Barnard's terminology, the zone of indifference for most people most of the time is quite narrow.[22] Achieving compliance requires some kind of reciprocal benefit, in the absence of a pervasive system of coercion, which itself would be costly to maintain. According to Banfield, "the terms upon which control may be acquired (assuming that it may be acquired at all) are established through a process of bargaining."[23] Dahl adds that "the relationship between leaders and citizens in a pluralist democracy is frequently reciprocal."[24]

Banfield's view of the virtual impossibility of achieving broad-scale control and coordination eventually became a foundation of neoconservative skepticism about liberal social reform. From Jeffrey L. Pressman and Aaron Wildavsky's complexity of joint action to Charles Morris's critique of Mayor John Lindsay's "arrogant overreachings," the message is that overambitious executives who are not mindful of the intractable character of social problems invite disappointment and defeat, if not outright disaster.[25] In *The Ungovernable City,* Douglas Yates tamed the rhetoric considerably and the argument a little, but his street-fighting pluralism is in the same vein. Mayors with limited resources should not undertake social crusades.[26]

Dahl's *Who Governs?* is connected to a somewhat different line of thought. It is, I contend, a contributor to an economistic paradigm, as exemplified in Paul Peterson's *City Limits*. Before turning to that discussion, let me summarize what I have said about the modernization paradigm and the view of power and leadership it encourages.

SUMMARY

According to Thomas Kuhn, a paradigm provides a set of assumptions and a way of seeing the world.[27] Because the assumptions themselves play a part in what we see or, perhaps more importantly, what we do not see, observation is never pure observation. It is colored by predisposition. That is the case with the modernization paradigm no less so than with others.

The modernization paradigm holds that the contemporary world is characterized by a high level of social differentiation and that the differentiated actors in this world (whether they be individuals, informal groups, formal organizations, or some larger social entity) enjoy considerable autonomy. The prevailing force is centrifugal: it is a natural tendency for complex arrangements to come apart. Imposing order and coordination on this world is difficult; achieving compliance is costly. No matter how skillful leaders are, they must have substantial resources, and even then, they lead mainly by bargaining and consent. Because control is costly, coalitions tend to be unstable. Typically they form and dissolve, issue by issue. In this pluralist scenario, a comprehensive plan of control is virtually impossible. Because subjects of power exercises are autonomous, they can resist and drive up the cost of obtaining their compliance. No elite group can monopolize sufficient resources and command enough know-how to establish a large and effective domain of control. Leadership consists of the capacity to mediate conflicts, to bargain in order to overcome differences by using mutually beneficial cooperation, and to anticipate what will garner popular approval. It follows, some might argue, that an overly ambitious agenda of public action will result in frustration. Neoconservatives were quick to use that characterization for liberal social reformers such as Mayor John Lindsay in New York. Furthermore, it could be argued that public officials, appointed as well as elected, have a self-serving interest in expanding public activity and that if that propensity is not curbed, society will suffer from political overload.[28]

THE ECONOMISTIC PARADIGM

Whereas the modernization paradigm offers a complex world in which centrifugal movement is prevalent, the economistic paradigm pictures the world as a market. Here also there is no command center and, in some respects, leadership does not much matter. The mobility of investment capital is the dominant feature, and the laws of the market shape the world. The primary exposition of this view is Paul Peterson. It should be noted that his *City Limits* acknowledges a debt not only to public-choice economists but also to structural Marxism.[29]

Structural Marxism, as the name implies, plays down the role of leadership in favor of attention to the laws of economic development. Structuralism is not the only Marxist position now current, but to try to unravel the various strands of Marxism and the process by which a new appreciation of autonomous state action has evolved would take us too far afield.[30] Suffice it for now to say that Marxism holds that cities are among the entities that are compelled to some degree to promote investment and thus to facilitate capital accumulation. This need to attract investment encourages the exploitation of have-nots and, in general, elevates the exchange value of property over its use value.[31] While those who are exploited by this process can counter it to some extent by engaging in a struggle to challenge the social legitimacy of the established order, the most telling imperative is that of capital accumulation.[32]

Peterson's *City Limits* is a purer rendition of the economistic paradigm for urban politics. In Peterson's account, the federal system produces an intergovernmental division of labor in which cities are particularly subject to the forces of economic competition. Cities are impelled to be highly responsive to investment interests and, for this reason, they avoid progressive measures of redistribution. The national government is therefore the body most responsive to social-welfare needs.[33]

Peterson's formulation of the city's position in the larger political economy is particularly significant for its bearing on his treatment of power and leadership. First, insofar as developmental policy and social welfare are concerned, he gives little emphasis to the particular conflicts that are such a pervasive part of the pluralist world depicted in the modernization paradigm. Peterson confines conflict to the arena of allocational policies (service distribution and employment rules). For the remainder, as "shareholders" in the city, citizens have a unitary interest in developmental policy and in avoiding welfare responsibilities as well. From this it follows, in Peterson's words:

> In the development arena, power is not best understood as a "zero-sum" game, where one person or group wins at the expense of another. Instead, power is better understood in systemic terms; it is the capacity of the community as a whole to realize its objectives. What is needed is not so much the capacity to enforce one's will over others as the leadership ability that can persuade others to contribute to a common cause.[34]

As an example of such leadership, Peterson turns to New Haven's Mayor Richard Lee. Because Dahl had described Lee, particularly in promoting redevelopment, as someone who activated latent support, Lee's leadership appears to be that of a facilitator rather than an overrider of opposition. Peterson's view of the social context, unlike the Marxist view, defines away conflict. Playing on Dahl's view of Mayor Lee as someone who activated latent support, Peterson transforms power from a cost-of-compliance problem to an efficiency problem. The transformation requires only that conflict not be present to a significant degree.

How does the community best act to further its shared interest in economic advancement? The external threat of economic competition presumably makes business executives and other relevant actors amenable to mayoral persuasion. Besides, Peterson adds, support for development enables business executives to enhance their reputations as civic leaders: "The politics of development is particularly enticing to otherwise apolitical businessmen, because successful effort on behalf of a project that benefits the community as a whole has a halo effect."[35]

Peterson's formulation by-passes the cost-of-compliance issue by defining the situation as consensual. This transforms the problem from one of overcoming opposition to one of surmounting the free-rider problem—how to get individuals to exert themselves on behalf of a collective good. This is the efficiency problem. Working deductively, Peterson solves the problem by positing an individual interest on the part of business executives in enhancing their reputations as civic leaders and in achieving a halo effect. Significantly, Peterson's argument is silent on the individual and group gains that may accrue from developmental projects. Civic reputations and halo effects fit nicely with a non-zero-sum scenario of power, and similarly, persuasion appears to be appropriate for the leadership role. By contrast, consideration of particular gains and benefits invites questions about who bears the costs and how economic losers in development fit into the picture. Focusing on these issues poses a different kind of leadership challenge, one that the economistic paradigm does not highlight. As Kuhn maintained, paradigms have a propensity to direct attention to some questions and facts and away from others. The economistic paradigm is no exception.

TAKING STOCK

Paradigm-guided research—which all research is according to Kuhn—is a mixture of assumptions and observations. Kuhn also suggests that each paradigm enables us to answer some questions but not others. A paradigm is ascendant as long as it directs attention to interesting questions and holds some promise of yielding answers. But as new questions emerge, perhaps from anomalous findings that become increasingly hard to dismiss, the ground is prepared for a paradigm shift. It should be remembered that a paradigm shift does not mean that findings from a previous paradigm have been invalidated; it only means that a new way of looking at the world is being attempted with the hope of generating new findings that bear on more pressing questions. This is not the occasion to try to trace the intellectual origins of the various paradigms, but it is in order to give some brief indication of how the modernization and economistic paradigms fit into the historical context. The modernization paradigm, with its pluralist scenario, could explain a world in which urban conflict was relatively low-key and in which the most visible cleavage was between city machines and good-government reformers. With the eruption of more intense conflict during the 1960s and the emergence of sharp cleavages along racial lines, the conventional modernization paradigm no longer seemed adequate. The political-overload/street-fighting-pluralism modification had some appeal for a time, but a subsequent lessening of overt conflict and a lowering of political temperatures left that revised version of the modernization paradigm with little to offer as a research agenda.

Marxism could explain conflict and even fluctuations in the intensity of conflict, but it faced several difficulties, not the least of which was its dubious legitimacy in the larger political arena. Marxism's appeal historically was tied to its joining of theory and practice. Structural Marxism does that poorly, all the more so when the political tide is running against radical change and events offer no promise of a crisis capable of supporting system transformation. At least in its vulgar interpretation, structural Marxism provides weak ground for political involvement and plays down the role of leadership.[36] It is not surprising, then, that some Marxist scholars have moved toward an increasingly flexible notion of the autonomy of politics and, I would argue, toward a renewed respect for the work of Max Weber.[37] This line of intellectual development has merged with historical sociology and is one of the sources that feed the emerging paradigm of regime theory.[38]

Paul Peterson's *City Limits* represents a different line of development. As the most influential work in the economistic paradigm, *City Limits* has an affinity with public choice as a school of thought. But that is not its primary appeal. Indeed, as indicated above, *City Limits,* by focusing on the city as a corporate unit and what is rational for that unit, fails to probe very much into the incentives that motivate individuals. It does not answer the question of why, given that behavior generally is to be understood as a matter of expedient self-interest, individuals would act on behalf of some larger good.[39]

Still, *City Limits* has a twofold appeal. It provides a plausible account of federalism from the New Deal up to recent years. Specifically, it suggests why city governments in particular are unreceptive to assuming responsibilities for welfare. It also offers an explanation of the tendency for city officials and business executives to form a close working alliance, including those circumstances in which a mobilized black electorate succeeds in putting a black mayor in city hall. Peterson's achievement is a significant one, strengthened by the fact that he has put together a parsimonious and logically consistent argument.

There are chinks in Peterson's armor, however. It is a deductive argument, and close observation of the facts turns up anomalies. Peterson's argument about cities in the federal system is ahistorical; it fails to account for a pre–New Deal period in which urban machines were more responsive to welfare concerns than the national government was.[40] Moreover, the present era of Republican presidential ascendancy, in which New Deal priorities have been overturned and megadeficits have put a squeeze on social spending, also fits poorly Peterson's view of federalism.

At the city level itself, Peterson's argument characterizes developmental policy as consensual, based on the city's unitary interest in economic advancement. Again, the facts fit imperfectly. Conflict often surrounds development, and much of the dispute involves the issue of which policy is best for the city.[41] Perhaps the most telling anomaly is the fact that urban-development policies have not diminished urban poverty, and cities are characterized by segmented economies in which a large proportion of the population appears to be blocked away from the benefits of economic growth and change.[42] A final specific inadequacy is that Peterson describes urban leadership as being engaged primarily in persuasion. Especially when viewed historically, that appears to be an anemic way of picturing the role of leadership.

This description and assessment of the modernization and economistic paradigms have focused on particular features and specific anomalies. The two paradigms also share a general feature, which I regard as more serious than anomalous findings. Neither points to the question of abuse of power, and that strikes me as a serious inadequacy. To be sure, structural Marxism focuses on class exploitation as the inevitable consequence of capitalism. But that is much too sweeping and too general to serve very well as a basis for evaluating specific urban regimes and their performance. It condemns a system, not the actions of specific agents within that system. To be sure, the Marxist response to this observation is to say, "That is the point." I beg off debating the issue on this occasion by asserting simply that we have choices less grand than acceptance or rejection of capitalism. To talk about urban regimes, as I propose to do, is to consider how local political arrangements are put together and altered. These arrangements can be more representative or less so. Put another way, they can be more faction-dominated or less so. In the Madisonian tradition, we have a responsibility to try to make them less so. The first step is to consider how factionalism and representativeness are at issue. This is the question that regime theory addresses, and the modernization and economistic paradigms do not.

In the case of the modernization paradigm, the conception of power as a matter of command and compliance treats abuse of authority as an unlikely event. Leaders can be unskillful and ineffective, but in the pluralist scenario overreaching the proper bounds of power in the service of factional advancement is seen as untenable over the long run. The dispersion of power assures that. Resistance can always drive up the cost of control and undercut the position of those who abuse their power.

The economistic paradigm treats power in a similar manner. In the developmental arena (redistributive policy is the opposite side of the same coin), Peterson explicitly refuses to treat power as the ability to enforce one's will over others. Instead, power is defined as a system capacity to act—it is "power to" rather than "power over." The challenge facing leaders is how to aggregate efforts for a common purpose. Viewed in this way, leadership can fail. It can, as in the pluralist scenario, be unskillful and ineffective, but there is no strong reason to worry about abuses of authority, because power is not defined as the capability of one element of the community to dominate and exploit another.

To treat power and leadership as a matter of efficiency undercuts the critical role of analysis. To be sure, the economistic perspective can serve to question how effective a city is in the developmental efforts it makes. But economics is an efficiency-driven discipline; it never speaks with confidence about matters of equity. It has little to say about conflict, and it tends to see politics as irrational.[43] Consequently, economics often treats equity as subordinate to efficiency. The favored rhetoric, whether in popular or technical terms, is that which talks about policies that result in virtually no one's being worse off and at least some being better off—hence, Peterson defines power in the developmental arena as non–zero sum.

That the modernization and economistic paradigms fail to direct attention to the possibility of the abuse of power does not mean that these paradigms have taught us nothing. By focusing on power as a cost-of-compliance problem, the modernization paradigm shows us that an elite group is unlikely to control a community by means of coercion and deception. By focusing on the need to aggregate efforts in support of a common purpose, the economistic paradigm indicates that authority can serve a worthy purpose and, indeed, that weak or ineffective authority can be detrimental to a community's well-being. What is needed, then, is a paradigm that (1) shows how power can be concentrated, although not in the form of a centralized command-and-control structure and (2) appreciates the good that authority can do while making us mindful of the ways in which it can be abused. A regime paradigm, coupled with the concept of preemptive power, can, I believe, meet these two needs.[44]

URBAN REGIMES

Regime theory has many antecedents. Martin Shefter's reinterpretation of machine politics; Harvey Molotch's work on "the growth machine"; John Mollenkopf's analysis of coalition building at the national level; the study of political incorporation by Rufus Browning, Dale Rogers Marshall, and David Tabb; a general body of literature on historical sociology with its roots in Marx and Weber; "the two faces of power" argument by Peter Bachrach and Morton Baratz, the discussion of sectarchy by Bryan Jones and Lynn Bachelor; and the work of Stephen D. Krasner and others in international politics—all are among the contributors to this emerging paradigm.[45] Important as these various works are, the two sources I have found most compelling are Floyd Hunter's *Community Power Structure,* as an antecedent of preemptive power, and Stephen L. Elkin's formulation of urban regimes as arising in a political-economy context.[46] Hunter's work I will return to later. Elkin's contribution is at the heart of the concept of regime itself.

According to Elkin, the task facing those who would govern is one of putting together arrangements that cope with the division of labor between state and economy. This means satisfying the principle of popular control of public authority while fostering a climate suitable for investment by privately controlled capital. Elkin thus takes into account the economic imperative that is so central in Peterson's analysis, but he does not treat it as a single, overriding determinant. Regime character is formed by an accommodation between the need for private investment and a community's political arrangements. Furthermore, this accommodation is not merely coexistence. Business interests attempt to shape politics, and they possess important political resources in their efforts. In the other part of this accommodation, along with seeking popular support, political actors pursue strategies that affect investment; governmental decisions do much to shape investment opportunities.

While accommodation is essential, the relationship between these two centers of activity is fraught with tension. Under regime theory, political conflict ceases to appear as an irrational distraction from the pursuit of a community's well-being. Instead, because community well-being involves an accommodation between two principles, one largely economic and the other political, struggle can be seen as the natural result of efforts by various groups to shape that accommodation on terms that are favorable to their interests. Conflict is thus part of the struggle to determine how the two principles, though in tension with one another, will be reconciled. While the structural boundaries of this struggle are set by the political-economy context, any particular settlement is subject to alteration. A change in either the economic situation or the political landscape can result in new or modified arrangements. The regime paradigm is therefore particularly well suited to consider questions of political change and continuity—change originating either in the economic or in the political sphere and continuity based in the persistence of a structural relationship.

Implicit in this view of the urban community is an understanding of leadership as an activity that involves the creation, maintenance, and modification of a governing regime—the prevailing arrangements through which economic and political imperatives are accommodated. As in the previous two paradigms, the leadership task is intertwined with a conception of power, and I now turn to that discussion.

PREEMPTIVE POWER

Elsewhere I have spelled out the connection between the concept of preemptive power and Floyd Hunter's *Community Power Structure;* I won't repeat that discussion here.[47] I will, however, remind the reader that the basic argument of Hunter's original study is quite compatible with the current emphasis on political economy. In looking at Atlanta, Hunter observed a formal division of authority between the public arena of government and the private arena of business ownership and investment. This formal division, Hunter argued, was bridged by an informal structure, for which he coined the phrase "community power structure." In an argument parallel to Robert K. Merton's analysis of the latent functions of the machine, Hunter argued that this informal structure persisted because it met a community need for leadership, for some group capable of responding to social change and of easing various forms of friction in the community.[48] Leadership consists of devising adaptive responses and mobilizing community resources so as to put those responses into effect. Note that Hunter does not argue that this group runs the community in command-and-control fashion. He is arguing only that some group keeps an eye on the need to modify community practices and puts together efforts to adopt what it regards as essential new policies.[49] This is the leadership function, which Hunter found in Atlanta to be filled by an informal structure that he regarded as highly unrepresentative.

The conception of power surrounding this leadership role is what I call preemptive power, and it involves two aspects. One is the power advantage that comes from occupying that role and being able to take the initiative and to frame proposed actions as *community* responses—to say, in effect, if the community acts, then its action will take *this* form. Alternative proposals can be and are made, but they are often piecemeal, or they may be attempts to veto proposed actions. Rarely are they part of a broad effort to exercise governing responsibilities. More importantly, even if they are broadly conceived, proponents may command too few resources to make them viable. That brings us to the second aspect of preemptive power, the capacity to hold together enough resources and positions of institutional strength to foreclose any rival group or coalition from exercising the power of governance. This is the least understood and least explored aspect of preemptive power. Yet it is precisely this capacity to bring together *and hold together* a coalition capable of exercising governing responsibilities that is at the heart of the concept of preemptive power. Interestingly enough, Hunter views this situation as contingent. His argument is not that an elite group inevitably dominates. Instead, he maintains that the insider coalition controls the leadership function not only because it is well endowed with resources but also because it works at making the most politically (in a broad sense) of these resources. Those on the outside are too fragmented, uninformed, and apathetic to counter the insider monopoly of the capacity to govern.

There are three sets of institutions that are key to the capacity to govern. Government itself is only one. Corporate business is a second, and Hunter regards it as inevitable that business interests will be part of any effective governing coalition. The third arena is the network of civic organizations which conducts much of the public debate on policy issues and harnesses and directs much of the volunteer activity in the community. *Community Power Structure* describes how business control extended to that arena in the Atlanta of the period immediately after World War II. It is in that arena, Hunter believed, that business presence could be, but was not, countered by a broader set of community interests.

In harmony with Bachrach and Baratz, one can argue within the regime paradigm that leadership has two faces. One is a policy face, leadership engaged in deciding particular policy questions. The other is a regime face, leadership engaged in creating, maintaining, and modifying the de facto governing arrangements of the community.

Regime leadership is important because formal public authority is weak. The operating assumption of the regime paradigm is that the authority of a community's official government is too weak to govern autonomously. As we have come to appreciate, a winning electoral coalition is not the same as a coalition capable of governing.[50] Consequently, a governing coalition can be created only by putting together an informal structure that joins public and private resources and institutions.

The question that this conclusion raises, then, is one of how the membership in the governing coalition is determined. That is what preemptive power is about, and a political-economy perspective on this question becomes important in providing an explanation for why significant business involvement is essential. Business control of credit and investment activity is simply too important to be by-passed.

The matter doesn't end there, however, because the question of popular control and the involvement of civic and community organizations of various kinds has much to do with exactly how the governing regime is shaped and how it conducts itself. Political and economic actors need to achieve cooperation. On the one side, business investment is intertwined with a variety of publicly provided services and facilities. On the other side, economic growth is a popular campaign theme. However, cooperation is not automatic. What everyone agrees on in the abstract quickly becomes a source of friction when it is made concrete. Group conflict and personal aspirations stand as formidable obstacles to any collective effort. Under these conditions, it is no easy task to see that policy goals are articulated and resources mobilized behind them. For a community to be governed, group conflict must be managed and personal ambition harnessed. Although governance does not entail comprehensive control, it does require that cooperation and exchange occur and that critical decisions be made.[51] That is what urban regimes are about, and it is through civic organizations and informal networks that much of the essential cooperation, exchange, and consequent mobilization of resources occurs.

The capacity to exercise leadership—whether preemptively or not—thus depends heavily on a community's associational life. The creation and shaping of networks of cooperation and exchange are important aspects of regime leadership, and such activities are not necessarily tied to the mayor's office.

Within the regime paradigm, leadership is a complex activity, occurring at various stages. The regime paradigm assumes that a stable structure of cooperation and exchange is widely useful to urban communities. That being the case, any coalition capable of providing that structure is powerful because of that fact. Community dependence on such a structure undergirds that power.[52] However, the members of the governing coalition are preemptively powerful only to the extent that they are able to monopolize enough resources and positions of institutional strength to prevent themselves from being displaced by a rival structure of cooperation and exchange. The difficulty of changing such a structure is what gives the incumbent coalition its distinctive power. If that structure can be changed easily, it holds no preemptive advantage.

It is important, then, to see that a preemptive advantage is contingent. This advantage can be modified. Moved one way, the situation heightens factional domination of the structure of cooperation and exchange. Moved another way, that role becomes more representative. Thus the regime paradigm puts business's role in community governance in a light quite different from the one shed by the economistic paradigm. Whereas Peterson sees the alliance between business leaders and city officials as an effort to promote the city's economic interest efficiently, the regime paradigm sees the potential for factional exploitation in such an arrangement, unless it is expanded to include a broad representation of community interests.

The question of representation assumes special importance in the regime paradigm because it is assumed that the policy face of leadership is governed by the regime face. Policy is shaped by the composition of the governing coalition *and* by the terms on which its members are related to one another. Put another way, because membership in the governing coalition is so coveted, members have a strong incentive to maintain the coalition, and its maintenance needs thus help to shape policy.

The reader should bear in mind that the preemptive-power argument does not hold that the governing coalition is free to control the tides of social change and to impose any policy solution of its own choosing. The claim is the much more modest one that the governing coalition shapes policy responses to social change. Its control is only that of adaptive *responses;* it does not control the *sources* of social and economic change.

The preemptive-power argument further holds that adaptive responses are always partial and incomplete. Policy is made by an unending succession of attempts to cope satisfactorily with an ongoing process of change. The process is very much one of trial and error, with the governing coalition determining not only which trials will be made, but also deciding what constitutes an error. If the governing coalition is inadequately representative, then its capacity to detect error is also inadequate. As Pressman and Wildavsky observed in their study of implementation: "Learning fails because events are caused and consequences are felt by different organizations."[53] If the governing coalition is a mediating agent between such external forces as economic competition among localities or various forms of social change, on the one side, and, on the other side, the impact of these changes on the mass public, then representation becomes enormously important. This is the reason regime composition and preemptive advantage are worth studying. The argument I am making, it should be noted, assumes that the response to external pressures, such as economic competition and various social changes, are political; they do not possess a technically defined character. The regime argument assumes there is no one best way, dictated by known facts. Priorities are too much at issue and policy solutions are too uncertain for technical solutions to hold sway.

The regime paradigm thus has us look at leadership in a way different from both the economistic and the modernization paradigms. Efficiency or effectiveness in countering centrifugal forces is not enough. It is by no means rendered irrelevant—a governing coalition still faces the challenge of being effective. But regime leadership is also subject to the critical test of how representative are the arrangements that it creates and maintains.

Regime leadership is also much broader than mayoral leadership. When elected executives assume office, they confront an established set of civic relationships—formal and informal organizations within the business community and within the broader community as well. Business and other community-based leaders constitute part of the force that shapes these civic relationships, and these relationships, I have suggested, are a major element in the picture of preemptive power.

Faced with a limited base of resources and a need for showing quick results, a newly elected mayor is to a great extent bound by existing civic relationships. Unusual skill and timely circumstances may afford a mayor some opportunity to reshape those relationships. Richard Daley, Fiorello LaGuardia, Richard Lee, and John Lindsay are among the mayors who appear to have been able to achieve some reshaping. But the preemptive-power argument tells us not to restrict our attention to the holders of governmental office. Other community actors are also important. Race relations in Atlanta, for example, have been powerfully shaped by business leadership.[54] In Flint, Michigan, the Charles S. Mott Foundation plays a central part in community affairs.[55] In Minnesota's Twin Cities, foundations and such business-backed organizations as the Citizens League play a major role in setting the civic agenda.[56] The examples could be multiplied.

THE REGIME PARADIGM AND REGIME LEADERSHIP

Regime leadership never operates with a completely free hand. Societal trends, the particular traditions of a community, and established institutions, as well as national policies and political alignments, provide a context within which urban regimes are formed, re-formed, and modified. Richard Daley did not create his centralized political structure out of whole cloth. Fiorello LaGuardia reshaped New York City's politics by capitalizing on the New Deal.

Each individual case is somewhat unique, reflecting the differing skills and visions of various urban leaders as well as the particulars of time and place. Yet, the building and reshaping of urban regimes are also constrained by society-wide forces. Thus, while regime character cannot be predicted from a set formula, it is possible to focus on some matters of general importance. These fall into two categories, one involving societal trends over time and the other cross-city comparisons.

As indicated earlier, those who employ the modernization paradigm see an overriding trend toward social differentiation and a consequent fragmentation of power. However, the concept of preemptive power calls into question the connection between social differentiation and dispersed power. Complexity does more than run up the costs of compliance and coordination. It also gives rise to new forms of exchange and organization; it leads to change in how people act together for shared ends.[57] With the rise and maturation of industrial society, personal and small-scale social action based on communal groups gives way to more impersonal and large-scale social action based on formal organizations. This increase in scale almost certainly contributes to a shift in political form, from legislative centered and ward based to executive centered and functionally oriented.[58]

In making a case for sectarchy rather than pluralism, Jones and Bachelor challenge Dahl's view that industrial society disperses resources. They see a trend in which advanced industrialism confers an advantage on large size and in which politics often consists of bargaining between powerful peak organizations in the various sectors of community life.[59] In a society of large-scale actors, the ability to act in a forceful and sustained manner is beyond the capacity of most small community-based groups. Hence the policy agenda is controlled by those who work through peak associations and other big entities.

Although the modernization paradigm colored Dahl and Banfield's interpretation of what they observed, both authors were aware of the change in the scale of urban political life. Banfield acknowledged this directly in arguing that civic controversies in Chicago grow out of the maintenance and enhancement needs of large-scale formal organizations. The picture is a complicated one, however. Relatively homogeneous suburbs and small cities are still able to represent the interests of modest property holders and neighborhood-oriented citizens, but such groups can easily find themselves left out of the decision processes of the large metropolis.[60]

By examining the secular trend of industrial society toward big entities and concentrations of resources, we can see how urban regimes can be constituted so as to leave a significant set of community interests unrepresented. In order to get a fuller picture, it is important, however, to consider cross-city differences as well as trends over time. The economistic paradigm focuses attention on differences in the economic position of cities. Cities with declining economies are impelled to court business assiduously; those with a strong investment position can pursue more varied development strategies. It follows also that cities that are heavily dependent on a single firm or industry are more constrained than are those that have diversified economies.[61]

The regime paradigm shifts the cross-city focus considerably by directing attention to community civic life. In this paradigm, investment strategies in the economic sector and electoral strategies in the political sector are not isolated activities. In some sense, they must be reconciled with one another. In an era of ward-based party politics, the urban machines provided the mediating mechanism. With the erosion and replacement of those old forms, the "nonpartisan" civic life of the community has become the arena in which issues are debated, cooperation is elicited, and forms of exchange are articulated.[62] It is in the shaping of a community's civic institutions that regime leadership is exercised. If only a city's commercial elite are active in this endeavor, then business priorities and concerns are likely to dominate the civic as well the economic sector. As large-scale enterprises, businesses individually and in their peak associations have the money, the professional staff, and the organizational capacity to play a dominant civic role. Of course, in a given community, it matters whether the commercial elite operates within a tradition of civic involvement and public unity or whether business enterprises with particular stakes in governmental policy go their individual ways.[63] But perhaps even more important is the question of whether nonbusiness interests are sufficiently organized and command enough resources to be a durable countervailing force in a community's civic life. Labor unions, churches, and ethnic associations are among the possible sources of a more diverse civic life; but it is not their mere presence that matters. The question is whether or not they are constituted in such a way as to take an active and independent part in civic affairs.[64] There is the further question of the presence and involvement of the educated middle class on a basis other than employment in large economic enterprises. The knowledge and professional skills of such a population can enhance the place of nonbusiness groups in a community's civic life.[65] Of course, the character of a regime is not just a matter of the composition of the groups that make up the governing coalition. Regimes also differ in the norms that guide their governing elites.[66] These elites may be disposed to be a closed group, or they may be disposed to operate more openly and inclusively.

In shaping urban regimes, leaders are constrained by the givens of the situation. But leadership is also capable of reshaping, within limits, these givens. The task of urban leadership is therefore not merely to build regimes that can govern effectively; they also have a responsibility to shape regimes that will govern equitably. This means giving attention to the community's associational life. Particularly as older neighborhood-based channels of representation are abandoned, efforts are needed to develop institutions through which diverse concerns and experiences can gain expression. Without these efforts, large business enterprises are likely to dominate a community's public life. Businesses not only control investment activity; they also are organizationally capable of establishing and running a system of civic cooperation and exchange that is narrowly attentive to business interests.

CONCLUSION

At this point it should be clear that paradigms influence how we view leadership as well as what questions we ask. Thus it is important to be aware of paradigmatic assumptions. They color our interpretation of what we observe, and they make some issues prominent while leaving others in the background.

The modernization paradigm highlights social differentiation and the centrifugal effect it has. Operating from a cost-of-compliance conception of power, this paradigm emphasizes the fragmenting effect that social differentiation has on the power of command. Leadership, it suggests, is a matter of overcoming a centrifugal tendency through skillful bargaining and persuasion, aimed at potential areas of agreement that cut across various lines of social differentiation.

Peterson's version of the economistic paradigm provides a logical extension of this classic pluralist view of leadership. Peterson simply argues that the competitive economic situation in which local governments are located gives various community interests a common stake in securing the economic well-being of their city as a territorial entity. This unitary interest in the city's economic standing, according to Peterson, transcends the pluralistic interests that social differentiation otherwise generates. In the treatment of the leadership task, the difference between the modernization and the economistic paradigms is mainly a matter of emphasis. Looking at the large and complex city of Chicago, Banfield accentuated Mayor Daley's brokerage role as a mediator among the community's competing interests. In looking at the developmental arena, Peterson gave cardinal attention to executive leadership in mobilizing community efforts. He cited New Haven's Mayor Lee as a prime example.

Neither the modernization paradigm nor Peterson's version of the economistic paradigm invites attention to the possibility of exploitation by a dominant group. In the modernization paradigm, dissatisfied groups can simply resist and drive up the cost of control, so that domination becomes impossible.[67] In Peterson's model, the external threat of economic competition promotes to the top priority a shared concern with the corporate body's financial well-being. Because this concern is shared by everyone, there is no room for exploitation.

Concern with exploitation is evident in structural Marxism, but it is largely an abstract, system-level concern—essentially beyond the actions and inactions of community-level leaders, except perhaps at the point of *system* crisis. Concern with exploitation is, however, incorporated into the regime paradigm. In this paradigm, because the governing coalition and the arrangements it rests on help to shape policy, it matters who makes up the governing coalition and how the members are related to one another and to the larger community. Leadership is not solely a matter of policy making; it is also a matter of building, maintaining, and modifying a governing regime. This is the leadership task shared by both elected officials and other community actors.

The notion of preemptive power that is embodied in the regime paradigm exposes the possibility of exploitation in the form of factional domination. However, it is important to understand just what form this possibility may take. The concept of preemptive power does *not* remove power as a cost-of-compliance problem from the scene. It does *not* deny that the capacity to command is highly fragmented. It does direct our attention to a different level of power or, in the words of Bachrach and Baratz, a different face of power.

While highlighting the possibility of factional domination, the preemptive-power argument does not treat such domination as inevitable. Indeed, it treats it as contingent. That is why leadership is so important in the regime paradigm. Preemptive power is a concept that draws both on the usefulness of power in serving community needs (in that sense, it has kinship with Peterson's view of power) and on the potential for abusing power. The assumption is that it is useful for the members of a community to be guided by some set of arrangements through which adaptive responses can be made to social change and through which potential conflict will be contained.[68] That such a structure is useful is, however, no guarantee that it will exist or that it will be used fairly.

The practical political question raised by the concept of preemptive power is one of how such power can be perpetuated if, in the eyes of various segments of the community, it is being wielded unfairly. The answer is complex, and it has been detailed elsewhere.[69] Suffice it to say here that the usefulness of governing arrangements means that segmented acts of resistance are easily overridden. To be effective, opposition has to be organized and coordinated. If it is to replace an established coalition, it has to be able to bring together and hold together a coalition of its own capable of assuming the responsibilities of governance. In short, it has to create an alternative regime that will be able to maintain itself over time. Passive resistance alone will not do. To effect significant change, the alternative regime has to be at least capable of withholding something vital from the existing coalition as a condition of being incorporated into a modified set of governing arrangements.

Most discussions of authority get entangled in a consideration of legitimacy and the assumption that authority entails a morally binding quality. I view authority in a somewhat different light. My argument is that the formal authority of local government is inadequate for effective governance. For that reason, an informal set of arrangements may fill that vacuum. To those who know little about these arrangements, their status may be cloudy. To those who do know about such an informal structure, it will be regarded as legitimate to the extent that it is perceived to be the best *available* arrangement for filling the community's needs.[70] If this structure entails cooperation with Daley's machine in Chicago, then the attitude may be one of "so be it." If it means an alliance with white business elites in Atlanta in order to hold racial demagogues in check, then again the attitude may be one of "so be it." This means, not that the authority of such an informal structure has a sacred quality, but that it appears to be the most practical way of meeting an important need for a workable form of governance. Much as inmates generally go along with a system of control in a prison because they prefer an orderly and predictable form of constraint to random violence and harassment, so elements of a community may cooperate with or acquiesce to an informal structure because they regard it as preferable to no structure at all.

Authority in the preemptive-power argument thus does not necessarily entail moral obligations. Such obligations may or may not be present. I frame the issue this way in order to make the point that a given structure is not necessarily weakened by pointing out its moral shortcomings. So long as it is regarded as the best available structure, those who are subject to its form of authority are likely to acquiesce. The structure can be challenged only by convincing enough people with enough institutional positions of strength that an alternative structure can be created and made to work, or by convincing substantial segments of the community that no authority is better than the existing structure. This puts an enormous burden on those who would oppose, a far greater burden than can be imagined from thinking about power in terms of the cost of compliance. Indeed, the urban-regimes paradigm reverses the impact of the cost factor on power relations. It emphasizes the cost of opposing and replacing a system of governance. This does not mean that the cost of achieving compliance is inconsequential for an established regime. It does mean, however, that an established regime is not easily replaced, and a challenge to it may be expensive.

At the same time, the preemptive-power argument does not treat any given system of authority as inevitable. Authority is contingent. Any system of governance can be weakened by showing that an alternative set of arrangements is possible, but change can be made only by showing that the alternative is better in some sense, whether moral or self-interested, *and* by showing that the alternative is workable. Preemption thus involves more than occupying a position of governing authority; it also entails securing a governing role in such a way that one cannot be easily displaced—driving up the cost to any challenge group. Preemptive power can be exercised only by those who control enough resources of the kind that are especially useful in governance and that cannot be readily duplicated. Leadership is the activity of bringing resources together in such a way that a set of governing arrangements is created and maintained. Responsible leadership entails the creation and maintenance of such arrangements in a way that does not serve the factional interest of some segment of the community at the expense of others. That is a particularly difficult task because there is always tension between representativeness and the capacity to govern. The first step, however, is to gain a clear understanding of what the task is and of the tensions it must deal with. That understanding, I believe, can be furthered by research conducted within an urban-regimes paradigm.

NOTES

1. Robert Dahl, *Who Governs?* (New Haven, Conn.: Yale University Press, 1961); Edward C. Banfield, *Political Influence* (New York: Free Press, 1961); Douglas Yates, *Ungovernable City* (Cambridge, Mass.: MIT Press, 1977); Barbara Ferman, *Governing the Ungovernable City* (Philadelphia: Temple University Press, 1985).
2. Paul Peterson, *City Limits* (Chicago: University of Chicago Press, 1981).
3. Edward C. Banfield and James Q. Wilson, *City Politics* (Cambridge, Mass.: Harvard University Press, 1963).
4. Banfield, *Political Influence,* pp. 246–47.
5. Dahl, *Who Governs?* p. 61.
6. Ibid., p. 62.
7. Raymond Wolfinger, *The Politics of Progress* (Englewood Cliffs, N.J.: Prentice-Hall, 1974); Russell Murphy, *Political Entrepreneurs and Urban Poverty* (Lexington, Mass.: D.C. Heath, Lexington Books, 1971).
8. Banfield, *Political Influence,* p. 263.
9. Dahl, *Who Governs?* p. 6.
10. Banfield, *Political Influence,* pp. 270–71.
11. This is the organizing theme for *City Politics;* see also Banfield's *The Moral Basis of a Backward Society* (New York: Free Press, 1958) and Everett C. Ladd, Jr., *Ideology in America* (Ithaca, N.Y.: Cornell University Press, 1969).
12. Dahl, *Who Governs?* p. 59.
13. Banfield, *Political Influence,* p. 252.
14. Ibid., p. 258.
15. Dahl, *Who Governs?* p. 204.
16. Ibid.
17. Robert Dahl, *Dilemmas of Pluralist Democracy* (New Haven, Conn.: Yale University Press, 1982), p. 33.
18. Banfield, *Political Influence,* p. 241.
19. Dahl, *Dilemmas of Pluralist Democracy,* pp. 32–36; see also Dennis Wrong, *Power* (New York: Harper Colophon Books, 1980), pp. 14–20.
20. See H. H. Gerth and C. Wright Mills, *From Max Weber* (New York: Oxford University Press, 1958), pp. 232–35. On the problem of achieving compliance in an organizational setting see also Michel Crozier, *The Bureaucratic Phenomenon* (Chicago: University of Chicago Press, 1964).
21. Dahl, *Dilemmas of Pluralist Democracy,* p. 33.
22. Chester Barnard, *The Functions of the Executive* (Cambridge, Mass.: Harvard University Press, 1938).
23. Banfield, *Political Influence,* p. 313.

24. Dahl, *Who Governs?* p. 89.

25. Jeffrey L. Pressman and Aaron Wildavsky, *Implementation,* 3d ed. (Berkeley: University of California Press, 1984); Charles Morris, *The Cost of Good Intentions* (New York: W. W. Norton & Co., 1980), p. 205.

26. Yates, *Ungovernable City,* pp. 146–65.

27. Thomas Kuhn, *The Structure of Scientific Revolutions* (Chicago: University of Chicago Press, 1970).

28. See, e.g., B. Bruce-Briggs, *The New Class?* (New York: McGraw-Hill, 1979).

29. Peterson, *City Limits,* p. xii.

30. But see Martin Carnoy, *The State and Political Theory* (Princeton, N.J.: Princeton University Press, 1984).

31. David Harvey, *Social Justice and the City* (Baltimore, Md.: Johns Hopkins University Press, 1973).

32. Norman I. Fainstein and Susan S. Fainstein, *Urban Policy under Capitalism,* vol. 22 of *Urban Affairs Annual Reviews* (Beverly Hills, Calif.: Sage, 1982), pp. 181–85.

33. See also Paul E. Peterson, Barry G. Rabe, and Kenneth K. Wong, *When Federalism Works* (Washington, D.C.: Brookings Institution, 1986).

34. Peterson, *City Limits,* p. 148.

35. Ibid., p. 142.

36. Note the shift away from economic determinism by Manuel Castells, *The City and the Grassroots: A Cross-Cultural Theory of Urban Social Movements* (Berkeley: University of California Press, 1983).

37. On trends in Marxist thought see Carnoy, *State and Political Theory.*

38. Among the important works in this area are Charles Abrams, *Historical Sociology* (Ithaca, N.Y.: Cornell University Press, 1982); Theda Skocpol, ed., *Vision and Method in Historical Sociology* (Cambridge: Cambridge University Press, 1984); and Charles Tilly, *As Sociology Meets History* (Orlando, Fla.: Academic Press, 1981).

39. Contrast the analysis of behavior within business firms presented in Richard M. Cyert and James G. March, *A Behavioral Theory of the Firm* (Englewood Cliffs, N.J.: Prentice-Hall, 1963).

40. Steven P. Erie, *Rainbow's End* (Berkeley: University of California Press, 1988).

41. See Clarence N. Stone and Heywood T. Sanders, eds., *The Politics of Urban Development* (Lawrence: University Press of Kansas, 1987).

42. Interestingly, one of the best discussions of this problem is in a book edited by Paul Peterson; see John D. Kasarda, "Urban Change and Minority Opportunities," in *The New Urban Reality,* ed. Paul E. Peterson (Washington, D.C.: Brookings Institution, 1985), pp. 33–67.

43. See, e.g., Charles L. Schultze, *The Public Uses of the Private Interest* (Washington, D.C.: Brookings Institution, 1977), p. 89.

44. On the concept of preemptive power see Clarence N. Stone, "Preemptive Power: Floyd Hunter's *Community Power Structure* Reconsidered," *American Journal of Political Science* 32 (Feb. 1988): 82–104.

45. Martin Shefter, "The Emergence of the Machine," in *Theoretical Perspectives on Urban Politics,* Willis D. Hawley et al. (Englewood Cliffs, N.J.: Prentice-Hall, 1976), pp. 14–44. (See also *Political Crisis/Fiscal Crisis* [New York: Basic Books, 1985]); Harvey Molotch, "The Growth Machine," *American Journal of Sociology* 82 (Sept. 1976): 309–31; John Mollenkopf, *The Contested City* (Princeton, N.J.: Princeton University Press, 1983); Rufus Browning, Dale Rogers Marshall, and David Tabb, *Protest Is Not Enough* (Berkeley: University of California Press, 1984); Peter Bachrach and Morton Baratz, *Power and Poverty* (New York: Oxford University Press, 1970);

Bryan D. Jones and Lynn W. Bachelor, with Carter Wilson, *The Sustaining Hand: Community Leadership and Corporate Power* (Lawrence: University Press of Kansas, 1986); and Stephen D. Krasner, ed., *International Regimes* (Ithaca, N.Y.: Cornell University Press, 1983).

46. Floyd Hunter, *Community Power Structure* (Chapel Hill: University of North Carolina Press, 1953); Stephen Elkin, "Cities without Power: The Transformation of American Urban Regimes," in *The Ambiguous Connection*, ed. Douglas Ashford (Chicago: Metheun, 1980); and Stephen L. Elkin, "Twentieth Century Urban Regimes," *Journal of Urban Affairs* 7 (Spring 1985): 11–28.

47. See note 44 above.

48. Robert K. Merton, *Social Theory and Social Structure*, rev. ed. (Glencoe, Ill.: Free Press, 1957).

49. Cf. Philip Selznick, *Leadership in Administration: A Sociological Interpretation* (New York: Harper & Row, 1957).

50. See Ferman, *Governing the Ungovernable City;* and more generally, see Stein Rokkan, "Norway: Numerical Democracy and Corporate Pluralism," in *Political Opposition in Western Democracies*, ed. Robert Dahl (New Haven, Conn.: Yale University Press, 1966), pp. 70–115.

51. Cf. Selznick, *Leadership in Administration*.

52. On power and dependence see Peter Blau, *Exchange and Power in Social Life* (New York: John Wiley, 1964); and Richard M. Emerson, "Power-Dependence Relations," *American Sociological Review* 27 (Feb. 1962): 31–40.

53. Pressman and Wildavsky, *Implementation*, p. 135.

54. See Clarence N. Stone, "Partnership New South Style: Central Atlanta Progress," in *Public-Private Partnerships*, ed. Perry Davis, *Proceedings of the Academy of Political Science*, vol. 36, no. 2 (New York: Academy of Political Science, 1986), pp. 100–110.

55. Jones and Bachelor, *Sustaining Hand*, pp. 183–84.

56. John Brandl and Ronnie Brooks, "Public-Private Cooperation in Urban Revitalization: The Minneapolis and St. Paul Experience," in *Public-Private Partnership in American Cities*, ed. R. Scott Fosler and Renee A. Berger (Lexington, Mass.: Lexington Books, 1982), pp. 163–99.

57. Douglass C. North, "Government and the Cost of Exchange in History," *Journal of Economic History* 44 (June 1984): 255–64; and see, e.g., Charles Tilly, Louise Tilly, and Richard Tilly, *The Rebellious Century* (Cambridge, Mass.: Harvard University Press, 1975).

58. Clarence N. Stone, Robert K. Whelan, and William J. Murin, *Urban Policy and Politics in a Bureaucratic Age*, 2d ed. (Englewood Cliffs, N.J.: Prentice-Hall, 1986), pp. 190–95, 214–18.

59. Jones and Bachelor, *Sustaining Hand*, pp. 203–10.

60. Michael N. Danielson and Jameson W. Doig, *New York: The Politics of Urban Regional Development* (Berkeley: University of California Press, 1982), pp. 77–78; Gary Miller, *Cities by Contract: The Politics of Municipal Incorporation* (Cambridge, Mass.: MIT Press, 1981); Stone and Sanders, *Politics of Urban Development;* Jones and Bachelor, *Sustaining Hand;* and Clarence N. Stone, *Economic Growth and Neighborhood Discontent* (Chapel Hill: University of North Carolina Press, 1976).

61. Jones and Bachelor, *Sustaining Hand*, p. 214.

62. Cf. North, "Government and the Cost of Exchange in History."

63. Stephen L. Elkin, *City and Regime in the American Republic* (Chicago: University of Chicago Press, 1987), pp. 61–82.

64. Jewel Bellush and Bernard Bellush, *Union Power and New York* (New York:

Praeger, 1984); Jones and Bachelor, *Sustaining Hand*, esp. pp. 214–15; and Shefter, *Political Crisis/Fiscal Crisis*.

65. See the various case studies in Pierre Clavel, *Progressive City: Planning and Participation, 1969–1984* (New Brunswick, N.J.: Rutgers University Press, 1986).

66. Cf. Krasner, *International Regimes*.

67. See the discussion of ''slack resources'' by Dahl, *Who Governs?* pp. 308–10.

68. Cf. Hunter, *Community Power Structure*, pp. 6, 9; see also Yves Simon, *A General Theory of Authority* (Notre Dame, Ind.: Notre Dame Press, 1962, 1980).

69. Stone, ''Preemptive Power.''

70. Cf. Kim Lane Scheppele and Karol E. Soltan, ''The Authority of Alternatives,'' in *Authority Revisisted*, Nomos 29, ed. J. Roland Pennock and John W. Chapman (New York: New York University Press, 1987), pp. 169–200.

8

The Iron Law of Oligarchy Revisited

Robert Harmel

Who says party leadership says iron law of oligarchy!

While that may be an exaggeration, it is a fact that during the past seventy-five years or so there have been many studies of party leadership, and few have failed to at least mention Robert Michels and his "iron law" ("Who says organization says oligarchy"). Whether due to Michels's writing or not, concern about the development of oligarchy within parties clearly continues today, both among scholars and among practitioners of parties. This is the case even though much change has occurred in the composition and roles of parties in many Western countries. Party reformers (e.g., in the U.S. Democratic party) and party founders (e.g., especially in the Greens party of Germany, as will be documented here in detail) have taken great pains to develop structures intended to assure internal party democracy and to offset the oligarchical tendencies that Michels thought inevitable.

The diamond anniversary of Michels's classic book seems an appropriate time to review the arguments and the evidence that have accumulated with respect to his theory and to begin to assess the extent to which elements of the "iron law" may still apply in today's postindustrial environment.[1] In this chapter we will (1) briefly review Michels's theory and many reactions to it, including some with empirical evidence; (2) add some empirical evidence of our own, based on analysis of cross-national data from the 1960s; and (3) document and analyze the attempts of the German Greens party to repeal the iron law in the age of postindustrialism.

MICHELS'S THEORY AND REACTIONS TO IT

MICHELS'S THEORY

Although Michels is best known for the version of the "iron law" that involves having working-class leaders of workers' parties eventually transformed into clones of their bourgeois counterparts, putting personal and organizational interests above ideology, his theory of party leadership is actually more elaborate than that.

Michels felt that the most important factor in the rise of oligarchical leadership (by which he meant the uncontrolled ability of a small clique to do with the party as it pleased) was the inability of the masses to give direction to their own movement. Because of the apathy and general lack of political skills among the masses, leadership was not only inevitable, but also necessary: "Since the rank and file are incapable of looking after their own interests, it is necessary that they should have experts to attend to their affairs. From this point of view it cannot be always considered a bad thing that the leaders should really lead."[2]

If virtue could be found in *having* leadership, however, there was no virtue to be found in the *distance* that would develop between the leaders and the led. This, too, was inevitable, according to Michels, mostly because of changes that would naturally occur in the expectations and the behavior of the leaders themselves. Leaders of working-class origins would become more educated in the ways of politics and of the middle-class life style. Before long, they would be indistinguishable from the leaders of bourgeois parties. The result of these changes would be a "loss of touch" between the objectives that the leaders would have for their organizations, on the one hand, and the interests of the party's followers and of the movement that preceded the party, on the other hand. In the end, the leaders' goals would be more conservative and maintenance oriented (and relatedly, more electorally oriented) than would the more radical, revolutionary, and ideologically correct preferences of the masses.

Through natural organizational processes, the leadership group would become professionalized, closed, and, because of its perceived indispensability, relatively "permanent." A small, cohesive, professionalized, and generally unrepresentative "clique" would ultimately rule the party, uncontrolled by its membership.

The lack of representation of the masses at the top would prove critically important precisely because of the growing importance, professionalism, and independence of the leaders. In short, in any *potential* dispute between leaders and led, leaders would win. In reality, however, the condition of the masses would make such disputes very infrequent if not impossible. The presence of the oligarchy was itself important, on the other hand, because of the distance that had developed between the positions of masses and leaders. If the leaders just naturally represented the orientations of the followers, the lack of need for consultation would be less important.

Although Michels's theory was undeniably rooted in his own experiences in Germany's Social Democratic party (SPD), he was not reluctant to claim that his theory had much broader applicability. After all, he argued, if oligarchy would arise in such a prodemocracy party as the SPD, it would be all the more likely to be present elsewhere, in parties that harbored no visible aspirations toward internal democracy: the "appearance of oligarchical phenomena in the very bosom of the revolutionary parties is a conclusive proof of the existence of immanent oligarchical tendencies in every kind of human organization which strives for the attainment of definite ends."[3]

Oligarchy would develop naturally because of the very nature of extensive organization, which itself was inevitable.[4] The masses needed and welcomed leaders. The leaders would naturally become socially and politically separated from their followers, with the eventual result being a small clique at the top, jealously guarding its own personal, organizational interests and without regard for the interests of the followers or for the goals of the movement from which the party had developed in the first place. All of this would happen with such regularity that it could reasonably be thought of as an "iron law" of oligarchy.

Reactions to Michels's Theory

Since Michels's writing, many of his propositions have found support in the empirical literature on political parties. Many examples of the general tendency toward oligarchy have been documented.[5] More specifically, evidence has been found to support Michels's contentions that as party organization develops, the party's leadership becomes professionalized,[6] the parliamentary wing of the party becomes dominant,[7] the movement's original objectives are subordinated to managerial and electoral concerns,[8] leadership becomes entrenched and conservative,[9] power is concentrated in a small group,[10] social "distance" develops between leaders and led,[11] and the mass members tend not to participate often or meaningfully.[12] Most of this evidence, however, comes in the forms of case analyses and general observations; relatively little of the supporting evidence has been derived from systematic cross-national research on political parties.

In spite of the supporting evidence and more general comments concerning the lasting importance and wide acceptance of Michels's argument, the "iron law" theory has also been the subject of criticism on a number of fronts, including definitional, logical, theoretical, and empirical.[13]

Some criticisms of Michels's work are definitional. Hans Daalder, for instance, has suggested that Michels's definition of oligarchy is too broad.[14] Inequality of influence, Daalder argues, is erroneously equated with oligarchy. Instead, "oligarchy consists not in the taking of many decisions by few men, but in the taking by few men of any decisions they care to take."[15] Leaders, militants, and voters may have different levels of influence, but that need not mean that a few leaders, totally uncontrolled, can make any decisions they wish to make. For instance, it is sometimes the case that factions in the leadership group will effectively control one another.

Relatedly, it has been argued from the elitist perspective that Michels took too narrow a view of democracy. "Democracy in the sense of a system of decision making in which all members or citizens play an active role in the continuous process is inherently impossible," Seymour M. Lipset has said in summarizing this view.[16] A broader and equally justifiable definition of democracy, such as "conflict of organized groups and of access by the ruled to their rulers," would put the internal politics of some parties in a much more favorable light.[17]

Other criticisms of Michels's theory have alleged that it is based on a number of false arguments. Daalder, for instance, has suggested that the "determinist fallacy" is in operation when Michels sees "too direct a link between social origins of politicians and class bias, in their politics," when, in fact, "social origin may but need not determine political sympathies."[18] This criticism seems somewhat misdirected (at least as applied to Michels specifically), because Michels himself argued strongly that the leaders of working-class parties tend to have working-class (not middle-class) origins,[19] and in fact lose sight of those social origins as they assume leadership; but a similar argument made by Samuel J. Eldersveld seems to be more on the mark:

> The basic assumption is that political elites in modern societies are always exploitative of the masses, that political leaders only follow their self interest. This has certainly not always been true. Many party leaders have been advocates of changes in society in order to improve the social and economic conditions of the masses.[20]

In other words, leaders of mass parties, regardless of social origins, do not always pursue "conservative" middle-class goals, as Michels assumed would happen when all leaders became bourgeois in life style.

Along similar lines, Lipset has noted that some believe that Michels was overdeterministic in assuming that leadership independence on some issues necessarily means lack of representation on all issues, when, in fact, the "consent of the governed" is necessary in voluntary organizations and leadership's fulfillment of membership interests on salient issues may result in consent to act independently in other areas.[21] And Eldersveld has charged that Michels was wrong in assuming that conservatism in leadership style always means nonrepresentation of the mass's wishes, when actually "conservative leadership is often a *response* to rank-and-file conservatism."[22]

Daalder has further suggested that the "iron law" is a victim of the "delusion of indispensability, which wrongly deduces an exclusive power position for those who fulfill functions that are socially indispensable."[23] Indeed, Michels claimed that "the leader's principle source of power is found in his indispensability."[24] The problem with this assumption, Daalder has suggested, is that the indispensable group may not be "sufficiently cohesive to exploit the full power resources of their seemingly strategic social position'' and/or that there may be ''countervailing powers there . . . to stop them from even considering this.''[25]

Some have suggested that Michels's theory is defective because it does not adequately account for variable features in the environment and in the parties themselves that may have an important influence on the form of party leadership. Eldersveld has suggested that Michels's theory is flawed because its author saw ''the party organization in a social vacuum,'' rather than in a situation of competing with other parties for votes: ''Parties are transformed in their leadership because they have to be responsive to social forces if they are to stay in power and win elections.''[26] And R. T. McKenzie has suggested that even when the masses do not have control of their own parties, this may be due to environmental reasons rather than the ''iron law'': ''In the British context there is another reason of greater importance: the conventions of the parliamentary system . . . require that Members of Parliament, and therefore parliamentary parties also, must hold themselves responsible solely to the electorate and not to the mass organization of their supporters outside Parliament.''[27]

Other authorities have argued that Michels did not go far enough in accounting for the influence of important ''internal'' factors, including especially the role of meaningful competition *among* the leaders of a given party. Lipset has noted: ''Michels was forced to deny that conflicts among factions, left and right wings, within the socialist movement or other parties, represented anything but struggles for the spoils of office, and, in fact, he hardly alludes to such controversies.''[28] So for Michels, intraelite squabbles and organized factionalism are largely irrelevant to the formation and practice of oligarchy. Klaus von Beyme has viewed factionalism very differently: ''if factionalism, particularly in its clientelist form, is not democratic, it can contribute to increasing internal democracy. It will certainly prevent the party leaders from monopolising all the communication channels within the party, as Michels once feared they would.''[29] At the least, Michels may have given too little credit to the impact of genuine controversy within the organization, which may keep oligarchical tendencies in check.[30] In summarizing the empirical reality in Europe today, Daalder clearly gives more support to von Beyme's than to Michels's view: ''Most European parties would seem to be comparatively open agencies that allow for a great deal of intra-elite conflict as well as for the rise of new elite groups in competition to older ones.''[31]

The empirical reality has been shown to deviate from Michels's theory in other ways as well. Although Michels treated all modern organization alike and argued that it would always lead to oligarchy, it has been demonstrated that organization is variable and oligarchy—at least the full-blown variety—is not inevitable. As Kay Lawson has noted: ''Duverger, while acknowledging the continuing truth of Michels's fundamental proposition, pointed out the numerous variations possible, both in organizational forms and in the extent and nature of oligarchy.''[32] (My own statistical analysis, later in this chapter, confirms Duverger's points.) As to the inevitability of oligarchy, numerous examples to the contrary have now been documented. The Dutch PvdA, for instance, has recently been analyzed by Steven B. Wolinetz, who found that, in spite of Michels's prediction of a one-way path to oligarchy for all parties regardless of structural tinkering, a set of reforms to bring about

> internal democracy has reduced the control of the leadership and made relationships inside the party more fluid than before. Although the leadership continues to lead the party, it must do so by facing up to, persuading (and occasionally threatening) the party congress and the council. The process is far more public than in the past. The character of the party leadership has also changed.[33]

In an earlier case study—one of the few full-scale empirical tests of Michels's theory—Eldersveld found that American political parties were, not oligarchies, but ''stratarchies,'' with meaningful circulation of party elites, with significant communication between leaders and led, and *without* the single elite cadre that Michels thought inevitable.[34]

Eldersveld began the report of his test of Michels's theory with these words: ''This theory has never been satisfactorily and systematically substantiated through empirical research.''[35] Although Eldersveld's own study made a classic contribution to the assessment of oligarchy theory by carefully documenting and explaining an exception to the ''iron law,'' the theory has still been insufficiently subjected to cross-national analysis.[36] In the next section of this chapter, I attempt to make a modest contribution to that enterprise, by employing comparative data not only to test many of Michels's assertions but also to further substantiate or refute some of the above arguments and ''findings,'' which are themselves in most cases based only on single-case analyses or ''general observation.''

ADDITIONAL CROSS-NATIONAL ANALYSIS

THE DATA TO BE USED

Data are now available with which to test some of Michels's more important assertions and hypotheses, along with some additional propositions derived from critiques of his theory. Kenneth Janda's International Comparative Political Parties (ICPP) Project produced judgmental data for 158 parties in 53 countries for the period 1950–62 (although most of the data used in the following analyses cover the more limited span of 1957–62). Janda defined a party as ''an organization at least one of whose goals is the placement of its avowed representatives in government offices,'' and he required that a party must have won at least 5 percent of the seats in the national parliament in two consecutive elections in order to be included in his study. The ICPP data cover one hundred variables, including several dimensions of organizational complexity and centralization of power, as well as related variables. Many of the latter are directly applicable to testing statements made by Michels and others concerning tendencies toward oligarchical leadership. Because Michels limited his own theorizing to modern democratic parties, I have included in the following analyses only the 53 competitive parties from the 15 Western democracies in Janda's data set.[37]

For purposes of these analyses, the related but nonredundant concepts of ''centralization'' and ''concentration'' of power are treated as separate dimensions of what Michels meant by oligarchy. By ''power'' I mean the ultimate responsibility for decision making. If the arrangements within the party are hierarchical, with the primary locus of power at the national (or central) level, power is ''centralized.'' ''Concentration'' of power is more closely related to Michels's notion of the small, single-minded clique. When the leadership is more collective, rather than singular, and when it allows representatives of different views to be included, power is *not* concentrated. The ICPP includes several indicators of centralization and one of concentration. The fact that an index of centralization (described below) and the measure of concentration are not empirically related at a magnitude that would suggest redundancy between the two concepts (the actual Pearson's r is .28) supports treating them separately in the following analyses.

Testable Assertions and Hypotheses

Among the characteristics that Michels thought were, or would eventually become, attributes of *all* mass democratic parties are (as put in our terms) complex organization, centralization and concentration of power, and a low level of membership participation.

> Democracy is inconceivable without *organization* [because] organization appears the only means for the creation of a collective will.
>
> A fighting party needs a *hierarchical structure.* It is indisputable that the *oligarchical* and bureaucratic *tendency* of party organization is a matter of technical and practical necessity.
>
> In the life of modern democratic parties we may observe signs of . . . indifference. It is only a small *minority* which *participates* in party decisions, and sometimes that minority is ludicrously small.[38]

For Michels, it would not necessarily be the case that all of these characteristics would be present at the inception of a party, but all would develop eventually. Complex organization, which would necessarily develop over time, would further necessitate the others.

> For technical and administrative reasons, no less than for tactical reasons, a strong organization needs an equally *strong leadership*.
>
> [*Oligarchical tendency*] is the inevitable product of the very principle of organization.
>
> With the advance of organization, *democracy* tends to decline.[39]

Strong organization was inevitable; centralization, concentration, and the decline of meaningful participation by the membership would inevitably flow from organization.

From the above, I infer the following testable assertions and hypotheses:

1. All mass democratic parties should display very high levels of organizational complexity, centralization of power, and concentration of power and low levels of meaningful membership participation.
2. Any variation that does exist in the above features should be explainable by age of party. Indeed, each of the above variables (if they are found to be variable) should be very highly correlated to age of the party.
3. Centralization of power and concentration of power should be related to organizational complexity (although, again, Michels assumed all to be universal, so that the concept of "relational variability" might not have actually been proposed by him in such terms). The level of membership participation should be negatively related to organizational complexity and to the centralization and concentration of power.

RESULTS: THE UNIVERSALITY OF OLIGARCHICAL TENDENCIES

Included in Janda's ICPP data are a number of indicators for organizational complexity, a number for decentralization, and one each for concentration of power and extent of membership participation. Although limitations of space prohibit me from providing frequency distributions for all of them here, analyses reported elsewhere do shed direct light upon the universality—or lack of it—of complex organization and of oligarchy among competitive parties.[40] The relevant findings can be summarized here.

On organizational complexity, Janda's data reveal that while large majorities of the parties have organizations that are highly articulated, intensive, and extensive, there is some variance in these dimensions. There is wide variance in the activity level of local party organs, the maintenance of records, and the pervasiveness of organization.

The ICPP data on centralization (i.e., nationalization) of power reveal that while the large majorities of parties are hierarchically structured, relatively closed in leadership and candidate selection, and nationalized in the formulation of policy, control of communications, and administration of discipline, there are parties that do not share these features of centralized power. In addition, there is wide variance among the parties on how and where (i.e., national, regional, or local levels) party funds are collected and allocated.

Whereas the concept of "centralization" captures the location of power among local, regional, and national party levels, "concentration" of power refers to "the number of individuals who constitute the top hierarchy and who are regarded as key decision makers" at just the national (or "central") level of the party.[41] As related to Michels, the more "concentrated" the leadership is, the more "oligarchical" (in the sense of "cliquish") it will be. While a large majority of Western competitive parties in Janda's sample have concentrated effective decision-making power in the hands of a very small group of leaders, nearly one-fifth of the parties are exceptions to this "rule."

Although centralization and concentration of power are more directly related to Michels's notion of oligarchy, stability of the same leadership personnel over time is another component of Michels's general concern with unaccountable leadership. Although Janda's data set does not include a direct indicator of the exact frequency of turnover among national party leaders (i.e., "heads") over a standard period of time, his variable of "leadership competition" does provide sufficient information with which to refute the universality of Michels's assertion that party leadership becomes entrenched and hardly ever changes, except through "natural" causes. One-fourth of the 53 parties in Janda's Western democracies experienced frequent turnovers through "overt" processes involving many members, just in the period from 1950 through 1962, and an additional 35.8 percent had experienced at least one overt change in leadership (although perhaps with fewer participants) during the same period. Janda's data alone, however, do not lend themselves to testing Michels's related assertion that turnovers that do occur involve something less than meaningful change.

Finally, Janda's data on the extent of membership participation, which Michels believed would be nonexistent or meaningless in all parties once oligarchy had been established, reveal that membership participation is indeed almost nonexistent in nearly two-fifths of the parties and quite low in another third. Large numbers of members are quite active in about one-tenth of the parties.

While the ICPP data certainly do not refute the general tendencies suggested by many of Michels's assertions concerning the development of highly organized parties that had effective power centralized and concentrated in the hands of a few, the data do negate any claim to the universality of those characteristics. In other words, there do seem to be exceptions to many features of the "iron law." To be fair to Michels, however, it is important to remember that his theory does allow for the absence of these characteristics during the earliest years of a party's development. If the "exceptions" are preponderantly among "young" parties, then Michels's assertions may yet go unshaken by this analysis.

Results: Party Age and Oligarchical Attributes

We have inferred from Michels that party age should be correlated positively with organizational complexity, centralization, and concentration of power and negatively with the level of meaningful participation by the membership. My own analyses, based on ICPP data and reported in table 8.1, reveal only two of the anticipated relationships. For these analyses, the six organization variables mentioned above are combined into a single "organizational complexity" measure, using the summated z-scoring technique; likewise, seven indicators of party nationalization are combined into a single index of "centralization of power."[42] First, the degree of organization is significantly related to party age in the expected direction; only "younger" parties (and one exceptional older party) have a low degree of complexity (see figure 8.1). This is precisely what Michels would have predicted. Second, Michels would have predicted that membership participation would decrease with age; the data suggest that this may be the case.

On the other hand, neither of the indices of centralization or concentration is similarly related to age. In fact, both variables are related (significantly so for centralization) to age in the *opposite* direction from what Michels would have

TABLE 8.1
Pearson Correlations for Party Age with Oligarchical Attributes

Age With	R	N	Probability
Organizational complexity	+.27	53	.02
Centralization of power	−.27	52	.03
Concentration of power	−.16	50	.13
Membership participation	−.33	38	.02
Leadership competition	+.20	53	.07

FIGURE 8.1 ORGANIZATION BY AGE

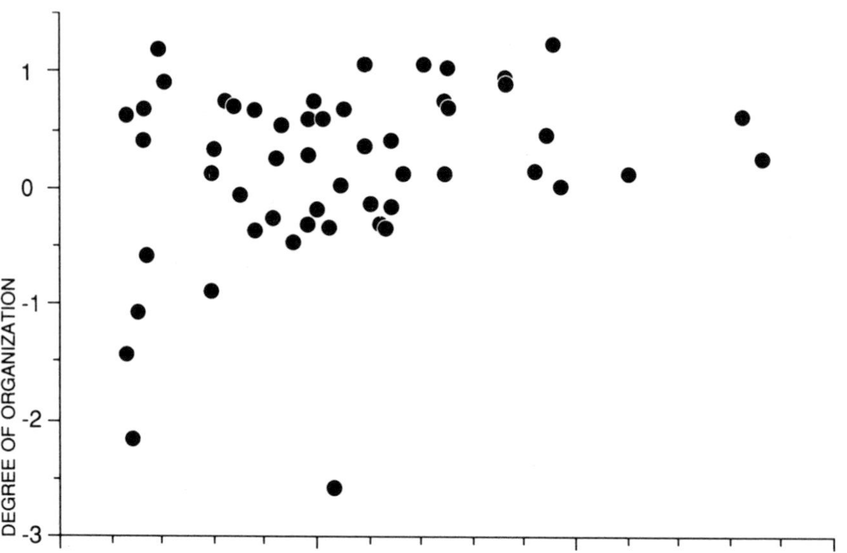

predicted. As indicated in figure 8.2, for example, older parties are actually more likely to be *de*centralized than are their younger counterparts. Even with the extremely decentralized American cases removed, the older parties of the other countries are still as likely as the younger parties to be decentralized.

From Michels's theory, we would also expect leadership turnover to decrease with party age; but I found an insignificant relationship in the opposite direction.

Although a truer test of Michels's theory would require longitudinal data (so as to avoid the cross-sectional fallacy) or at least data for parties covering the full range of ages (the range for the ICPP data is artificially truncated by the "cutoff" requiring seats in the legislature), these analyses are certainly sufficient to raise doubts about Michels's contention that all mature parties would have oligarchical traits.

RESULTS: ORGANIZATION AND OLIGARCHY

From such statements as "with the advance of organization, democracy tends to decline," "the increase in the power of the leaders is directly proportional with the extension of the organization," and "a strong organization needs an equally strong leadership," it is easy to infer from Michels that he would

FIGURE 8.2 CENTRALIZATION BY AGE

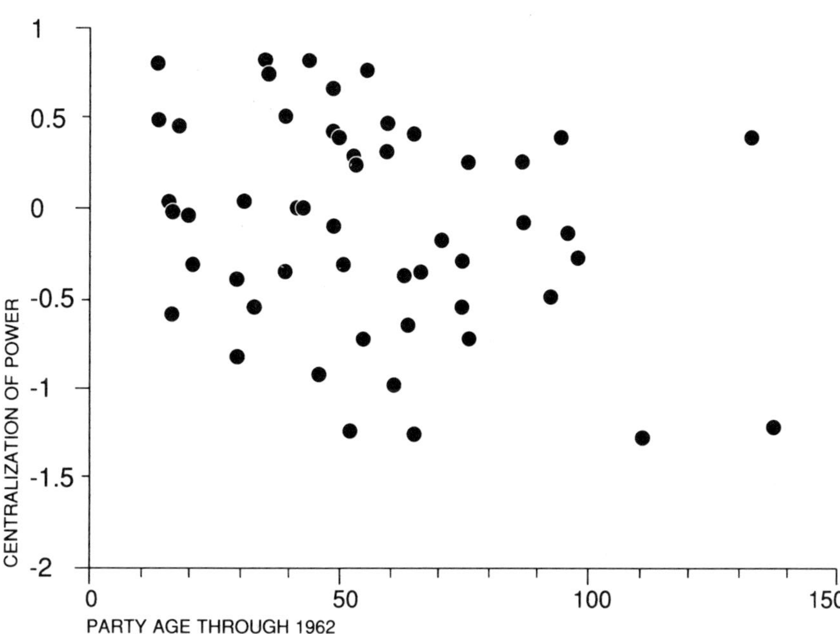

expect organizational complexity to be positively correlated with oligarchical attributes such as centralization and concentration of power.[43] In fact, the degree of organization is *not* significantly correlated with either of those "power" dimensions, and the strength of relationship with centralization is close to zero (see table 8.2). As is clear from figures 8.3 and 8.4, many parties have a high degree of organization but low levels of centralization and concentration.

TABLE 8.2
PEARSON CORRELATIONS FOR ORGANIZATIONAL COMPLEXITY WITH OLIGARCHICAL ATTRIBUTES

	ORGANIZATIONAL COMPLEXITY
Leadership centralization	+.04 p=.39; n=52
Leadership concentration	−.20 p=.08; n=50

The Pearson correlation coefficient for Leadership Centralization with Leadership Concentration is +.28, p=.02, n=49.

FIGURE 8.3 CENTRALIZATION BY ORGANIZATION

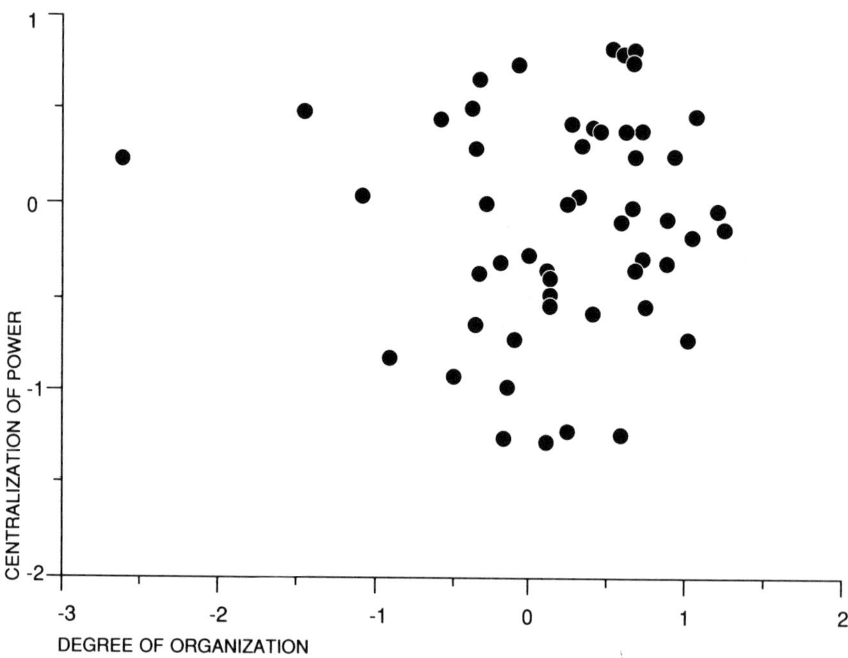

FIGURE 8.4 CONCENTRATION BY ORGANIZATION

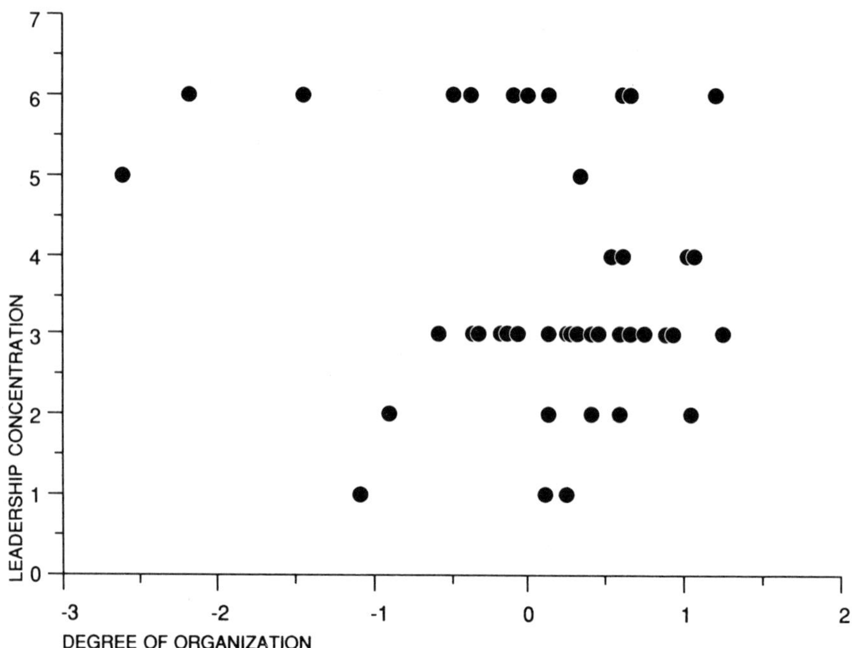

RESULTS: TESTS OF ALTERNATIVES

As is now evident, Michels's theory fails the test of cross-national substantiation in several of its elements. Most important, perhaps, are the findings that (1) oligarchy—operationalized here as two-dimensional: centralization and concentration of power—is variable and not universal, and, relatedly, (2) organizational complexity alone is far from sufficient to explain either centralization or concentration. I have already listed a host of possible reasons why the theory might fail. Two of them allege incomplete specification of the theory, and they are particularly well suited to being addressed with the ICPP data.

Specifically, it has been suggested that Michels's theory is flawed by (1) not taking the party's environment into account and (2) not giving enough credit to organized factionalism within the party as an inhibiter to oligarchy. The first of these suggestions is addressed in table 8.3, which consists of results of analyses of variance, with "country" (as a surrogate for "national environment") as the grouping variable.[44] It is clear from these data that the environment can go far in helping to explain variance on several dimensions related to the concept of oligarchy. This is especially true for centralization of power, where 77 percent of variance in centralization can be explained by national-level environmental factors, as opposed to internal factors such as degree of organization; this is also true to a lesser but still substantial degree for the other dimensions.

As for the contribution of factionalism, table 8.4 presents the results of correlation analyses for centralization and concentration of power with two common types of organized party factionalism. Although centralization is not related to either ideological or issue-based factionalism (and frankly, there is no particularly compelling reason to expect that it would be), concentration of power is significantly related, negatively, to both.[45] In other words, the higher the factionalism, the lower the concentration. It is plausible to infer that in parties that have well-organized factions with opposing views, a "compro-

TABLE 8.3
ANALYSES OF VARIANCE*

CRITERION	ETA-SQUARED	NONMISSING N
Organizational complexity	.51	53
Centralization	.77	52
Concentration	.42	50
Membership participation	.34	38
Leadership competition	.26	53

*Broken down by country for fifteen countries. For Membership Participation, the number of countries with sufficient nonmissing values for analysis of variance is 13.

TABLE 8.4
PEARSON CORRELATIONS FOR ATTRIBUTES OF OLIGARCHY WITH TWO TYPES OF INTERNAL FACTIONALISM

	IDEOLOGICAL FACTIONALISM*	ISSUE FACTIONALISM*
Centralization of power	−.03 p=.44; n=39	−.20 p=.12; n=38
Concentration of power	−.27 p=.05; n=38	−.44 p=.00; n=37

*For a description of the data for factionalism see Kenneth Janda, *Political Parties: A Cross-National Survey* (New York: Free Press, 1980), pp. 119–21.

mise'' collective leadership will be necessary. In such an arrangement, it would seem difficult to conclude that a single cohesive leadership ''clique'' could run the party without being checked.[46]

RESULTS: SUMMARY AND CONCLUSION

The weight of the evidence from my own analyses of ICPP data clearly leads to the conclusions that (1) oligarchy is not inevitable and (2) where it does arise, organizational complexity (i.e., the ''iron law'') is not sufficient to explain it. Other environmental and internal factors (including the degree of factionalism) must be taken into account in explaining different leadership forms within political parties.

THE GREENS: ATTEMPTED REPEAL IN THE POSTINDUSTRIAL AGE

In establishing that Michels's theory does not hold for all parties in all types of environments, we are not, of course, justified in denying that the theory could hold true in *particular* contexts. While it is not an object of this chapter to isolate all of the contexts (if any) in which Michels's theory might apply, it is my purpose in this final section of the chapter to assess the applicability of the ''iron law'' to one particular type of party in one specific context.

Michels built his theory largely from observations of German parties, particularly the SPD. At one point, he specifically took note of his assessment that ''the German people in especial exhibits to an extreme degree the need for someone to point out the way and to issue orders. . . . There exist among the Germans all the preconditions necessary for such a development: a psychical predisposition to subordination, a profound instinct for discipline.''[47] Given that Michels found the iron law to be particularly well suited to understanding the German parties of his day, it seems particularly appropriate to end this paper with an analysis of an attempt to break Michels's law within today's Germany.

The party that I will consider is the Greens party, a party of a "new type," not so much because of its structure and not just because of its program, but primarily because of the nature of its base of support. From the Greens' experience, I ultimately hope to learn something about the applicability of Michels's theory, which was written to cover parties in the "industrial" age, to parties that might better be described as "postindustrial."

THE GREENS AND COMMITMENT TO INTERNAL DEMOCRACY

During the nearly seven decades between Michels's analysis of the SPD and the founding of the Greens party (in 1980), much changed in the world and, importantly, in German society. But one of the enduring features of German "movement" politics was clearly the concern over the tendency toward oligarchy in political parties. Like the SPD, the Greens began as a movement and "changed" into a party. But with the advantage of hindsight and, especially, Michels's treatise and all of the attention it generated, the leaders of the Greens' movement were determined to avoid the oligarchical tendencies that had spoiled Michels's love affair with the SPD. Formed as an amalgamation of existing, somewhat disparate organizations and lists, mostly at the local and state levels, Die Grünen was to be an "antiparty" party.

Even the idea to "go national" was troubling to some supporters of the ecological causes, but it reflected a desire to "express the unity intrinsic to ecological policies, and secondly, to provide continuity and coherence to dispersed citizen groups who might in the absence of a party lose their dynamics and directions."[48] It also involved the political calculation that the movement might be most successful in affecting government policy if it faced the national parties on their own turf.[49] This was not, however, to be a party of the "old type," like all of the existing parties in Germany. Specifically, it was to be "a counter model to the established parties, which are perceived to be bureaucratic oligarchies."[50] It was to be an "antiparty" party, a "movement party," a "network party," a "party unlike the others," a new type of party controlled from below and maintaining the primacy of the "grass roots" over elected officials and representatives. In short, it was to be the first German party to successfully repeal Michels's iron law of oligarchy.

As important to the character of the Greens as its name and ecological program has been its commitment to internal democracy. In fact, one student of the party, Don Schoonmaker, has suggested that it is "*first and foremost* a party of democratic renewal."[51] According to the party's own preamble, adopted in Dortmund in June 1980, "Our politics is determined by the view that the ecological crisis can only be solved through democratic means—that is, with the active assent of the people. We must set about seeking a solution to the crisis soon if we want to prevent an undemocratic solution.''[52] The party's politics is further described as being ''ecological,'' ''social,'' ''nonviolent,'' and ''grass roots.''

> Grass roots, because we stand for direct democracy. Through this method decisions about public affairs will be the most effectively understood. This form of democracy allows itself to work best more on the local level. We reject the evergrasping bureaucracy which leaves the citizen helpless against increasing arbitrariness and the growing abuse of power by the economic and state machinery.[53]

In designing the party, great pains were taken to include mechanisms that would provide for participatory democracy at all levels and grass-roots inputs on all types of issues (including foreign policy), assure control of party officials and parliamentary representatives by the grass roots, avoid ''antidemocratic tendencies toward oligarchization, bureaucratization, routinization, and the growth of a professional elite,'' and—as if that wouldn't be difficult enough under any circumstances—to do so ''while working within the framework of the old politics.''[54] More specifically, internal democracy was to be achieved through a decentralized structure that would emphasize grass-roots democracy and a nonprofessionalized collective leadership, which could be controlled from ''below.''[55]

Although the general structure resembles that of the established German parties (with organs at the national, state, and local levels), the distribution of power is very different. Instead of answering to the national level, the state and local branches of the Greens are given complete autonomy ''regarding program, finances, and personnel.''[56] Furthermore, in keeping with the idea that the party is an extension of the movement, the local level is to be the most powerful; ideally, it would have the greatest resources and the most responsibilties.[57]

Grass-roots democracy (or *Basisdemokratie*) was to be implemented, in part, by making all party meetings, including those of the parliamentary groups, at all levels open to all members of the party. Minorities are guaranteed equal opportunities to affect the opinion-formation process, and even nonmembers who represent related groups or ''initiatives'' may speak and introduce motions.

As one inhibiter to oligarchization, the leadership of the Greens was made undeniably ''collective'' (i.e., ''unconcentrated''):

> Fragmentation of power prevails. The party is governed, first, by decisions of the ''federal delegate assembly'' that meets annually and consists of delegates from local and country groups. A ''federal

> committee'' . . . with 50 elected members meets about every six weeks. A ''federal executive committee,'' consisting of 11 members and 3 cochairpersons, is elected annually by the delegates' assembly and meets two or three times during six week intervals. In addition, the . . . representatives of the Greens in the federal parliament elect their own leadership.[58]

To the extent that it is even reasonable to speak of a ''top'' in such an arrangement, it is occupied by the three speakers of an extraparliamentary organization and, when the party holds seats, three speakers of the parliamentary group *Fraktion*.[59]

To keep the leadership from becoming professionalized, rotation is mandated after two years in an office, the number of party offices held at one time is limited to one, and monetary rewards for party service are kept to a minimum: for example, no salary is paid to party officials, and part of the salary of a Bundestag member is returned to the party. The rotation principle requires representatives in the Bundestag and in the land parliament to give up their seats after serving two years of a four-year term to make way for fellow Greens who were lower on the list. Direct control over the parliamentary group is implemented through the requirement that all representatives make a full accounting of their activities—this may not include advising private industry—and through the ''imperative mandate.''[60] The latter, which has been in effect since 1983, requires that the parliamentary group follow the dictates of the federal assembly and the federal committee, under penalty of expulsion.[61]

There can be little question that the Greens constitute a party structured to break the iron law. But even *if* the Greens are ultimately successful in staving off the dreaded oligarchical form that Michels felt was ''inevitable,'' can that success necessarily be attributed to the carefully shaped antileadership structure of the Greens? Michels thought that structural arrangements, no matter how carefully designed, could not hold back the forces of oligarchy. Oligarchy had, after all, arisen in the SPD itself in spite of well-intentioned arrangements to prevent it. After Michels's time, other failed attempts to structure against hierarchical, professionalized leadership have been documented.[62]

Other factors may, however, bolster the structural inhibiters and enhance the Greens' chances for success in beating back any oligarchical tendencies. Acute factionalism, for instance, is likely to assure continued adherence to the principle of collective leadership and to deconcentration of power. And the fact that the Greens are a ''postindustrial'' party, drawing support heavily from Germany's ''new middle class,'' may mean that the necessities for internal democracy are in far greater supply than Michels thought would ever be the case. In short, both internal factionalism and a ''postindustrial'' environment could potentially be more important than the antioligarchy structure itself in enabling the Greens to break the iron law.

THE GREENS AND INTERNAL FACTIONALISM

The Greens began as a collection of disparate groups that had one thing in common: a deep commitment to ecological issues. The problems of trying to integrate the various groups into a single party became evident during its first year of existence, as a number of prominent conservative members, including Herbert Gruhl, left the party over its leftist tendencies and its commitment to direct democracy for Germany. The departures left the remaining Greens only slightly more homogeneous. In a 1985 study, Werner Hulsberg described the most prominent factions:

> On the right of the party are the *eco-libertarians,* who advocate a radical politics without reference to class and declare war on the "dictatorial jacobinism of the socialists." On the left of it are the *eco-socialists,* who insist on the relationship between social and ecological questions, and on the need to resist and defeat the bourgeois state. In the middle are the *political realists,* who argue for compromise with the SPD and feasible "policies of reform" to one side; and the *fundamentalists* to the other, closer in temper to the eco-socialists but divided from them over the issue of relations with the labour movement.[63]

Each of these factions has identifiable leaders; none has the support of a majority within the party.[64] In recognition of the fact that the dominant rift is strategic rather than ideological, however, it is much more common to think of the Greens as effectively bifactional (between "Realos" and "Fundis"), with each major faction split less decisively. Although the question of cooperation with the SPD has been the most visible point of dispute, "the two sides also argue over everything from policy to trivia."[65] When viewed in this way, the fundamentalists may be seen as having had a majority among the leadership during the mid 1960s, although the realists have been seen as doing somewhat better in the documents issued from the annual party conferences.[66] Currently, the factions are truly competitive with one another, both in the membership—even though the other *voters* are much more likely to be realists than fundamentalists—and in the leadership. As long as this remains the case, it is unlikely that the party will be home to a single-minded leadership "clique" of the type Michels thought inevitable for all parties.

THE GREENS AND THE "POSTINDUSTRIAL MASS"

Michels described a "mass" membership that began with little interest or skills in politics and that would become even more apathetic as the process of oligarchization progressed. For Michels, the mass was not a pretty thing to describe: "indifferent and apathetic," with a "trust in authority that verges on the complete absence of a critical faculty," "useless" without leadership.[67] Indeed, leadership in a mass organization did not have to be imposed; it was welcomed: "In collective movements, with rare exceptions, the process is natural and not 'artificial.' Natural above all is the movement itself, at whose head the leader takes his place, not as a rule of his own initiative, but by force of circumstances. No less natural is the sudden collapse of the agitation as soon as the army is deprived of its chief."[68] As the leaders became better educated in the ways of politics and as a natural tendency among the masses toward "hero worship" took hold, the masses would be even less well equipped, even if they wished it, to ward off oligarchy. The "superiority" of the leaders over the masses would be solidified on such grounds as money, heredity, and "formal instruction," with the last being the most important: "Now the most superficial observation shows that in the parties of the proletariat the leaders are, in matters of education, greatly superior to the led."[69] An apathetic and uneducated mass would be led by an interested, skilled minority. As long as the state of the mass remained so deplorable—and Michels held up no hope for the alternative—the development of an indispensable, and consequently oligarchical, leadership would be inevitable.

For Michels, the form of the organization, especially the roles of leaders and led within the organization, clearly reflected what he saw to be the nature of the masses in industrial society, with their lack of education being the key ingredient.

The "masses" from which today's Greens party draws its members and many of its voters is quite different from the German masses as described by Michels in 1911. By the time the Greens were founded in 1980, German society, and Western societies generally, had moved or were moving from the "industrial" period to a period that, for want of a better term, has simply been called "postindustrial." Among the component changes—the most important of them from the perspective of Michels's theory—was a tremendous extension of higher education throughout the population. According to Ronald Inglehart, there have been monumental political consequences in the forms of "changing values and political styles."[70]

In postindustrial society, according to Inglehart's view, advanced education joins with electronic media and a largely urban population to produce significantly higher levels of political information and skills among the general population. The consequences for political participation, organization, and leadership are evident in this comparison:

> The institutions that mobilized mass political participation in the late 19th and early 20th century—labor union, church, and mass political party—were typically hierarchical organizations in which a small number of leaders or bosses led a mass of disciplined troops.

> The newer mode of participation is capable of expressing the individual's preferences with far greater precision than the old. It is more issue-oriented participation, based less on established bureaucratic organizations than on ad hoc groups; it aims at affecting specific policy changes rather than simply supporting "our" leaders.
>
> . . . .
>
> It is new in the sense that only recently has a large percentage of the population possessed the skills required for this form of participation. And it is new in that it relies less heavily on a permanent and relatively rigid infrastructure.[71]

The attitude toward leadership in this new mode of participation is, according to Inglehart, "elite challenging," as opposed to the earlier "elite directed" variety.[72]

According to William M. Chandler and Alan Siaroff, the Greens party is clearly a product of postindustrialism and the associated change in values ("postmaterialism"), as had been other "new" participatory forms that preceded the Greens:

> It is worth noting that the radicalism and discontent of the late 1960s and early 1970s created a formative political experience in unconventional direct action politics for many young Germans who would later provide a core of activists in new forms of participation. This experience was certainly conducive to the spread of Burgerinitiativen and the pursuit of single-issue protests. New modes of participation that bypassed and partially displaced the established parties later crystallized in the form of the antiparty Greens.[73]

Indeed, recent studies have shown that the membership and the voting support of the Greens are drawn primarily from the types of people most likely to have the new participatory skills and attitudes. Greens' support tends to come from those who are young, highly educated, urban (or from university towns), and "new middle class."[74] A 1981 survey found that 67 percent of the Greens' supporters considered themselves "strongly interested" in politics, in comparison to 24–31 percent for other parties, and 70 percent were "ready to participate actively in organizing and staging nationwide peace protests."[75] Ferdinand Muller-Rommel has found Greens' voters to be well above the norm in participatory skills and better able than the average voters to both anticipate and evaluate political issues and governmental policies.[76]

So, the Greens party is a "postindustrial" party in the sense that its members and supporters are far more educated and skilled politically and are much more likely to have proparticipatory and elite-challenging attitudes than was allegedly true for all mass parties in the preceding "industrial" age. At the very least, it must be observed that this "basis" of the Greens is far different from the apathetic, unskilled, uninformed mass of Michels's SPD. The postindustrial, postmaterialist members see far less need for strong leadership (in fact they are likely to rebel against it), are far less prone to "hero worship," are far more "independent" in thought and politics, and place far greater value on participating meaningfully in their own governance. As long as the party continues to draw its membership primarily from the young, well-educated "new middle class," it would seem to be among the parties most likely to succeed in achieving internal democracy.

THE GREENS VERSUS OLIGARCHY: THE RECORD THUS FAR

Although the Greens party is still relatively young, so that even Michels might not have expected full-blown oligarchy to have developed yet within a party so committed to denying oligarchy, the party's success record with respect to such matters is already a "mixed bag," including some possible indications of oligarchical tendencies.[77]

There are some signs that, while they fall far short of indicating a fully established oligarchy, could signal the first stages that Michels described.

1. The much-heralded rotation system has come under attack, especially as applied to parliamentary delegates. Some state and local parties have already suspended rotation, and only a few years after the Greens won their first seats in the national parliament, one observer noted that "the argument for professional leadership seems to be gaining" in order to deal effectively with the leaders of other parties.[78] He further noted that "even with rotation, the Greens are developing a sizable group of full-time professional politicians."[79]

2. Michels predicted that parliamentary professionalization within a party would come at the expense of organizational leaders and dedicated party supporters within that organization. In the Greens, there have been reports of serious conflicts, since 1983, between the party organization and the parliamentary *Fraktion,* in a relationship that is marked by "mistrust."[80] A hint of potential problems ahead may be found in the deputies' perceptions of their own role. According to Otto Schily, who is one of the three co-leaders of the *Fraktion,* the overwhelming majority of Green deputies see parliament as more than just a forum for "fundamental opposition."[81] As Frankland has argued: "If the deputies of the Greens utilize parliament as more than a forum and become actively involved with the decision-making in regard to the complex specialized issues on the parliamentary agenda, then serious strains are likely with organization activists, given the radical democratic values of the Greens."[82]

3. Michels thought that as the organization developed and leadership became professionalized, "distance" would develop between leaders and led—socially as well as politically. Social distance has not developed between the Greens' leaders and members, perhaps because the whole party is "new

middle class'' rather than working class. Both leaders and led are young and highly educated.[83] Neither is there a marked difference politically between leaders and members. Currently the only significant distance seems to be between voters, on the one side, and activists and leaders, on the other side. This distance, however, is due less to the professionalization of the leadership than to the expansion of the Greens' electorate to include voters who are less likely to be committed to the totality of the Greens' program and who, in some cases, belong to the working class rather than to the new middle class.[84] If the leadership should, with the support of the party's electorate, place even more emphasis on its electoral goals at the expense of the ''fundamentalists,'' the party's activists could indeed find themselves distanced from the leadership. That has not happened yet, but in the 1987 national elections the Greens increased their share of the votes to 8.3 percent (from 5.6 percent in 1983). Afterward, a ''realist'' leader noted the momentum and declared: ''The Greens must grow. . . . Now that we'll be back into the Bundestag for four more years, we'll have time.''[85] The thought undoubtedly sends chills through fundamentalists, the most prominent of whom was quoted in 1982 as saying ''I sometimes fear that the Greens will suddenly win 13 [percent] and turn into a party which competes for power. We should rather remain at 6 or 7 percent and remain uncompromising in our demands than be ministers.''[86]

4. Michels thought that with professionalized leadership would come a decline in the size of the always-small group of active participants within a party. Although there is no evidence of decline as yet, the general rule of low participation seems to apply even to ''postmaterialist'' groups, including the Greens: ''Most decisions [in the Greens] are made by county assemblies, where a natural selection between active and passive members of the party seems already to be taking place. It has been variously estimated that about 20 to 30 percent of the party membership participate in these assemblies, and about 10 percent of the members become active party workers. Thus, first indications are that even among the new social movements oriented toward postmaterialist values, only a relatively small number of activists constitute the continuous base of participatory democracy.''[87]

But while there are signs that Michels himself might interpret as evidence that the iron law is working within the Greens, the party's structure, bolstered by its members' genuine commitment to internal democracy, has generally worked well enough that Horst Mewes has recently concluded that the members still tend to prevail over the party's leaders and that in spite of the chinks in the antioligarchy armor, ''the parliamentary group of the party continues to discourage the creation of . . . [elite] leadership groups by annual elections of its leaders, as well as by fostering decision-making by the entire membership.''[88] And while only a minority of the members actively participate in decision making, the fact remains that most members are better equipped than are their counterparts in ''older'' parties to arrive at independent evaluations of their leaders' actions and to "control" those leaders if and when they would deviate markedly from the members' wishes.

The biggest potential threat, ironically, remains the possibility of success in expanding the party's electorate. As E. Gene Frankland has argued, and the fundamentalists would agree: "If additional electoral support is generated from those who are *not* young, highly educated, new middle class, 'post-materialists,' the imperative to hold and broaden one's votes would make the Basis even more contourless and the Greens less of an 'anti-party' party in practice (if not in rhetoric)."[89] That is precisely why the Greens are not likely to ever become a party "like the others," however. To the extent that the Greens party comes to look and *act* like an established party, it is more apt to lose its base of support to the SPD and, effectively, to collapse. Becoming a large, "establishment," perhaps even oligarchical, party does not seem to be a viable option for the Greens. The party exists *because* it is different.

CONCLUSION

It has been our purpose here to review arguments and evidence and to bring new evidence to bear on Michels's "iron law of oligarchy." Although some of what Michels argued in 1911 has withstood the test of time, the weight of the argument and the evidence leads to the conclusion, as James M. Burns has stated, that "Michels' theory was no law, much less an 'iron' law."[90] While Michels's theory may not be proven wrong in all contexts, it is far too simplistic, especially in failing to account for variable contexts. In suggesting one potentially important avenue of explanation, Michels's theory is useful. In suggesting that that path is the only one, it is highly misleading. In suggesting that *tendencies* to oligarchy are universal, so that concerned activists must be vigilant to prevent oligarchy from forming, Michels would possibly be correct; there is nothing in this study to suggest otherwise. But to go further, as Michels does, and suggest in despair that oligarchy is inevitable, regardless of efforts to the contrary, is clearly wrong. The Democratic party in the United States is not headed by an oligarchical clique. And in Michels's homeland, the Greens, with an antioligarchical structure bolstered by acute factionalism and an elite-challenging membership, have at least an even chance of avoiding the "inevitable."

It has not been my purpose here to consider the ramifications of success in adhering to internal democracy, whether generally or specifically for the German Greens. It may be worthwhile just to note in passing, however, that it is sometimes argued in the United States that "too much" internal democracy has made the Democratic party, in particular, ineffective if not obsolete.[91] And simply as food for thought, it may be interesting to consider whether the Greens' triple wallop of factionalism, elite-challenging attitudes, and antioligarchical structure might condemn the party to a future of confused direction, internal squabbling, amateurism, and, ultimately, failure in accomplishing the party's "external" policy goals. It is very possible that when the full story of the Greens is told someday, it will tell of a party whose major difficulties were tied to too little, not too much, leadership; difficulties tied to a fragmented, collective leadership group that could not give clear direction, rather than to a single-minded clique that had too much power; to a membership that had too little, not too much, willingness to follow. Then again, it could be the story of a party's developing a new type of leadership style, which was consistent with internal democracy and was still capable of helping the party to accomplish external policy objectives. It is important to observe the Greens' experience precisely because it may be duplicated in other postindustrial parties, and even established parties have shown an interest in attracting the type of voters and members that have so far made the Greens distinctive. If the Greens' approach to organization and leadership (or more accurately, nonleadership) were adopted more broadly, the ramifications could be profound not only for the internal operations of the parties but for the practice of government as well.

Seventy-five years after Michels's "iron law" was formulated, it must be concluded that it wasn't a very effective law after all. Some parties have sucessfully broken it in the past, and the period of postindustrialism seems to have brought with it a whole new set of loopholes.

NOTES

The research for this chapter was funded by a Summer Grant (1987) from the College of Liberal Arts at Texas A & M University and by a Departmental Development Grant from the College of Liberal Arts to the Department of Political Science. Data used herein are from the International Comparative Political Parties (ICCP) Project, Kenneth Janda principal investigator. Janda made the data available to me, but they are also available from the Interuniversity Consortium for Political and Social Research. I owe intellectual debts to the students in Political Science 620, a graduate seminar in comparative politics that I taught during 1986, and to Stephen Babalola, a Ph.D. student in political science at Texas A & M.

1. The first German edition of Robert Michels's work was published in 1911; the first Italian edition, in 1912; the first English edition, in 1915.
2. Robert Michels, *Political Parties: A Sociological Study of the Oligarchical Tendencies of Modern Democracy* (New York: Free Press, 1962), p. 112.
3. Ibid., p. 50.
4. Ibid., p. 70.
5. Seymour M. Lipset, M. Trow, and J. Coleman, *Union Democracy* (Glencoe, Ill: Free Press, 1956); and Lipset, "Introduction," in Michels, *Political Parties,* p. 32.
6. Knut Heidar, "The Norwegian Labor Party: Social Democracy in Periphery of Europe," in *Social Democratic Parties in Western Europe,* ed. William E. Patterson and

Alastair H. Thomas (New York: St. Martin's Press, 1977), p. 295; and David Hine, "Leaders and Followers: Democracy and Manageability in the Social Democratic Parties of Western Europe," in *The Future of Social Democracy: Problems and Prospects of Social Democratic Parties in Western Europe,* ed. William E. Patterson and Alastair H. Thomas (Oxford: Clarendon Press, 1986), p. 263.

7. Leon D. Epstein, *Political Parties in Western Democracies* (New York: Praeger Publishers, 1967), p. 311; Klaus von Beyme, *Political Parties in Western Democracies* (Aldershot, Eng.: Gower, 1985); James Q. Wilson, *Political Organizations* (New York: Basic Books, 1973), p. 241; R. T. McKenzie, *British Political Parties: The Distribution of Power within the Conservative and Labour Parties* (New York: Frederick A. Praeger, 1963), pp. 635–38.

8. Lipset, "Introduction," p. 19; von Beyme, *Political Parties in Western Democracies,* p. 164.

9. Von Beyme, *Political Parties in Western Democracies,* pp. 235–36.

10. Lipset, "Introduction," p. 32.

11. Heidar, "Norwegian Labor Party," p. 295; von Beyme, *Political Parties in Western Democracies,* p. 236.

12. Von Beyme, *Political Parties in Western Democracies,* p. 235.

13. For examples see Lipset, "Introduction," pp. 20–25.

14. Hans Daalder, "Parties, Elites, and Political Development in Western Europe," in *Political Parties and Political Development,* ed. Joseph La Palombara and Myron Weiner (Princeton, N.J.: Princeton University Press, 1966), p. 70.

15. Ibid.

16. See Lipset, "Introduction," p. 34, for a discussion of this view.

17. Ibid., p. 36.

18. Daalder, "Parties, Elites, and Political Development," pp. 70–71.

19. Although Daalder does not specifically attribute this flaw in the "oligarchical theory" directly to Michels, it is reasonable to infer from the context that it is intended as a reference to Michels.

20. Samuel J. Eldersveld, *Political Parties in American Society* (New York: Basic Books, 1982), p. 161.

21. Lipset, "Introduction," pp. 28–31.

22. Eldersveld, *Political Parties in American Society,* p. 161.

23. Daalder, "Parties, Elites, and Political Development," p. 72.

24. Michels, *Political Parties,* p. 111.

25. Daalder, "Parties, Elites, and Political Development," p. 72.

26. Eldersveld, *Political Parties in American Society,* p. 161.

27. McKenzie, *British Political Parties,* p. 645.

28. Lipset, "Introduction," p. 36.

29. Von Beyme, *Political Parties in Western Democracies,* p. 238.

30. Lipset, "Introduction," pp. 35–36.

31. Daalder, "Parties, Elites, and Political Development," p. 71.

32. Kay Lawson, *The Comparative Study of Political Parties* (New York: St. Martin's Press, 1976), p. 9.

33. Steven B. Wolinetz, quoted by Hine in "Leaders and Followers," p. 279.

34. Samuel J. Eldersveld, *Political Parties: A Behavioral Analysis* (Chicago, Ill: Rand McNally, 1964).

35. Ibid., p. 119.

36. Russell J. Dalton, "Political Parties and Political Representation: Party Supporters and Party Elitism within Nations," *Comparative Political Studies* 18 (1985): 267–99.

37. The fifteen western democracies in these analyses are the United States, the United Kingdom, Australia, New Zealand, Canada, Ireland, Austria, France, West Germany, Greece, Denmark, Iceland, Sweden, Netherlands, and Luxembourg.

38. Michels, *Political Parties,* pp. 61, 79, 72, 86; italics added.

39. Ibid., pp. 73, 72, 70; italics added.

40. Frequency distributions for the variables discussed here are included as tables 1.1 through 1.5 in Robert Harmel, "Michels + 75: The Iron Law of Oligarchy Revisited," a paper prepared for delivery at the 1987 annual meeting of the American Political Science Association, the Palmer House, Chicago, Sept. 3–5, 1987. While the later tables are based on just the fifty-three Western democratic parties studied here, similar tables based on all of the parties in the ICPP Project may be found in Kenneth Janda, *Political Parties: A Cross-National Survey* (New York: Free Press, 1980).

41. Janda, *Political Parties,* p. 116.

42. The variables used for these analyses are described fully in Janda, *Political Parties.* The indicators that were combined for the index of organizational complexity are: structural articulation, intensiveness of organization, extensiveness of organization, frequency of local meetings, maintaining records, and pervasiveness of organization. The indicators contributing to the centralization index are: nationalization of structure, selecting the national leader, selecting parliamentary candidates, allocating funds, formulating policy, controlling communications, and administering discipline.

43. Michels, *Political Parties,* pp. 70, 71, 73.

44. Although "country" itself is hardly satisfying as an explanatory variable, it is used here as a surrogate for all of the relevant factors that vary at the national (or "system") level, rather than at the party or subparty levels. In analyses covering all competitive parties in twenty-eight democratic countries, which have been reported in detail elsewhere (Robert Harmel and Kenneth Janda, *Parties and Their Environments: Limits to Reform?* [New York: Longman, 1982], it was found that the specific environmental factors of modernity, population size, nature of the electoral system, breadth of franchise, length of experience with democracy, and degree of party competition may together account for a large portion of the environment's impact on the complexity of party organization. Similarly, the size of the country and the vertical and horizontal structures of the government can account for a substantial part of the environment's influence on the internal distribution of power within parties (i.e., centralization).

45. Analyses for "strategic" factionalism are not included here only because of insufficient data: see Janda, *Political Parties.*

46. The exact relationship between factionalism and oligarchy is more complex, and it deserves a more thorough treatment than can be presented here. Although the literature that I cite in this chapter treats factionalism as a *causal variable* affecting the presence or absence of oligarchy, an alternative view might see the presence of factions (or at least those of a particular type and role within the party) as an *indicator* of the lack of oligarchy or at least of its "concentration" dimension. Thus, any relationship between factionalism and concentration of power would then be tautological rather than causal. Seeing merits in both approaches, I have chosen here to treat the relationship as presented in the existing literature. Either way, the presence of factionalism and its relationship (whether tautological or causal) to deconcentration of leadership cast doubt on the inevitability of forming a single, cohesive leadership clique within a political party.

47. Michels, *Political Parties,* p. 89.

48. Horst Mewes, "The West German Green Party," *New German Critique,* Winter 1983, pp. 51–85; see also Ferdinand Muller-Rommel, "The Consolidation of a New Party in Germany: The Greens and the German Party System in the 1980s,"

paper presented at the joint sessions of the European Consortium for Political Research (ECPR), Amsterdam, Apr. 10–15, 1987.

49. Mewes, "West German Green Party," p. 56.

50. E. Gene Frankland, "Interpreting the 'Green' Phenomenon in West German Politics, 1977–1983," paper presented at the annual meetings of the Midwest Political Science Association, Milwaukee, Wis., Apr. 29–May 2, 1983, p. 18.

51. Don Schoonmaker, "The 'Greens' in West Germany: Between Movement and Party," a paper presented at the 1983 annual meeting of the American Political Science Association, Chicago, Sept. 1–4, 1983, p. 3; italics added.

52. Schoonmaker, "The 'Greens'," app. I.

53. Ibid.

54. Horst Mewes, "The Green Party Comes of Age," in *Comparative Politics Annual Edition 1987/88* (Guilford, Conn.: Dushkin, 1987), p. 111; this originally appeared in *Environment,* June 1985, pp. 12–17, 33–39. P. M. R. Stirk, "Sect, Party, or Social Movement: Some Observations on the Problems of Group Identity in the Greens," paper presented at the Political Studies Association Annual Conference, Aberdeen, Scotland, Apr. 1987, p. 10.

55. Muller-Rommel, "Consolidation," p. 10.

56. Frankland, "Interpreting the 'Green' Phenomenon," p. 18.

57. Schoonmaker, "The 'Greens'," p. 13; Thomas Poguntke, "New Politics in Western Democratic Countries," paper presented at the ECPR workshop the Role of Small Parties in Western European Party Systems: A Comparative Approach, Amsterdam, Apr. 1987, p. 7.

58. Mewes, "Green Party Comes of Age," p. 116.

59. Muller-Rommel, "Consolidation," p. 10.

60. Stirk, "Sect, Party, or Social Movement," p. 10.

61. Mewes, "Green Party Comes of Age," p. 116.

62. E.g., PASOK; see Hine, "Leaders and Followers," p. 285.

63. Werner Hulsberg, "The Greens at the Crossroads," *New Left Review,* July/Aug. 1985, p. 22.

64. Ibid., pp. 12, 27.

65. *Wall Street Journal,* Jan. 27, 1987, p. 30.

66. E.g., see *New York Times,* Sept. 29, 1986, p. A4.

67. Michels, *Political Parties,* pp. 87, 89 (with special reference to Germans), 90.

68. Ibid.

69. Ibid., p. 107.

70. Ronald Inglehart, *The Silent Revolution: Changing Values and Political Styles among Western Publics* (Princeton, N.J.: Princeton University Press, 1977).

71. Ibid., pp. 299–300.

72. Ibid., pp. 3, 299–300.

73. William M. Chandler and Alan Siaroff, "Postindustrial Politics in Germany and the Origins of the Greens," *Comparative Politics,* Apr. 1986, p. 311.

74. See Muller-Rommel, "Consolidation," pp. 11, 14.

75. Mewes, "West German Green Party," p. 68.

76. Muller-Rommel, "Consolidation," p. 4.

77. Depending on which of alternative birthdates is used, Michels's SPD was either twenty or thirty-six years old in 1911, when his book was first published.

78. Mewes, "Green Party Comes of Age," p. 115.

79. Ibid., p. 116.

80. Frankland, "Interpreting the 'Green' Phenomenon," p. 22.

81. Ibid., p. 31.

82. Ibid., p. 35.

83. Schoonmaker, ''The 'Greens','' p. 19; Frankland, ''Interpreting the 'Green' Phenomenon,'' p. 31.

84. Hulsberg, ''Greens at the Crossroads,'' p. 19; Frankland, ''Interpreting the 'Green' Phenomenon,'' p. 35.

85. Joschka Fischer, quoted in *Washington Post,* Jan. 27, 1987, p. 30.

86. Petra Kelly, quoted in Stirk, ''Sect, Party, or Social Movement,'' p. 7, from *Der Spiegel,* June 14, 1982, p. 53.

87. Mewes, ''Green Party Comes of Age,'' p. 115.

88. Ibid., p. 116.

89. Frankland, ''Interpreting the 'Green' Phenomenon,'' p. 35.

90. James M. Burns, *Leadership* (New York: Harper & Row, 1978), p. 314.

91. E.g., see Harmel and Janda, *Parties and Their Environments.*

9

Leadership in the International System: Bismarck and Washington Compared

Manus I. Midlarsky

Leadership in the international system is a difficult issue to treat effectively precisely because there has been so little of it. In democratic political systems such as that of the United States, there exists a plethora of leaders, both good and bad, effective and ineffective, within which one can make comparisons. It is no accident therefore, that journals such as *Presidential Studies Quarterly* contain numerous articles and even entire issues devoted to the subject of leadership, largely of the presidential variety.

In contrast, one finds few if any direct analyses of expressly international leadership; those that exist are almost wholly devoted to the leadership exerted by a particular national leader acting on the international scene. Franklin D. Roosevelt, Harry S. Truman, Winston Churchill, and Joseph Stalin are instances of national leaders who readily come to mind. Rarely is there a leader who, after being prominent on the national stage, also becomes an acknowledged international leader for virtually all major international actors. The one fairly recent exception is Otto von Bismarck, who assumed the leadership of the European continental system after the formation of the German Empire in 1871. Here, a national leader had risen to such heights of power and prestige that even his erstwhile enemies acknowledged his leadership of the sytem. As Prosper Mérimée put it, "Unfortunately there is only one great man in each century and Bismarck is the one in ours."[1] And when George F. Kennan published his magisterial *The Decline of Bismarck's European Order* in 1979, it was not Prussia's or Germany's order that was the object of his inquiry; as the title of the book suggests, it was a European order. Given the centrality of Europe to the international politics of the period, this was tantamount to an international order as well.

If we seek to analyze the workings of leadership in the international system, Bismarck becomes a useful point of departure, especially if we also compare him with at least one other leader of stature, in this instance George Washington. This second comparative emphasis is chosen because again, of all of the possibilities, Washington comes closest to having acted on a multiunit stage. The thirteen formerly British colonies of North America were hardly a unified entity when Washington assumed leadership. It is quite possible that they could have gone their separate ways, as, in fact, one bloc of states did later, in 1861. Thus, there is at least this shared element between the two leaders: each one acted on a multiunit stage that he had done much to unify. This is in contrast, say, to Charles de Gaulle, who even during wartime and especially after his second accession to power in 1958 saw himself almost exclusively as a leader of France.[2] But beyond these similarities (admittedly somewhat superficial) exists one that goes to the heart of the basis for successful international leadership. Despite the obvious differences between their styles of leadership—Bismarck, the autocratic and charismatic leader, and Washington, the quintessential democratic leader with no real evidence of charisma—a basic similarity will be revealed which characterizes these two as archetypal international leaders.[3] This is the norm-reflecting property, in contrast to the establishment of normative systems that are characteristic of other leaders (e.g., Mao, Lenin, Hitler), especially those of the charismatic transforming variety.[4]

TYPES OF LEADERSHIP

It is fairly common to distinguish among the various types of leadership authority such as charismatic, bureaucratic, and legal-rationalistic, as did Max Weber, or between transforming and transacting leaderships, as did James MacGregor Burns.[5] In the former instance, the typology is based on the sources of power and authority. Whether the leader draws upon the charisma of his own personality (Muammar al-Qaddafi) or a power base within the bureaucracy (Stalin) or the legitimacy of a legally sanctioned process (Jimmy Carter), it is primarily the source of this power and authority which is singled out.[6] On the other hand, the distinction between transforming and transacting refers to the purposive aspects of leadership. Transforming leaders seek to make substantial and fundamental changes in the systems that they lead (Hitler, Lenin, Stalin), whereas transacting leaders make the typical sorts of exchanges or bargains that are characteristic of leadership in times of "normalcy" (Carter).

All successful leaders may, to varying extents, exhibit several characteristics, which Thomas E. Cronin lists as:

- Self-knowledge/self-confidence
- Vision, ability to infuse important, transcending values into an enterprise
- Intelligence, wisdom, judgment
- Learning/renewal
- Worldmindedness/a sense of history and breadth
- Coalition building/social architecture
- Morale-building/motivation
- Stamina, energy, tenacity, courage, enthusiasm
- Character, integrity/intellectual honesty
- Risk-taking/entrepreneurship
- An ability to communicate, persuade/listen
- Understanding the nature of power and authority
- An ability to concentrate on achieving goals and results
- A sense of humor, perspective, flexibility.[7]

As we shall see, the character and integrity of Bismarck have been called into question by some observers, and Washington's self-confidence, especially during the early years of his military leadership, was not very high. But with these caveats, the preceding characteristics may be said to apply to both leaders. Additionally and most importantly, the two leaders display the norm-reflecting property that distinguishes them from others with whom they have been compared.

The norm-reflecting category combines elements both of the sources of power and of the purposes to which it is put. By "norm-reflecting" I mean a style of leadership that manages to capture the fundamental norms of a system and to articulate these norms in a very clear and recognizable manner. In this sense, the norm-reflecting leader does not merely reflect the basic principles of a society (to some extent all leaders do that); he or she also sharpens his or her awareness of these norms and operates with them in a highly successful manner, sometimes in novel ways. To this extent there is a creative and even a transforming aspect to the norm-reflecting leader, but only within the limits of what is allowed by these basic norms. These leaders do not introduce new normative systems.

I distinguish here between the creative use of existing norms (the norm-reflecting property) and the introduction of new normative systems. Indeed, as we shall see, the international system is not receptive to such transforming efforts except within relatively narrow limits. Hitler's efforts to introduce a new normative system and to assume international leadership outside of the narrow confines of the German-speaking population of central Europe were doomed to failure, as were the comparable later efforts of Stalin outside of the east European arena. Even the relatively innocuous (when compared to those of a

Hitler or a Stalin) attempted transformations of a Dag Hammarskjöld, in seeking to strengthen the political influence of the United Nations, probably led to his early demise at the hands of those who were unwilling to countenance a more centralized and effective international leadership. In the following comparison between Bismarck and Washington, I shall not only explore their individual styles of leadership, but I shall especially emphasize the interface between individual leaders and the normative environments from which they derive.

OTTO VON BISMARCK

Bismarck's greatness as a leader generally was manifested in two ways. First, he successfully unified Germany under conditions that were highly advantageous, first, to Prussia and, then, to the united Germany that emerged under Prussian leadership. Second, having achieved these goals, he was able to keep the peace in Europe, with Berlin as its diplomatic center. Indeed, so pervasive was his influence that a contemporary observer, the editor of the Russian newspaper *Moskovskie Vyedomosti,* commented in 1886: "The German Chancellor has acquired, together with his deserved fame, a certain mythological quality. His hand is suspected in all the events of our time; he is viewed as the possessor of the talisman before which all obstacles dissolve and all locks open. Without his agreement, one is given to understand, one may neither lie down nor stand up; he runs the whole world."[8]

Bismarck's main wish when he became first minister to Wilhelm I of Prussia in 1862 was to achieve an equality with Austria within the German-speaking portions of Europe. As Edward Crankshaw, the most recent English-language biographer of Bismarck, put it, "For ten years now his one devouring preoccupation had been the elevation of Prussia to a position of at least equality with Austria. If Austria refused to admit this equality—formalized by Prussian hegemony over all Germany north of the River Main—then she would have to be coerced."[9]

A consequence of the Congress of Vienna in 1815 and of the system that Prince Metternich had devised was Austria's near hegemony over these principalities. Bismarck fervently desired to change that condition. His first maneuverings toward the Danish War of 1864 were to reflect his extraordinarily acute perceptions of his environment and an ability to use these perceptions to further Prussia's, and of course his own, interests.[10] Although he had earlier offended Austria by engineering Prussia's refusal to participate in a Congress of Princes sponsored by Vienna, he was very quick to do an about-face and woo Vienna for a joint action against Denmark in order to "free" the largely German-speaking provinces of Schleswig and Holstein from Denmark's rule. This was to be a major hallmark of Bismarck's style: opportunism combined with an ever-present readiness to change policies as the needs of the moment might require.

Crankshaw put it thus: "The trick was quite simple: it was to stop what he was doing and do the opposite without asking whether he could afford to lose face. He was one of the very few public men to understand that if you do not care about face you have nothing to lose."[11] Bismarck realized that opportunities were fleeting moments in history or as he would say, "he listened for God's footfall, and seized the hem of His garment as it brushed by invisibly."[12]

A golden opportunity had been presented when the Danish king proclaimed a unitary constitution in 1863, incorporating Schleswig as a part of Denmark, now to be equal to the rest. This "affront" to German nationalism could be harnessed by Bismarck to Prussian advantage only if Prussia were not isolated in her action against Denmark. Now we see Bismarck's enormous flexibility in making overtures to Austria to join him in his crusade on behalf of German nationalism. The fact of a recent rift meant nothing to him.

Bismarck's ready understanding of his political environment also is evident here. With Russia absorbed in the latest Polish crisis and grateful to Bismarck for Prussia's earlier support against the Poles and with Britain requiring a continental ally to act effectively, Bismarck only needed to concern himself with France. And he did this in typical Bismarckian fashion by dropping hints to Napoleon III that Prussia was prepared to allow French access to the left bank of the Rhine.[13] Of course, in this, as in other instances, he "scattered promises so as not to carry them out."[14] With both Russia and France unprepared to act, all Bismarck needed was one major ally, in this instance Austria, and he then could move against Denmark.

Yet even here, in the midst of what would appear to have been some reckless gambling, Bismarck exhibited a prudent caution. Instead of immediately invading the duchies of Schleswig and Holstein with his *own* troops, Bismarck sought to have Saxon and Hanoverian troops, representing the Confederation of German States, invade Holstein. Troops of these lesser German states would be far less threatening to the great powers than those of Austria and Prussia. Additionally, these troops would enter only Holstein, which was almost completely German-speaking, in contrast to Schleswig, which had a fairly large Danish component. It was only after Holstein had been occupied successfully, without serious bloodshed and also without serious opposition from the great powers, that Austrian and Prussian troops entered Holstein and then moved against Schleswig as well.[15] It was Bismarck's keen appreciation of the system's possibilities, combined with flexibility and caution, which yielded success in this, as in his next venture of war with his former ally, Austria. And finally, war would come with Bismarck's undeclared yet nominal supporter, France. Napoleon III, who enjoyed the humbling of France's ancient enemy, Austria, would later experience the same consequence himself, after Sedan.

Although the goals would change after 1871 and the unification of Germany, the methods were the same. Now, instead of war to unify Germany under a Prussian hegemony, the goal was to keep the peace, with Berlin as Europe's diplomatic center. Here, the shifting alliances, deviousness, and ready *volte-face* were again to be characteristic of Bismarck's *modus operandi*, but now with stability as the goal. For example, even as the *Dreikaiserbund* was uniting Austria-Hungary, Germany and Russia, in a rather loosely knit Three Emperors' League between 1873 and 1878 (which was strengthened in 1881 and continued until 1887), with the purpose now of diplomatically isolating France, Bismarck had prepared an even stronger commitment to mutual defense between Germany and Austria-Hungary alone (consummated in 1879). Or consider the Reinsurance Treaty of 1887 between Germany and Russia, which was designed to replace the *Dreikaiserbund* on behalf of Germany's interests in the east; or even consider the occasional alliance overtures to France that the French could not seriously accept, given the continued German retention of Alsace-Lorraine, but that nevertheless would keep them off guard and perhaps less ready to plan for a war of *revanche*. These alliances—whether hinted at, consummated, or overlapping—were the mechanisms by which Bismarck sought to keep the peace in Europe precisely on his own terms. The fact that he intended to honor none of these commitments or, more accurately, that he would honor them only if it suited his purpose, distinguishes his diplomacy from that of Kaiser Wilhelm II later in the century.

After Wilhelm II dismissed Bismarck in 1890, German reliance on Austria-Hungary was to be virtually complete. From a generally European—and in that sense international—diplomacy, Germany now moved toward an exclusively bilateral policy. It was this stark contrast in policy which was to do much to escalate the 1914 summer crisis into world war, for the Balkan entanglements of Austria-Hungary now also were to become those of Germany after the assassination of Archduke Francis Ferdinand and the issuance of the "blank check" to the Austrians to do as they wished with Serbia. Germany promised continued support to Austria-Hungary, come what may. Bismarck, of course, never would have stepped into that quagmire.

Which norms can be said now to have been reflected so clearly by Bismarck's policies? Clearly, the norm of randomness is one that emerges most decisively. It was a randomness in timing and a choice of alliance partners (and their rejection) that Bismarck used so effectively, both in the unification process and in the keeping of the peace thereafter. Here is a characteristic of the balance-of-power system that Bismarck captured and made his own. A randomness and hence an unpredictability that Morton Kaplan explicitly put forward as the memoryless property of that system: "Permit defeated or constrained essential national actors to re-enter the system as acceptable role partners or act to bring some previously inessential actor within the essential actor classification. Treat all essential actors as acceptable role partners."[16] Two empirical tests of this essentially random and memoryless property of the nineteenth-century alliance system have confirmed its empirical validity.[17]

As manifested by Bismarck, first, his ostensibly unyielding hostility to Austria gave way quickly to the allied Austro-Prussian war against Denmark in 1864. This was followed almost immediately by war with his former ally, Austria, in 1866, to be succeeded finally by war with his nominal supporter, France, in 1870. Prior friendships or enmities did not in any way affect his decision making. After the formation of the German Empire, the shifting and overlapping alliances continued, but this time with the goal of preventing war, or at least one of *revanche,* by France against the new Germany. The methods were a honed, refined, and exquisitely applied version of the time-honored classical balance of power; but now they were being used for the interests of first Prussia and then Germany.

Yet another perspective exists from which to view Bismarck's policies. This is the concept of randomness as put forward by information theory.[18] According to this view, the greater the randomness of a sequence (numbers, letters, policies), the greater its complexity and incompressibility. This means that the sequence is not reducible to any simpler form or, put another way, there exists no formula or code that will reproduce the sequence other than the sequence itself. The randomness or, in this interpretation, the complexity of the sequence of Bismarck's policies was such that it is highly unlikely that one could reduce it to a simpler form. In this sense, of course, it was unpredictable, and it gave, first, Prussia, and, later, Germany a distinct advantage in their international affairs. It was only when these policies become predictable, after Bismarck's departure from the scene, that the dangers of systemic war were heightened. A polarization was allowed to develop wherein first, the Dual Alliance between Austria-Hungary and Germany was allowed to become a fixture of international life (nominally the Triple Alliance after Italy's accession in 1882), to be followed in 1894 by the Franco-Russian alliance and, later, the Triple Entente after the accession of England in 1907. Instead of a random alternation in partners and timing, a fixedness and consequently a polarized alliance system was allowed to set in. This of course made the systemic aspect of World War I more likely to occur. In this sense, the policies after 1890 constituted a strong departure from previous norms; they were radically different from the earlier ones of Bismarck. Wilhelm II was the revolutionary, but he was not a leader of consequence. Bismarck was a leader of consequence, but he was not a revolutionary.

In his randomness and unpredictability, Bismarck did not introduce innovations into the system. As I noted earlier, these elements were found throughout the nineteenth-century European system of alliances. What Bismarck did better than anyone else, at least in his own time, was to comprehend this essential property of the system and to reflect its use to the point where deviousness, half-truths, and lies could be the instrument of policy just as well as the bold truth, which Bismarck also used effectively. In other words, the precise means for attempting the goal of unpredictability, hence surprise, against an opponent were unimportant as long as that goal was achieved.

Another element of Bismarck's policies was especially evident after 1871, but had also been present earlier; it deserves comment. This was his attempt to establish international hierarchies that were conducive, if not to peace, at least to the absence of systemic war. This finding emerged from several studies of the role of the hierarchical equilibrium in preventing systemic war.[19] The hierarchical equilibrium has two components: (a) two or more hierarchies (alliances or loosely knit empires), including several small powers and a great power at the head of each, and (b) a relatively large number of small powers independent of any of the alliances headed by the great powers. Although Bismarck did not maintain such a hierarchy for very long, especially after 1871 (it was incorporated within the new Germany), at the root of his policies was an effort to establish just such a relationship with allies. As A. J. P. Taylor put it, "He controlled his allies: he did not cooperate with them. There indeed was the deepest element. In international affairs, as in domestic politics, Bismarck disliked equals; he sought for satellites."[20] Even when the close ally was another great power, as was the case with Austria-Hungary after 1879, Bismarck made efforts, which were frequently successful, to dictate the policies of that ally.

A basic reason for the success of this hierarchical property in preventing systemic war is the absence of memory associated with the hierarchy. The great power is free to act as it pleases in its relations with other powers without the necessity for responsiveness to its own allies and their traditional foreign-policy concerns or "memories." A striking illustration of the absence of alliance memory is found in the Cuban missile crisis of 1962 in which the Cubans were not allowed by the Soviets to crusade against United States "imperialism" in the Caribbean. At each such attempt, the Soviets quickly curtailed these efforts. Thus, the crisis could proceed as a superpower confrontation without any of the past local animosities that the Cubans had felt toward the United States. In contrast, the 1914 summer crisis allowed the historic parochial interests of southeastern Europe to exert a truly extraordinary and disproportionate effect on the outbreak of World War I.

In the latter instance, the interests of the Austro-Hungarians in the Balkans and especially Serbia were allowed to influence the course of events leading to war between the Dual Alliance and the Triple Entente. It was precisely the perceived dependence of the German decision makers on the Austro-Hungarians in 1914 which led to Germany's issuance of the blank check to Austria-Hungary to do as it wished with Serbia and which escalated the summer crisis of that year immeasurably. Bismarck, however, as we have seen, "scattered promises so as not to carry them out."[21] Thus, his dependence on Austria-Hungary was in reality minimal, and in time of crisis, it probably would have had little impact on the outcome. Bismarck's policies approximated the consequences of hierarchy in minimizing dependence on an ally, and even when at war prior to 1871, Bismarck took special care to minimize the risk of an emergent systemic war. This, of course, was especially true after 1871.

A reason for the success of the second component of the hierarchical equilibrium—namely, a large number of small independent powers—is that their presence leads to the possibility of positive-sum or at least constant-sum games, instead of the destructive zero-sum variety. There exists a long history of the use of small sovereign states as vehicles of cooperation. The entire settlement at the Congress of Vienna turned on the future of the small countries in relation to the great powers. Poland, which already had been dismembered during the late eighteenth century, continued under Russian, Prussian, and Austrian control. A portion of Saxony and of the left bank of the Rhine went to Prussia, and Austria received territories in Italy. The existence and disposition of these smaller entities avoided the breakdown of the Congress of Vienna and the possibility of a widespread war. What was perhaps even more important was the role of the so-called secondary powers in maintaining peace in central Europe.[22] This was because Austria and Prussia were continually vying for the support of these smaller states and principalities (e.g., Saxony, Hanover, Hesse-Electoral, Baden, Bavaria, Württemberg). The presence of a large number of these sovereign entities could allow one country to ally, say, with Austria, while another allied with Prussia. This hierarchical equilibrium in miniature in central Europe very likely contributed to the prevention of systemic war in Europe as a whole.

As the small powers in central Europe were being absorbed into the united Germany, Bismarck still maintained an emphasis on the positive-sum game with potential allies or supporters. He was quick to support Russia against the insurgent Poles with the expectation that Russia would give him a free hand in the coming wars of unification. He induced Austria to cooperate with him in the invasion of Denmark with the expectation that both powers would gain territory. France was constantly manipulated into covert support of Bismarck's efforts (until 1870) by the hint of additional territories that France would obtain on the Rhine if Prussia were not stalled in its ventures. This process continued well after 1871. A positive-sum political process, or at least the promise of one, was substituted for the physical presence of small powers, and as in the approximation to the consequences of an international hierarchy, this did much to prevent the onset of systemic war both before and after the unification of Germany.[23]

GEORGE WASHINGTON

I begin with the observation that Washington, like Bismarck, played a key role in unifying his country and then kept the peace very much on his own terms.

Here, however, the similarity ends abruptly. In contrast to Bismarck's genius, which all observers, including his worst enemies, acknowledged, Washington was not thought to be a brilliant man. "His mind was great and powerful," said Thomas Jefferson, but it was not "of the very first order. . . . It was slow in operation, being little aided by invention or imagination, but sure in conclusion."[24] Washington himself on more than one occasion noted his "inferior endowments from nature."[25]

In the successful performance of his duties, Washington also differed markedly from Bismarck. Bismarck erred hardly at all in his relentless quest for Prussian greatness and (in consequence) German unity, especially after he had found his sure footing as chief minister to the Prussian king, Wilhelm I. Washington's armies suffered a succession of disasters and defeats partly through his own mistakes.[26] While Bismarck needed military help from virtually no one, it may be fair to say that if the French had not come to the aid of Washington's armies, the United States today might be some latter-day version of the "United Colonies of North America." Unlike Bismarck, whose charismatic personality was said to exert a nearly hypnotic spell over listeners such as Wilhelm I, Washington was not so abundantly endowed. As a speaker he "never outgrew a heavy, somewhat clumsy manner," and as a writer he lacked elegance.[27] He inspired respect among his troops and followers but he did not inspire devotion; to that extent, he shared a similarity with Bismarck.

What, then, accounts for Washington's being venerated first as the commander of the continental armies and later as president? As Douglas S. Freeman, in his introduction to one of his six volumes on the life of Washington, observed: "The transformation of the quiet Virginia planter into the revered continental commander is . . . beyond documentary explanation."[28] Drawing upon Emile Durkheim, Barry Schwartz has offered the theory of Washington as a symbolic leader.[29] Durkheim observed:

> In the present day just as much as in the past, we see society constantly creating sacred things out of ordinary ones. If it happens to fall in love with a man and if it thinks it has found in him the principal aspirations that move it, as well as the means of satisfying them, this man will be raised above the others and, as it were, deified. . . . And the fact that it is society alone which is the author of these varieties of apotheosis, is evident since it frequently chances to consecrate men thus who have no right to it from their own merit.[30]

From this perspective, Washington was chosen more for what he was *not* than for what he was, because it was the republican and Whig tradition which found in him the object of veneration. In its military garb, this tradition demanded, first, that Washington *not* be the superb military commander that would appear to be required. The image of Oliver Cromwell was in the people's minds as one who did indeed demonstrate military genius and at the same time usurped power. Because of the Americans' basic distrust of all political authority and especially standing armies, a Cromwell-type leader was especially distasteful.[31] The citizen-soldier, not the charismatic leader-hero, was to be at the heart of the Continental Army. Moreover, the colonists had a religious belief in the rightness of their cause in the war against Britain; it was as if the "hand of Heaven" were directing their Revolution.[32] Under these circumstances, all that was required was that the virtue of the combatants be harnessed by the republican leader. A military hero was not necessary for victory, and indeed, as the Provincial Congress of the colony of New York stated to Washington a few weeks after his appointment, "We have . . . the fullest assurances, that whenever this important contest shall be decided, . . . you will cheerfully resign the important deposit committed into your hands, and re-assume the character of our worthy citizen."[33]

Upon becoming president, Washington passed from the status of republican military hero to moral symbol. All of the Whig virtues of justice, temperance, courage, honesty, integrity, sobriety, and rationality were seen to be reflected by Washington, in addition to his principal public virtue of the forbearance of power. In the Anglo-American Whig tradition, especially as it developed in the colonies, power was to be distrusted in the extreme. Indeed, the maintenance of individual liberty, so precious to the Revolutionary colonists, was dependent on the restraint of power. Power was thought of as having an "encroaching nature," as "elastic," "grasping," and "tenacious." It was also "restless," "aspiring," and "insatiable."[34] Washington's eight years of military command, during which he obeyed Congress and did not in any way attempt to usurp authority, was a strong affirmation of civilian control of the military. This was in the republican Whig tradition, which, as we shall see, provides a strong contrast to Bismarck's policies.

Washington's haste in relinquishing his commission to Congress at the end of the war further distanced him from the image of the power-hungry military hero to be distrusted and feared. The necessity for persistent appeals by his countrymen to take up the presidency further augmented the trust and veneration of Americans. At his funeral, the most striking eulogies pointed to his willingness to resign his commission and finally, as a capstone to his republican career of military and civic virtue, to refuse a third term as president, which probably would have assured his becoming the first American monarch. As Schwartz put it, "The ultimate grounds of Washington's veneration is not prowess, but morality; not achievement, but virtue. . . . Against [the European] conception, with its emphasis on entitlement, privilege, and strength, the ideal of heroic leadership that took root in eighteenth-century America stressed the republican virtues of obligation, sacrifice, and disinterestedness."[35] Or according to the German scholar Johannes Kuhn: "It is not easy for Europeans to comprehend the significance of a man like

Washington. We are too accustomed to seek human greatness in unusual talents and gifts of an individual nature.''[36]

The Old Testament leaders, such as Joshua, Gideon, David, and principally, Moses, were the standards against which Washington was compared in the eulogies. Given the religious convictions of the early colonists and especially their view of themselves as latter-day Children of Israel, this is to be expected. But Washington also was compared favorably to more contemporary leaders, such as Alexander, Caesar, Cromwell, Peter the Great, and Napoleon. All of these leaders exhibited the sins of intemperance and the thirst for power and conquest so clearly absent from Washington's career. As such, he was symbolic of the deepest religious and political traditions of the American people.

In this sense, he also was the quintessential norm-reflecting leader, but of a very different set of norms than was Bismarck. Whereas Bismarck in many respects conformed to the Weberian model of the charismatic leader, Washington in most respects was its antithesis. Yet, the fundamental similarity is that both deeply reflected the particular norms of their time and place and acted upon those norms successfully without introducing any significant changes. (Structurally, of course, the sovereignty and unification of both the United States and Germany were fundamental changes, but they respectively grew out of norms of freedom and nationalism that already had been entrenched in both societies before these leaders came on the scene.)

Each leader was firmly rooted in his party and in his class. Bismarck was ever a Junker who derived his domestic political philosophy from the agrarian, conservative squirearchy of East Prussia. Although this led to an early intolerance of the more cosmopolitan and industrialized regions of the west, bordering the Rhine, he ultimately learned to appreciate the contributions of industry and finance to Prussian and, later, German power. Washington was a member of the Virginia squirearchy, which he, unlike Bismarck, was eager to return to permanently. (Bismarck frequently expressed interest in returning to his estate, but he seldom did so except when ill.) Washington also was a Whig, with a deep attachment to the values of that ideology and party. From this perspective, too, there was no necessity for the introduction of any normative change.

There is an irony in the absence of normative change in the new Germany of 1871, especially as highlighted by Washington's career. For although Bismarck had his quarrels with the military, which he typically won, nevertheless he failed to establish the principle of the supremacy of the civilian authority over the military, which Washington confirmed so emphatically in his relations with Congress. Bismarck was content to win his battles with Helmuth von Moltke (ultimately Chief of the German General Staff), on an individual basis, without ever establishing the principle of civilian control.[37] Perhaps Bismarck did not even want to establish this principle, for he himself was so proud of obtaining the (largely honorary) rank of lieutenant general in the Prussian army that he wore the uniform on virtually all occasions. Or perhaps he thought that civilian supremacy could not be established in the Prussianized environment of the new Germany. For whatever reason, this failure was to have a grave impact on the Germany of Bismarck's creation.

After Bismarck's fall from power, a new military figure, perhaps even more formidable politically than Moltke, arrived on the scene in the form of Alfred von Tirpitz. Without the constraints of civilian control, the navy bills that Tirpitz demanded were repeatedly passed, thus alarming the British, spurring a naval arms race, and eventually forcing Great Britain to join with France and Russia to form the Triple Entente. It was the dominating figure of Tirpitz, without a Bismarck to stand in his way, along with other concessions to the military, which hastened the coming of World War I and the unraveling of the edifice that Bismarck had created.

There is a double irony in that the German navy was virtually useless in deciding the outcome of World War I, especially after 1916 and the Battle of Jutland. If the steel and other material that had been used in building these great capital ships had been diverted to the production of artillery and other useful ordnance, the outcome of the war might have been very different, and it might have been decided at a much earlier stage.

And what of Washington's foreign policies after he became president? Perhaps they can be summarized by his Farewell Address, which counseled against all foreign entanglements. His alliance policies could be represented by the single number zero. Surely this represents a stark contrast to the endlessly complex and incompressible policies of Bismarck. Yet here, too, as in the norm-reflecting (non-norm-creating) property, there is a basic similarity. In both cases, the operational code is incompressible. There could be no simpler representation of their operational codes than the codes themselves. Put another way, despite the vast differences in practice, there is a purity of policy expression in both cases, a policy that specifies either no activity of a certain type or random activity that is incapable of reduction to simpler forms. Perhaps this in itself is one hallmark of greatness, to be compared with, for example, Churchill's unwavering antagonism toward Nazi Germany or Metternich's single-minded pursuit of a conservative monarchical order in early-nineteenth-century Europe.

Yet in a fundamental way, the similarity goes deeper still. Despite the existence of many alliances, Bismarck, as Taylor so aptly put it, "scattered promises so as not to carry them out."[38] Thus the entanglements were more illusory than real, more for the preservation of German options and the isolation of France than for any real international commitment. In practice, Bismarck's degree of real entanglement was very close to zero, in accordance with Washington's prescription.

RICHARD M. NIXON

As an epilogue to this comparison it is intriguing to consider the adoption of certain Bismarckian-type policies by a leader in an American context. Probably the most effective expression of this synthesis was the presidency of Richard Nixon. The truncation of his second term by other, but perhaps related, events will provide a commentary on the success of this type of synthesis.

It is clear from Nixon's choice of Henry Kissinger to be national security advisor and, later, secretary of state that Nixon at least at some level appreciated the intricacies and unpredictabilities of Bismarckian-type policies. Kissinger, after all, had written widely about the European states system and had expressed his appreciation for certain of the stabilities inherent in the nineteenth-century European system.[39] The Nixon-Kissinger approach to policy reflected many of these elements.

First, on the negative side, there was the deviousness, for example, of the bombing of Cambodia and the subsequent invasion of that country. The duplicity shown by Nixon and Kissinger would have been worthy of Bismarck. Yet there was much that was positive, as in the three major policy successes of the Nixon administration, namely, the signing of the ABM Treaty with the Soviet Union in 1972, the opening to China, and the laying of the foundation of the Camp David Accords after the 1973 Arab-Israeli War. Each of these was to reflect the unpredictability and essential randomness to be found in Bismarck's reflection of essentially European norms but now to be found in an American foreign-policy-making context.

The ABM Treaty was a classic instance of reaching an accord with a longstanding enemy. Despite Nixon's long record of anti-Communist rhetoric and activity (and perhaps, in a sense, because of it), he could, in a surprising fashion, reach an accord with an old enemy, much as Bismarck did with Austria in 1873 and the *Dreikaiserbund*. The opening to China was a classic illustration of the random shifting of alliances, even among former combatants, as Morton Kaplan's memoryless rule of the balance-of-power system suggests. And the efforts to introduce the memoryless condition in the Middle East—or the institutionalization of forgetting—is a classic illustration of the attempt to use nineteenth-century methods in a twentieth-century context, perhaps in a highly successful manner.[40] All of these events were unexpected at the time, and in this sense of unpredictability, they also conform to the Bismarckian and nineteenth-century European tradition.

Yet this grafting of the European tradition on the American, although highly successful in the foreign-policy arena, failed in the domestic context, as perhaps our analysis of Washington might have foretold. Watergate and the unfortunate and ludicrous incident of White House uniforms that appeared to be from a Gilbert and Sullivan operetta also seemed to emerge from a European tradition of secrecy, duplicity, and the signs of privilege (even in Britain, the

Official Secrets Act comes close to this), not to mention the violation of constitutional principles for very narrowly defined "reasons of state." If President Nixon had been able to confine these borrowed practices to our now-active involvement in international affairs and to omit them from the domestic scene entirely, then his presidency probably would have been far more successful.

Within the frame of reference of this study, one can ask, What were the particular norms that were being reflected by the Nixon policies? Clearly, in a sense, they were borrowed from Kissinger's interpretation of the nineteenth-century environment; whether Nixon selected Kissinger in advance to implement those policies or was later influenced by his national security advisor is substantially irrelevant. In the international environment, these policies were, for the most part, highly successful; domestically, they were not. (The Cambodian case traverses both arenas.) Perhaps we can understand the latter syndrome by the importation of the former into an inappropriate domestic context.

The international environment of Bismarck's day, as at present, is one based on the preservation of the security interests of the state. Carried to its extreme as the sole raison d'être of interstate policy, it becomes the practice of realpolitik, whether used by Bismarck, by Kissinger, or earlier by the master craftsman, Metternich. According to this view, which is somewhat akin to that of Thomas Hobbes, the security interest of the state frequently must be ensured at the expense of other states, which is of course a zero-sum process. Thus, chicanery is justified by realpolitik, as are false promises or any other means that can yield the desired end of state security. Bismarck's world of central Europe was one in which Prussia, at virtually all points in her history, was surrounded by relatively large potential enemies, namely, Russia, Austria, France, Denmark, Poland, and Sweden. At some point in that history, Prussia was at war with every one of these states, either singly or in combination. This historical and geopolitical environment shaped Bismarck's world view and ultimately was probably used by him to justify his policies. For at all times in his adult life, he was a committed Pietist.

The United States, of course, was hardly in that position, because it had emerged to sovereignty in relative isolation from the European powers. Thus Washington could recommend the avoidance of foreign entanglements with the full knowledge that this injunction was consistent with and perhaps would even maximize the security of the United States. The avoidance of the world of European realpolitik and its derogation of virtue also was consistent with the domestic environment, which demanded such virtue. Although the United States emerged full bore into that world of foreign entanglements during the twentieth century, thus suggesting the use of some of Bismarck's methods, the *domestic* normative environment of the United States had changed much less. The domestic virtues of legality and adherence to constitutional principles still were in full force. Nixon's reflection of an inappropriate European-originated normative environment within the domestic context, then, was doomed to failure.

CONCLUSION

I have compared Bismarck and Washington as leaders, and I have included Nixon as an instance of a successful international leader who either willingly or inadvertently imposed an alien normative standard on the domestic environment, to his ruin.[41] A final question arises as to reasons for the likely failure of a uniform normative standard imposed on international life. (The failure of the League of Nations and the present political impotence of the United Nations are cases in point.) In providing an explanation, I will avoid the fairly obvious and, in the final accounting, analytically trivial explanation of differing cultural-normative systems among the world's nations. One need only look to the Swiss example or to that of Belgium or, indeed, China throughout much of its history to counter that argument. Perhaps the successes of our leader-illustrations will provide a clue.

In all instances of international leadership treated here, the successful leader took immediate and effective advantage of opportunities the system offered.[42] Bismarck immediately saw a golden opportunity in the Danish king's proclamation of a unitary constitution, as he saw an opportunity for exploitation in Napoleon III's grandiosity, vanity, and need for foreign victories, coupled with ill health, which could have seriously impaired his judgment. A decision by one foreign monarch and the health of another are essentiallly random events in the international system. Such events can provide threats or opportunities as they are responded to by national leaders. Washington saw the essentially randomly generated geopolitical isolation of the fledgling United States as an opportunity for the unhampered growth and development of the new country. For Nixon and Kissinger, the ending of the Vietnam War and the onset and termination of another—the 1973 Middle East War—presented opportunities (again random events) for, respectively, the opening to China and the laying of the foundations for the Camp David Accords, which included as a consequence, the vastly increased influence of the United States in the Middle East.

Here, the random universe of the international system is a generator of opportunities for the astute national leader. The imposition of a new normative system on such a chaotic universe, on the other hand, would generate difficulties of such an excessive order that they might prove unmanageable, as demonstrated by the failure of the League of Nations and the political impotence of the United Nations. The last such moderately successful effort was the Congress of Vienna, which led to the Congress system that degenerated fairly quickly into the random formation and termination of alliances typical of a balance-of-power system.[43] The fact that the Congress system was so loosely constructed that both democratic Britain and autocratic Russia could participate initially and then each one shortly thereafter could go its own way without war suggests the limits of what may be tolerably imposed on an international system repeatedly exposed to serious random disturbances. Each of our successful leaders was far too prescient to attempt to impose a normative order on such a system. Indeed, the hallmarks of both Bismarck's and Washington's successes were creative national leadership, consistent with the existing domestic norms but without any real normative innovations, and an equally creative international leadership, which maximized the randomly generated opportunities. If Nixon could have maintained the former condition while continuing his successful adherence to the latter, then he would have been a formidable leader indeed.

NOTES

1. Quoted in Edward Crankshaw, *Bismarck* (New York: Viking, 1981), p. 1.

2. For an analysis of de Gaulle's leadership from a quasi-Weberian perspective see Monique Clague, "Conceptions of Leadership," *Political Theory* 3 (Nov. 1975): 423–40.

3. Kenneth W. Thompson develops the notion of a tension between the need for a mystique for the charismatic leader and the simultaneous need for support at the grass roots. For Bismarck, the latter was not a necessity in the autocratic Prussia of his day, whereas Washington was not a charismatic leader. Thus, the following comparison between the two leaders is not affected by this tension. See Thompson, "The Dilemmas and Antinomies of Leadership," *Presidential Studies Quarterly* 14 (Winter 1984): 35–42.

4. For a treatment of non-Western leadership see Lucian W. Pye, "Mao Tse-tung's Leadership Style," *Political Science Quarterly* 91 (Summer 1976): 219–35. Robert C. Tucker analyzes the problem of personality in general, with a special emphasis on the creative leader, in his "Personality and Political Leadership," ibid., 92 (Fall 1977): 383–93. Other highly useful perspectives on leadership which explore the personality dimensions of the individual leader are Erwin C. Hargrove's *Presidential Leadership: Personality and Political Style* (New York: Macmillan, 1966) and Jameson W. Doig and Erwin C. Hargrove's "'Leadership' and Political Analysis," in *Leadership and Innovation: A Biographical Perspective on Entrepreneurs in Government*, ed. Jameson W. Doig and Erwin C. Hargrove (Baltimore, Md.: Johns Hopkins University Press, 1987), pp. 1–23. In the following analysis, the interface between the leader and the societal normative structure is the focus of investigation, instead of the individual leader per se.

5. See Weber's *The Theory of Social and Economic Organization*, trans. A. M. Henderson and Talcott Parsons (New York: Free Press, 1964), and Burns's *Leadership* (New York: Harper & Row, 1978).

6. A fascinating problem attendant upon charismatic leadership is its institutionalization. For an analysis of this process in the context of Mao's, Qaddafi's, and Castro's leadership see Jean C. Robinson, "Institutionalizing Charisma: Leadership, Faith and Rationality in Three Societies," *Polity* (Winter 1985): 181–203.

7. See Thomas E. Cronin, "Thinking and Learning about Leadership," *Presidential Studies Quarterly* 14 (Winter 1984): 28.

8. Quoted by George F. Kennan in *The Decline of Bismarck's European Order: Franco-Russian Relations, 1875–1890* (Princeton, N.J.: Princeton University Press, 1979), p. 177.

9. Crankshaw, *Bismarck,* 132.

10. For excellent treatments of Bismarck during the period of unification and beyond see Erich Eyck, *Bismarck and the German Empire* (London: George Allen & Unwin, 1950); Otto Pflanze, *Bismarck and the Development of Germany: The Period of Unification, 1815–1871* (Princeton, N.J.: Princeton University Press, 1963); and A. J. P. Taylor, *Bismarck: The Man and the Statesman* (New York: Knopf, 1955).

11. Crankshaw, *Bismarck,* p. 394.

12. Ibid., p. 4.

13. Ibid., p. 168.

14. A. J. P. Taylor, *The Struggle for Mastery in Europe, 1848–1918* (Oxford: Oxford University Press, 1971), p. 278.

15. For descriptions of these events see James Joll, "Prussia and the German Problem, 1830–66," in *The New Cambridge Modern History,* vol. 10, ed. J. P. T. Bury (Cambridge: Cambridge University Press, 1964), pp. 493–521; and G. Roloff, "Bismarck and German Unity," in *The Cambridge Modern History,* vol. 11, ed. A. W. Ward, G. W. Prothero, and Stanley Leathes (Cambridge, Eng.: Cambridge University Press, 1934), pp. 432–66.

16. Morton Kaplan, *System and Process in International Politics* (New York: Wiley, 1957), p. 23.

17. See Manus I. Midlarsky, "Absence of Memory in the Nineteenth-Century Alliance System," *American Journal of Political Science* 27 (Nov. 1983): 762–84, and "Equilibria in the Nineteenth-Century Balance-of-Power System," ibid., 25 (May 1981): 270–96.

18. See Gregory J. Chaitin, "Randomness and Mathematical Proof," *Scientific American* 232 (May 1975): 47–52.

19. These studies are found in Manus I. Midlarsky, *The Onset of World War* (Boston, Mass.: Unwin Hyman, 1988), and "A Hierarchical Equilibrium Theory of Systemic War," *International Studies Quarterly* 30 (Mar. 1986): 77–105.

20. Taylor, *Struggle for Mastery,* p. 280.

21. Ibid., p. 278.

22. For a description of this process see Henry A. Kissinger, *A World Restored: Metternich, Castlereagh and the Problems of Peace, 1812–1822* (Boston, Mass.: Houghton Mifflin, 1957), pp. 235–36.

23. Midlarsky, "Equilibria in the Nineteenth-Century," p. 290.

24. Thomas Jefferson, "Letter to Walter Jones," in *A Jefferson Profile, as Revealed in His Letters,* ed. Saul K. Padover (New York: John Day, 1956), p. 227.

25. Quoted by Barry Schwartz in "George Washington and the Whig Conception of Heroic Leadership," *American Sociological Review* 48 (Feb. 1983): 20.

26. See John W. Daniel, "Oration by Hon. John W. Daniel," *History of the Washington National Monument and Washington National Monument Society,* 57th Cong., 2d sess., Senate Document, vol. 21, no. 224 (Washington, D.C.: Government Printing Office, 1903), pp. 260–85, esp. 274–75.

27. Dixon Wecter, *The Hero in America: A Chronicle of Hero Worship* (New York: Scribner's, 1941), p. 102.

28. Douglas S. Freeman, *George Washington,* vol. 3 (New York: Scribner's, 1951), p. xiii.

29. Schwartz, "George Washington."

30. Emile Durkheim, *The Elementary Forms of the Religious Life,* trans. Joseph W. Swain (New York: Free Press, 1954), pp. 212–13.

31. Schwartz, "George Washington."

32. Quoted by Catherine L. Albanese in *Sons of the Fathers: The Civil Religion of the American Revolution* (Philadelphia: Temple University Press, 1976), p. 83.

33. *Virginia Gazette,* no. 1249, July 15, 1775, p. 3.

34. For the development of these ideas see Jackson Turner Main, *The Antifederalists: Critics of the Constitution, 1781–1788* (Chapel Hill: University of North Carolina Press, 1961), p. 127; and Cecelia M. Kenyon, "Men of Little Faith: The Anti-Federalists on the Nature of Representative Government," *William and Mary Quarterly* 12, 3d ser. (Jan. 1955): 3–43.

35. Schwartz, "George Washington," pp. 28, 30.

36. Johannes Kuhn, "Address to George Washington Bicentennial Banquet, Dresden," in *History of the George Washington Bicentennial Celebration* (Washington, D.C.: United States George Washington Bicentennial Commission, 1932), p. 142, quoted in Schwartz, "George Washington," p. 30.

37. Crankshaw, *Bismarck,* pp. 287–94.

38. Taylor, *Struggle for Mastery,* p. 278.

39. See, e.g., Kissinger, *A World Restored.*

40. See Midlarsky, "Absence of Memory," pp. 782–83.

41. I do not claim that all of President Nixon's behavior in the Watergate incident derived from his international posture. Certainly there were deeper psychological reasons for this behavior. Nevertheless, to the extent that he sought personal and political status and the freedom to engage in whichever policies he chose, for whatever narrowly defined political purpose, his extensive involvement in Bismarckian-type international affairs must have exerted some impact on his overall decision making. For a treatment of the Nixon presidency and others from a psychological perspective see, e.g., James D. Barber, *The Presidential Character,* 2d ed. (Englewood Cliffs, N.J.: Prentice-Hall, 1977).

42. One might recast this statement in the form of a "situation favorability," which has been found to be correlated with leadership effectiveness in groups, along with perceived environmental uncertainty. See Delbert M. Nebeker, "Situational Favorability and Perceived Environmental Uncertainty: An Integrative Approach," *Administrative Science Quarterly* 20 (June 1975): 281–94.

43. One could interpret this as a collegial leadership which has been found to be successful in the Swiss experience but obviously has had limited historical application. See Thomas A. Baylis, "Collegial Leadership in Advanced Industrial Societies: The Relevance of the Swiss Experience," *Polity* 13 (Fall 1980): 33–56.

PART 3

Leadership in an Institutional Context

10

Presidential Leadership of Congress: The Role of Legislative Skills

George C. Edwards III

The government of the United States is not a fertile field for the exercise of presidential leadership. Nowhere is this more clear than in dealing with Congress. Every president bears scars from his battles with the legislature. Each finds that his proposals often fail to pass and that legislators champion initiatives to which he is opposed. Yet, this predicament makes presidential leadership all the more necessary.

The peculiar merging of powers between the two institutions established by the Constitution prevents either one from acting unilaterally on most important matters. Moreover, the differences in the constituencies, internal structures, time perspectives, and decision-making procedures of the two branches guarantee that the branches will often view issues and policy proposals differently.[1] As a result, these features of our political system, as well as the conflicts they generate, virtually compel the president to attempt to lead Congress.

Extraconstitutional processes, such as the preparation of an elaborate legislative program in the White House, have evolved in response to the system's need for centralization. Yet such changes only provide instruments for presidents to employ as they try to obtain support from the legislature. These instruments carry no guarantee of success and are no substitute for leadership.

As we would expect, presidential-congressional relations have attracted considerable scholarly attention over the years. Furthermore, the volume of commentary on them in the press is little short of overwhelming. Despite this activity, we have a long way to go before we can claim to understand presidential leadership in Congress.

Many of the scholarly writings on presidential-congressional relations focus on topics such as the appropriate powers of each branch.[2] Others describe and analyze the institutions and processes involved in interactions between the president and Congress.[3] These are unquestionably important matters, but works on them are not principally concerned with the question of leadership.

Although interest in leadership has increased during recent years, it remains an elusive phenomenon. There is little consensus even on what leadership is. According to James MacGregor Burns, "Leadership is one of the most observed and least understood phenomenon on earth."[4] Barbara Kellerman lists ten different definitions of political leadership.[5]

Our lack of understanding of presidential leadership is not without costs. The media abound with inferences about the impact of presidential leadership, references to "mandates," "deals," threats, and the like—all of which are based on little or no systematic evidence and seemingly little reflection. More than a few academics have fallen into the same trap. As a result, discourse on presidential-congressional relations in both the press and the academy is less illuminating than it might be. An aide to President Carter expressed his frustration at our confusion when he compared the Carter and Reagan administrations:

> I could not help but laugh when [President Reagan] got credited with great legislative victories, when he succeeded in getting a twenty-five percent reduction in taxes over a three year period. Contrast that with what we had to do, with the windfall profits tax, the largest tax increase in the history of the republic. . . . And we got it through. The public perception was that when we did it, it was because we did not screw up; when they did it, it was because of their legislative brilliance.[6]

Gerald Ford was recently asked what, from his perspective, could be done to improve presidential-congressional relations. The response of the former president, who had served in Congress for a quarter century, longer than any other chief executive, is poignant testimony to the need to devote more attention to the question of presidential leadership in Congress. He simply replied, "I don't know."[7]

Another disadvantage of our lack of understanding of executive-legislative relations is the potential for distortion of both our expectations and our evaluations of presidential leadership. The notion of the dominant president who moves the country (including Congress) through his strong and effective leadership has deep roots in our political culture. Those chief executives whom we revere, such as Washington, Jefferson, Jackson, Lincoln, Wilson, and both Roosevelts, have taken on mythic proportions as leaders. Moreover, even though we are frequently disillusioned with the performance of presidents and even though we recognize that stalemates are frequent in our political system, we eagerly accept what appears to be effective presidential leadership, as in the case of Ronald Reagan in 1981, as evidence on which to renew our faith in the potential of the presidency. After all, if presidential leadership "works" some of the time, why doesn't it work all of the time?

Such an orientation directly influences our expectations and evaluations of the president. If it is reasonable to expect successful leadership from the White House, then failures of leadership are simply personal deficiencies. If problems arise because the leader (the president) lacks the proper will, skills, or understanding, then solutions to our perennial leadership needs are straightforward and simple. All we have to do is to elect a person to the presidency who is willing and able to lead. Since the system is malleable under the appropriate leadership, it will function smoothly with the right leader in the Oval Office. We can indulge in high expectations of the president, and we can freely criticize him if he fails to bend Congress to his point of view. The blame lies clearly in the leader, rather than in the environment of leadership. We need not concern ourselves with broader forces in American society that may influence executive-legislative relations. Because these conditions may be complex and perhaps intractable, the focus on the individual as leader simplifies both our analysis and our evaluation of problems of governing.

What, on the other hand, if presidential leadership is not the preeminent factor in executive-legislative relations? What if the potential of presidential leadership is less than holders of the conventional wisdom believe and the president actually operates at the margins in obtaining support in Congress? What if our national preoccupation with the chief executive is misplaced and our belief in the impact of the individual leader is largely a myth, a product of a search for simple solutions in an extremely complex and purposefully inefficient system in which the founding fathers' handiwork in decentralizing power prevails over even the most capable leaders?

If such a description is accurate, our expectations of the president should be less extreme, and our disappointment in his failure to lead Congress successfully should be less severe. In addition, we should focus our attention less exclusively on the president and more on the context in which the president seeks to lead Congress. We should recognize that major changes in public policy require more than just the "right" person in the job and that they do not necessarily turn on a president who fails to deliver. It does not follow that failures of presidential leadership may never be traced to the White House or that we should patiently accept the outcomes of executive-legislative relations. It does mean that we must better understand presidential leadership of Congress if we are to think sensibly about the role of the chief executive in our political system.

DIRECTOR OR FACILITATOR?

Many discussions of presidential "leadership" in Congress focus on the overall success or failure of presidents in obtaining passage of their proposals, as in accounts of Franklin Roosevelt's Hundred Days or Lyndon Johnson's Great

Society years. Most of the rest of the work in the area is in the form of case studies emphasizing the role the president's leadership skills have played, for better or worse, in the passage of a particular presidential policy. Implicit in such work is the notion that the president's leadership is a critical variable, often *the* critical variable, in determining outcomes in Congress.

Yet the premise on which this research is based begs the essential question of whether the president can indeed move Congress to do his will. Although no one seriously disputes the proposition that the White House can make a difference in Congress, we shall see that there is substantial reason to doubt that this impact is usually of great magnitude. Similarly, if Congress is sometimes responsive to the president's leadership, we should not assume that he can exercise such leadership at any one time, under any conditions. These are fundamental questions of presidential leadership that bear investigation, not presumption.

To guide our examination of presidential leadership in Congress, it is useful to contrast two broad perspectives on the presidency. According to the first, the president is the director of change. Through his leadership he creates opportunities to move in new directions, leading others where they otherwise would not go. In the role of director, he is out in front, establishing goals and encouraging others to follow.

A second perspective is less heroic but nevertheless important. According to it, the president is primarily a facilitator of change. He exploits opportunities to help others go where they want to go anyway. In the facilitator role, the president reflects and carries widely held views, using his resources to achieve his constituency's aspirations.

The director creates a constituency to follow his lead, while the facilitator endows his constituency's views with shape and purpose. The director restructures the contours of the political landscape to pave the way for change, while the facilitator exploits opportunities that are presented by a favorable configuration of political forces.

There is a third alternative, of course. This is the president who is disposed not to lead. Although such a description may accurately characterize some occupants of the Oval Office, it is not a useful heuristic device for our purposes. We may learn a great deal about leadership from those who do not succeed in their efforts, but we can learn little from those who fail to try.

We have, then, two different conceptions of leadership. First is the director, who moves mountains and influences many independent actors. He has the more formidable task because he establishes the legislative agenda and convinces an otherwise reluctant Congress to support his policies. Second is the facilitator, who, in contrast, works at the margins, influencing a few critical actors and taking advantage of the opportunities for change already present in his environment. In both cases the president exercises leadership. Yet the scale of the leadership is clearly different. The range and scope of the director's influence is broad, while that of the facilitator is narrower.

The director and the facilitator types are not meant to be representations of a division in the literature. Instead, they represent different emphases that are reflected in writings on the presidency, sometimes explicitly, but often implicitly. Moreover, the two perspectives are not neat categories. Our goal is neither to classify presidents nor to resolve an academic dispute. Instead, we employ these types to increase our understanding of leadership by exploring its possibilities. Moreover, once we understand the possibilities of leadership, we are in a better position to assess the performance of presidents.

Because of the prominence of the debate over the "great man" interpretation of history, it is useful for us to distinguish the leadership types we employ from the polar positions that characterize this issue. For the sake of convenience, let us turn to the nineteenth century, when the two sides assumed their best-known forms.

In his famous *Heroes and Hero-Worship and the Heroic in History*, published in 1841, Thomas Carlyle argued that great men alone were responsible for the direction of history. The environment of the hero, it seems, is generally malleable and is thus receptive to leadership. Viewing history from quite a different perspective, various schools of social determinists, including the Spencerians, Hegelians, and Marxists, saw history as an inexorable march in one direction, with change occurring only when the culture was ripe for it. Great men, they concluded, could not have acted differently than they had. This view is pictured perhaps most memorably in Tolstoy's portrayal of Napoleon in *War and Peace*.

Most people would agree that both of these perspectives are inadequate, and we have no need to become mired in this ancient debate. Our contrasting leadership types are much less extreme. For us, the issue is, not whether leadership matters, but how much and under what conditions. We must recognize, however, that it is not sufficient to conclude that sometimes the environment is receptive to change, whereas at other times it is not. This simply begs the question of whether leaders are able to exert a significant influence on the environment in such a way as to create the opportunity for change.

Our concern is akin to Sidney Hook's in his contrast between the "eventful man," whose actions influenced subsequent developments along different lines than if he had not acted, and "event-making man," an eventful man whose actions are consequences of outstanding capacities, rather than of the accidents of position, and who not only appears at but also helps to create the forking points in the road of history.[8]

Both the director and the facilitator types fall within Richard E. Neustadt's persuasive presidency.[9] Neustadt's outstanding contribution to the study of the presidency has alerted us to the fact that the president is not in a position to command and that he has to make the right choices and use his resources wisely to achieve his goals. What has remained unresolved is just what the potential of presidential leadership is. Is it possible to be a director? Are presidents in control of their resources, or are they highly dependent upon their environment? Answers to these questions are fundamental to understanding presidential leadership of Congress; they take on even greater significance in light of the view of presidential influence implied by the extraordinarily high expectations that Americans have of their chief executive. Our goal is to dig deeper into presidential-congressional relations and to achieve a richer understanding of how and under what conditions presidents persuade, what we can reasonably expect of chief executives, and how we should evaluate their performances.

LEGISLATIVE SKILLS

There are many facets of presidential leadership in Congress, and there are potentially important resources, such as party and public support, that may ease the burden of leading. The component of leadership that is of principal interest to us here, however, is the president's skill in dealing directly with Congress.

In 1981, Ronald Reagan's dramatic budget and tax proposals passed through Congress largely unscathed. Many observers commented upon his personal skills in dealing with Congress and offered them as at least a major reason for the president's success.[10] Yet in 1983, Republicans in the House refused even to propose, much less to vote for, the president's budget. This presents a fascinating puzzle. Had President Reagan's legislative skills diminished substantially over the preceding two years, or had they, in fact, not been a very significant factor in his early victories? More broadly, Are these skills at the core of presidential leadership, or are they significant only at the margins of coalition building, taking a back seat to more fundamental contextual factors such as a party's strength in Congress and the president's public support? Can legislative skills provide a foundation for the director, or can they only serve to support a facilitator?

There is more involved here than merely an isolated, albeit important, empirical question. The emphasis on personal skills—what James MacGregor Burns has called the "skill mystique"[11]—has important consequences for the way we evaluate the president and, more broadly, how we orient ourselves to politics. If problems of leadership simply represent personal failures, then we need not cast our sights far for a solution. All we have to do is to find a president who is skillful at persuasion and manipulation. Then, with a strong and effective leader at the helm, the ship of state will sail smoothly. We need not concern ourselves with broader forces in the polity that may influence public policy making.

If, on the other hand, presidential leadership skills constitute one of many factors, not necessarily the only factor, that influence policy making, our understanding of the presidency must be richer and our expectations of it less demanding. We should not devote our attention exclusively to the chief executive. Instead, we must focus on the context in which the president seeks to achieve his goals, always mindful of the other institutions and actors with independent power in regard to policy making. It follows directly from this orientation that there are significant constraints on what presidential skills can accomplish. Thus, change must usually involve more than an upgrading of skills through on-the-job training or a change in the occupant of the Oval Office.

THE CONVENTIONAL WISDOM

The attribution of significance to presidential legislative-leadership skills is a well-entrenched aspect of much of the writing, both popular and scholarly, on presidential-congressional relationships. Authors can chronicle and study presidential acts, and it is only natural to ascribe importance to them. The tendency of the press to focus on the more unusual aspects of these relationships, such as presidential bargaining and arm twisting, which implies that what they are presenting is typical, only reinforces the conventional wisdom.

Moreover, many reporters and correspondents, trained to focus on individual personalities and what is "new," rather than on patterns of behavior, perceive presidential success in Congress as resulting from a president's legislative skills.[12] For example, Robert Pierpoint, an experienced network White House correspondent, recently wrote of how he thought Lyndon Johnson would have garnered support for the 1977 nomination of Theodore Sorensen as director of the CIA:

> Good morinin', Mr. Chairman, this is yore President. . . . Not too well, thank you. I'm a mit unhappy that you don't seem to like my new Director of the CIA. At least that's what I read in the press. . . . Yeah, Senator, I know all that. Knew it before I nominated him. . . . Senator, I want to tell you something I been thinkin' about. You know all them military bases you got out there in Hah-wai-ee? Well, I been wonderin' if some of them bases might not be better off somewhere else . . . say Alasaka . . . or Gu-Wam. . . . No, Senator, I haven't made any decisions yet. But I do know those bases are pretty important to your people out there. . . . Oh, is that right, you've changed your mind about my appointment to head the CIA? Thank you, Senator, I thought yu'd see it my way!

Pierpoint then concludes that "that's the kind of power a president has" and criticizes President Carter for not exploiting it.[13]

The statements of participants in the legislative process also sometimes buttress the view that legislative skills are central factors in explaining presidential success in Congress. According to Lyndon Johnson, for example, "There is only one way for a President to deal with the Congress, and that is continuously, incessantly, and without interruption."[14] He believed that "merely placing a program before Congress is not enough. Without constant attention from the administration most legislation moves through the congressional process at the speed of a glacier."[15]

Some scholars have also emphasized personal legislative skills.[16] Paul Light engaged in a more systematic study of the question than most other commentators, and he concluded that legislative skills are intervening variables operating within the boundaries of presidential success set by presidential approval on the part of the public and by party strength in Congress. Presidents are more likely to obtain passage of their proposals, Light found, when they introduce their programs early and lobby for them than when they introduce programs late and fail to lobby for them.[17]

REASONS FOR SKEPTICISM

Despite these assertions and findings, there are a number of reasons to doubt the significance of presidential legislative skills in influencing Congress to support White House proposals. If presidential legislative skills have limited impact on congressional voting, we should not find systematic differences among presidents with different legislative skills in the support they received in Congress. If, on the other hand, legislative skills are an important tool of presidential leadership in Congress, then presidents with the most highly developed legislative skills should consistently receive more support than less skilled chief executives. In an intensive study of the presidents from Eisenhower through Reagan, employing four different measures of presidential support, ranging from the inclusive to the exclusive, I found that there was little variance between presidents who were highly skilled, such as Lyndon Johnson, and others who had a reputation for much more modest levels of skill, such as Jimmy Carter.[18]

In a recent study, Jon Bond and Richard Fleisher provided a strong critique of the use of case studies to "test" the importance of presidential legislative skills. Then they employed systematic data from 1953 to 1984 on the success of presidents in winning votes and found that skilled presidents were no more likely to win than were less skilled chief executives.[19]

Reexamining the research by Light, I found that although it is important as a step toward placing the significance of presidential legislative skills in the proper perspective, we must be cautious in accepting its specific findings. Light's study was limited to nonincremental domestic policy; it attempted to explain only passage of legislation (a boxscore), rather than support from members of Congress; and it lacked clear operational definitions for crucial terms such as "nonincremental" and "lobbying." Moreover, the number of programs involved was quite small, and the author tested the impact of White House lobbying by comparing the success of proposals that were lobbied with those that were not lobbied at all. Because it is difficult to imagine a significant, that is "nonincremental," presidential policy proposal that the White House simply ignores, it is unlikely that we can learn much about the importance of legislative skills from such a comparison.

Moreover, Light has pointed out an interesting and seemingly paradoxical phenomenon. The essence of his argument for our purposes is that presidents are more successful when they are less skilled and less successful when they have refined their skills.[20] The reasonable conclusion to draw from this analysis is not the perverse one that legislative skills are detrimental to obtaining legislative support. Instead, we might infer that legislative skills are of relatively modest significance in relation to other factors in explaining congressional behavior.

Misperceptions of history may also contribute to an undue emphasis on presidential legislative skills. This is especially true regarding two of the most prolific periods of presidential legislative success, Franklin Roosevelt's Hundred Days and Lyndon Johnson's Eighty-ninth Congress. The first piece of legislation Roosevelt proposed in 1933 was a bill to control the resumption of banking. According to James MacGregor Burns, "the milling representatives could hardly wait to act." Even during the forty-minute debate in the House, shouts of "Vote! Vote!" echoed from the floor. The *Republican* leader Bertrand H. Snell exclaimed in support, "The House is burning down and the President of the United States says this is the way to put out the fire."[21] There was little need for personal legislative skills in this environment.

Yet even in 1933, Roosevelt faced congressional resistance to his programs. The second bill he proposed gave the federal government the power to effect governmental economies to cut the deficit. The prospects of such a policy frightened veterans' organizations, which deluged Congress with telegrams in opposition. There was open revolt against the president in Congress on his second bill! It only passed the House when sixty-nine economy-minded Republicans voted with the president. Ninety Democrats, including seven party leaders, deserted FDR at this early stage in the Hundred Days. Things were not any better in the Senate, and it took the first fireside chat and the popular proposal to repeal prohibition to solidify Democratic ranks.[22] The president, in other words, took his case to the people, rather than to Congress, in order to obtain passage of his legislation.

FDR went on to serve longer in the White House than anyone else, but most of these years were not legislatively productive ones. Indeed, Burns has entitled his discussion of presidential-congressional relations during the late 1930s "Deadlock on the Potomac."[23] Either Roosevelt had lost his legislative skills, which is not a reasonable proposition, or other factors were more significant in determining congressional support.

John Kennedy and Lyndon Johnson are generally viewed as having had substantially different legislative skills and relationships with Congress. Yet, their visible differences were not considered important by the leading participants in legislative process. According to Henry Hall Wilson, the chief White House liaison aide to the House for both Kennedy and Johnson, the approach of the two presidents to the House was "practically identical."[24] Similarly, Mike Manatos, the White House liaison to the Senate for both presidents, has argued that it did not make any difference on the Hill which president he represented. His appeals for support were treated in the same way.[25]

Congressional leaders John McCormack, Carl Albert, Charles Halleck, and Everett Dirksen, Johnson aides Lawrence O'Brien, Joseph Califano, and Mike Manatos, executive branch official James Sundquist, and numerous scholars agree that had he lived, Kennedy would have gotten much the same from Congress as Johnson did and that the basic explanation for Johnson's phenomenal success in 1965 and 1966 was the increase in the number of liberal Democrats in Congress as a result of the 1964 elections.[26] Significantly, Kennedy's and Johnson's legislative liaison aides do not argue to the contrary in their published memoirs or in their oral histories in the Kennedy and Johnson presidential libraries.

The historian and White House aide Arthur Schlesinger, Jr., is also skeptical about the significance of legislative skills. Comparing Presidents Kennedy and Johnson, he has concluded that

> when Johnson lost 48 Democratic House seats in the 1966 election, he found himself, despite his alleged wizardry, in the same condition of stalemate that had thwarted Kennedy and, indeed, every Democratic President since 1938. Had the sequence been different, had Johnson been elected to the Presidency in 1960 with Kennedy as his Vice President, and had Johnson then offered the 87th Congress the same program actually offered by Kennedy, the probability is that he would have had no more success than Kennedy—perhaps even less because he appealed less effectively to public opinion. And, if Johnson had died in 1963 and Kennedy had beaten Goldwater by a large margin in 1964, then Kennedy would have had those extra votes in the House of Representatives, and the pundits of the press would have contrasted his cool management of Congress with the frenetic and bumbling efforts of his predecessor. In the end, arithmetic is decisive.[27]

Johnson, of course, was aware of the overwhelming importance of party affiliation in the passage of legislation. After the results of the 1964 congressional elections were in, he called his chief legislative liaison aide, Lawrence O'Brien, and said to him: "We can wrap up the New Frontier program now, Larry. . . . We can pass it now."[28]

Similarly, party remained the dominant factor in the Reagan administration's relations with Congress. In contrasting President Reagan's difficulties with Congress in 1983/84 with his more productive experience in 1981/82, Tom Loeffler, the House Republicans' chief deputy whip, commented: "The difference is that in 1981 and 1982 the White House was more capable of pushing the president's program through Congress simply because the makeup of the House was different."[29]

Ronald Reagan also benefited from the nature of the times. Although 1981 was hardly a repeat of 1933, there was a definite sense of the need for immediate action to meet urgent problems. In its first issue following Reagan's inauguration, the *Congressional Quarterly Weekly Report* declared that "one of Reagan's biggest advantages is the sense of both parties in Congress that the nation's problems are now very serious indeed."[30]

Similarly, David Stockman, a principal architect and proponent of Reagan's budgeting and tax proposals, remembers that when the president announced his "Program for Economic Recovery" to a joint session of Congress in February 1981, "the plan already had momentum and few were standing in the way." Reagan was "speaking to an assembly of desperate politicians who . . . were predisposed to grant him extraordinary latitude in finding a new remedy for the nation's economic ills . . . not because they understood the plan or even accepted it, but because they had lost all faith in the remedies tried before."[31]

Scholars who have examined congressional leadership from within Congress have reached similar conclusions about the relative importance of skills and party seats. In their path-breaking examination of leadership in the House of Representatives, Joseph Cooper and David Brady concluded that institutional context is more important than personal skills or traits in determining the influence of leaders. They found no relationship between leadership style and effectiveness. Indeed, they argue that style is determined more by the institutional context in which leaders find themselves than by their own personal traits. At the bottom line, the impact of institutional context on the power and style of leaders is determined primarily by party strength.[32]

Presidential skills must compete with other more stable factors that affect voting in Congress in addition to party. These include ideology, personal views and commitments on specific policies, and constituency interests. By the time a president is ready to intervene on a vote, most members of Congress have made up their minds on the basis of these other factors. As Lawrence O'Brien wrote to Lyndon Johnson in 1965, "Normally we enter into a tough count with a minimum of 175 votes, about which we need not worry."[33] O'Brien's memo indicates that Johnson could depend on 175 votes out of the maximum of 218 necessary for a majority. If not everyone voted, which was usually the case, the number of votes needed to win would, of course, be less than 218. So Johnson needed to add at most 43 votes to his dependable coalition—only about one-fifth of the necessary total. We should also keep in mind that these figures are for "tough counts," not the typical vote. On less controversial measures he undoubtedly needed even fewer votes, if he needed any at all.

Thus, presidential legislative skills are likely to be a critical factor only for those members of Congress who remain open to conversion after other influences have had their impact. Although the size and composition of this group varies from issue to issue, it will almost always be a minority in each chamber. Sometimes the number will be large enough to make a noticeable difference, but often it will not. At times a few votes will be crucial in affecting the outcomes on an issue. Whatever the circumstances, the impact will usually be on a relatively modest scale. Thus, although potentially important, conversion is not likely to be at the core of changes in policy.

In an interview near the end of President Reagan's first two years in office, Richard Cheney, chairman of the House Republican Policy Committee and President Ford's White House chief of staff, attributed the president's success in 1981 to the 1980 election results, public support, the assassination attempt, and the fact that Reagan proposed policies that Republicans in Congress believed in, not to the Reagan White House's personal dealings with members of Congress.[34]

In sum, despite the conventional wisdom that attributes substantial importance to presidential legislative skills in determining presidential support on congressional votes, there is good reason to be cautious in accepting this conclusion at face value. Other factors are likely to exercise more influence on congressional voting.

This conclusion is compatible with that of authors who stress historical context as the prime determinant in the success of presidential attempts to lead Congress.[35] Such analyses are very helpful in explaining the challenges and opportunities that different presidents have faced in their leadership efforts and thus in placing legislative skills in perspective. Whether we want to analyze a particular presidency or a potential source of influence, it is important that we understand that the president does not operate in a political or institutional vacuum.

At the same time, we must recognize that macro-level conclusions about historical context are inherently limited. To argue, for example, that there is a higher probability for success when the president is of the dominant party in Congress and there is consensus on the need for policy change is certainly correct. Yet such a conclusion is virtually a truism that explains very little about the impact of legislative skills or any other source of influence.

Arguments about the significance of historical context do not provide the basis for inferences about the impact of legislative skills or other leadership tools. It is important that we dig beneath the veneer of macro-level conclusions to explain the role of legislative skills. Similarly, it is necessary to round out our own evaluation of presidential legislative skills. To understand the role they play in presidential leadership in Congress, we must focus on presidents' efforts to exercise them.

A CLOSER LOOK

In the preceding section we saw that there is little correlation *in the aggregate* between the personal legislative skills of presidents and the support they receive in Congress. Yet we have it on good authority that legislative skills can make a difference. The prevailing patterns of voting may mask important variations.[36]

Although we have seen that legislative skills are not likely to influence Congress broadly, we need to obtain a more complete understanding of their role in presidential leadership. To do so, we must examine some of the most prominent elements of legislative skills more closely to see both their advantages and, equally important, the constraints on their use.

There is no lack of observers who criticize presidents for their lack of skill and urge that they be more adroit in their leadership. Implicit in such commentary are the notions that skills are always available for use and that all the president has to do is to reach into his inventory and employ the appropriate means of persuasion. But are things really so straightforward? If so, why do presidents fail to exploit these devices, and why do they end up so frequently in a stalemate with Congress?

Focusing on the limits of legislative skills will help to explain the absence of an aggregate relationship between skills and support. Because it is obvious that "deals," presidential appeals, consultation, and the like should increase the probabilities of support, findings such as those cited in the previous section may seem puzzling. Yet if presidents cannot employ legislative skills as readily as the conventional wisdom suggests, then their lack of broad impact is not surprising.

Legislative skills come in a variety of forms. Some, such as bargaining, personal appeals, and consultation, are oriented at what we might term the "tactical" level. In other words, the president and his aides employ them to obtain one or a few votes at a time. Other skills, such as setting priorities, exploiting "honeymoon" periods, and structuring votes, have broader consequence because they may affect most or all members of Congress at the same time. Space limitations prohibit a detailed consideration of every component of legislative skill, but we can examine examples of each type. Because we are especially interested in the question of broad change, we will devote our attention primarily to legislative skills that, at least in theory, have the potential to move the greatest number of members of Congress to support the president.

If these skills, when properly employed by the president, will reliably provide him with the tools to create new possibilities for change, we will have support for the argument that the president can play the role of director. However, if they are limited to aiding the president on the margins of coalition building and in exploiting opportunities that arise from other factors, then we will see the presidency in a different role, that of the facilitator.

BARGAINING

Bargaining is perhaps the component of presidential legislative skills that receives the most attention from commentators on the presidency. Richard Neustadt placed bargaining at the core of his model of presidential power. He argues that the president must bargain even with those who agree with him in order to ensure their support, because most people in government have interests of their own beyond the realm of policy objectives.[37]

Because of the negative aura of bargaining, participants often deny that they have engaged in it. For example, Ronald Reagan claimed that during the fight to sell AWACs planes to Saudi Arabia in 1981, "no deals were made. None were offered. I talked strictly on the merits of the proposal."[38] At the same time, the *Wall Street Journal* ran a story entitled "Some Senators Say They Were Promised White House Favors to Vote for Awacs."[39]

Similarly, two of the leading White House lobbyists of the 1960s, Henry Hall Wilson and Mike Manatos, could reflect on their respective experiences that "you'd never see anything so crude as a trade," and "I've never been involved in anything that would even approach a payoff."[40] Yet Clark Clifford, a Johnson intimate and, later, secretary of defense, described White House interaction with Congress as follows:

> President Johnson calls in a senator and he says, "Joe, . . . does that law partner of yours still want to be a federal judge?" "Oh," he says, "he certainly does." "Well," he says, "you know I've been thinking about that lately and we're going to talk about that. But in the process of talking about that, I want to talk with you about the fact that I think we've got to increase our Social Security program." "Well, Mr. President, I've spoken against that." "Well, I know, Joe. But times have changed. And you think about it awhile. . . . Let a week go by, you call me." Joe calls him in a week and says, "Mr. President, I've been thinking about that and I think there's a lot of merit to your position. And I believe I can change on . . . Social Security. I want to come over and talk to you. And, incidentally, I talked to my partner, and he is just tickled to death." That's the way our government runs . . . you're constantly trading assets back and forth to get your program.[41]

There can be no question that many bargains occur and that they take a variety of forms.[42] Some officials are very explicit about bargaining. Reagan's budget director, David Stockman, termed the trading that went into passing the Gramm-Latta II Budget Act in 1981 "an open vote auction." Regarding the 1981 tax cut, he recalled that "the last 10 or 20 percent of the votes needed for a majority of both houses had to be bought, period."[43]

Sometimes bargains consist of trading White House support on one policy for congressional support on another, as when President Reagan agreed to raise price supports for sugar in order to obtain support from Louisiana representatives for his budget cuts in 1981. Or when he promised to continue production of A-10 warplanes in exchange for the support of Long Island Republicans for the 1982 tax increase.[44] To obtain passage of the 1964 tax cut and the 1968 tax surcharge, President Johnson had to agree to limits on expenditures.[45] President Kennedy was forced to support the Communications Satellite Act of 1962 to please Senator Robert Kerr, whose aid the president needed on a number of issues.[46]

More common are bargains involving compromising on one aspect of a policy or trading support on two provisions of the same policy. In order to avoid a congressional veto of the sale of missiles to Saudi Arabia in 1986, President Reagan deleted the most controversial weapons from his request. Presidents are quite accustomed to compromising on the provisions of policies, especially on those they want to see passed and thus require a majority vote. On policies they oppose, the threat of a veto is a powerful weapon. Because the White House only requires one-third plus one vote in one of the chambers to sustain a veto, it can be more insistent on behalf of its policy preferences.

Yet another type of trade involves the "clarification" of policies. President Carter accepted clarifying provisions in order to gain passage of the Panama Canal treaties. Similarly, during the battle over the sale of AWACs to Saudi Arabia in 1981, President Reagan sent Congress reassurance that the planes would be used only for defensive purposes, and he specified conditions the Saudis would have to meet to receive the planes.

In still other incidents, the president may provide a discrete benefit, such as campaign aid or an appointive position for a constitutent in exchange for a legislator's support, as when the White House promised Republican representatives that Vice-President George Bush would make campaign appearances in exchange for support for the 1982 tax increase.[47] Lyndon Johnson's regular trades with Everett Dirksen have become legendary.[48]

Much of the bargaining that occurs is implicit trading on accounts. In effect, members of Congress exchange their support for the president for the administration's responsiveness to their requests for assistance. The White House tries to get members of Congress in its debt by providing favors and sympathetic hearings. Many members, in turn, try to create favorable impressions in the White House of their support for the president, sometimes writing and reminding him of their votes. For the White House, a member of Congress who is indebted to the president is easier to approach and ask for a vote. For the member, previous support increases the chances that a request will be honored. Thus, officeholders at both ends of Pennsylvania Avenue want to be in the other's favor. Although services and favors increase the president's chances of obtaining support, they are not usually exchanged for votes directly.[49]

Instead of offering bargains, the White House here is trying to create good will as a foundation for its future appeals for support. One Reagan liaison aide called the Office of Congressional Liaison "a service organization," while its director, Max Friedersdorf, said that its objectives were to "establish good, sympathetic relations with all members . . . [so that] when you go back and ask for a vote, you'll have an entree, and they'll give you a fair hearing."[50]

Echoing liaison aides of the past three decades, one of Friedersdorf's successors in the Reagan administration explained the relationship of implicit bargaining with Congress as follows: "It's a two way street. Members call us with problems and wanting information, and we have to get back to them as quickly and as accurately as possible. That's so they depend on us and have confidence in us, so that when we call them later on for a vote, they are willing to listen."[51]

Despite the record of bargaining and the prominent attention it receives from observers of the presidency, it occurs less often and plays a less critical role in the creation of presidential coalitions in Congress than the conventional wisdom would indicate.[52] This is especially true when we focus on trading support on two or more policies or on providing discrete benefits for representatives and senators

To begin with, the president does not have to bargain with every member of Congress to receive his or her support. On controversial issues, on which bargaining may be useful, a substantial portion of each chamber can be written off as implacable opponents. Unless the president is willing to sacrifice the substance of his policy, which is self-defeating, he will rarely be able to bargain with his firm opponents.

Equally important, the president almost always starts with a sizable core of party supporters, and he may add to this group those of the opposition party who agree with him on ideological or policy grounds. Others may support him because of relevant constituency interests or his standing with the public. Thus, the president only needs to bargain if this coalition does not provide him with a majority (two-thirds on treaties and veto overrides), and he need bargain only with enough people to provide him with that majority.

When the president needs to bargain, he is faced with a number of significant limitations on his ability to do so. Perhaps the foremost limitation on bargaining during the 1970s and the 1980s is the scarcity of resources. When budgets are tight, presidents must choose between policies, rather than build coalitions for several policies through logrolling. In other words, they find it difficult to obtain support from, say, urban interests for policies to aid rural areas, and vice versa, when the budget can support only one policy.

President Kennedy included a wide range of educational programs in his 1963 omnibus education bill to encourage education groups to work for each other's programs.[53] In 1964, President Johnson conceived the idea of trading the food-stamp program for his farm bill. Thus, he called members who supported each program and told them to support each other's bill.[54] Both Kennedy's and Johnson's strategies worked, but they could only exploit these strategies because of the availability of slack resources to fund the programs.

In addition, even in the best of times, there are limits to the number of appointive positions, public-works projects, and other discrete benefits the White House can offer to members of Congress. Moreover, much of what the president can offer in bargaining is ultimately in the hands of the bureaucracy or other members of Congress. Consequently, he must often bargain within the executive branch or within Congress before he can bargain with a particular member of Congress whose vote he needs. This saps the president's time, energy, and bargaining resources. In addition, once credit has been built up between a department (which has done a favor) and a member of Congress, it may be drawn upon by the department without the president's approval.

There is a special burden in bargaining with members of the opposition party. All bargains are not equal. Rewarding one's usual opponents for short-term support is much costlier than rewarding one's supporters, since the former action may not only alienate supporters who did not receive benefits but also may give opponents greater strength in the future. Rewarding supporters, on the other hand, may make them more effective in advancing the president's policies, thereby multiplying the positive effect of bargains. Thus, presidents are constrained in bargaining with the opposition. According to Barefoot Sanders, who headed the White House Office of Congressional Relations during part of the Johnson administration, "there's very little you can do for Republicans in a Democratic administration."[55]

Sometimes what members of Congress want is not the president's to give. A representative told one high-ranking White House official that he would vote to sustain an important presidential veto "if, and only if, we would get a CAB route into his town." The official responded: "Congressman, that is impossible. We can't touch regulatory agencies." Therefore, the member voted against the president.[56]

Even when presidents can make bargains, they may choose not to do so. Raising price supports on sugar or spending scarce funds on A-10 planes that the Pentagon planned to phase out was certainly inconsistent with Ronald Reagan's policy goals. Such deals entail costs for presidents, who are generally willing to tolerate only so much. President Reagan's firm stand against compromise on his military budget has been a central feature of his administration's legislative relations.[57] In 1961, Congressman D. B. Saund of California was angered by President Kennedy's closing of a veterans' hospital in Saund's district, and in retaliation, he opposed an important provision of the president's foreign-aid bill. Nevertheless, Kennedy refused to reopen the inadequate and unsafe hospital in return for Saund's support on foreign aid (his opposition was ultimately successful).[58]

The president may find bargaining incompatible with his temperament or his orientation toward policy making. Jimmy Carter did not believe in developing measures on the strength of bargains.[59] According to one White House aide, Carter, when asked to negotiate with a member of Congress, might reply: "I don't know why I should spend my time kissing that fellow's ass when he is playing politics and what I want to do is right. Why should I have to compromise when he is using only a political view? I don't understand."[60] Although the president would eventually talk to the member, his reluctance to "deal" is clear.

The president may even inhibit others from concluding compromises. When President Reagan left Washington to attend an economic summit conference abroad, the Senate proceeded to pass a budget for the next fiscal year, a reorganization of the joint chiefs of staff, and a gun-control bill. Moreover, the Finance Committee unanimously reported out a major tax-reform bill. Some observers thought that the absence of the president, whom they saw as a partisan and polarizing figure, more concerned with ideological assertions than with practical compromises, allowed the natural forces of conciliation on Capitol Hill to assert themselves.[61]

There is also no guarantee that a tendered bargain will be accepted. The members may not desire what the president is offering, or they may be able to obtain what they want on their own. This is, of course, particularly true of the most powerful members, whose support the president may need the most. In 1982, congressional leaders and White House officials, including the president, invested weeks in intense negotiations over the budget. Yet when the air cleared, agreement was absent.[62]

Sometimes members of Congress do not want to trade at all. This may be due either to constraints such as constituency opinion or to personal views. In 1961, Congressman Jim Delaney cast the vote that was responsible for holding the federal aid-to-education bill in the House Rules Committee. He wanted to include aid to parochial schools, which President Kennedy opposed. The president desperately needed Delaney's vote, but Delaney was not interested in bargaining on other subjects. As Lawrence O'Brien, chief of legislative liaison, exclaimed: "He didn't want a thing. I wish he had."[63]

The very nature of bargaining also limits its utility. If many direct bargains are struck, word will rapidly spread, everyone will want to trade, and persuasive efforts will fail. Thus, most of the bargains that are reached are implicit.[64] The lack of respectability that surrounds bargaining also encourages implicitness. This has drawbacks, however. The terms of an implicit bargain are likely to be less clear than those of an explicit one, inceasing the likelihood for misunderstanding and subsequent ill will when the member of Congress wishes to reap his or her reward for having supported the president.[65] Thus, Ronald Reagan enraged some members of Congress in 1982 when he first agreed to cuts in his proposed defense budget in order to obtain support for the tax increase and then proclaimed that he was not bound by the second and third year of the cuts after the tax bill had been passed.[66]

As a result of the limitations on bargaining, the White House initiates relatively few bargains. Most of the pressure for bargaining actually comes from the Hill. When the White House calls and asks for support, representatives and senators frequently raise a question regarding some request that they have made.[67] In the words of an Eisenhower aide, "Every time we make a special appeal to a Congressman to change his position, he eventually comes back with a request for a favor ranging in importance from one of the President's packages of matches to a judgeship or cabinet appointment for a worthy constituent."[68]

Sometimes members of Congress go to great lengths to create bargaining resources for themselves. Congressman Harold Rogers, a long-time supporter of the MX missile, absented himself when the House Appropriations Committee voted on the president's request to purchase twenty-one additional missiles. He missed the vote, not because of a change of heart about the weapon, but to create leverage for himself to influence the support program for tobacco, a policy of great concern to his constituents. Because the MX was important to the president and because the vote was close, the White House wasted no time in arranging a meeting to hear the congressman's complaint.[69]

The budget director, David Stockman, was quite candid about the concessions that members of Congress demanded in return for their support for the 1981 tax cut, including special breaks for oil-lease holders, real-estate tax shelters, and generous loopholes that virtually eliminated the corporate income tax. "The hogs were really feeding," he declared; "the greed level, the level of opportunism, just got out of control."[70] For obvious reasons, the White House does not want to encourage this tendency among members of Congress.

SETTING PRIORITIES

An important aspect of a president's legislative strategy can be establishing priorities among legislative proposals. The goal of this effort is to set Congress's agenda. The danger is that the president's priority programs, if he is not able to focus Congress's attention on them, may become lost in the complex and overloaded legislative process. An aide to Gerald Ford once remarked: "Congress needs time to digest what the President sends; time to come up with independent analysis; time to schedule hearings and markups.

Unless the President gives some indication of what's truly important, Congress will simply put the proposals in a queue."[71]

Setting priorities is also important because presidents and their staff can lobby effectively for only a few bills at a time. Moreover, the president's political capital is inevitably limited, and it makes sense to focus it on the issues he cares about most. Otherwise, this precious resource may be wasted, as when Jimmy Carter "spent his political capital to a deficit on pork barrel projects" in 1981, which was not one of his priority items.[72]

Jimmy Carter has been widely criticized by the media and by scholarly commentators for failing to set legislative priorities, especially in light of the scale, diversity, complexity, and controversial nature of his initial legislative program. Carter actually proposed about the same percentage of new and large programs as Presidents Kennedy and Johnson and actually fewer new programs than Johnson. Yet, his critics argue, Carter's failure to rank his legislative proposals made his legislative program seem larger than it was.[73] This problem was aggravated by the fact that so much of his program, including energy, tax and welfare reform, health insurance, and social-security financing, fell within the jurisdiction of the House Ways and Means Committee and the Senate Finance Committee. Without guidance on priorities, the proposals clogged the pipeline and stretched his prestige too thin.

There are fundamental obstacles to focusing congressional attention on a few top-priority items, however. In 1981, Ronald Reagan focused attention on his priorities by asking for relatively little, but in the first year of his second term the budget, tax reform, the MX missile, farm credit, sanctions against South Africa, aid to Nicaraguan rebels, and much more crowded the congressional agenda. Max Friedersdorf, the head of Reagan's legislative liaison team in both 1981 and 1985, explained, "In '81, during the whole course of the year, we only had three major votes," and they were spaced out. By May 1985, however, "we've had five or six votes. The circuits have been overloaded."[74]

Several forces are at work here. First, the White House can put off dealing with the full spectrum of national issues for a period of months at the beginning of the term of a new president, but it cannot do so for four years. Eventually it must make decisions about these issues. By the second year the agenda is full and more policies are in the pipeline as the administration attempts to satisfy its constituencies and responds to unanticipated or simply overlooked problems.

Moreover, the president himself will inevitably be a distraction from his own priorities. There are so many demands on the president to speak, appear, and attend meetings that it is impossible to organize his schedule for very long around focusing attention on his major goals, especially when he has been in office for a long time. For example:

> At the beginning of a two-week period in June, 1979 the President [Carter] met with a congressional delegation to try to rally its support

> for an expected close vote on the implementation of the Panama Canal Treaty. . . . In the course of it, Carter told two congressmen that he would "whip his [Senator Ted Kennedy's] ass" if the latter tried to run against him. This statement became a big story on the evening news. . . . [Two days later] the President introduced his proposals for national health insurance. Before any campaign could be launched to back his legislation, the President left for Vienna to sign the SALT agreements. When he returned he addressed Congress and the nation on the subject of SALT. . . . The President's next appearance on the news took place the following day, when he spoke at a ceremony after the completion of a solar panel for the White House hot-water system. There he urged the nation to give its attention to this important alternative to oil. Three days later he left for a world economic conference.[75]

Similarly, President Reagan wanted to focus attention on tax reform in 1985. Yet during a short trip to Alabama he had to react to a Senate vote that day on his funding request for aid to the rebels in Nicaragua and to the Supreme Court's decision on a school-prayer case that had originated in Alabama. As one presidential aide put it, "You can't go to Alabama and not mention the school prayer decision, and if you go to Alabama and mention the school prayer decision, don't think you are going to get covered on tax reform."[76]

In 1986 the president was again pushing for aid to the contras, but his efforts were overtaken by other events. According to the White House's communications director, Patrick J. Buchanan, "the Philippines intruded and dominated for two weeks, making it difficult for us to get the contra aid campaign off the ground." In addition, the president had to give a nationally televised speech on behalf of his defense budget, and the Challenger space-shuttle disaster also distracted attention from the president's priorities. Thus, as one White House aide put it, "the hardest thing to do is not to get into a reactive mode and have your schedule dictated to you by events, rather than dictating events and having a schedule reflective of your priorities."[77]

Second, Congress is quite capable of setting its own agenda. The changes in Congress during the last generation—changes in its aggressiveness, its institutional capabilities, and the freedom of individuals and groups to act—have made it more difficult not only for the president to persuade Congress but also to focus its attention.[78] The public expects Congress to take the initiative, and members of Congress have strong electoral incentives to respond.[79] Thus, when President Carter sent his large legislative program to Congress, it had to compete for space on the agenda with congressional initiatives. As a presidential aide put it, "Congress was scheduled up before most of the items arrived."[80]

This aggressive role on Congress's part is not unusual. A list of the major legislative actions of the Ninety-ninth Congress (1985/86) includes the reauthorization of the Clear Water Act, the Safe Drinking Act, and the "Superfund" hazardous-waste cleanup bill, sanctions against South Africa, the reorganization of the Pentagon, an anti–drug abuse bill, a major revision of immigration law, the Gramm-Rudman-Hollings anti-deficit bill, revisions of the law on gun control, the first authorizations for water projects in a decade, an extension of daylight-saving time, and expanded protection against age discrimination. On none of this legislation did the White House take the lead. Instead, it reacted to congressional initiatives. Even the historic Tax Reform Act of 1986 was as much a product of long-term congressional momentum and committee leadership as it was of presidential agenda setting. In 1987 the president found Congress already working on his two primary domestic-policy initiatives for his last two years in office, catastrophic health insurance and welfare reform.

Finally, presidents may not want to set priorities and concentrate attention on a few items. Lyndon Johnson is often viewed as being careful to set priorities for Congress, but when we examine his legislative activity more closely, we find that there is less to his priority setting than we might expect. In his memoirs, Johnson wrote: "One of the President's most important jobs is to help Congress concentrate on the *five or six dozen bills* that make up his legislative program" (italics added).[81] Wilbur Cohen has recalled that Johnson gathered his administration's legislative liaison people together about ten days after his inauguration in 1965 and told them he wanted *all* of his legislative proposals passed that session (italics added).[82] Lawrence O'Brien, the head of the Office of Congressional Relations, has remembered: "Certainly we didn't worry about overburdening our friends in Congress" in 1965.[83] According to Johnson's chief Senate lobbyist, Mike Manatos, the president had a master list of sixty to eighty bills that included priorities, but he carefully followed and pushed each piece of legislation on the list.[84] This hardly sounds like careful setting of priorities on a few bills and then focusing congressional and public attention on them. Instead, Johnson was more concerned about moving legislation through Congress rapidly to exploit the favorable political environment.[85]

It is considerably easier for a president with a short legislative agenda, such as Ronald Reagan, to set priorities than it is for a chief executive with a more ambitious agenda. It is also an advantage if the opposition party is in disarray and lacks alternatives to the president's agenda, a situation that the Republicans enjoyed in 1981 as the Democrats were reeling from Reagan's electoral victory and their loss of control in the Senate.

MOVING FAST

Related to setting priorities is being ready to send legislation to the Hill early in the first year of the term of a new president in order to exploit the "honeymoon" atmosphere that typically characterizes this period. Lyndon

Johnson explained: "You've got to give it all you can that first year. . . . You've got just one year when they treat you right and before they start worrying about themselves."[86] Moreover, it is to the advantage of presidents if they are ready to replace enacted requests with additional items of their legislative program.[87] In other words, it is best to keep Congress concentrating on the president's proposals.

First-year proposals have a considerably better chance of passing Congress than do those sent to the Hill later in an administration. Kennedy, Johnson, and Reagan took advantage of this opportunity, while Eisenhower, Nixon, Ford, and Carter did not. Moreover, most presidents are not ready with a second wave of proposals. The exception, as we might expect, was Lyndon Johnson.[88]

Once again, although moving legislation fast will enhance the prospects of its passage, there are good reasons why many presidents are not able to do so. For example, Jimmy Carter's proposals for energy, welfare reform, and the containment of hospital costs were complex and controversial policies that took a long time to draft and to clear relevant offices in the White House. He could not turn to a well-established party program, as Kennedy and Johnson could. As one Carter aide put it:

> We did not come into office with a handful of already developed programs. If anything, we had a set of ideas that took more than their share of time. There was no set of experts working on hospital cost containment when we came in, and energy was a mess. We had to start the programs all over from scratch. We were the ones who had to canvass the executive branch for ideas. We were also the ones that had to look for some potential solutions.[89]

There is an alternative to the methodical, time-consuming drafting of legislation, of course. The president might choose simply to propose a policy without thorough analysis in order to exploit the favorable political climate of his honeymoon. This appears to be the strategy of the Reagan White House regarding the budget cuts that Congress passed in 1981. The departments, including cabinet members, and their expertise were kept at a distance in the decision-making process. According to the budget director, David Stockman, "None of us really understands what's going on with all these numbers."[90] The legislation for Lyndon Johnson's 1964 War on Poverty is often faulted for being understood by virtually no one.[91]

Although the "move it or lose it" strategy may increase the probability that legislation will be passed and although it may not affront the sensibilities of someone with Ronald Reagan's concern for details, it is not difficult to understand why someone with Jimmy Carter's temperament may eschew such a process. Taking time to draft proposals does not gurarantee that they will be well conceived, but it is by no means clear that rapid drafting of legislation is in the best interests of the nation.

STRUCTURING CHOICE

Unlike bargaining, and similar to setting priorities and moving quickly, structuring the choices facing Congress has the potential to influence many votes at the same time. Framing issues in ways that favor the president's programs may set the terms of the debate on his proposals and thus the premises on which members of Congress cast their votes. Because mandates are infrequent, however, presidents must typically rely on framing issues one at a time.

The White House is generally quite interested in influencing the terms of debate on issues. As one top Reagan advisor put it, "I've always believed that 80 percent of any legislative or political matter is how you frame the debate."[92] Usually this involves emphasizing features of a policy other than its immediate substantive merits and making these other features more prominent in the decisional calculus of members of Congress.

The key vote on the Reagan budget cuts in 1981 was on the rule determining whether there would be a single up or down vote in the House. Once the rule had been passed, the White House could frame the issue for or against the popular president, and the broad nature of the reconciliation bill shifted the debate from the losses of individual programs to the benefits of the package as a whole. Although Reagan could not win a string of important individual votes on cutting social-welfare programs, by structuring Congress's choice, he needed to win only one vote; then he could avoid much of the potential criticism for specific reductions in spending.

In 1985 Ronald Reagan asked Congress to appropriate funds to build twenty-one additional MX missiles. He had been unable to win the money he had sought in 1984, when the debate had focused on the utility of the missiles as strategic weapons. He succeeded the next year, however, after the terms of the debate changed to the impact that building the missiles would have on the recently begun arms-control negotiations with the Soviet Union in Geneva. Senators and representatives who lacked confidence in the MX's contribution to the national security of the United States were still reluctant to deny American negotiators the bargaining chips they said they required. A senior Pentagon official said: "By the end, we gave up on technical briefings on the missile. . . . It was all based on the unspoken bargaining chip. Without Geneva, we would have died right there."[93]

The program that the president proposed had not changed. The MX was the same missile, with essentially the same capabilities in 1985 as it had had in 1984. What had changed were the premises on which members of Congress based their votes. The burden of proof had switched from the administration

(''MX is a useful weapon'') to its opponents (''canceling the MX will not hurt the arms-control negotiations''). Structuring of choices, not conversion, is what made the difference.

It is important to distinguish structuring choices from setting the agenda. Changes in the agenda may occur without changes in public policy. Agenda setting is only one stage in the policy-making process; by itself, it does not determine the outcomes of the process. In structuring choices, the same issues remain on the agenda, as in the case of the MX, but the questions asked about them change.

Portraying policies in terms of consensual criteria and playing down divisive issues are often at the core of efforts to structure choices for Congress. Federal aid to education had been a divisive issue for years before President Johnson proposed the Elementary and Secondary Education Act in 1965. To blunt opposition, he successfully changed the focus of debate from teachers' salaries and classroom shortages to fighting poverty, and from the separation of church and state to aiding children. This change in the premises of congressional decision making eased the path for the bill.[94]

Similarly, Richard Nixon articulated general revenue sharing as a program that would make the government more efficient and would distribute benefits widely. He deemphasized the allocational aspect of the policy, which redistributed federal funds from traditional Democratic constituencies to projects favored by the Republicans' middle-class constituents.[95] During the Cold War, Dwight Eisenhower employed the consensual symbol of national defense to obtain support for aid to education (the National *Defense* Education Act) and for building highways (the Interstate and *Defense* Highway Act).

Because of the diverse perspectives of members of Congress, presidents often portray the same issue in different terms for different audiences. On a tax question, Lyndon Johnson might emphasize budget balancing with Republicans and personal loyalty with Democrats.[96] Likewise, in appealing to Republican senators on the AWAC issue in 1981, Ronald Reagan stressed party and personal loyalty and the necessity for Republicans to be united so as to preserve their ability to govern. Equally important, he emphasized the president's need for credibility in the conduct of foreign affairs. ''Vote against me,'' he said privately on several occasions, ''and you will cut me off at the knees.'' To Democrats the president invoked the bipartisan tradition of American foreign policy.[97] On votes to override vetoes, presidents often appeal to their party cohorts not to undermine their party leader and to the opposition party on more substantive grounds.

Although structuring choices can be a useful tool for the president, there is no guarantee that he will succeed by using it. Although there are occasions on which a president can exploit an external event, such as arms-control negotiations, to structure legislators' choices on a single issue, he cannot rely on his environment to be so accommodating. Moreover, the White House must advocate the passage of many proposals at roughly the same time, further complicating its strategic position.

In addition, opponents of the president's policies are unlikely to defer to his attempts to structure choices on issues. Policies are very complex, and they typically affect many different interests, which inevitably evaluate programs from their diverse perspectives. Moreover, interests in the United States are more numerous, more politically active, and richer in resources than ever before. The rise of single-issue groups has only exacerbated this situation. Organized interests are ready and able to fight vigorously to be heard and to show how the trade-offs involved in policy choices involve far more than the dimensions of evaluation that the president has proposed. One can hardly get by with projecting a decrease in aid for college students as merely a deficit-reduction matter, for example. Opponents immediately raise other aspects of the issue, ranging from equity to economic growth.

As when making appeals, one can only go to the well so often. In 1986 there was another battle over the sale of arms to Saudi Arabia, during which the president argued that a defeat on this highly visible foreign-policy issue would undermine his international credibility and destroy his role as mediator in the Middle East. Despite all his efforts, the president was able to garner only thirty-four votes in the Republican-controlled Senate.[98]

Attempts to structure decisions may actually hurt the president's cause if they are too heavy-handed and thus create a backlash. In 1986, Ronald Reagan was engaged in his perennial fight to provide aid to the "Contras" in Nicaragua. The president equated opposition to his aid program with support for the Sandinistas. More graphically, the White House's communications director, Patrick J. Buchanan, wrote an editorial in the *Washington Post* that characterized the issue in stark terms: "With the contra vote, the Democratic Party will reveal whether it stands with Ronald Reagan and the resistance or [Nicaraguan President] Daniel Ortega and the communists." These overt efforts to structure the decision for Congress were not successful. Instead, they irritated members of Congress and provoked charges of Red baiting on the part of the White House.[99]

LACK OF SKILL

The reverse side of the question of how much legislative skills matter is that of how much a president's program can be hurt by lack of skills. Certainly the press often reports presidential blunders and attributes significance to them. Yet even if the White House bungles the handling of an issue, does it follow that members of Congress will vote against other presidential programs out of irritation about the earlier behavior? We have no evidence to support such an assertion, and it strains credibility to think that very many members of

Congress would override their own policy views and the pressures of party and constituency and oppose the president out of pique. As a Nixon aide argued: "The mistakes you make will follow you, but they aren't that important in the long run. . . . We made some mistakes on welfare reform, but I doubt that they affected the revenue sharing bills."[100]

A Carter assistant also cautioned against attributing too much influence to poor personal legislative relations: "When we came in, I don't think there was any question that we were viewed as country bumpkins. I don't doubt that it affected Congress. But in comparison to what? Was that as important as the close election? Was that as critical as the drop in popularity? Or Bert Lance?"[101]

On the other hand, the White House can certainly irritate members of Congress, and this is not necessarily cost free. If the president mishandles an issue, he may alienate some potential supporters, swing votes that could go either way. Ronald Reagan riled House Republicans with his handling of tax reform in 1985, and he found himself literally pleading for support after an initial and highly embarrassing defeat as a result of their abandoning him.

Moreover, bungling an issue may provoke a more general estrangement. Jimmy Carter's efforts to cut water projects in 1977 irritated Congress for years.[102] Although we may not be able to pinpoint the consequences of this disaffection, it is not unreasonable to argue that at least some members of Congress were less willing to grant him the benefit of the doubt for awhile on issues on which they were undecided.

Equally important, the absence of skills can undermine efforts to exploit windows of opportunity for the passage of legislation, and it can hinder even the recognition of these opportunities. Because presidents are not in a strong position to create opportunities for legislative success, exploiting opportunities becomes especially significant.[103] Indeed, taking advantage of opportunities may be the most important skill of all.

Interviews with former Speaker of the House Carl Albert are instructive on this point. He argued that Johnson's tenaciousness, his intensity in pushing legislation, was his great talent. Although pressed by the interviewer for specifics on Johnson's legislative skills, Albert could only respond that the president just kept pushing.[104] Russell Renka reached a similar conclusion. After studying Johnson's legislative relations in great detail, he found that the president possessed no special legislative touch. Nevertheless, Johnson moved more legislation through Congress than other contemporary presidents.[105] He understood the opportunity that the Eighty-ninth Congress presented to him, and he seized it.

CONCLUSION

We have seen that presidential legislative skills are not closely related to presidential support in Congress. Upon close examination, we have also seen that these skills are limited in their potential for obtaining support from senators and representatives. In essence, presidential legislative skills operate in an environment that is largely beyond the president's control. In most instances, presidents exercise their skills at the margins, not at the core, of coalition building. This is consistent with Paul Light's finding that "according to the White House staffs, the President's political power is only marginally related to internal resources and bargaining skills."[106]

Despite these findings, we should not conclude that presidents should ignore their legislative skills or that these skills never matter. Certainly presidents have successfully intervened with a bargain or an amenity, occasionally winning a crucial vote because of such an effort. Moreover, making strategic decisions such as setting priorities and proposing legislation shortly after Inauguration Day will increase the probability of obtaining congressional support. The important point is that these skills should be placed in their proper perspective. They do not appear to be a predominant factor in determining a president's support in Congress on most roll-call votes, despite commonly held assumptions to the contrary. Presidential legislative skills are more useful in exploiting discrete opportunities than in creating broad possibilities for changes in policy. They help the president play the role of facilitator rather than director.

Even when the environment is favorable for the White House, there are usually severe limits on the exercise of skills. The Reagan administration, for example, could press hard for its budget and tax policies in 1981, but otherwise it had a very limited agenda. When the issue of the sale of AWACs to Saudi Arabia arose, the White House initially handled it clumsily and had to come from behind to win a victory that should never have been in doubt. The White House was simply preoccupied with other matters and could not devote its attention and its "skills" to the next item on the agenda.

Finally, our conclusions have broad implications for how we view presidential leadership. Although we often attribute what we see as failures of presidential leadership to inadequacies in the president's leadership skills, there are much broader and much more important forces at work. It seems appropriate, then, that we adjust our expectations of presidential leadership accordingly and come to grips with the fact that presidential legislative skills are rarely at the core of policy making in the American political system.

Moreover, if presidents typically operate at the margins of coalition formation and if their legislative skills are essentially limited to being employed in exploiting rather than creating opportunities for leadership, we should devote more effort to examining other influences on Congress, such as party leadership and public opinion, and place less emphasis on personal skills. This personalization of politics can distract our attention from factors that play a larger role in explaining presidential success in Congress; it can also greatly oversimplify our understanding of executive-legislative relations.

NOTES

1. See George C. Edwards III, *Presidential Influence in Congress* (San Francisco, Calif.: W. H. Freeman, 1980), pp. 35–48.

2. An excellent example is Louis Fisher's *Constitutional Conflicts between Congress and the President* (Princeton, N.J.: Princeton University Press, 1985).

3. An excellent example is Stephen J. Wayne's *The Legislative Presidency* (New York: Harper & Row, 1978).

4. James MacGregor Burns, *Leadership* (New York: Harper & Row, 1978), p. 2.

5. Barbara Kellerman, "Leadership as a Political Act," in *Leadership: Multidisciplinary Perspectives*, ed. Barbara Kellerman (Englewood Cliffs, N.J.: Prentice-Hall, 1984), p. 70.

6. Quoted by Mark Peterson in "Domestic Policy and Legislative Decision Making," a paper presented at the annual meeting of the Midwest Political Science Association, Chicago, Ill., Apr. 1985, p. 32.

7. Remarks made at the United States Military Academy, West Point, N.Y., Apr. 30, 1986.

8. Sidney Hook, *The Hero in History* (Boston, Mass.: Beacon Press, 1943), chap. 9.

9. Richard E. Neustadt, *Presidential Power: The Politics of Leadership from FDR to Carter* (New York: John Wiley, 1980).

10. See, e.g., the essays in Norman J. Ornstein, ed., *President and Congress; Assessing Reagan's First Year* (Washington, D.C.: American Enterprise Institute, 1982).

11. James MacGregor Burns, *The Power to Lead* (New York: Simon & Schuster, 1984), p. 38.

12. Similarly, Thomas E. Patterson found that the press, when covering elections, emphasizes electoral skills rather than issues, believing that the skills are what makes the difference. See *The Mass Media Election* (New York: Praeger, 1980), pp. 51–52. F. Christopher Arterton found that reporters view elections as contests between individuals. See *Media Politics* (Lexington, Mass.: D. C. Heath, 1984), pp. 63–64.

13. Robert Pierpoint, *At the White House: Assignment to Six Presidents* (New York: Putnam's, 1981), p. 119.

14. Doris Kearns, *Lyndon Johnson and the American Dream* (New York: Harper & Row, 1976), p. 226.

15. Lyndon B. Johnson, *The Vantage Point* (New York: Popular Library, 1971), p. 448.

16. See, e.g., Barbara Kellerman, *The Political Presidency* (New York: Oxford University Press, 1984).

17. Paul Light, "Passing Nonincremental Policy: Presidential Influence in Congress, Kennedy to Carter," *Congress and the Presidency* 9 (Winter 1981/82): 61–82.

18. Edwards, *Presidential Influence in Congress*, chap. 7.

19. Richard Fleisher and Jon Bond, "Presidential Leadership Skill and Success in Congress," paper presented at the annual meeting of the Southern Political Science Association, Atlanta, Ga., Nov. 1986.

20. Paul C. Light, *The President's Agenda* (Baltimore, Md.: Johns Hopkins University Press, 1982).

21. James MacGregor Burns, *Roosevelt: The Lion and the Fox* (New York: Harcourt, Brace & World, 1956), pp. 166–67.

22. Ibid., pp. 167–68.

23. Ibid., pp. 337–42.

24. Transcript of Henry Hall Wilson oral history interview, April 11, 1973, by Joe B. Frantz, pp. 6–7, LBJ Library.

25. Transcript of Mike Manatos oral history interview, Aug. 25, 1969, by Joe B. Frantz, pp. 13–14, LBJ Library.

26. Transcript of John McCormack oral history, Sept. 23, 1968, by T. Harrison Baker, pp. 20, 39–40, LBJ Library; transcript of Carl Albert oral history interview no. 3, July 9, 1969, by Dorothy Pierce McSweeny, p. 4, LBJ Library; Eric F. Goldman, *The Tragedy of Lyndon Johnson* (New York: Dell, 1974), p. 68; transcript of Charles Halleck oral history inteview, Mar. 22, 1965, by Stephen Hess, p. 27, John F. Kennedy Library; Lawrence F. O'Brien, *No Final Victories* (New York: Ballantine, 1974), pp. 106, 145–49, 188–89; Richard Bolling, *Power in the House* (New York: Capricorn Books, 1974), pp. 218, 229; Joseph A. Califano, Jr., *A Presidential Nation* (New York: Norton, 1975), p. 155; Mike Manatos oral history, pp. 14, 29–30, 57–58, see also p. 32; James L. Sundquist, *Politics and Policy* (Washington, D.C.: Brookings Institution, 1968), pp. 476–82; Joseph Cooper and Gary Bombardier, "Presidential Leadership and Party Success," *Journal of Politics* 30 (Nov. 1968): 1012–27; Aage R. Clausen, *How Congressmen Decide* (New York: St. Martin's, 1973), p. 146. See also Rowland Evans and Robert Novak, *Lyndon B. Johnson: The Exercise of Power* (New York: New American Library, 1966), p. 364.

27. Arthur M. Schlesinger, Jr., *Robert Kennedy and His Times* (New York: Ballantine, 1978), p. 742.

28. O'Brien, *No Final Victories,* p. 180.

29. "White House Lobbyists Find Congress Is Less Supportive," *Congressional Quarterly Weekly Report,* June 16, 1984, p. 1429.

30. "Numerous Factors Favoring Good Relationship between Reagan and New Congress," ibid., Jan. 24, 1981, p. 172.

31. David A. Stockman, *The Triumph of Politics* (New York: Harper & Row, 1986), pp. 79–80; see also p. 120.

32. Joseph Cooper and David W. Brady, "Institutional Context and Leadership Style: The House from Cannon to Rayburn," *American Political Science Review* 75 (June 1981): 411–25.

33. John F. Manley, "White House Lobbying and the Problem of Presidential Power," paper presented at the annual meeting of the American Political Science Association, Washington, D.C., Sept. 1977, p. 27. For a similar argument regarding the Eighty-seventh Congress see Neil MacNeil, *Forge of Democracy* (New York: McKay, 1963), pp. 258–59.

34. Interview with Richard Cheney, Princeton, N.J., Nov. 19, 1982.

35. See, e.g., Erwin C. Hargrove and Michael Nelson, *Presidents, Politics, and Policy* (Baltimore, Md.: Johns Hopkins University Press, 1984), chap. 3; Stephen Skowronek, "Presidential Leadership in Political Time," in *The Presidency and the Political System,* ed. Michael Nelson (Washington, D.C.: CQ Press, 1984), pp. 87–132.

36. William H. Riker and Donald Niemi, "Stability of Coalitions on Roll Calls in the House of Representatives," *American Political Science Review* 56 (Mar. 1962): 58–65.

37. Neustadt, *Presidential Power,* chap. 3.

38. Quoted in "Reagan Reaction to AWACs Vote," *Congressional Quarterly Weekly Report,* Oct. 31, 1981, p. 2136; see also Laurence I. Barrett, *Gambling with History* (New York: Penguin Books, 1984), pp. 160, 162.

39. Albert R. Hunt, *Wall Street Journal,* Oct. 14, 1981, p. 10.

40. Henry Hall Wilson oral history interview, p. 10; Mike Manatos oral history interview, p. 20.

41. Quoted in Kellerman, *Political Presidency,* p. 25.

42. See, e.g., Edwards, *Presidential Influence in Congress,* pp. 129–31.

43. Stockman, *Triumph of Politics,* pp. 208–9, 214–15, 251, 253, 260–61, 264–65. See also "White House's Lobbying Apparatus . . . Produces Impressive Tax Vote Victory," *Congressional Quarterly Weekly Report,* Aug. 1, 1981, pp. 1372–73.

44. Barrett, *Gambling with History,* pp. 160–61, 365; William Greider, "The Education of David Stockman," *Atlantic,* Dec. 1981, p. 50; see pp. 36 and 39 for other examples.

45. Transcript of Carl Albert oral history interview no. 4, Aug. 13, 1969, by Dorothy Pierce McSweeny, pp. 2–3, LBJ Library.

46. Transcript of Mike Mansfield oral history interview, June 23, 1964, by Seth P. Tillman, pp. 28–29, John F. Kennedy Library.

47. Barrett, *Gambling with History,* p. 365.

48. See, e.g., Kearns, *Lyndon Johnson and the American Dream,* pp. 182–83; Jack Valenti, *A Very Human President* (New York: Norton, 1975), pp. 182–83; Russell D. Renka, "Legislative Leadership and Marginal Vote-Gaining Strategies in the Kennedy and Johnson Presidencies," paper presented at the annual meeting of the Southwestern Political Sciences Association, Houston, Tex., Apr. 1978, pp. 28–30.

49. See Edwards, *Presidential Influence in Congress,* pp. 1351–41.

50. See Arthur Maass, *Congress and the Common Good* (New York: Basic Books, 1983), pp. 50–53.

51. Quoted in "Reagan's Team on the Hill Getting Members' Praise for Hard Work, Experience," *Congressional Quarterly Weekly Report,* May 21, 1981, p. 749.

52. M. B. Oglesby, quoted by Gerald M. Boyd in "The Presidential Line to and from Capitol Hill," *New York Times,* Feb. 3, 1985, p. 2E.

53. Sundquist, *Politics and Policy,* pp. 206, 210.

54. Jack Bell, *The Johnson Treatment* (New York: Harper & Row, 1965), p. 189.

55. Transcript of Barefoot Sanders oral history interview, Mar. 24, 1969, by Joe B. Frantz, tape 2, p. 6, LBJ Library; see also tape 3, p. 36.

56. Wayne, *Legislative Presidency,* p. 160.

57. See, e.g., Barrett, *Gambling with History,* pp. 152–54; "Congress Struggles to Quit, but Does Not Finish," *Congressional Quarterly Weekly Report,* Oct. 16, 1984, pp. 2415–16.

58. O'Brien, *No Final Victories,* p. 122.

59. Hargrove and Nelson, *Presidents, Politics, and Policy,* p. 119.

60. Quoted by Mark Peterson in "The President's Legislative Program: More Than Meets the 'Aye'?" paper presented at the annual meeting of the Midwest Political Science Association, Chicago, Apr. 1984, p. 23.

61. See Steven V. Roberts, "Congress Activity and Reagan's Absence," *New York Times,* May 10, 1986, p. 8.

62. For an account of these negotiations see Barrett, *Gambling with History,* chap. 20.

63. O'Brien, *No Final Victories,* pp. 129–30, 136–37; Theodore C. Sorensen, *Kennedy* (New York: Bantam Books, 1966), pp. 404–5.

64. Johnson, *Vantage Point,* p. 457; Kearns, *Lyndon Johnson and the American Dream,* p. 236, "Turning Screws: Winning Votes in Congress," *Congressional Quarterly Weekly Report,* Apr. 24, 1976, pp. 947, 949.

65. Stanley Kelly, Jr., "Patronage and Presidential Legislative Leadership," in *The Presidency,* ed. Aaron Wildavsky (Boston, Mass.: Little, Brown, 1969), p. 273.

66. Steven R. Weisman, "Reaganomics and the President's Men," *New York Times Magazine,* Nov. 21, 1982, p. 109; see also pp. 90, 92.

67. "Turning Screws," pp. 947, 949, 954.

68. Quoted by Gary W. Reichard in *The Reaffirmation of Republicanism* (Knoxville: University of Tennessee Press, 1975), p. 173.

69. Jonathan Fuerbringer, "Pressures and Rewards Face House Members on MX Vote," *New York Times,* Mar. 26, 1985, p. 1.

70. Quoted by Greider in "Education of David Stockman," p. 51.

71. Quoted in Light, *President's Agenda,* p. 156.

72. Interview with Jack Watson, Oct. 19, 1985, West Point, N.Y.

73. See Light, *President's Agenda,* pp. 119-26, 156-57.

74. Quoted by Bernard Weinraub in "Back in the Legislative Strategist's Saddle Again," *New York Times,* May 28, 1985, p. 10.

75. Michael Baruch Grossman and Martha Joynt Kumar, *Portraying the President* (Baltimore, Md.: Johns Hopkins University Press, 1981), pp. 99-100; see also p. 314.

76. Quoted by Gerald M. Boyd in "Rethinking a Tax Plan Strategy," *New York Times,* June 12, 1985, p. 14.

77. Quoted by Dick Kirschten in "For Reagan Communication Team . . . It's Strictly One Week at a Time," *National Journal,* Mar. 8, 1986, p. 594.

78. See, e.g., Edwards, *Presidential Influence in Congress,* pp. 193-95.

79. See, e.g., Adam Clymer, "Majority in Poll Expect Congress to Cut Spending," *New York Times,* Nov. 17, 1985, sec. 1, p. 1.

80. Quoted by Light in *President's Agenda,* p. 54.

81. Johnson, *Vantage Point,* p. 448.

82. "Discussion," in William S. Livingston, Lawrence C. Dodd, and Richard L. Schott, eds., *The Presidency and the Congress* (Austin, Tex.: Lyndon B. Johnson School of Public Affairs, 1979), pp. 300-301.

83. O'Brien, *No Final Victories,* p. 183.

84. Mike Manatos oral history interview, pp. 21-22, 50-51.

85. See William E. Leuchtenburg, *In the Shadow of FDR* (Ithaca, N.Y.: Cornell University Press, 1983), p. 146.

86. Quoted by Harry McPherson in *A Political Education* (Boston, Mass.: Little, Brown, 1972), p. 268.

87. Light, *President's Agenda,* pp. 58-59.

88. Ibid., pp. 44-49, 58-59.

89. Quoted ibid., p. 218, see also pp. 49-51, 55-56.

90. Quoted by Greider in "Education of David Stockman," p. 38.

91. See, e.g., Daniel P. Moynihan, *Maximum Feasible Misunderstanding* (New York: Free Press, 1969), p. 87; John C. Donovan, *The Politics of Poverty,* 2d ed. (Indianapolis, Ind.: Bobbs-Merrill, 1973), p. 40; and James L. Sundquist, ed., *On Fighting Poverty* (New York: Basic Books, 1969), p. 29.

92. Quoted by Gerald M. Boyd in " 'General Contractor' of the White House Staff," *New York Times,* Mar. 4, 1986, p. A22.

93. Quoted in "MX Debate: It's Not Over," *New York Times,* Mar. 30, 1985, pp. 1, 8; see also, "Senate Hands Reagan Victory on MX Missile," *Congressional Quarterly Weekly Report,* Mar. 23, 1985, pp. 515-23.

94. See, e.g., Carl Albert oral history interview no. 3, pp. 8-9.

95. See, e.g., Richard P. Nathan, Charles F. Adams, et al., *Revenue Sharing: The Second Round* (Washington, D.C.: Brookings Institution, 1977).

96. Bell, *Johnson Treatment,* pp. 93-94; Johnson, *Vantage Point,* p. 85.

97. Quoted by Barrett in *Gambling with History,* pp. 275-76; see also Albert R. Hunt, "Out of the Fire," *Wall Street Journal,* Oct. 29, 1981, pp. 1, 10; "Senate

Supports Reagan on AWACs Sale,'' *Congressional Quarterly Weekly Report*, Oct. 31, 1981, pp. 2098–3000.

98. Steven V. Roberts, ''Senate Upholds Arms for Saudis, Backing Reagan,'' *New York Times*, June 6, 1986, pp. A1, A10. The thirty-four votes did sustain his veto, however.

99. ''Reagan Loses Ground on 'Contra' Aid Program,'' *Congressional Quarterly Weekly Report*, Mar. 8, 1986, pp. 535–36.

100. Quoted in Light, *President's Agenda*, p. 29.

101. Quoted ibid., p. 29.

102. Barbara Sinclair, *Majority Leadership in the U.S. House* (Baltimore, Md.: Johns Hopkins University Press, 1983), p. 119.

103. See Mark Peterson, ''Congressional Response to Presidential Proposals: Impact, Effort, and Politics,'' paper presented at the annual meeting of the Midwest Political Science Association, Chicago, Apr. 1986, pp. 29–30.

104. Carl Albert oral history inteview no. 3, pp. 7, 11, and no. 4, pp. 22, 25; Transcript of Carl Albert oral history interview no. 1, Apr. 28, 1969, by Dorothy Pierce McSweeny, pp. 22–23, LBJ Library; Transcript of Carl Albert oral history interview no. 2, June 10, 1969, by Dorothy Pierce McSweeny, p. 14, LBJ Library.

105. Russell Renka, ''Comparing Presidents Kennedy and Johnson as Legislative Leaders,'' paper presented at the annual meeting of the Southern Political Science Association, Savannah, Ga., Nov. 1984, p. 18, table 4. See Light, *President's Agenda*, p. 57, on the size of Johnson's legislative program.

106. Paul C. Light, ''The President's Agenda: Notes on the Timing of Domestic Choice,'' *Presidential Studies Quarterly* 11 (Winter 1981): 70.

11

Coalition Leadership, Government Stability, and Macroeconomic Policy in European Democracies

John D. Robertson

Leadership entails a degree of authority in combination with insight, talent, and an understanding of the preferences and motives of others. This has led scholars to focus on individuals who have been asked under specific conditions to succeed at tasks involving the coordination of people performing different roles and functions. Weber drew attention to the institution of leadership under conditions of rationality, but he reinforced, through the concept of charisma, the individualistic concept of political leadership.

Students of comparative government—particularly students of contemporary democracies—have begun to develop a broader concept of leadership. This broader conception focuses on the constitutional dynamics that give rise to institutional, rather than individual and personal, leadership. In this chapter, I focus on one aspect of institutional leadership—the formation of governing coalitions of political parties in parliamentary democracies.

Coalition leadership within parliamentary democracies has long been equated with longevity of tenure. The durability of parliamentary executives is said to be as a positive feature of modern democracies, because duration affords a greater opportunity for policy coherence and because it reduces public discontent with democratic institutions. During the recent periods of economic malaise afflicting contemporary democracies, the durability of the parliamentary system seems to have been a significant advantage, especially in comparison to the experiences of interwar Europe and the French Fourth Republic.[1]

Arend Lijphart has recently challenged the claim that cabinet durability is of major consequence for the health of the democratic regime.[2] Instead, he contends that if "cabinet durability can stand for anything, it stands for a preponderance of executive power in executive-legislative relations.''[3] While the legislature's ability (and willingness) to dismiss the cabinet in parliamentary democracies is not a very common occurrence, the constraining effect of parliament is always present. ''When the legislatures are not completely controlled by the executive . . . fundamental power of censuring and thereby dismissing the cabinet does play a role—either directly, or, more often, indirectly, in limiting the duration of cabinets.''[4] Consequently, he notes, ''cabinets that do not enjoy a long life are unable to develop the kind of cohesion and control that would enable them to stand up to the legislature.''[5] William Mishler and Anne Hildreth (1984) offered empirical support for this, based on their cross-national analysis of legislatures. They concluded that in ''wealthier nations, representative and effective legislatures with relatively open and competitive party systems ensure relatively high levels of turnover in government.''[6]

Rockman has reminded us that ''relationships between the executive and the legislatures are anything but simple, because nowhere are the executive and legislature homogeneous entities.''[7] Nevertheless, the critical contest in parliamentary systems concerns the ''futurity principle'': the matter of deciding in whom to entrust the future of the public interest.[8] This choice is between a legislature, with its representative focus but with complicated configurations of parties, and the executive, with authority that is less representative but more concentrated and more efficiently brought to bear on policy matters. In building governing coalitions, therefore, legislative parties must decide upon a formula for national leadership that has major consequences for the future course of public policy and, at a more fundamental level, for the stability of the political system.

If the durability of the parliamentary executive bears directly on policy content and leadership consistency, then the process of choosing a form of executive leadership may explain the connection between executive leadership and the stability of public policy. Robert L. Peterson et al. (1983, p. 55) have elaborated upon this in their analysis of executive-coalition building.[9] In the ongoing struggle over the future course of policy,

> government formation is the transfer of the treatment of an issue from administrative and legislative decision making arenas to an interparty and intergroup arena. Issues which have proved insoluble within the government, within the parliament and/or through interaction between them lead to the collapse of the incumbent and are the subject of bargaining in the formation of a new coalition. Once the new coalition is formed on the basis of these (and other) issues, they are returned to administrative and parliamentary arenas for further action, and the process continues. . . . Thus policy is the basis for coalition, and coalition is the basis for policy.

Within this context, I will explore three questions. First, what are the various styles of executive-coalition leadership that emerge from the arena of negotiations over the formation of new cabinet governments? Second, what policy changes follow from choices regarding the final shape of the executive coalition? Third, what implications can be drawn for national political leadership among contemporary parliamentary democracies? In addressing these three questions, I shall attempt to explain how the phenomenon of coalition formation in multiparty parliamentary democracies determines political leadership, to the extent that such political leadership at the national level is based on the formal institutional configuration of power.

THE THREE STYLES OF COALITION LEADERSHIP

Three basic types of governing coalitions emerge from the arena of governmental negotiations: the minority coalition, the minimum winning coalition, and the oversized coalition. The three criteria for the success of policy in regard to executive-coalition leadership are the capacity of coalition cabinets (1) to shape legislative coherence, (2) to direct the legislature toward a policy agenda that it would otherwise not be willing or capable of pursuing, and (3) to endure long enough to realize both the coalition parties' principal policy priorities as well as to provide primary constituencies with critical distributional rewards.[10] The basic issue that I address in this chapter is how the types of governing coalitions affect the policy success of the executive coalition.

The type of governing coalition is determined by the configuration of political parties that end up being included in a governing coalition. The configuration depends upon the proportion of seats in the principal chamber of the legislature and upon the number of parties within the coalition.[11] The type of coalition, in turn, defines the extent to which a coalition can affect policy by ultimately garnering the support of various political parties within the legislature.

Three basic styles of coalition leadership emerge from the three basic types of governing coalitions. First is the *hegemonic* style, in which the cabinet coalition contains no parties beyond the number necessary to achieve a majority of legislative votes in parliament and consequently in which the cabinet enjoys a dominant role in shaping the policy agenda (the minimum winning coalition). Second is the *consensual* style, in which the cabinet coalition contains at least one or more over the minimum needed to ensure the cabinet a majority of votes in the legislature. Here the cabinet's role in the shaping of the policy agenda is constrained by the fact that the prime minister must seek a consensus among conflicting interests that are represented by the political parties within the cabinet (the oversized coalition). Third is the *consultative* style, in which the governing coalition contains too few parties to ensure the cabinet a majority of votes in the legislature. Here the cabinet's role is severely limited by the fact that the prime minister must consult with his/her extracabinet coalition support within the legislature on policy matters (the minority coalition).

Lijphart has reported that the life of a cabinet is related to the type of governing coalition. The average duration of minimum winning coalitions is 46 months (compared to 74 months for single-party majority coalitions), 23 months for oversized coalitions, and 19 months for minority coalitions.[12] Minimum winning coalitions are therefore in a better position to develop and implement a coherent policy agenda, while oversized and minority coalitions, *ceteris paribus*, are in a more difficult position. Lijphart has concluded that "we can expect greater legislative independence when cabinets are oversized [and minority] rather than minimal winning."[13] Carrying this argument one step further, we may reason that minimum winning coalitions are indicative of the executive's ascendancy over the public policy, while minority and oversized coalitions reflect the legislature's control over the distribution of critical resources. Thus, the type of executive-coalition that emerges from the arena of cabinet negotiations can be understood not simply as the final formula that rational actors in a gaming strategy agree to but also as an indication of the extent to which the legislature will allow executive-coalition leadership in the policy process.

The process by which executive-coalitions are ratified by various political parties is conditioned by two contextual factors: decisional factors and systemic factors. Decisional factors are limits on founding coalitions that stem from the representative structure of parliaments. They consist of the hyperpluralist axis and the economic polarization axis.[14]

Hyperpluralism, according to Lawrence C. Dodd, is a condition within parliamentary representative systems in which (1) political parties and their elites are confronted by a high degree of uncertainty about the preferences, priorities, and programmatic demands of the other political parties and (2) the diversity of issue preferences that are represented in the legislature is so large as to constrain the flexibility of party elites in shaping a compromise over the formation of a new coalition executive.[15] Economic polarization is the convergence of two potentially volatile politicoeconomic conditions: sharp ideological polarization among parties along a traditional Left-Right economic continuum and high rates of inflation and unemployment.[16]

The systemic factors are those structural, cultural, and historical traits that constrain the decision-making process by defining acceptable roles and procedures for shaping resolution within the bargaining arena. These factors exist at the institutional level; they shape inter- and intraparty negotiations and thereby affect the leadership capacity of party elites.

Gregory Luebbert (1986) has identified three general patterns of decision making and conflict resolution (the systemic factors) among multiparty parliamentary democracies: the consensual pattern, the conflictual pattern, and the competitive pattern. The *consensual* pattern of decision making is characterized by the influence of firmly entrenched traditions of extragovernmental channels into the policy-making arena, which, in effect, expands the field of actors within negotiations over governmental formats, program development, and policy course. Minority coalitions are far more likely to emerge from avenues of negotiation over governmental formations in parliamentary democracies that traditionally practice the consensual pattern of decision making. Because several extragovernmental channels afford political parties avenues to the policy-making arena, political elites are not compelled to compromise their specific preferences in order to gain membership within a governing coalition as a means of representing and protecting the interests of their constituencies.[17] Thus, these democracies are more likely to be characterized by consultative style of executive leadership.

The *conflictual* pattern of decision making among parliamentary democracies is characterized by a high level of ideological polarization among political parties in the party system, high degrees of fractionalization in the party system, and a number of antisystem parties, which exacerbate polarization and complicate the formation of coalitions. Without extragovernmental channels into the policy-making arena, the effect of polarization, fractionalization, and antisystem pressure is to force resolution through larger-than-necessary coalitions. Such "oversized" coalitions are often designed to temper by coopting the more polarized and conflictual tendencies among the political parties.[18] Thus, multiparty parliamentary democracies that are traditionally constrained by conflictual patterns of policy making are also more likely to have oversized governing coalitions.

The *competitive* pattern of decision making is characterized by the absence of both political polarization and extragovernmental channels into the policy-making process. With a high degree of legitimacy therefore granted to formal institutions of policy making and with a strong commitment to cabinet government—governments built upon effective majorities—this pattern of decision making is more likely to accommodate minimum winning coalitions or single-party cabinets, that is, the hegemonic style of executive-coalition leadership.[19]

A number of factors influence the decisional and systemic factors in coalition formation. These include (1) established patterns of collaborations among party elites; (2) assessments of the stability of the preferences and priorities of potential partners in a coalition; (3) the stability of the issues that are represented in the legislature; (4) the condition of the macroeconomy (especially inflation and unemployment) and how it influences the welfare of a particular party's constituencies; (5) the potential for influencing policy (and particularly macroeconomic policy) without having to actually commit a party to a parliamentary administration; and (6) the advantages or disadvantages of remaining outside government while your ideological adversary gains entry.

These conditions, shaped as they are by the electoral laws of the democracy, the constitutional norms and provisions of the nation, and the cultural traditions of society, help to determine the style of executive-coalition leadership within a particular democracy.

Developing measures of hyperpluralism and economic polarization and drawing on Luebbert's classification of parliamentary representation democracies, I have elsewhere shown that minimum winning coalitions, which afford a hegemonic style of executive-coalition leadership to parliamentary representative systems, are more likely to emerge from the arena of cabinet negotiations that are relatively free from economic polarization. Oversized coalitions are more likely under a more complex set of circumstances in which economic polarization is relatively high and hyperpluralism characterizes the parliamentary party system. Minority coalitions, as expected, are most likely to be found in democracies that are characterized by consensual patterns of decision making.[20]

SOME PRELIMINARY EVIDENCE OF THE EFFECTS OF COALITION LEADERSHIP

Does it matter if a parliamentary representative democracy, over an extended period of time, is characterized by a particular style of executive-coalition leadership? To explore this question, in the present study I shall rely upon a sample of ten multiparty democracies that traditionally have practiced coalition-executive leadership—namely, those European democracies that practiced coalitional rule during the years between 1958 and 1984. Excluded from the sample were (1) recent democracies (Spain, Portugal, Greece), (2) countries closer to the "Westminster" model of parliamentary democracy (Great Britain, New Zealand, Australia, and Canada), (3) democracies whose process of coalition formation is strongly influenced by presidential power (France V), and (4) those democracies whose cultural/historical dynamics of the party system are outside the European experience. Iceland was also omitted because of the lack of reliable data. The sample is therefore the set of "representational" party democracies (Ireland being the only omission)—democracies that are characterized by strong party-constituency linkages and parliaments in which majorities are difficult to obtain and infrequent in occurrence.[21]

While there are many places in which one could begin to explore the impact that such a leadership style may have, two of the more important critical dimensions of democratic performance are (1) the stability of government and (2) the stability of macroeconomic policy. First, the style of coalition leadership and the type of cabinet coalition should be associated with the stability of cabinet administration. This, as we have noted already, is generally the case.[22] A parliamentary representative democracy that typically is governed by a minimum winning executive cabinet coalition (or single-party majoritarian cabinet) will endure longer than one in a democracy that relies upon minority or oversized coalitions. Generally, the consultative and consensual style of coalition leadership offers too many opportunities for (and too few structural supports against) political opposition, from either within or outside the coalition. This, however, may not be the case for democracies that are characterized by the systemic factor of consensual decision making. For instance, in Norway and Sweden, two of the three democracies in which the consensual patterns of decision making is common, cabinet stability is generally maintained.[23] Thus, we should expect to see the frequency of incidents of the cabinet-collapse/government-formation sequence to be highest among countries in our sample that are less prone to achieving a hegemonic style of coalition leadership. However, this may have to be qualified because of the existence of democracies with legitimate extraparliamentary channels into the policy-making process.

The second pattern we would expect to observe is a strong association between the style of coalition leadership and the stability of macroeconomic policy. Joel D. Aberbach, Robert D. Putnam, and Bert A. Rockman have distinguished between two forms of governmental leadership: the centripetal and the centrifugal.[24] The *centripetal* form is governmental leadership affected by a minimal amount of external influence, while a *centrifugal* form is governmental leadership more sensitive to external constraints. According to Aberbach and his colleagues, centripetal governmental leadership "energizes" policy with ideological and partisan preferences, while centrifugal governmental leadership provides the "ballast" that tends to reduce the influence of ideology and partisanship upon policy. This distinction is empirical; whether "energy" or "ballast" is more or less appropriate at a specific point in time is entirely dependent upon a range of issues that go beyond the present analysis. The distinction also does not necessarily mean that one form of government is beyond the "rationalization of parliament," as Karl D. Bracher has termed the growing expertise in modern parliamentary democracies.[25] This rationalization has given rise to expert commissions, committees, and administrative agencies and thereby has radically transformed the old classic-liberal concept of representation.

Rather, the centripetal/centrifugal dichotomy helps to highlight the importance of the style of coalition leadership. A hegemonic style of coalition leadership, for instance, should enhance to a greater degree the executive's capacity to influence the ever-growing and increasingly sophisticated bureaucracy via policy change, more than coalition styles that depart from this ideal—for example, the minority-consultative and oversized-consensual arrangements. Therefore, despite the general tendency of bureaucrats to inject stabilizing "ballast" into the policy process (a tendency that, Bracher has argued, has weakened political representation throughout European parliamentary democracies), we should nonetheless expect the hegemonic style of coalition leadership to be able to overcome this structural transformation of modern democracy and provide more opportunity for policy change and energy. So the governing coalition can provide the energy that, *ceteris paribus*, the bureaucracy is incapable or unwilling to generate.[26]

The particular domestic and international politicoeconomic malaise that has afflicted the advanced industrial democracies since 1973 means that the relationship between macroeconomic policy change and executive-coalition leadership style, on the one hand, and government stability and executive-coalition leadership style, on the other, may have been disrupted. Hence I have examined these relationships for the period 1958 to 1984 and separately for the periods 1958 to 1973 and 1974 to 1984. Table 11.1 summarizes these expected results and the overall logic of coalition leadership.

In the following analysis, cabinet stability is operationalized as the number of government-collapse/government-formation episodes during the period 1958–84, within a given country.[27] The number of collapse/formation episodes corresponds to the number of coalition formations (including formations of one-party majority cabinets) noted in table 11.2. Policy change is operationalized according to the example of John D. Robertson and Sue W. Cutcomb and is defined as the standard deviation in the average annual rate of change in final expenditures for public consumption for a given country, 1958–84.[28]

The style of executive-coalition leadership (CLS) within a given representational parliamentary democracy may be assessed by the following formula:

$$CLS = \frac{1}{12 \cdot N} \sum_{i=1}^{N} \sum_{j=1}^{12} P_a \qquad (11.1)$$

in which i is the year, j is a particular month during a given year, P_a is the proportion of seats, cumulatively, that a given cabinet (a) will either need to add to or subtract from the cabinet in order to obtain a hegemonic style (a minimum winning cabinet). The value of 12 is the number of months in a given year, and the N is the total number of years in the time period (27 in this case, 1958 through 1984). This follows Dodd's formula for coalition type.[29] The value of P_a is determined by first ascertaining what proportion of the seats within the principal chamber of the legislature the cabinet coalition controls. If the coalition is a minority coalition (<50.1 percent of seats in the legislature), a determination is then made as to which combination of parties would provide the cabinet with a proportion as close as possible to 50.1 percent. The sum of each of these parties (or party, if only one is necessary or possible) as a proportion of seats within the legislature is then determined, and this becomes the value of P_a. This is the proportion of seats that a cabinet would need to become a minimum winning coalition. The value for P_a in this example would be negative, as the coalition is short a certain proportion of seats to obtain a majority. If a coalition

TABLE 11.1
THE LOGIC AND IMPLIED EFFECTS OF COALITION LEADERSHIP IN MULTIPARTY PARLIAMENTARY DEMOCRACIES

COALITION STRUCTURE	STYLE OF EXECUTIVE COALITION LEADERSHIP	PARTY DECISION MAKING AND CONFLICT RESOLUTION (CONTEXT OF COALITION FORMATION)	HYPERPLURALISM AND ECONOMIC POLARIZATION IN LEGISLATIVE ARENA (DECISIONAL CONTEXT OF COALITION FORMATION)	PREDICTED STABILITY OF EXECUTIVE COALITION	PREDICTED EFFECT ON MACROECONOMIC POLICY CHANGE	COUNTRY EXAMPLES 1958–84
Minimum winning	Hegemonic	Competitive	Minimal	Stable	Energy	Germany, Luxembourg, Ireland[1]
Oversized	Consensual	Conflictual	Prominent	Instable	Ballast	Belgium, Finland, Netherlands, Italy
Minority	Consultative	Consensual	Nondeterminant	Stable	Ballast	Denmark, Norway, Sweden

[1]Based on modal structure of coalitions during the period 1958 through 1984. Ireland has no modal structure during this period, and its categorization here reflects its departure from hegemony (see table 11.2).

TABLE 11.2
EXECUTIVE COALITION FORMATIONS EMERGING FROM CABINET NEGOTIATIONS IN TEN EUROPEAN PARLIAMENTARY DEMOCRACIES, 1958–84

	TYPES OF EXECUTIVE COALITION FORMATIONS				
Country	Single-Party Majority Cabinets	Minority Cabinets	Minimum Winning Cabinets	Oversized Cabinets	Total (%)
Belgium	0	5	9	10	24 (16.6)
Denmark	0	11	2	0	13 (9.0)
Finland	0	7	2	13	22 (15.2)
Germany	0	0	8	0	8 (5.5)
Ireland	5	5	1	0	11 (7.6)
Italy	1	11	3	14	29 (20.0)
Luxembourg	0	0	6	0	6 (4.1)
Netherlands	0	2	7	9	18 (12.4)
Norway	0	7	2	0	9 (6.2)
Sweden	0	3	1	1	5 (3.4)
Total Sample	6	51	41	47	145
Percentage	4.1	35.2	28.3	32.4	

has one or more parties in its configuration beyond what would be necessary to obtain a minimum majority of seats in the legislature, a determination is made as to which of the parties (or party) would provide the largest reduction in parliamentary seats while also providing the coalition a minimum winning status. The value of P_a in this case would be positive, as this would represent the largest proportion of the seats in the cabinet which is above that needed for a minimum winning status.

A value of P_a less than zero is a coalition that must depend upon a consultative style of coalition leadership. A value of zero for the index indicates a hegemonic style (a minimum winning coalition or a single-party majority cabinet coalition), requiring no additions or subtractions from the coalition. A value larger than zero depicts a cabinet coalition style which is less hegemonic and more consensual in its style of executive-coalition leadership.

The advantage of this measure over the alternative of using the difference between total proportions of seats that the cabinet controls within the legislature and 50.1 percent is critical. A minority cabinet, for instance, may have 48 percent of the parliamentary seats, yet the only political party available to it if it wishes to seek minimum winning status may have 25 percent of the seats. The alternative measure would suggest that the minority cabinet is "almost" minimum winning ($48 - 50.1 = -2.1$). Yet in fact, it is much further from being minimum winning. A political party that controls a quarter of the seats in the legislature will demand sizable payoffs in order to join the present coalition.[30] The political compromise and its attendant costs may be too great for the coalition. Or the ideological distance between the cabinet's predominant ideological preference and the party may be too great.[31] Thus, the value of P_a would be -25, a value more closely approximating the situation within which the coalition finds itself. Similar examples can be constructed for oversized coalition cabinets.

For any given year between 1958 and 1984, a particular month's value of P_a would be that of the coalition last formed. For each year, the sum total of all months' value of P_a for a given year was calculated, and the mean value of P_a for the year was derived. Over the full twenty-seven years between 1958 and 1984, the mean annual value of P_a assesses the style of coalition leadership and the extent of that style within executive-legislative relations.

A second measure of executive-coalition style was derived from the first measure. This second measure is the extent to which an operative executive-coalition style deviates from hegemony ($-H$). The equation for deriving this second measure of coalition style is

$$-H = \frac{1}{12 \cdot N} \sum_{i=1}^{N} \sum_{j=1}^{12} |P_a| \qquad (11.2)$$

in which, instead of including the directionality of P_a, we use the absolute value of P_a. This allows us to determine the cumulative extent to which the coalition style in executive-legislative relations for a country over a time period deviated from simple hegemony (0). This second measure assesses whether a hegemonic style of coalition leadership has significantly different effects from the other two styles on the stability of macroeconomic policy and the stability of the government. Over an extended period of time, the mean value of P_a may approach zero (hegemony), but it may actually entail several minority coalitions as well as several oversized coalitions, such as is the case for Italy. While equation 11.1 allows us to gauge the typical operative style of coalition leadership within the country over the time period, it would not allow us to assess the absolute departure from hegemony. All things being equal, we would expect that the hegemonic style of coalition leadership would be most likely to inject the "energy" or change into macroeconomic policy necessary for policy change, while either consultation or consensual styles of executive leadership would be associated with more policy "ballast" or stability over an extended period of time. Equation 11.2, with its use of the absolute value of P_a, provides such an assessment.

Table 11.3 presents the values for the typical coalition style, as well as the degree to which the coalition style typically departed from hegemony, for the sample of ten multiparty democracies between 1958 and 1984. Table 11.4 presents the Pearson correlation coefficients among coalition leadership style, departure from hegemony, the number of cabinet-collapse/cabinet-formation

TABLE 11.3
MEAN STYLE OF AND MEAN EXTENT OF DEPARTURE FROM HEGEMONIC STYLE OF EXECUTIVE COALITION LEADERSHIP IN MULTIPARTY DEMOCRACIES

	1958–84		1958–73		1974–84	
COUNTRY	COALITION STYLE	DEPARTURE FROM HEGEMONY	COALITION STYLE	DEPARTURE FROM HEGEMONY	COALITION STYLE	DEPARTURE FROM HEGEMONY
Belgium	.048	.048	.010	.007	.110	.114
Denmark	−.145	.146	−.087	.087	−.240	.240
Finland	.055	.135	.022	.128	.190	.146
Germany	.012	.012	.020	.020	0	0
Ireland	−.013	.013	−.010	.010	−.018	.018
Italy	.014	.082	.033	.062	−.015	.113
Luxembourg	0	0	0	0	0	0
Netherlands	.086	.093	.056	.056	.134	.152
Norway	−.064	.064	−.040	.040	−.103	.103
Sweden	−.056	.056	−.029	.029	−.098	.098

episodes, and the degree of change in macroeconomic policy. The correlations are presented separately for the three separate time periods: 1958–84, 1958–73, and 1974–84. Table 11.5 presents partial correlation coefficients, controlling for consensual democracy, across each time period. (Consensual democracy is a binary [dummy] variable, with Sweden, Denmark and Norway coded as zero).

While these results must be considered tentative because of the small number of observations, several distinctive patterns emerge. Turning first to table 11.3, three substantively significant patterns emerge for the full time period (1958–84). The more consultative the typical coalition style within a multiparty democracy, the more "energized" or changed (PC) is the macroeconomic policy ($r = -.68$), a conclusion contrary to our expectations. Second, underscoring the first observation, yet again contrary to our general expectation, we see that the greater the departure from the hegemonic style of coalition leadership ($-H$), the more energized is the macroeconomic policy ($r = .44$). Third, the greater the departure from hegemony, the greater is the incidence of cabinet collapse (CS), confirming one of our expectations ($r = .43$). These three patterns generally hold up for the time period 1958–73 but are attenuated for the more turbulent period of 1974–84. During the latter period, (1) there is no relationship between executive-coalition style and policy change ($r = -.02$); (2) there is a very strong positive relationship between coalition style and cabinet collapse ($r = .69$); (3) there is a reversal in the direction of the relationship between the degree of departure from hegemony and policy change ($r = -.48$); and (4) there is a weakening of the relationship between the degree of departure from hegemony and cabinet stability ($r = .36$). It would

TABLE 11.4
PEARSON CORRELATION COEFFICIENTS (N = 10)

	1958–84					1958–73					1974–84			
	PC	CS	CLS	–H		PC	CS	CLS	–H		PC	CS	CLS	–H
PC	--	--	--	--	PC	--	--	--	--	PC	--	--	--	--
CS	–.0396 (p = .457)	--	--	--	CS	.1434 (p = .346)	--	--	--	CS	–.2086 (p = .282)	--	--	--
CLS	–.6766 (p = .016)	.3307 (p = .199)	--	--	CLS	–.6427 (p = .023)	.3822 (p = .138)	--	--	CLS	–.0176 (p = .481)	.6940 (p = .013)	--	--
–H	.4401 (p = .102)	.4321 (p = .106)	–.1791 (p = .310)	--	–H	.3586 (p = .154)	.5857 (p = .038)	–.0364 (p = .460)	--	–H	–.4835 (p = .078)	.3632 (p = .151)	–.2242 (p = .248)	--

Variables: PC = Degree of macroeconomic policy change
CS = The number of cabinet collapse/cabinet formation episodes
CLS = Coalition leadership style
–H = Departure from hegemonic style of coalition leadership

seem that under conditions of general politicoeconomic turbulence, coalition arrangements that depart from hegemony are less able to generate change and energy in macroeconomic policy, and are less able to generate stability of coalition leadership as well.

Before we draw any conclusions about the relationships between coalition style, change in macroeconomic policy, and cabinet stability, we must first control for the effect that one important systemic factor—consensual patterns of decision making—is expected to have in shaping these relationships. As we have seen, democracies that are characterized by consensual decision making are far more prone to opt for minority governments. We expect that a minority coalition within such a democracy may not be equivalent to a minority government within a democracy that is not characterized by consensual decision making. A minority coalition within the former democracies may require a consultative style, but the corporatist institutional structures characteristic of these democracies and the strong consensus-building tradition within their parliaments may serve to weaken the relationship between the style of coalition leadership and policy change, as well as the relationship between the style of coalition leadership and cabinet durability. In other words, if Luebbert is correct and these democracies are characterized by "party concessions [that] will not then be party-to-party concessions, and therefore highly risky for party leaders, but will also be concessions among the interest groups directly concerned with the government and parties," then the type of coalition style becomes spurious by being related to both policy instability and to duration of the coalition.[32] In any event, the consultative style within consensual democracies can be expected to be associated with more stability and less, not more, policy change than in the democracies that do not traditionally practice consensual decision making.

Table 11.5 supports this line of reasoning. During the period 1958–84, we can see that the partial correlation between policy change and coalition style improves somewhat (–.72) in comparison to the simple correlation presented in table 11.3. A similar finding holds for the partial between the departure from hegemony and the stability of cabinet governments (.61) as compared to the relationship reported in table 11.4. The partial for the relationship between the departure from hegemony and policy instability declines notably (.36) from that reported in table 11.4. This pattern of change is repeated in the critical time period 1974–84.

We may draw four central conclusions from tables 11.4 and 11.5. First, the more the style of coalition leadership assumes a consensual pattern (i.e., an oversized coalition), the less macroeconomic policy will assume an energetic nature. Second, the greater the departure from hegemony in the style of executive-coalition leadership, the more frequent are the episodes of coalition collapse/coalition formation. Third, when we control for specific time periods associated with peculiar politicoeconomic turbulence and uncertainty, a depar-

TABLE 11.5
PARTIAL CORRELATION COEFFICIENTS, CONTROLLING FOR CONSENSUAL DECISION-MAKING DEMOCRACIES* (N = 10)

	1958–84					1958–73					1974–84			
	PC	CS	CLS	–H		PC	CS	CLS	–H		PC	CS	CLS	–H
PC	--	--	--	--	PC	--	--	--	--	PC	--	--	--	--
CS	.1013 (p = .398)	--	--	--	CS	.3853 (p = .153)	--	--	--	CS	–.4144 (p = .134)	--	--	--
CLS	–.7160 (p = .015)	.0295 (p = .470)	--	--	CLS	–.6008 (p = .044)	.0489 (p = .450)	--	--	CLS	–.4029 (p = .141)	.6067 (p = .042)	--	--
–H	.3624 (p = .169)	.6118 (p = .040)	.1837 (p = .318)	--	–H	.3341 (p = .190)	.7222 (p = .014)	1420 (p = .358)	--	–H	–.4099 (p = .137)	.7213 (p = .014)	.2188 (p = .286)	--

Variables: PC = Degree of macroeconomic policy change
CS = The number of cabinet-collapse/cabinet-formation episodes
CLS = Coalition leadership style
–H = Departure from hegemonic style of coalition leadership

*Consensual democracy is a dummy variable; Sweden, Denmark, and Norway are coded as 0; the seven other nonconsensual democracies are coded as 1.

ture from hegemony reduces the opportunities for macroeconomic energy and innovation, and a consensual style of executive-coalition leadership increases the prospects of confronting frequent cycles of cabinet collapse/cabinet formation. And fourth, unlike democracies that opt for minority cabinets and the consultative style of coalition leadership, parliamentary democracies that are traditionally associated with patterns of conflictual decision making appear more likely to stabilize policy and executive leadership, particularly in periods of politicoeconomic turbulence (e.g., 1974–84).

COALITION LEADERSHIP IN PERSPECTIVE

The study of executive-coalition leadership and its implications for the performance of contemporary representational parliamentary democracies has only recently become the object of systematic cross-national analysis. As the findings presented in this paper suggest, there are three critical implications that follow from such an analysis which lend themselves to the broader study of comparative contemporary democracies.

First, the stability and diversity of the party system have consequences for the democratic polity that go beyond the persistence and survival of modern politics. Instable patterns of issue representation (e.g., fragmentation, fractionalization and polarization of the party system) also constrain the capacity of executive-coalitional leadership within contemporary democracies. By contributing to the final form that coalition cabinets assume, the features of the party system clearly determine not only the stability of the cabinet executive but also, indirectly, the contours of macroeconomic policy over time. Therefore, choices bearing upon the nature of electoral laws and constitutional provisions for issue representation have implications for the nature of executive-coalition leadership that also determine the nature of policy changes.

Second, despite the fact that the configuration of coalitions does constrain the latitude that parliamentary executives have in alternating macroeconomic policy, there are systemic-level factors that can compensate for what would otherwise be weak executive-coalition leadership in representational parliamentary democracies. Consensual democracies, which often have a consultative (i.e., minority) style of executive-coalition leadership, nonetheless have demonstrated a greater capacity to stabilize the contours of public policy and have also remained relatively free from coalition instability. During the entire time period studied the three consensual democracies in the sample—Denmark, Norway and Sweden—averaged only 1.67 government collapses during a five-year period, while the remaining seven nonconsensual democracies averaged 2.99 per five-year period during the same span of time. Therefore, the relationship between policy change and executive-coalition style should not be considered outside the systemic factors that also shape executive-legislative relations.

Executive-coalition leadership is a product of the party system–legislative arena and the systemic factors associated with particular representational parliamentary democracies. Leadership patterns are additionally conditioned by the particular politicoeconomic environment that confronts party elites in their decisions both to agree on a final formula for the parliamentary executive and eventually to influence the contours of macroeconomic policy. A hegemonic style of coalition leadership does not inject macroeconomic policy with energy during periods when the politicoeconomic environment is stable (e.g., 1958–73). However, a hegemonic style of executive-coalition leadership during more turbulent periods (e.g., 1974–84) is, except in consensual democracies, a stimulus to changes in macroeconomic policy. Hence, the hegemonic leadership style is both more stable during stable economic times and more adept at responding to rapidly changing economic circumstances.

What does this analysis suggest about the broader concept of political leadership at the national level of government in multiparty democracies? Within the context of institutional leadership, the role of the bureaucracy and the particular skills, attitudes, and experiences of the members of the executive coalition will play a major role in shaping the contours of macroeconomic policy and the stability of coalitions.[33] Nonetheless, beyond such factors lie critical influences that are often underestimated when exploring the effects of political leadership. It is precisely these factors—the particular configuration of power and authority within executive-legislative relations as manifested by the style of executive-coalition leadership—that consumes our attention in this chapter. And within this context, the most prominent question to emerge is why certain styles of executive-coalition leadership influence macroeconomic policy in ways inconsistent with our initial expectations. More specifically, these findings raise the question: What broader explanations can account for why a hegemonic style of coalition leadership "stabilizes" macroeconomic policy generally while "energizing" such policy during more turbulent periods of economic activity?

The answer seems to lie in the executive-legislative relationship within multiparty parliamentary democracies. The legislative assembly is the arena within which the rules governing executive leadership are constituted. Thus the resulting executive coalition incorporates the aggregate of agreements, bargains, and compromises between the various contending interests within the legislative arena that gave rise to the particular coalition. Then the executive coalition will reflect the style of leadership that is, at the moment the bargain is made, the one that most closely approximates a Pareto optimality among the various interests within the bargaining arena. It would then follow that the actual style of leadership and, more specifically, the influence of the executive coalition on the factors of change in macroeconomic policy would be generally consistent with the preferences of the parties to the bargain.

For minimum winning coalitions, the preference of the parties to the bargain is for an executive that reaches an equilibrium among the contending interests within the decision-making and policy-implementation phase of the policy process. Such an equilibrium is maintained to the extent that the executive is granted the latitude to explore policy options when the environmental conditions demand it; yet because of the delicate balance between the parties in the minimum winning coalition, the coalition will refrain from significant alternations in policy in the absence of a clear need. Restraint, therefore, dominates the hegemonic style in general. For the consensual executive, built around the structure of an oversized coalition, ballast becomes the outgrowth of a clear alignment of contending interests within the executive coalition. Unable to reach such a clear agreement in the legislative arena, the parties to the bargain seek to preserve their particular interests by expanding the representation in the coalition to ensure a reflection of their particular interests in policymaking. An unstable and dynamic economic environment will only exaggerate and clarify policy differences between parties and interests within the coalition, as well as raise the specter of increasing costs that are associated with uncertain outcomes. An oversized coalition faces the likelihood not only of disintegrating but also of being unable to mobilize the very consensus necessary to manufacture and sustain the leadership required to innovate policy. Ballast (or deadlock) results under either environmental condition.

The distinctive leadership styles of executive coalitions and the respective patterns of influence on macroeconomic policy may be conceived as the products of interaction of two elements that are present in any democratic polity but that are particularly critical in multiparty parliamentary democracies. These are (1) decision-making rules governing the strategy of consent and (2) executive-legislative relations in the context of sanctioning executive leadership. In order to understand coalition leadership and its influence on policy, the legislature and the executive will have to be understood in terms of a clear division of labor. In the legislative arena, the negotiation and bargaining over the final form of executive leadership occurs. The executive must (collectively) act to realize the preferences of those parties that have sanctioned the executive coalition.

James M. Buchanan and Gordon Tullock suggest that decision-making rules are designed around either the principle of unanimity or that of majority rule.[34] The principle of unanimity holds that decisions at the legislative level that bear upon the final form of the executive coalition include the input of as many interests as possible. At the executive level, it would similarly mean that as many party interests as possible be involved in deciding specific strategies and tactics in order to realize the interests of those parties that have sanctioned the coalition. As we have seen, the structural effect of such an arrangement is to opt for an oversized executive coalition that will have a stabilizing effect on policy in general but no role during more turbulent periods.

Where the arena of bargaining lies outside the legislature, yet where the principle of unanimity still applies, as in the special case of consensual democracies, the style of executive leadership is consultative (rather than consensual), and the policy effect is generally that of energy. Where, however, rules of decision making and strategy of consent favor the principle of majority rule in the legislative arena and where such a strategy is complemented at the executive level, the structural effect is that of a minimum winning executive coalition, with a consequent minimal effect on macroeconomic policy in general, though an energetic influence during turbulence.

Table 11.6 summarizes this logic. The resulting patterns of relations in the legislature between political parties (consensual, conflictual, and competitive), the conditions of hyperpluralism and economic polarization, and the rules of decision making are presented in the first row of table 11.6. In the second row, the particular coalition structure (minority, oversized, or minimum winning) and the corresponding style of coalition leadership within the executive level are presented according to the specific rule of decision making that characterizes strategies of consent and conflict resolution among political parties. Finally, the third row depicts the expected (and observed) change in macroeconomic policy that should follow from a particular alignment of a rule of decision making, the pattern of relations between political parties, the dynamics of hyperpluralism and economic polarization, coalition structure, and coalition leadership. Each cell is consistent with the previous logic of coalition leadership outlined in table 11.1

Political leadership has long been associated with the charismatic qualities of particular individuals. Frequently, the starting point for understanding the nature of political leadership has been the skills of communication and persuasion possessed by those who occupy critical authority roles. However, in parliamentary representative democracies, in which parties and their elites are compressed into arenas of political conflict that may be far more turbulent and fragmented than in "majoritarian" or "Westminster" democracies, executive coalitions play a critical role in shaping the contours of policy through the channels of executive-legislative relations. While individuals within these coalitions may certainly play a significant role in shaping the course of macroeconomic policy and in determining the serviceability of a particular coalition, the institutional dynamics that bear upon these individuals places a higher premium on understanding the particular nature of the relationship between institutional structure, policy outcome, and democratic reforms. However, as is suggested by the cases of Norway, Sweden, and Denmark, the particular dynamics of political culture seem also to affect the nature of political leadership in contemporary parliamentary democracies.

TABLE 11.6

COALITION LEADERSHIP IN THE CONTEXT OF EXECUTIVE-LEGISLATIVE RELATIONS AND DECISION-MAKING RULES AMONG POLITICAL PARTIES IN MULTIPARTY PARLIAMENTARY DEMOCRACIES

		Decision-Making Rules and the Logic of Consent among Political Parties in the Context of Building Executive Coalitions	
		Unanimity Rule	Majority Rule
	Legislative role: arena of bargaining	Consensual or conflictual inter- and intraparty decision making and conflict resolution	Competitive intra- and interparty decision making and conflict resolution
Executive-legislative roles in the context of coalition leadership		Probability greater under conditions of hyperpluralism and economic polarization (see table 11.1)	Probability greater under conditions of minimal hyperpluralism and economic polarization (see table 11.1)
	Executive role: arena of coalition leadership	Oversized coalition structure with a consensual leadership style, or a minority coalition structure with a consultative style (see table 11.1)	Minimum-winning-coalition structure with a hegemonic style of executive leadership (see table 11.1)
Marginal effects on macroeconomic policy change		Energy (consultative); ballast under conditions of macroeconomic turbulence (ballast overall for the conflictual subset of multiparty democracies) (see table 11.1)	Ballast generally; energy under conditions of macroeconomic turbulence (see table 11.1)

NOTES

The research for this paper was supported by a Departmental Development Grant at Texas A & M University. I would like to thank Charles Cnudde, Bryan Jones, Gary Marks, Carol Mershon, and Kaare Strom for their helpful comments on earlier versions of this paper.

1. Harry Ekstein, *The Evaluation of Political Performance: Problems and Dimensions* (Beverly Hills, Calif.: Sage Publications, 1971); Ted Robert Gurr and Muriel McClelland, *Political Performance: A Twelve Nation Study* (Beverly Hills, Calif.: Sage Publications, 1971); Lawrence C. Dodd, *Coalitions in Parliamentary Government* (Princeton, N.J.: Princeton University Press, 1976); Ekkart Zimmermann, "Government Stability in Six European Countries during the World Economic Crisis of the 1930s: Some Preliminary Considerations," *European Journal of Political Research* 15 (Apr. 1987): 23–52; Robert Harmel and John D. Robertson, "Government Stability and Regime Support: A Cross-National Analysis," *Journal of Politics* 48 (Nov. 1986): 1029–40.
2. Arend Lijphart, *Democracies: Patterns of Majoritarian and Consensus Government in Twenty-One Countries* (New Haven, Conn.: Yale University Press, 1984).
3. Ibid., p. 163.
4. Ibid., p. 165.
5. Ibid.; also see Dodd, *Coalitions,* p. 5.
6. William Mishler and Anne Hildreth, "Legislatures and Political Stability: An Exploratory Analysis," *Journal of Politics* 46 (Feb. 1984): 25–59.
7. Bert A. Rockman, "Legislative-Executive Relations and Legislative Oversight," *Legislative Studies Quarterly* 3 (Aug. 1984): 390; see also Anthony King, "Modes of Executive-Legislative Relations: Great Britain, France, and West Germany," *Legislative Studies Quarterly* 1 (Feb. 1976): 11–36.
8. S. E. Finer, "Princes, Parliaments, and the Public Service," *Parliamentary Affairs* 33 (Autumn 1980): 367.
9. Robert L. Peterson, Martine De Ridder, J. D. Hobbs, and E. F. McClellan, "Government Formation and Policy Formation: Patterns in Belgium and the Netherlands," *Res Publica* 25 (Autumn 1983): 55.
10. See Gerhard Loewenberg and Samuel C. Patterson, *Comparing Legislatures* (Boston, Mass.: Little, Brown, & Co., 1979), pp. 231–79.
11. Dodd, *Coalitions,* pp. 54–70.
12. Lijphart, *Democracies,* p. 81; also see Dodd, *Coalitions,* pp. 156–81, and John D. Robertson, "The Political Economy and the Durability of European Coalition Cabinets: New Variations on a Game-Theoretic Perspective," *Journal of Politics* 45 (Nov. 1983): 932–57.
13. Lijphart, *Democracies,* p. 80.
14. John D. Robertson, "Economic Polarization and Cabinet Formation in Western Europe," *Legislative Studies Quarterly* 11 (Nov. 1986): 533–49; Kaare Strom, "Minority Governments in Parliamentary Democracies: The Rationality of Nonwinning Cabinet Solutions," *Comparative Political Studies* 17 (July 1984): 199–227; Gregory Luebbert, *Contemporary Democracy: Policymaking and Governing Coalitions in Europe and Israel* (New York: Columbia University Press, 1986), pp. 45–89; Dodd, *Coalitions,* pp. 44–114.
15. Dodd, *Coalitions,* pp. 34–70. For further elaboration of the decisional context of cabinet formation, a succinct and cogent overview can be found in Lijphart, *Democracies,* pp. 46–66. The classic formal theoretical analysis of coalition formation is William Riker's *The Theory of Political Coalition* (New Haven, Conn.: Yale University

Press, 1962). Additional perspectives on game theory include William A. Gamson, "A Theory of Coalition Formation," *American Sociological Review* 26 (June 1968): 373–82; Abram De Swaan, *Coalition Theories and Cabinet Formation* (Amsterdam: Elsevier, 1973); and Robert Axelrod, *Conflict of Interest* (Chicago: Markham, 1970). For a recent examination of the conflict-of-interest component within the decisional context of cabinet formations see Eric C. Browne, Dennis Gleiber, and Carolyn S. Mashoba, "Evaluating Conflict of Interest Theory: Western European Cabinet Coalition, 1945-1980," *British Journal of Political Science* 14 (Jan. 1984): 335–51. Among the most compelling of recent studies on the topic is that of Peterson et al. They argue that the formation of government in parliamentary democracies "necessarily involves policy considerations as part of the process of mapping areas of agreement and creating a payoff structure through policy agreements" (p. 81); they also identify three stages of cabinet formation. According to the logic of their framework, the decisional context, as described above, would, for the most part, fall into the second stage identified by Peterson et al. (1983). They depict this stage as characterized by "a shift from determining who is to participate [in government] to negotiations about the substance of policy" (p. 58). Based on their case studies of one Dutch and two Belgium cabinet negotiations, they describe the second stage as where "the agreement to govern is hammered out as negotiations discuss key policies to be pursued by the new government" (p. 58), concluding that this stage is "generally the most time consuming and associated with the greatest apparent difficulties" (p. 80).

16. Robertson, "Economic Polarization."

17. Strom "Minority Governments"; Luebbert, *Contemporary Democracy,* pp. 43–65.

18. Luebbert, *Contemporary Democracy,* pp. 83–86; Dodd, *Coalitions,* pp. 41–48, 57–62.

19. Luebbert, *Contemporary Democracy,* pp. 71–83; Dodd, *Coalitions,* pp. 127–55.

20. Luebbert, *Contemporary Democracy,* pp. 71–83; Dodd, *Coalitions,* pp. 127–55; and John D. Robertson, "Economic Issues and the Probability of Forming Minority Coalitions Cabinets," *Social Science Quarterly* 66 (Sept. 1985): 687–94.

21. G. Bingham Powell, Jr., "Party Systems and Political System Performance: Voting, Participation, Government Stability and Mass Violence in Contemporary Democracies," *American Political Science Review* 75 (Dec. 1981): 861–79.

22. Luebbert, *Contemporary Democracy,* pp. 68–70.

23. See Strom, "Minority Governments"; and Luebbert, *Contemporary Democracy,* pp. 68–70.

24. Joel D. Aberbach, Robert D. Putnam, and Bert A. Rockman, *Bureaucrats and Politicians in Western Democracies* (Cambridge, Mass.: Harvard University Press, 1981).

25. Karl D. Bracher, "Problems of Parliamentary Democracy in Europe," in *Comparative Legislative Systems: A Reader in Theory and Research,* ed. Herbert Hirsch and M. Donald Hancock (New York: Free Press, 1971), pp. 343–59.

26. Also see John D. Robertson and Sue W. Cutcomb, "Parliamentary Executive-Legislative Relations and the Implications of Cabinet Stability: 'Ballast' and 'Energy' in Macroeconomic Policy," *Western Political Quarterly* 40 (Mar. 1987): 7–27. For further elaboration of the role that bureaucratic leadership may play in constraining the executive's capacity to influence policy see B. Guy Peters, "The Problem of Bureaucratic Government," *Journal of Politics* 43 (Jan. 1981): 56–82.

27. See Zimmerman, "Government Stability," pp. 32-33; and John D. Robertson, "Toward a Political-Economic Accounting of the Endurance of Cabinet Administrations: An Empirical Assessment of Eight European Democracies," *American Journal of*

Political Science 28 (Nov. 1984): 695–97. Data on the collapse of governments and the configuration of parties within each of the coalitions within the ten countries over the years 1958 through 1984 were collected from the *Keesing's Contemporary Archives* (New York: Longman); various volumes, 1954–84.

28. Data were collected from the Organization for Economic Cooperation and Development, *Economic Outlook* 40 (Dec. 1986): 161.

29. Dodd, *Coalitions,* pp. 117–19.

30. Ian Budge and Michael Laver, "Policy, Ideology, and Party Distance: Analysis of Election Programmes in 19 Democracies," *Legislative Studies Quarterly* 11 (Nov. 1986): 607–18; and Norman Schofield and Michael Laver, "Bargaining Theory and Portfolio Payoffs in European Coalition Governments, 1945–1983," *British Journal of Political Science* 15 (Apr. 1985): 26–49.

31. Giovanni Sartori, *Parties and Party Systems: A Framework for Analysis* (Cambridge: Cambridge University Press, 1976).

32. Luebbert, *Contemporary Democracy,* p. 68.

33. See, for instance, Mattei Dogan, ed., *The Mandarins of Western Europe: The Political Role of Top Civil Servants* (New York: John Wiley & Sons, 1975); Edward Page, *Political Authority and Bureaucratic Power: A Comparative Analysis* (Knoxville: University of Tennessee Press, 1985); G. Guy Peters, "Politicians and Bureaucrats in the Politics of Policy-making," in *Bureaucracy and Public Choice,* ed. Jan-Erik Lane (Beverly Hills, Calif.: Sage Publications, 1987), pp. 225–82; and William A. Niskanen, Jr., *Bureaucracy and Representative Government* (Chicago: Aldine Publishing Co., 1971).

34. James M. Buchanan and Gordon Tullock, *The Calculus of Consent: Logical Foundations of Constitutional Democracy* (Ann Arbor: University of Michigan Press, 1971).

12

Bureaucratic Leadership in Public Organizations

Kenneth J. Meier

Herbert Kaufman, in *Time, Chance, and Organizations,* presents a theory of organizational development and survival in which leadership plays no role.[1] According to Kaufman, organizations die because they develop resource problems; resource problems result because organizations do not adapt to changes in their environment. Organizations that are able to adapt and survive do so because "they are lucky," not because bureaucratic leaders make conscious decisions that improve the organization's chances of survival. Although Kaufman's thesis appears radical, it is only an extreme presentation of one branch of organizational sociology that emphasizes environmental determinism. This school of thought treats organizations as black boxes that react to environmental pressures. The key relationships are between the organization and its environment, not between actors within the organization.[2]

Although Kaufman's argument has some intuitive appeal because it eliminates a part of organizations that is difficult to measure and analyze, it has implications that are difficult for students of bureaucracy to accept. Such a view would hold that the activities of the Environmental Protection Agency would be no different if Anne Burford were the administrator than if William Ruckelshaus were in charge. The Consumer Product Safety Commission should have no greater chance of survival if Susan Kennedy were its leader than if S. John Byington were its head.[3]

These two illustrations stretch credulity, but constructing a leaderless theory of organization is entirely plausible. In all of public administration, leadership is one of the more difficult phenomena to study. Leadership studies in bureaucracy are beset with problems similar to leadership studies of the presidency. Essentially, research is limited to case studies as the mode of analysis; theory building is difficult with samples of N = 1 and little comparative analysis. Although the behavioral revolution has had only a modest impact on public administration, it completely by-passed the study of bureaucratic leadership.[4]

My objective in this chapter is to set bureau leadership within a theoretical context that will permit some comparative analysis. I will produce a series of testable hypotheses, and I will do so within the structure of organizational systems theory.[5] This approach will not reject the assumption that environments have a major impact on public organizations; the impact of the 1980 election on the federal bureaucracy was simply too great to make this assumption implausible.[6] Rather, the environment will be assumed to structure the choices that individuals in an organization can make. Leadership will be viewed as a series of strategic choices by members of the organization's dominant coalition.[7] These strategic decisions fall into two general groups—decisions concerning the organization's response to environmental demands and decisions concerning how to structure the organization internally.

ORGANIZATIONAL GOALS

Public organizations are goal-oriented collectivities; that is, they exist to pursue some end.[8] Much organization theory literature stresses that the primary goal of organizations is survival.[9] Such a view of public organizations, however, is incomplete, because public organizations are not free to pursue all possible strategies to achieve survival. Public organizations are created by other political actors for the purpose of attaining some policy end. The elected chief executive, the legislature, and other political actors specify the general policy domain of a public organization.

This theory assumes that all public organizations have policy goals as well as survival goals.[10] The environmental establishment of goals does not mean that public organizations have no influence over the policy goals they pursue; clearly, public organizations are political actors that can influence their own goals. Economic theorists and bureaucratic observers argue that bureaus aggressively seek to expand their policy domains.[11] Similarly, some bureaus seek to restrict their policy domain by eliminating policy goals; the Department of Housing and Urban Development, for example, actively sought to eliminate its disaster housing program during the late 1970s, and the Army Corps of Engineers resisted demands to regulate coastal wetlands for long periods of time before court rulings forced it to act.

Despite an ability to influence their own goals, public organizations are not free agents. Public organizations cannot pursue any possible goal that might ensure their survival. The Agricultural Research Service, for example, could not decide next year to establish policies related to munitions research; nor could the Army Corps of Engineers realistically propose policies that would serve welfare mothers as a clientele.

POWER IN ORGANIZATIONS

According to Norton Long, power is the lifeblood of administration.[12] To achieve policy goals that are established by their environment, public organizations need power.[13] Power for an organization has two essential components—resources and autonomy.[14] Resources include money, legal authority, personnel, and other inputs necessary to deliver goods or services to the environment. Without adequate resources, public organizations cannot attain their goals; the limited resources of the Securities and Exchange Commission (SEC), for example, means that the SEC must rely on voluntary self-regulation to implement many of its policies.

Resources are not the only component of power, however. The Social Security Administration spends more than $200 billion a year, yet is not a powerful organization because legislation severely limits its discretion. Power also requires autonomy, discretion in the use of resources, and a sphere of influence that is recognized by other policy actors. To develop power, and thus to have a reasonable chance of attaining policy goals, the organization must have both resources and autonomy. The Social Security Administration, with vast resources and little autonomy, is a weak organization; the SEC, with substantial autonomy but few resources, is also a weak organization. Without power, public organizations may well resemble those organizations at the mercy of their environments described by Kaufman.

POWER AND LEADERSHIP

The role of leadership in organizations is to acquire power for the organization. A leader's success in gaining resources and autonomy should determine, in part, the organization's ability to survive and achieve its policy goals. The actions of an organization's leaders can contribute to resources or autonomy by affecting any of three variables—cohesion, expertise, and clientele support.[15] Cohesion is the degree of commitment that the organization's members have to the organization and its goals. Expertise is the specialized knowledge that an organization develops to use in the policy-making or implementing process. Clientele support is the political support for the organization in its environment.

The bureau leadership's actions to increase cohesion, expertise, or clientele support are subject to constraints placed on the organization by its environment. The objective of an organization's leadership is to extract resources and autonomy from the environment. Four strategic choices face an organizational leader. First, how will the leadership attempt to gain the organization's members' support for the organization's goals, that is, what *membership inducements* will be offered?[16] Second, what *policy objectives* will the organization pursue? Third, how will the organization seek to implement the organization's policy objectives? What will the *implementation strategy* be?

Fourth, what efforts will be made to build support for the organization in its environment? That is, what will the organization's *coalitional strategy* be?

These four strategic decisions have both internal and external ramifications. Internal aspects of these decisions affect the internal operations of the organization; external dimensions concern the relationship of the organization to its environment. Strategic decisions about policy goals, implementation strategy, and coalitional strategy affect an organization's external activities. Decisions concerning policy goals, implementation strategy, and membership inducements have implications for an organization's internal structure. The four strategic decisions and their relationship to bureaucratic leadership are shown in figure 12.1.

STRATEGIC DECISIONS

INDUCEMENTS TO MEMBERS

Strategic decisions regarding the inducements offered to members seek to affect two variables linked to organizational power. The creative use of inducements can increase the commitment of members to the organization and its goals; that is, it can augment cohesion. Inducements can also be used to develop expertise and other policy skills so that the organization can gain autonomy in its policy operations.

The inducements that the leadership offers to members can best be viewed as exchanges between the leadership and the organization's members. Leadership must offer individuals something of value to attract members to the organization and to gain their cooperation after they join. In this view, support for leadership comes from below in the organization similar to Barnard's conception of organizational authority.[17]

Any organization has a wide variety of incentives that it can offer to potential members to gain their cooperation. A review of the literature on exchanges reveals four categories of organizational incentives—material, solidary, purposive, and coercive.[18]

Material incentives are tangible benefits that an organization offers to its members. These benefits include, but are not limited to, salary and fringe benefits. For example, office space or research resources might also be material incentives. Access to material resources varies from organization to organization. Expanding public organizations will have greater material incentives to offer employees than will contracting organizations. Public organizations rely heavily on material incentives to attract employees, but the impact of material incentives can be overestimated.[19] Leadership can affect the availability of material incentives if it is more or less successful in gaining support from those portions of the environment that control the organization's resources.

FIGURE 12.1
STRATEGIC DECISIONS AND BUREAU LEADERSHIP

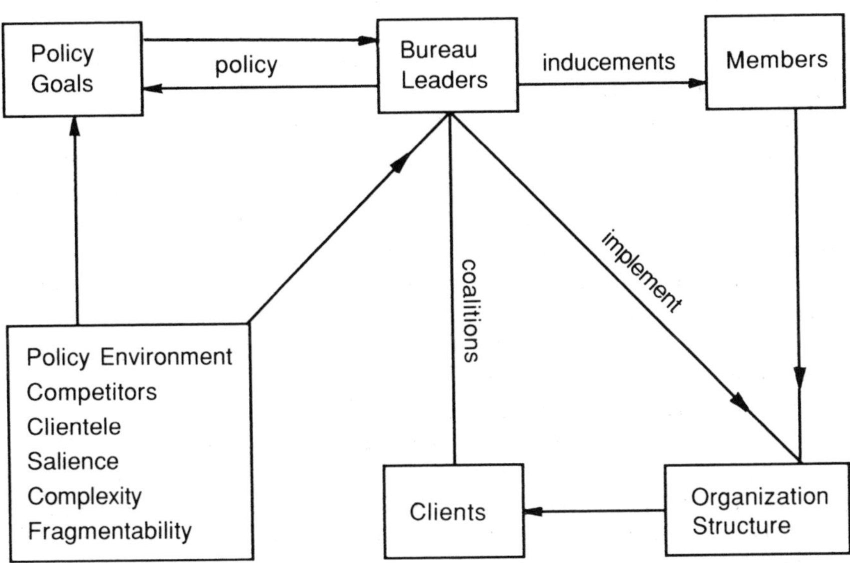

Solidary benefits are "intangible rewards arising out of the act of associating."[20] Solidary benefits can be offered to all members of the organization, or they can be offered selectively to some members. The collegiality of the organization, the status of the organization, and a sense of organizational membership are benefits offered to all employees. Status in the organization, however, is offered to some employees but not to others. Certain public organizations rely heavily on solidary benefits to maintain employee loyalty; the Forest Service and the Marine Corps are two such organizations.

Leadership can increase solidary benefits by manipulating informal elements in an organization. Individual members of the organization can be granted greater status in terms of position or promotion. Decision processes can be made more participatory to gain employee support. The socialization of the organization's employees to supportive values can make reliance on solidary benefits easier to maintain.[21]

Purposive incentives are "intangible rewards that derive from the sense of satisfaction of having contributed to the attainment of a worthwhile cause."[22] For a governmental bureau, purposive incentives are linked to the bureau's policy goals. If an individual identifies with the organization's goals, then that individual will become attached to the organization regardless of the material incentives. The early Peace Corps was a classic example of an organization able to attract talented individuals by appealing to purposive incentives. The Civil Aeronautics Board under Alfred Kahn was able to recruit quality economists by allowing them to work toward their goal of deregulation.[23]

Governmental organizations are more likely to attract individuals who are receptive to purposive incentives than are private-sector organizations. Individuals who pursue Master of Public Administration degrees (a public-sector degree) are more likely to empathize with the plight of others, more likely to be innovative, to be interested in the "public interest," and to be interested in public service than are students in Master of Business Administration programs.[24] The former are also more likely to be motivated by challenging work than by higher pay.[25] Other studies show that public employees have different political values than the general population.[26]

Effective leadership can use purposive incentives to improve agency cohesion. Delegating decision responsibility to individuals can develop a commitment among those individuals to the programs that they administer. This principle has even reached the status of law, as in Miles' Law, "Where one stands [on an issue] depends on where one sits."[27]

Not all incentives used to gain member cooperation are positive. Public organizations can also rely on coercion to gain compliance with the leadership's goals. Organizational leaders can threaten to deny benefits to individual members and may prevent pay raises or access to key decisions. The most dramatic coercive incentive is termination; although not frequently used in the public sector, the threat of termination, especially due to a reduction in force as the result of a political transition, is a strong motive for cooperating with new agency leaders.

One little-studied method of coercion is to deny employees the purposive benefits of the organization. Anne Burford, as head of the Environmental Protection Agency, distrusted career civil servants. As a result, she tried to centralize decision making and to deny career employees the purposive benefits of program control.[28] The results were a drop in morale and active employee resistance to Burford's policies.

Every bureaucratic leader can to some extent manipulate the mix of incentives offered to employees. If leaders offer a mix that will increase cohesion or encourage individuals to develop expertise, then the power position of the organization will be improved. Improvements in the organization's power position should translate not only into greater impact on public policy but also into a greater probability of survival.

Policy Objectives

Although legislative bodies set the basic policy objectives of governmental organizations, bureau leadership can still affect these objectives. The Tennessee Valley Authority (TVA) was charged with two policy goals when it was created—developing public electrical-power programs in the Tenenssee River valley and stimulating changes in agricultural production. The early TVA leadership allowed the agricultural programs to be co-opted by the land-grant universities in the region, thus gaining political support that was used to pursue its public-power goals.[29] Similarly, the Federal Reserve (FED) frequently chooses among a wide variety of economic goals in an effort to stabilize the United States economy. In 1978, Federal Reserve Chair Paul Volcker radically altered the FED's goals by permitting interest rates to float and by committing the organization to a monetarist strategy of controlling money aggregates.[30] After inflation declined, Volcker again changed the goals, forsaking monetarism for his own brand of economic pragmatism.

The discretion available to bureau leaders varies from bureau to bureau. The Environmental Protection Agency has a detailed authorizing law that requires specific actions to be taken when certain conditions occur. Goals and timetables for reaching the goals are expressed in law.[31] The Federal Trade Commission (FTC), on the other hand, has vague operating legislation, so that its goals can change dramatically over time. The range of goal discretion in these two agencies is aptly demonstrated by events following the 1980 elections. James Miller, chair of the FTC, was able to redirect the FTC away from consumer activism to a free-market orientation; but Anne Burford was not able to redirect EPA policies to become more supportive of business interests.[32] Burford, as a result of detailed EPA legislation, had inherently less discretion in setting policy goals than did Miller.[33]

In some cases, external constraints are such that agency goals are changed profoundly by actors outside the agency. The Army Corps of Engineers historically has pursued with vigor its goal of constructing water projects.[34] After President Carter's famous water-project hit list was overruled, however, no new water projects were authorized for the corps. The congressional decision not to authorize new projects effectively changed the corps's short-term goals from construction to project maintenance.

A bureau leader's ability to influence agency goals is similar to the president's power to persuade.[35] The bureau leader must convince both employees and external political actors that different policy goals are more appropriate. The ability to convince others is one aspect of personal power within the organization. In a study of organizational influence, French and Raven cite five sources of organizational power—legitimate, reward, coercive, referent, and expert.[36]

Legitimate power is the right of bureau leaders to make certain decisions as a result of their hierarchical positions. Because all bureau leaders have this power, it can be treated as a constant in analyzing differences in bureau leadership.[37] Reward power is the ability to dispense or deny rewards to individual members of an organization. Within this theoretical framework, reward power could refer to the ability of bureau leaders to use solidary and purposive incentives to bind employees to the organization. Even normal utilitarian incentives can be manipulated somewhat to improve employee motivation. Coercive power is the ability of leaders to deny rewards, using the fear of punishment as a motivator. Such methods are clearly short-term and can have only a brief motivating impact; but any long-term effort to lead an organization, even a military organization, by coercion alone would be unsuccessful.[38]

Referent power is power that results because organization members identify with the organization leader. A person's personality, charisma, and reputation can all contribute to referent power. Perhaps the success of such bureaucratic politicians as Elmo Zumwalt and Hyman Rickover can be attributed to their referent power. Michael Pertschuk's reputation as a strong consumer advocate served to create cohesion in the FTC while it was under attack by probusiness advocates in the late 1970s.[39]

Finally, expert power is power that is derived from superior knowledge; this knowledge could be about policy, program implementation, political considerations, or technical factors. Although bureaucratic organizations are repositories of expertise—a fact that should make superior expertise on the part of bureau leaders rare—instances of leaders who possess expert power are common. Jack Knott, in a perceptive discussion of leadership in the Federal Reserve, found that Arthur Burns was able to use his reputation as a macroeconomic expert to convince other organization members to support his policy recommendations.[40] Similarly, Alfred Kahn, when appointed to head the Civil Aeronautics Board, was already a well-known expert on regulation. He was able to present persuasive arguments to other commissioners and staff on the merits of deregulation.[41]

Leadership decisions regarding policy goals, in summary, can serve to build organizational cohesion, a vital source of bureau power. As noted above, governmental employees are likely to hold strong policy positions, particularly about the objectives that their bureau seeks. A bureau leader's ability to express progressive policy goals can attract support from bureau employees. Russell Train's stress on the vigorous enforcement of environmental laws could not but have increased the motivation of environmentalists working for the EPA; Anne Burford's emphasis on less vigorous enforcement served to alienate the same individuals.

Implementation Strategy

Bureau leaders make strategic decisions about how to structure an organization and how to implement its policy objectives. Implementation strategies are as numerous as organizations, so no complete catalogue is possible.[42] Several examples illustrate some options that bureau leaders might consider when making decisions about implementation strategy.

The Environmental Protection Agency, the Occupational Safety and Health Administration (OSHA), and other social regulatory agencies must usually decide between two general forms of implementation. With a command-and-control system, a bureau specifies both its objectives and the means to reach them. The EPA, for example, specifies not only how much pollution an individual plant must remove from its emissions but also the method of removing the pollution. The alternative implementation strategy that is advocated by most economists is to set objectives and to use incentives to encourage industry to reduce pollution; a pollution tax would be one such mechanism.[43]

When policies are applied to individuals, the organization must decide how to interact with the public. At one extreme the organization can treat its rules and application procedures as rigid and allow no deviation, to "go by the book."[44] At the other extreme, the organization might bargain with individuals on how much compliance will be acceptable. Air and water pollution emissions limits are often negotiated on a case-by-case basis between businesses and local enforcement officials.[45]

A structural decision with implications for policy implementation is the centralization of decision making. An agency can retain control over decisions in the central office so that policy is consistent from case to case; economic regulatory agencies are often highly centralized. Other organizations decentralize their decision making so that field units can act autonomously vis-à-vis the central staff. The Agricultural Stabilization and Conservation Service and a wide variety of other agriculture programs are implemented on such a decentralized basis.[46] Decentralized implementation procedures should result in greater policy variation and more adaptation to local conditions.[47]

Implementation decisions might also include a definition of what constitutes compliance.[48] Compliance with public policies is rarely automatic, and organizations determine by enforcement actions what an acceptable level of compliance is. Most states, for example, have adopted informal rules that permit drivers to exceed the 65-mile-per-hour speed limit by small amounts. National banks and their holding companies can only engage in "businesses related to banking"; the Federal Reserve, through a series of definitions, has defined what compliance with this policy entails.

Finally, implementation decisions include the choice of tactics by the agency. Under its first administrator, William Ruckelshaus, the EPA adopted the implementation tactic of filing lawsuits against the most visible polluters to serve as an example to others. OSHA's head, Thorne Auchter (1981–84), eschewed lawsuits and stressed voluntary compliance and a partnership between federal regulators and business, a much different tactic from the strict enforcement of minor rules that characterized OSHA before 1976.[49]

Strategic leadership decisions regarding implementation tactics can contribute to a bureau's power by affecting either cohesion or expertise within the bureau. Tactics that stress the strict enforcement of laws are more likely to encourage cohesion on the part of agency employees. In such circumstances, employees are part of a unit with common goals, rather than individual operators negotiating the best deal.

Strategic leadership decisions regarding implementation tactics can also develop bureau expertise. J. Edgar Hoover was instrumental in developing the expertise of the Federal Bureau of Investigation (FBI) crime labs; these labs enhanced the FBI's reputation for the scientific investigation of crimes.[50] Eula Bingham, herself an expert on occupational health, stressed health rather than safety regulation at OSHA; under this policy, OSHA developed some expertise as a knowledgeable regulator on health issues.[51]

Coalition Strategy

Coalition strategy is nothing more than a series of decisions about how the organization will interact with its environment, that is, what political coalitions the organization will form to increase its ability to achieve policy goals and to survive. The first coalitional strategy that a bureau leader must make is to define the target of coalitional efforts. Several potential targets are possible—program beneficiaries, members of Congress, other executive-branch personnel, and so forth.

Each potential target may be enticed into a policy coalition through inducements that at an abstract level resemble the inducements used to gain employee cooperation.[52] Purposive appeals can attract political support from individuals who share goals similar to those of the bureau. The Agricultural Research Service, for example, has programs to improve the productivity of pecan trees, a goal near and dear to the heart of Rep. Jamie Whitten of Mississippi.

Utilitarian appeals can result in the bureau's providing tangible benefits in exchange for political support. The National Institutes of Health, for example, fund research grants; in turn, grant recipients are active in lobbying Congress for more funds for health research. Solidary inducements might include the ability to meet and be seen with Washington's movers and shakers. A visit by the secretary of education to local schools or a commencement address at a university will build credits with individuals who can be contacted later. Finally, coercion plays a role in coalitional behavior. If a bureau requests support from its clientele for a legislative hearing, that clientele can ignore the request only at the risk of losing its benefits.

The inducements offered to potential coalition targets can vary in intensity and can be a mix of different inducements. The nature of regulatory coercion provides a good illustration. A regulatory bureau can either seek clientele support from those it regulates, or it can seek support from the more diffuse and less-well-organized group of consumers who favor strict regulation.[53]

Policy outputs will reflect this decision. The SEC relies heavily on support from its regulatees, and it permits a great deal of self-regulation; the EPA, on the other hand, has rejected the concept of self-regulation during most of its history. A bureau can pursue both strategies. The Food and Drug Administration (FDA) in 1981 adopted a fast-track method of approving breakthrough drugs in an effort to reduce criticism by the pharmaceutical industry, but retained its rigid testing requirements for other drugs to maintain support from advocates of strict regulation.

The mix of incentives used in coalitional exchanges is illustrated by the land-grant universities. The utilitarian incentives offered to farmers through research on crop and animal productivity are fairly obvious. Less obvious are those universities' solidary appeals through extension conferences or the purposive appeals they make about family farming as a noble way of life.[54]

Bureau leadership and its impact on coalitional behavior is empirically visible through the relationships that bureau leaders develop with various potential clientele. First, some bureau leaders have stronger ties to interest groups than do other leaders. Earl Butz and Richard Lyng were secretaries of agriculture with long-term ties to farming interest groups and agribusiness; John Block and Bob Bergland did not have these ties. Second, some bureau leaders have or can develop stronger connections with members of Congress. A bureau leader that is recruited from a congressional staff position, as some regulatory commissioners are, is likely to have good relationships with key members of Congress.

Third, some bureaucratic leaders have greater access to power centers within the executive branch. Access to the president or to officials in the Office of Management and Budget can provide key legislative and budgeting support. State agencies often propose legislation that reflects their support from the governor.[55] President Carter's support for civil-service reform was crucial to Office of Personnel Management (OPM) director Alan Campbell's efforts to build a legislative majority for the Civil Service Reform Act of 1978. Similarly, threats of a veto by President Carter prevented the passage in 1979 of an act to restrict the Federal Trade Commission and resulted in the passage of a more moderate act in 1980.[56] Fourth, a bureaucratic leader might have strong ties to administrative officials that actually implement the policy. Mary Schweitzer, a long-time head of the federal rehabilitation program, was revered by state vocational rehabilitation directors. Her successor, Bob Humphries, lacked this rapport and had ongoing difficulties in gathering support for his administrative actions.

In sum, leadership in a bureaucracy is important because bureau leaders make strategic decisions regarding member inducements, policy goals, implementation strategies, and coalitional strategies. These strategic decisions affect the organization's ability to develop political support, cohesion, and expertise. Political support, cohesion, and expertise in turn affect the organization's ability to extract resources and autonomy from its environment. The greater the extraction of resources and autonomy, the more likely that the organization will achieve its policy goals and the more likely that it will survive.

Individual leadership actions, however, are not unconstrained. The membership inducements that are offered may limit coalitional strategies; decisions about policy goals may restrict options concerning strategies to implement policy. The major constraint on bureau leaders, however, is the political environment. To this environment and the nature of the constraints, I now turn.

THE ENVIRONMENT

A bureau's political environment can be divided into two parts. One part, the density of the environment, includes two factors: (a) the number of competitors and (b) the number of potential clientele. The other part may be designated the nature of the issue; it includes the bureau's policy goals and their salience, complexity, and fragmentability. Each aspect of the bureau's environment merits separate discussion.

COMPETITORS

Although public organizations are often thought to have monopolies over their policy domains, in many cases competitors or potential competitors exist. A potential competitor might be another agency. The Army Corps of Engineers has long had a competitive relationship with the Bureau of Reclamation for the control of water projects. The Federal Trade Commission and the Antitrust Division of the Department of Justice are competitors for the control of some parts of federal antitrust policy.

In many cases agencies perform a generic function in a specialized area so that other agencies with different specializations might be able to perform the same function. For example, agencies that discipline members of a licensed occupation adjudicate disputes; the process of discipline is little different from the adjudication function that courts and other adjudicatory agencies perform. Courts are a likely competitor of these agencies, just as other dispute-resolution mechanisms (e.g., arbitration) are.

Potential competitors are not limited to public-sector organizations. Private-sector organizations can often perform services similar to those performed by public organizations.[57] Private organizations now provide state and local governments with fire protection, garbage disposal, tax assessments, and even corrections.[58] State workers' compensation systems illustrate the range of options; in some states, workers' compensation insurance is provided solely by private companies; other states provide insurance via a state agency with a monopoly on the sale of insurance; still other states have competitive systems whereby both a state agency and private firms can sell workers' compensation insurance.

The greater the number of potential competitors a bureau has, the more difficult are the tasks facing the bureau's leadership. Potential competitors are interested in the same resources and autonomy that the bureau seeks. With competition, the strategic decisions of the bureau's leadership become more crucial. Poor decisions will result in a bureau's losing resources to other competitors and possibly even losing control over a policy area completely. A public organization with no potential competitors bears fewer risks when it makes strategic decisions.

Potential Clientele

Potential clientele are individuals who might be served some way by the bureau. Although every person in the United States could conceivably be a potential client of every agency, some agencies have a larger potential clientele than others. Agencies that provide services to the elderly, for example, have a larger potential clientele than do agencies that provide services to railroad workers. The larger a bureau's potential clientele, the more potential political support the bureau can attract. A large potential clientele increases the strategic options available to bureau leadership in terms of coalition formation. Agencies that have a small potential clientele will be less able to build the support necessary for survival.

The size of potential clientele is not the only variable of concern.[59] A bureau's coalitional options increase if the potential clientele is organized and self-conscious,[60] receives tangible benefits from the bureau, is prestigious, and is divided into several organized groups. A bureau facing an environment with few potential clientele or with clientele that are not organized, not self-conscious, and lack prestige must rely on other strategic decisions to gain power for the organization.[61] Coalitional decisions are unlikely to greatly improve this organization's potential for survival.

Issue Salience and Issue Complexity

"A highly salient issue is one that affects a large number of people in a significant way."[62] A complex issue is one that requires specialized knowledge and training to understand the factual questions involved. William Gormley has argued that issue salience and issue complexity interact in regulatory policies and determine which political actors are likely to dominate policy decisions.[63] Gormley's logic can be applied to policy decisions all bureaus face. If an issue is salient, politicians and "public" interest groups are more likely to be involved, since the potential political gains from success on such an issue are large. Nonsalient issues are likely to be left to the discretion of the bureau and those immediately affected by the policies.

Complex issues place a premium on expertise, and such an environment favors bureau autonomy, since bureaus are the primary repositories of expertise. Combining salience and complexity into four general types of policy, Gormley argues that each will result in having different actors participate. Salient but noncomplex issues will be the sphere of influence of politicians since these issues offer great potential political gains but impose few costs in terms of learning the policy area.

A salient but complex issue will involve the bureau as a key actor, subject to intervention by other actors to the extent that they can develop expertise. A complex but not salient issue will be left almost entirely to the bureau, with decisions being made at upper levels in the bureaucracy. Finally, issues that are neither salient nor complex will also be left to the discretion of the bureau, with decision-making authority vested in lower levels of the bureaucracy.[64]

Gormley's hypotheses can be linked to the importance of leadership decisions. Complex issues require that the leadership make decisions that will enhance expertise in order to be effective. Salient issues require that leadership pay more attention to strategic decisions regarding coalitional building. In short, the nature of the issue influences the optimal strategy for bureau leadership.

Issue Fragmentability

Policy issues vary in their degree of fragmentability. A fragmentable issue is one that can be subdivided into many parts and addressed one part at a time. Agricultural price supports is a fragmentable issue since it can be addressed as a research problem, an excess-supply problem, a marketing problem, an income problem, and in a variety of other ways. The death penalty is an issue that is not fragmentable in that one either has a death penalty or does not have one; it is difficult to have part of a death penalty.[65]

Fragmentable issues increase a bureau's coalitional opportunities. With a fragmentable issue, bureaus can attract support from various individuals by trading off parts of the policy area. The Department of Agriculture, for example, can attract the support of universities for its agriculture policies by stressing the research nature of the "farm problem." Additional university research on farm productivity can be funded with little influence on the marketing, income maintenance, or production policies of the department. Fragmentable issues allow bureau leaders more options in terms of developing clientele support.

CONCLUSION

In this essay I have outlined an alternative theory of bureaucratic leadership. The emphasis was on leadership and the role it could play in increasing the policy impact and the survival potential of the organization. In the process of outlining the theory, a series of testable hypotheses were generated. Before reiterating the hypotheses, we should note that this theory is intended to be an empirical theory, capable of being used in either single case studies of organizations or in cross-organizational studies. Each hypothesis will incorporate crucial variables that will affect the ability of an organization to survive. Survival might be enhanced by improving the power setting of the organization, measured as increases in resources or autonomy.[66] Survival might also be enhanced by improving clientele support, expertise, and organizational cohesion, which in turn generate increases in resources or autonomy. Finally, some variables make the exercise of strategic decisions by leadership more crucial to the organization; under certain environmental conditions, leadership decisions can have life-or-death consequences for the organization.

In this essay, I have generated sixteen testable hypotheses:

H_1. The increased use of solidary incentives by organizational leadership will increase organizational cohesion.[67]

H_2. The increased use of purposive incentives by organizational leadership will increase organizational cohesion.

H_3. Coercive inducements have only a short-term impact; the use of coercive inducements will result in decreased organizational cohesion.

H_4. The greater the range of goal discretion available to the organization, the more crucial leadership decisions will be to organizational survival.[68]

H_5. The greater the referent power possessed by the bureau leader, the greater the impact that the bureau leader will have on policy goals.[69]

H_6. The greater the expert power possessed by the bureau leader, the greater the impact that the bureau leader will have on policy goals.

H_7. Implementation strategies affect the ability of organizations to form coalitions to increase clientele support.[70]

H_8. Implementation strategies, particularly those that increase the participation of employees in making decisions, affect the cohesion of the organization.

H_9. Implementation strategies, particularly those that emphasize the development of skills, affect the expertise of the organization.

H_{10}. Leadership decisions regarding appropriate coalitional strategies can result in greater public support for the agency.[71]

H_{11}. Leadership with long historical ties to clientele groups will increase the public support for the agency.[72]

H_{12}. The more competitors the organization's environment contains, the more crucial leadership decisions are to organizational survival.

H_{13}. The larger the potential clientele of the organization, the greater the public support for the organization will be.

H_{14}. In organizations without positive clientele support in the environment, bureau leadership, to survive, must develop ties to other political actors.

H_{15}. The more complex the organization's issue environment, the greater is leadership's potential to develop expertise as a bureau power source.

H_{16}. The more salient the organization's issue environment is, the more potential clientele support the bureau leadership can attract to the organization.

NOTES

1. Herbert Kaufman, *Time, Chance, and Organizations: Natural Selection in a Perilous Environment* (Chatham, N.J.: Chatham House, 1985).

2. This view of organizations has many names, including "open systems theory" or "structuralism." The origins of this approach can be traced back at least to Max Weber, *From Max Weber: Essays in Sociology,* trans. H. H. Gerth and C. Wright Mills (New York: Oxford University Press, 1946); perhaps the best advocate of this approach to organization theory is Charles Perrow, *Complex Organizations: A Critical Essay* (Glenview, Ill.: Scott, Foresman, 1979). Although most scholars who approach organizations from this viewpoint pay little attention to leadership, the position argued by Kaufman is an extreme one.

3. The Consumer Product Safety Commission (CPSC) was able to survive a sunset review of its performance in 1978 in part because Byington resigned. The success of the CPSC at its 1981 reauthorization was a function of Kennedy's ability to focus the CPSC on more significant consumer protection issues. See Kenneth J. Meier, *Regulation: Politics, Bureaucracy and Economics* (New York: St. Martin's, 1985), p. 105.

4. On the behavioral revolution in public administration see James L. Perry and Kenneth L. Kraemer, "Research Methodology in *Public Administration Review,* 1975–1984," *Public Administration Review* 46 (May/June 1986): 215–26. There are some leadership studies that have been conducted in psychology which are noted below. These are within the realm of another discipline, however. Public-administration scholars have done only modest empirical work in the area of leadership.

5. To completely change theoretical perspectives to, say, organizational behavior would hardly be addressing the concerns that Kaufman raised. In this chapter, in short, I will deal with the concerns raised by Kaufman within a theoretical approach that is similar to his.

6. Howard Ball, *Controlling Regulatory Sprawl* (Westport, Conn.: Greenwood Press, 1984); George C. Eads and Michael Fix, *The Reagan Regulatory Strategy* (Washington, D.C.: Urban Institute, 1984).

7. H. Fiedler and M. Chemers, *Leadership and Effective Management* (Glenview, Ill.: Scott, Foresman, 1974).

8. Talcott Parsons, *Structure and Process in Modern Society* (New York: Free Press of Glencoe, 1960).

9. Lawrence B. Mohr, "The Concept of Organizational Goal," *American Political Science Review* 77 (1973): 470–81; Amitai Etzioni, *Modern Organizations* (Englewood Cliffs, N.J.: Prentice-Hall, 1964); Stanley E. Seashore and Ephraim Yuchtman,

"Factorial Analysis of Organizational Performance," *Administrative Science Quarterly* 12 (Dec. 1967): 377–95.

10. I am not convinced that public organizations always have survival goals. Under the leadership of Alfred Kahn, the late Civil Aeronautics Board aggressively pursued policies intended to eliminate the agency. With the rise of deregulation and privatization as public issues, many individuals within governmental organizations may well have the death of their organization as their primary goal. See Martha Derthick and Paul Quirk, *The Politics of Deregulation* (Washington, D.C.: Brookings Institution, 1985).

11. William Niskanen, *Bureaucracy and Representative Government* (Chicago: Aldine, 1971); Matthew Holden, " 'Imperialism' in Bureaucracy," *American Political Science Review* 60 (Dec. 1966): 943–51.

12. Norton E. Long, "Power and Administration," *Public Administration Review* 9 (Autumn 1949): 257–64.

13. The same generalization is true for individuals seeking personal goals in an organization.

14. Francis E. Rourke, *Bureaucracy, Politics, and Public Policy* (Boston: Little, Brown, 1984); Kenneth J. Meier, *Politics and the Bureaucracy* (Monterey, Calif.: Brooks/Cole, 1987).

15. Rourke, *Bureaucracy.*

16. This presentation is essentially a strategic-contingencies approach to organizations. See Fiedler and Chemers, *Leadership and Effective Management.*

17. Chester Barnard, *Functions of the Executive* (Cambridge, Mass.: Harvard University Press, 1938).

18. Although many of these incentive typologies were developed to explain exchanges in voluntary organizations such as interest groups, they are clearly applicable to public bureaucracies. The typologies are presented by C. W. Gordon and N. Babchuk in "A Typology of Voluntary Associations," *American Sociological Review* 24 (1959): 22–29; Amitai Etzioni, *A Comparative Analysis of Complex Organizations* (New York: Free Press, 1961); James Q. Wilson, *Political Organizations* (New York: Basic Books, 1973); C. K. Warriner, "The Problem of Organizational Purpose," *Sociological Quarterly* 6 (1965): 138–46; Meyer N. Zald and David Jacobs, "Compliance/Incentive Classifications of Organizations," *Administration and Society* 9 (1978): 403–24.

19. If material incentives were the only incentives offered by public agencies, then most individuals would probably prefer to work in the private sector, where material rewards are generally higher. The more interesting aspects of public bureaucracies are their use of nonmaterial incentives.

20. Wilson, *Political Organizations,* p. 33.

21. The Forest Service uses personnel rotation and socialization to develop an identification with the Forest Service. See Herbert Kaufman, *The Forest Ranger* (Baltimore, Md.: Johns Hopkins University Press, 1960). All organizations do this somewhat. Anthony Downs, *Inside Bureaucracy* (Boston: Little, Brown, 1967), argues that over time, all bureaucracies create pressures to become advocates of the programs that the bureau administers. Although some of these pressures might be based on material incentives, some are clearly based on an individual's need to belong to an organization.

22. Wilson, *Political Organizations,* p. 34.

23. Derthick and Quirk, *Politics of Deregulation.*

24. John Nalbandian and J. Terry Edwards, "The Values of Public Administrators," *Review of Public Personnel Administration* (Fall 1983): 114–27; Hal G. Rainey, "Reward Preferences among Public and Private Managers," *American Review of Public Administration,* Fall 1982, p. 293.

25. Jane L. Pearce and James L. Perry, "Federal Merit Pay: A Longitudinal Analysis," *Public Administration Review* 43 (July/August 1983): 318.

26. Milton C. Cummings, M. Kent Jennings, and Franklin P. Kilpatrick, "Federal and Nonfederal Employees," *Public Administration Review* 27 (Dec. 1967): 393–402; Joel D. Aberbach and Bert A. Rockman, "Clashing Beliefs within the Executive Branch," *American Political Science Review* 70 (June 1976): 456–68.

27. Rufus E. Miles, "The Origin and Meaning of Miles' Law," *Public Administration Review* 38 (Sept./Oct. 1978): 399–403.

28. Meier, *Regulation.*

29. Philip Selznick, *TVA and the Grassroots* (Berkeley: University of California Press, 1947).

30. Donald F. Kettl, *Leadership at the FED* (New Haven, Conn.: Yale University Press, 1986).

31. Alfred Marcus, "Environmental Protection Agency," in *The Politics of Regulation,* ed. James Q. Wilson (New York: Basic Books, 1980), pp. 267–303.

32. See Meier, *Regulation.*

33. Miller even had to persuade a majority of the FTC commissioners to his view, and yet he was more successful than Burford, who was the sole hierarchical head of the EPA.

34. Arthur Maass, *Muddy Waters* (Cambridge, Mass.: Harvard University Press, 1951).

35. Richard Neustadt, *Presidential Power* (New York: John Wiley & Sons, 1960).

36. J. French and B. Raven, "The Bases of Social Power," in *Studies in Social Power,* ed. D. Cartwright (Ann Arbor, Mich.: Institute for Social Research, 1959), pp. 150–67.

37. Some bureau leaders might be more effective than others in using hierarchical power. This suggests that some individuals simply have more leadership ability than others. Without resurrecting trait theories of leadership (e.g., decisiveness results in better leadership), see R. Stogdill, *Handbook of Leadership: A Survey of Theory and Research* (New York: Free Press, 1974), this suggestion is clearly correct. Eliot Richardson appeared to be able to lead organizations with a variety of goals. Don Noble, the head of the ill-fated Synthetic Fuels Corporation, was unable to use the formal powers at his disposal. A comparison of the leadership of John Powell and Eleanor Norton Holmes at the Equal Employment Opportunity Commission would illustrate similar powers being used with vastly different impacts on the organization.

38. Military and paramilitary organizations have the greatest ability to use coercive exchanges; but in fact, they are the organizations that rely most on solidary exchanges. Much effort is used to build group solidarity in military organizations. The coercive power of the organization remains, but emphasis on pride of membership may be a more important source of organizational commitment.

39. Michael Pertschuk, *Revolt against Regulation* (Berkeley: University of California Press).

40. Jack H. Knott, "The FED Chairman as a Political Executive," *Administration and Society* 18 (Aug. 1986): 197–232.

41. Derthick and Quirk, *Politics of Deregulation.*

42. See Lawrence J. O'Toole and Robert S. Mountjoy, "Interorganizational Policy Implementation: A Theoretical Perspective," *Public Administration Review* 44 (Nov./Dec. 1984): 491–503.

43. See Robert W. Poole, *Instead of Regulation* (Lexington, Mass.: Lexington Books, 1982). These strategies are not mutually exclusive. The EPA has used incentives in introducing pollution offsets, bubbles, and emissions' banking. These

incentives-based controls supplement a system that is essentially a command-and-control one. Federal antitrust policy also has a hybrid implementation structure. Federal antitrust laws can be enforced either by federal agencies or by private individuals who are seeking damages. The treble damage awards that are possible in private suits serve as an incentive for private individuals to file antitrust actions.

44. Eugene Bardach and Robert A. Kagen, *Going by the Book* (Philadelphia: Temple University Press, 1982).

45. Paul B. Downing and James N. Kimball, "Enforcing Pollution Control Laws in the United States," *Policy Studies Journal* 11 (Sept. 1982): 55–65.

46. An even more extreme position in decentralization is privatization. In this situation, policy implementation is delegated to the private sector, and individual citizens decide for themselves what services to provide. Federal grant programs that have few federal requirements might be interpreted as a similar implementation strategy. A frequent decision at the federal level is whether to have a federal agency implement the policy or to rely on state governmental agencies to implement the policy. The use of states as proxy administrators has become fairly frequent in welfare policies, environmental policies, and health-care policies. See Christopher C. Hood, *The Limits of Administration* (New York: John Wiley & Sons, 1976); Michael Reagan, *Regulation: The Politics of Policy* (Boston, Mass.: Little, Brown, 1987).

47. Such a result might be either positive or negative. In situations in which local conditions affect the ability to operate a successful program, such as local-job-creation projects, decentralization might be a plus. In other situations, in which one seeks uniform nationwide application, such as in discrimination policies, a centralized form of administration might be more appropriate.

48. James E. Anderson, *Public Policy-Making* (New York: Praeger, 1984).

49. Frank F. Thompson, "Deregulation by the Bureaucracy: OSHA and the Augean Quest for Error Correction," *Public Administration Review* 42 (May/June 1982): 202–12.

50. Rourke, *Bureaucracy.*

51. Meier, *Regulation.*

52. This view of coalitions is similar to the view of policy networks expressed by Hugh Heclo, "Issue Networks in the Executive Establishment," in *The New American Political System,* ed. Anthony King (Washington, D.C.: American Enterprise Institute, 1978), pp, 87–124; and by Paul A. Sabatier, "Toward a Strategic Interaction Framework of Policy Evaluation and Learning," paper presented at the annual meeting of the Western Political Science Association, 1983, in that loose coalitions of interests form around issues.

53. This issue is addressed by Marver Bernstein in *Regulating Business by Independent Commission* (Princeton, N.J.: Princeton University Press) and by George Stigler in "The Theory of Economic Regulation," *Bell Journal of Economics and Management Science* 2 (Spring 1971): 3–21, who, in their capture theory of regulation, argue that regulatory agencies will rationally seek to attract the regulated industry rather than the general public. That regulatory agencies are able not only to exercise choice but also to reject close ties with the regulated can be seen from the many recent critiques of capture theory. See Lawrence S. Rothenberg, "Reassessing Capture Theory," paper presented at the 1985 annual meeting of the American Political Science Association; Jeffrey E. Cohen, "The Dynamics of the 'Revolving Door' on the FCC," *American Journal of Political Science* 30 (Nov. 1986): 689–708; Paul J. Quirk, *Industry Influence in Federal Regulatory Agencies* (Princeton, N.J.: Princeton University Press, 1981).

54. Ross B. Talbot and Don F. Hadwiger, *The Policy Process in American Agriculture* (San Francisco, Calif.: Chandler Publishing, 1968).

55. The Department of Regulation and Licensing in Wisconsin proposed occupational-regulation reforms in 1986 that would have transferred much authority from regulatory boards, made up of members of the regulated profession, to the career staff of the agency. After the 1986 election, when a conservative Republican replaced a liberal Democrat as governor, the department altered its request and asked that more authority be transferred to the boards, rather than to the career staff.

56. Meier, *Regulation,* p. 110.

57. E. S. Savas, *Privatizing the Public Sector* (Chatham, N.J.: Chatham House, 1983).

58. David Lowery, ''Public Choice When Services Are Costs,'' *American Journal of Political Science* 26 (Feb. 1982); 57–75.

59. Rourke, *Bureaucracy.*

60. A self-conscious clientele sees the common identity that it shares with other clientele members. Consumers are a clientele that are not always conscious that they share similar interests. Physicians, on the other hand, are normally self-conscious about their shared interests.

61. Closer ties with members of Congress, the generating of support from the president, and the developing of a reputation for neutral competence are only three possible options.

62. William T. Gormley, ''Regulatory Issue Networks in a Federal System,'' *Polity* 18 (Summer 1986): 598.

63. Ibid.

64. Ibid., pp. 599–603.

65. There is of course the option taken by many states, to enact a death penalty and then never use it. In this case, the death penalty is a symbol rather than an actual policy.

66. For an illustration see Kenneth J. Meier, ''Measuring Organizational Power,'' *Administration and Society* 12 (Nov. 1980): 357–75.

67. Cohesion might be made operational by turnover rates for the organization, by the number of vacancies that are unfilled, or by survey research methods. The type of incentives offered by leaders could be determined by a content analysis of leadership statements to members of the organization. A secondary method might also be a survey of employees on the incentives that were offered.

68. Goal discretion might be measured by the length of the authorizing statute or by the ratio of the length of the authorizing statute to the length of administrative rules issued by the agency. Statutes could also be content-analyzed for specificity in policy goals.

69. Referent power and expert power might be determined by a content analysis of agency heads' careers. Evidence of expertise would not be difficult to categorize; examples of referent power might include other leadership positions, the rapidity of rise to the top of the organization, or reputational surveys.

70. Hardcore implementation strategies, such as going by the book, will reduce the ability of the organization to attract clientele. Decentralization will probably increase clientele support. Philip Selznick, in *TVA and the Grass Roots* (Berkeley: University of California Press, 1947), illustrates how implementation techniques can affect the power setting of an organization.

71. No direction is specified by this hypothesis since bad leadership decisions regarding coalitional strategies can result in a decrease in public support.

72. This can be measured by analyzing the career pattern of the agency head. Prior experience with clientele groups or employment by Congress or the president should improve relationships with these political actors.

Concluding Comments

13

Two Conceptions of Political Leadership Revisited

Bryan D. Jones

As one reads through the essays composing this volume, one can almost feel the tension between the two conceptions of leadership. Both seem so compelling. One approach views leaders as responding rationally to incentives in structured situations. The other approaches the leadership problem as an exercise in creativity in ambiguous situations, in which problems and solutions can be imaginatively joined and new political realities defined for followers.

The results that Fiorina and Shepsle present for such matters as representation and agenda control seem to be formal and deductive analyses of what all of us have observed in representative assemblies and local meetings. Robertson makes clear, in a way that is intuitively appealing, that the manner in which governing coalitions are constructed in a legislative bargaining process affects national macroeconomic policy. In his ambitious essay, Wildavsky argues that the type of political culture (regime) has more impact on leadership style than does the "situation." Understood rules and norms govern leadership as well as followship. "When you know more about what a third baseman is likely to do by knowing his personality than by understanding the rules and customs of baseball, one of you is crazy," writes Wildavsky.

But wait a minute. Where did the rules and customs of baseball (or politics) come from? Abner Doubleday may be the founding father of our summer pastime, but who invented the steal, the bunt, or the split-fingered fast ball? Could we conceive of a different baseball game, coming out of the same "constitution" but having a different incremental history? The development of the rules and customs, in politics or in baseball, can be conceived as responses to very peculiar circumstances, generally involving a probabilistic union of situation (defined culturally, following Wildavsky) and personality (limited by culture, but more as a probability distribution than an unvarying parameter).

Now the second conception of leadership begins to come into focus. Baumgartner sees political leaders as capable of manipulating debate and engaging in rhetoric in order to impose their definitions of policy initiatives. But the success of these activities is in proportion to the ambiguity of the political situation. Harmel looks for lawlike oligarchy in the structure of party organizations, and instead he finds organizational variety. "Oligarchy is not inevitable," he writes; maybe this applies to all political structure. In his review of presidential leadership in Congress, Edwards concludes that the technical details of constructing coalitions are not very important; presidential success cannot be explained in terms of techniques. It is in this vein that Hargrove issues his dictum: "Political leaders create new possibilities in history."

In the introductory essay to this volume, I set out three aspects of political leadership that have to be addressed if a more comprehensive theory of political leadership is ever to be developed. They are (1) a role for maximizing behavior within set institutional structures; (2) the specification of conditions under which political actors can modify and redefine existing institutions, customs, and incentive structures; and (3) a recognition of the connection between the political and the economic worlds.

LEADERSHIP AND INNOVATION UNDER UNAMBIGUOUS RULES

Wildavsky is right; the first step toward wisdom in the study of political leadership is to understand the rules that structure political action. The formal approaches to leadership that are described by Shepsle and Fiorina are attempts to model carefully these rules and to trace out their impacts. Right again; without such careful attention to the rules and the incentives that they generate, we cannot realize the full range of strategies that can be generated by the interaction between rational maximization and the rules.

But there is a second step to wisdom. This is the recognition of change and evolution in the structure of rules. There are two kinds of changes: those generated internally and those generated through an interaction between internal processes and changing external circumstances.

Contemplate, first, internal change. One can conceive of a carefully modeled dynamic system of human interaction that looks very different as time progresses. It is possible, I believe, to show that change in the system results from rational maximization under the structure of the rules.

This may not be an easy notion to accept. Maximizers within a set structure would seem to present an invariant picture of the political process. But maximization, like any decision process, is not static. Something new is invariably introduced, some innovation that gives the innovator an advantage under the rules. Such innovation can change the customs, the informal structure, and even the formal structure as constitution makers struggle with the impacts of the innovation. The rules in effect at any given time act as a mechanism of selection, eliminating some innovations and favoring others. Call them innovators, or call them entrepreneurs; they are the political leaders who are able to use the given structure to maximum advantage. We don't know what makes these individuals create. But given that they do create, we can see that they are maximizers; they are making the rules that define individual or group success work for them.

We have, then, a political actor facing a structured incentive system but serving up novel ideas. Trials become important; through trial proposals and pilot projects, political innovations are winnowed. One can conceive of a probability distribution of potential political innovations that are subjected to a selection process, the selection process of political rules. These innovations maximize success for the entrepreneur, but they also modify the system of rules and customs in minor and major ways. Hence, the next innovator will face a slightly changed (or, sometimes, not so slightly changed) system of rules.

If we focus only on internal change, "situation" means the system of rules facing an innovator at a particular moment. If our innovator or leader is an elected politician and if the rules of success incorporate the standard public-choice assumption of the maximization of votes, then he or she may try out several different strategies. These strategies can involve interelection behavior (writing a record on which to run) or campaigns. Our politician can try out all sorts of new policies or campaign strategies from the set of available ones. Some don't work; he will either discard them or he will lose. He is doing his best to maximize, but—and here is the major point—he may not be able to do so. Because this random process of trial and selection is an essential feature of the system, it seems silly to call this a "lack of information." It is true that he may not know exactly what mass preferences he is trying to serve with his policy proposals, but this is not the key to understanding the system. Creativity, trial, and error are fundamental to the political process, even when the process is very structured. The result is a system in which political leaders try a lot and fail a lot, yet are maximizers in the sense that the system of rules selects the most successful strategies.

LEADERSHIP IN AMBIGUOUS AND CHANGING SYSTEMS

If we went no further than this, we could argue that such a system can result in the maximum satisfaction of voter preferences through a process of trial and error, with the system of election and policy-making rules acting as the great winnower. The problem, however, is more complicated than this, for three reasons. The first is the influence of external events. The second is the vagueness and instability of mass preferences. And the third is the complexity and ambiguity of the rules that govern policy making.

It ought to go without saying that external events can alter the inputs into a system or the very limits of the system itself. The increasing number of females in the labor force, for example, alters the inputs to the system. Politicians face a different distribution of preferences, and they serve up different policies to respond to the change; an example is day care. Yet the rules of the game have not changed. On the other hand, the party reforms after 1968 certainly changed the electoral calculus; both inputs and structure were altered.

The vagueness and instability of mass preferences is, as I noted in my introductory essay, probably a misnomer. It is not difficult to discern generally what voters want; the problem is to get them to see that your policies will provide what they want. Voters do not have to have any direct income from policies if general macroeconomic policies will add income indirectly. Convincing voters of the connection between their goals and your policies is, at root, an attempt to manipulate social understandings of policy causation; to forge a connection between policy and outcome in the mind of the voter.

This is possible because of the third factor, the rules that govern policy making. Rules in politics involve both rules of the game itself and the policy-and-effect connection. Rules in politics are more complex and ambiguous than those in baseball, to recall an earlier analogy. But the cause-and-effect process is also more complex and more ambiguous. It is reasonably easy to discern the success of the split-fingered fast ball, I suppose. If it works, it wins games (and gets the pitcher more money). But what about the supply-side effects of a tax cut? Now, clearly, there is a role for promotion and hucksterism in the case of the split-fingered fast ball. But just as clearly there is an even greater role for rhetoric in the case of a tax cut. The reason that political leadership creates new possibilities is that political leaders can forge new courses of action through the use of political rhetoric. To work, this rhetoric must link the new policy with old goals in the minds of voters.

TWO CONCEPTIONS? OR TWO DIFFERENT POLITICAL REALITIES?

It is possible that the two conceptions of political leadership are not so antagonistic as they seem at first glance. There is a probabilistic component to all maximizing behavior, even in situations characterized by low ambiguity. This probabilistic component comes from the trying out of new political ideas by leaders. Most will be rejected; some will be accepted. But the system would nevertheless maximize. The something that is maximized would depend on the structure of the system, but the satisfaction of voter preferences is what would result in the idealized models of public-choice theorists. This notion of maximization, however, is considerably different from that currently employed by most public-choice theorists. Its essential components are creativity and a selection process that is enforced by the existing set of rules.

Many political systems are neither infused with ambiguity nor buffeted by change for long periods of time. Congress is probably such a system, which may explain why so much of the work in public choice is directed at that institution. Other systems are not so favored, and the selection function of rules that causes actors to resemble maximizers are less important, and political rhetoric and new definitions of the situation are more important. Change in the former systems comes about primarily through the actions of policy entrepreneurs and the system of rules governing policy success. Change in the latter systems comes about from this source as well as from the use of political rhetoric to define new courses of action.

There is a final component of political leadership and social change. That is social inertia. Political actors tend to treat the existing political settlement as given, until either external events or, more likely, imaginative political leadership transforms the old understandings into new power realities. The concept of regime, especially as developed in the urban-politics literature by Elkin, Stone, and others, directs attention to this basic aspect of political life. The not-infrequent result is a gradual social change underlying a disjoint political process. San Antonio provides a fascinating example. In the mid 1970s, its regime changed from a governing system of locally oriented Anglo businessmen to one based on an alliance between the Mexican-American community and nationally and internationally oriented businessmen.

THE TASK AHEAD

It has become increasingly clear that the task of understanding political leadership lies in specifying the relationship between individual entrepreneurial actions in structured and unstructured situations. Entrepreneurship is important in both situations, but it takes on critically different forms. Political systems are changed by both types of political entrepreneurs. The transactional entrepreneur offers up new policies or strategies within the existing set of rules, strategies that will subtly modify the system. Transforming entrepreneuers define new political realities for followers. We may not, as social scientists, even understand just how specific strategies get incorporated into the policy process. We should, however, be able to understand change and continuity of systems through the ideas of internal versus external change, a probability distribution of policy proposals, and transactional versus transforming leadership and entrepreneurship.

What are the essential features of both leaders and structure that combine to distinguish, in the words of Hargrove, transactional from transforming leadership? One cannot be a transforming leader unless the situation is right. On the other hand, social systems probably do not get transformed unless they have a leader who is able to define new political realities for followers.

The contribution of this volume of leadership studies from various corners of the discipline of political science emphasizes the ancient notion of unity within diversity. It also points to the need for more thought about this unity in studies of leadership. It seems clear that political scientists are developing concepts and theories that can fruitfully be used to study leadership. It seems just as clear that the process of achieving success in subdisciplinary areas—a form of transactional entrepreneurship—has hindered the knowledge and the development of this unity. If, when a truly serious, comprehensive theory of political leadership is presented, this volume is cited as a stimulus to transforming entrepreneurship, it will have more than served its purpose.

The Contributors

FRANK R. BAUMGARTNER is assistant professor of political science at Texas A & M University. He is the author of *Conflict and Rhetoric in French Policymaking* (forthcoming). His current work concerns the generation of political controversies in advanced democracies, focusing on nuclear energy policy.

GEORGE C. EDWARDS III is professor of political science at Texas A & M University. He has served as president of the Presidency Research Section of the American Political Science Association. Among his most recent books are *At the Margins: Presidential Leadership of Congress, Presidential Leadership, National Security and the U.S. Constitution,* and *The Presidency and Public Policy Making,* and he is currently at work on a book on public approval of the president.

MORRIS P. FIORINA is professor of government at Harvard University. He has written widely on American politics, with special emphasis on electoral and legislative politics. His books include *Representatives, Roll Calls, and Constituencies, Congress—Keystone of the Washington Establishment,* and *Retrospective Voting in American National Elections*. His book *The Personal Vote: Constituency Service and Electoral Independence* (coauthored with Bruce Cain and John Ferejohn) received the Legislative Studies Association's 1987 Richard F. Fenno Prize for the best book published in the field of legislative studies.

ERVIN C. HARGROVE is director of the Vanderbilt Institute for Public Policy Studies at Vanderbilt University. He taught at Brown University from 1960 to 1976. He is author of *Presidential Leadership, The Power of the Modern Presidency, Presidents, Politics and Policy,* and *Jimmy Carter as President* and editor of *TVA: Fifty Years of Grass Roots Bureaucracy, The President and Council of Economic Advisers,* and *Leadership and Innovation: A Biographical Perspective on Entrepreneurs in Government.*

BRYAN D. JONES is professor and head of the Department of Political Science, Texas A & M University. He is coauthor of *The Sustaining Hand: Community Leadership and Corporate Power* and author of *Governing Buildings and Building Governments*.

KENNETH J. MEIER is professor of political science at the University of Wisconsin-Madison. He is the author of *The Political Economy of Regulation: The Case of Insurance* and *The Politics of Bureaucracy.* His current research focuses on the role of bureaucracy and representation in educational policies that affect minority students.

MANUS I. MIDLARSKY is Moses and Annuta Back Professor of International Peace and Conflict Resolution at Rutgers University. He was formerly professor of political science and founding director of the Center for International Relations at the University of Colorado, Boulder. He was the founding president of the Conflict Processes Section of the American Political Science Association. He is the author of *On War: Political Violence in the International System, The Disintegration of Political Systems: War and Revolution in Comparative Perspective,* and *The Onset of World War* and the editor of *Inequality and Contemporary Revolutions* and *The Handbook of War Studies.*

JOHN D. ROBERTSON is associate professor of political science at Texas A & M University. His current research interests concern the impact of government formation in parliamentary democracies on macroeconomic policies.

KENNETH A. SHEPSLE is professor of government at Harvard University. He has written extensively on rational choice models of the political process.

CLARENCE N. STONE is professor of government and politics at the University of Maryland. He is the author of *Economic Growth and Neighborhood Discontent: System Bias in the Urban Renewal Program of Atlanta* and of the forthcoming *Civic Cooperation in Atlanta*. He is also the coauthor of *Urban Policy and Politics in a Bureaucratic Age* and coeditor of and contributor to *The Politics of Urban Development.*

AARON WILDAVSKY is professor of political science and public policy at the University of California, Berkeley. He is the author (with Richard Ellis) of *Dilemmas of Early American Presidents From Washington Through Lincoln.*

Index